UNIVERSITY OF
WINCHESTER

A

Being the Norse Voya~
Settlement to Iceland,
and North America

GWYN JONES

A New and Enlarged Edition, with contributions by
Robert McGhee, Thomas H. McGovern and
colleagues, and Birgitta Linderoth Wallace

Oxford   New York

OXFORD UNIVERSITY PRESS

Oxford University Press, Walton Street, Oxford OX2 6DP

Oxford New York Toronto
Delhi Bombay Calcutta Madras Karachi
Kuala Lumpur Singapore Hong Kong Tokyo
Nairobi Dar es Salaam Cape Town
Melbourne Auckland

and associated companies in
Beirut Berlin Ibadan Nicosia

Oxford is a trade mark of Oxford University Press

First published in 1964. Second edition published
simultaneously in hardback and as an Oxford University
Press paperback 1986.

British Library Cataloguing in Publication Data
Jones, Gwyn, 1907–
The Norse Atlantic saga: being the Norse voyages
of discovery and settlement to Iceland,
Greenland, and North America.—New and enl.ed.
1. Norse literature
I. Title   II. McGhee, Robert
839'.6'08   PT72210.E5
ISBN 0–19–215886–4
ISBN 0–19–285160–8 Pbk

Library of Congress Cataloging in Publication Data
Jones, Gwyn, 1907–
The Norse Atlantic saga.
Bibliography: p.   Includes index.
1. Iceland—Discovery and exploration.
2. Greenland—Discovery and exploration.   3. America—
Discovery and exploration—Norse.   I. Title.
G302.J6   1986   909'.09821   85–21781
ISBN 0–19–215886–4
ISBN 0–19–285160–8 (pbk.)

Set by Promenade Graphics Ltd.
Printed in Great Britain by
Richard Clay (The Chaucer Press) Ltd.
Bungay, Suffolk

Preface

The Norse Atlantic Saga, a narrative and descriptive account of the Norse, or Viking, voyages of discovery and colonization westward across the North Altantic Ocean, to Iceland, Greenland, and the eastern seaboard of North America, was first published by the Oxford University Press in 1964. This new edition has been substantially enlarged and reshaped, and in the event reset, to take account of the many gains in knowledge and interpretation made during the intervening twenty-two years. Scholars have continued to study the documentary and cartographical evidence, with consequences as gratifying as the new editions of sagas, annals, and supportive texts listed in the Supplementary Note to Appendix VIII and, at the other extreme, as creditable as the final discrediting of the Vinland Map. Advances in underwater archaeology, together with the technical skills of Scandinavian boatbuilders and sailors, have extended our knowledge of the Norsemen's ships and seafaring arts and demonstrated in decisive fashion the practicability of their Atlantic crossings. Our picture of the life and death of the Norse colonies in Greenland is at once more detailed and more coherent than it was, and our knowledge of the culture and habitat of the Ancestral or Archaic Indians and the Palaeo-Eskimos of North America, though still far from complete, has become decidedly more secure. And, finally, we know beyond all doubt that the Norsemen *did* reach North America and establish a short-lived but identifiable base at L'Anse aux Meadows in northern Newfoundland.

These considerations, along with others as diverse as new light on the modes and sites of paganism in Iceland and the not always beneficial relationship in later centuries between farming practice and Church ownership of land in Iceland and Greenland, are responsible for the main overall difference between this *Norse Atlantic Saga* and its predecessor. The documentary evidence remains, as it ever must, both indispensable and precious, for not only was it this which set the subject in train and established its historical and geographical context, but for as long as man retains his deep-rooted interest in his past it

will continue to illuminate the findings of science and techno-
logy with that extra dimension of human interest which named
persons and recorded actions, whether factual, prototypal, or
even in part fictive, seem, however unfairly, to enjoy in fuller
measure than the chronicles of anonymity. This in no way
diminishes the importance and interest of the scientific evidence, embracing as it does the findings of archaeology, anthropology, and the entire palaeo-ecological complex, which by
virtue of the ever-increasing accuracy and refinement of their
techniques are now seen to be our main, and perhaps our only,
source of new enlightenment. My acquaintance with northern
archaeologists and their fellows, which I have always held to be
one of the crowning blessings of my working life, began with
Kristján Eldjárn and Sigurður Thórarinsson in Iceland in the
late 1940s, continued with Jørgen Meldgaard, C. L. Vebaek,
Knud Krogh, Bent Fredskild, and H. M. Jansen in Greenland,
Olaf Olsen in Denmark (who with Ole Crumlin-Petersen raised
the Skuldelev ships from the waters of Roskilde Fjord in the
early 1960s, and is now Denmark's State Antiquary and Director of her National Museum), the Norwegians Helge and Anne
Stine Ingstad, and more recently Robert McGhee of the
Archaeological Survey of Canada (National Museum of Man,
Ottawa), the anthropologist Thomas H. McGovern of Hunter
College, New York, and Birgitta Wallace of Parks Canada
(Archaeology, Historic Properties) and presently Director of
the L'Anse aux Meadows Project. Evidence of the learning
and generosity of all these (as of many others) will be found
plentifully in the pages that follow, and the last-named three,
with their contributions on pp. 281–3, 268–76, and 285–304,
have conferred authority and the voice of first-hand experience where a non-archaeologist, however well-provided for in
other areas, could at best contribute piracy and plagiarism.
True, these have never been offences for which authors have
swung at the yard-arm, but the entry and subsequent progression of European man first into the Island Countries of the
Western Atlantic, and then into the New World, is of such
importance and interest to the peoples of both continents that
I count myself most fortunate in being allowed to convey to
my readers the authoritative summaries of fact and interpretation presented in Appendixes IV, V, and VII by three

of the foremost contributors to our present state of knowledge.

Among further changes are the four-parted Introduction,
designed to make the volume more self-contained because
more self-explanatory; the updating and expansion of the three
chapters of Part One, The Story; such checking of the translations (pp. 141–248) as my re-readings of the texts have suggested; while only half of the original six Appendixes have
survived among the present eight. There are four new plates
(nos. 26–9); the number of text-figures has increased from fourteen to thirty, and of maps from five to eight.

Which brings me to my debts and obligations. Various of
these are expressed in context; others were listed in my original
Preface. Here I can only repeat from my *History of the Vikings*
my consciousness of my many Viking-style raids on other men's
riches, and trust that every bibliographical reference will be
held indicative of gratitude and esteem. To the roll-call of
archaeologists and their colleagues already mentioned I offer
the same warm thanks as ever. Alas, that in a few cases my
words will not be heard. If I single out the three friends who are
also my contributors, that is their due and my happiness. Peter
Schledermann, Pat Sutherland, Magnús Einarsson, and William E. Taylor, Jr., of Canada; Eleanor Guralnick and Robert
T. Farrell of the United States; Hilmar Foss and Ólafur Halldórsson of Iceland; and my colleagues and neighbours Harold
Carter and Ifor Enoch here in Wales, have all shown me much
kindness. *Gott ey ǫldum mǫnnum, gott ey ærum mǫnnum!* But
my warmest thanks I owe to Mair, my wife, who—to echo King
Alfred's heartfelt sentence of long ago—amidst the other various and manifold cares of the kingdom, helped me provide a
reputable typescript for the press, and thereafter read proof and
shared with me the making of the Index.

Among institutions I owe thanks to the British Council, the
Archaeological Institute of America and its Chicago Society,
the Canadian Archaeological Association, the Smithsonian
Institution, the Universities of Cornell, Iowa, Wisconsin, and
McMaster, the American-Scandinavian Foundation, the
Museum of Science and Industry of Chicago, for travel, hospi-
tality, the opportunity to air my own views and listen to those of
others, and a deal of scholarly contact otherwise beyond my

reach. My debts to the National Museum of Denmark and to the sister colleges of the University of Wales at Aberystwyth and Cardiff have grown with the years. Among newer friends and for access to recent scholarship it is a pleasure to mention Parks Canada and its helpful researchers.

I am grateful to Peter Fisher (translator) and Hilda Davidson (commentator) for the use of generous extracts of copyright material from their translation of and commentary upon Saxo Grammaticus's *History of the Danes*, 2 vols. (D. S. Brewer: Rowman and Littlefield, 1979 and 1980). The Board of Regents of the University of Wisconsin System, the Editor of *Arctic Anthropology*, and the international team drawn from Greenland, Iceland, Great Britain, and the United States (their names will be found on p. 268) have by an international act of benevolence made me free of the material reproduced in Appendix IV. My obligations in respect of artists and illustrations are in general expressed where the plates, text figures, and maps are listed. Robert McGhee's 'Remarks' at the conclusion of Appendix V are reproduced by permission of the Society for American Archaeology from *American Antiquity*, 49. 1 (1984).

GWYN JONES

1986

Contents

APPENDIXES

Illustrations

LIST OF TEXT FIGURES

THE MAPS

following page 311

Introduction
Home Truths and Far Horizons

I. CAUSES AND EFFECTS

THE sequence of voyages across the North Atlantic Ocean which carried the Norsemen, or Vikings, from their Scandinavian homelands by way of the Faeroes and the British Isles to the discovery of Iceland by c.860–70, to south-west Greenland by c.986, and to the discovery and attempted colonization of some part of the east coast of North America (Helluland, South Baffin Island; Markland, coastal Labrador; and Vinland the Good, northern Newfoundland and somewhat further south) by the millennial year AD 1000, was of immediate and practical concern to the peoples of Scandinavia, of prime though for the time being unrealized significance to the course of European history, and as we now know, a meridian point in the history of mankind. For when the Greenlander Thorvald Eiriksson and the Icelander Thorfinn Karlsefni, whether we regard them as authenticated historical characters or the named prototypes of their nameless contemporaries—when these and their ships' crews in their continuing search for new land 'habitable and trespassable' in the west made contact with the native populations of North America (whose separate odyssey had brought them by way of Siberia and Alaska and thereafter south and east throughout the American continent)—it was then, and only then, that 'two human populations expanding around the globe in opposite directions met for the first time'.[1] It was a meeting which had been at least 12,000 years and some 500 generations in the making. Like their Indian and Eskimo predecessors, the Norsemen too came to explore, colonize, and possess for ever. But for a variety of reasons, of which a warlike and well-equipped native population was the most compelling, this did not happen. In the words of *Eiríks Saga Rauða*: 'It now seemed

---

[1] Robert McGhee, 'Contact Between Native North Americans and the Medieval Norse: A Review of the Evidence', *American Antiquity*, 49. 1 (1984), p. 22.

clear to Karlsefni that though the quality of the land was admirable, there would always be fear and strife dogging them on account of those who already inhabited it. So they made ready to leave, setting their hearts on their own country.' So clear was the lesson, and so lasting its effect, that a European acquaintance with North America was delayed for a further five hundred years, and the honour of the discovery remained all that while with the Norsemen alone.

But before a traveller's tale, a home truth, serving at such a heady moment to remind us that before mainland European man could set foot on the shores of Iceland, Greenland, and North America, there must have existed the impulse, the opportunity, and the means to get him there, attempt something purposeful (if only to survey and survive), and get back home with his tidings. Few things come to pass in that chequered and obscured chronicle of events we call History without a traceable cause and context; and the Norse Atlantic voyages west conform to rule. They were not rash, haphazard, and isolated ventures, though the written records sometimes tempt us to think that they were. They arose out of their place and time, and were the product of a set of conditions conducive to geographical discovery and attempted colonization. The place was Scandinavia, and more especially the western ocean-facing seaboard of Norway, and the time was roughly consonant with the so-called Viking Age, and especially with that aspect of it known as the Viking Movement.

The Viking Age is the name bestowed by modern historians on the three and a quarter centuries c.760–1080, when what was happening in Scandinavia was of decisive consequence for the shape and texture of the peoples we now know as Danes, Swedes and Norwegians, and the territories we know as Denmark, Sweden, and Norway, and of inescapable and for the most part painful concern to their European neighbours. This was because political, economic, climatic, dynastic, and in the widest sense social events and conditions in the Viking lands during the Viking Age made it impossible for the Viking peoples to remain cooped up inside their disparate and often inhospitable homelands. So, like a host of peoples before and since, they overspilled their natural boundaries, and as seekers of land and loot made a deep and hurtful mark upon other countries and peoples. It was this overspill, in large measure violent and acquisitive, conducted by folk with a language, religion, and legal system different from the peoples they maltreated, that for reasons of scholarly convenience and historical propriety is called the Viking Movement.

It manifested itself in a variety of ways and over a wide area, in warfare, piracy, trade, colonization, the seizure of goods and people (the freedom-loving Vikings were inveterate slavers), fishing- and hunting-grounds, territories small as a farm or extensive as a kingdom. The Swedes moved by way of the Baltic into the country we now call Russia, and proceeded by way of the great Russian rivers and waterways to usurp power and seize booty at Novgorod, Bulgar and the Volga bend, Kiev, and so down to the Caspian and the Muslim world and the palaces and emporia of Constantinople itself. As the Age advanced, the Danes pressed south and south-west to assault the British Isles, the Frankish Empire, and even the islands and cities of the Mediterranean. Of their campaigns and conquests, the sea ivory, furs, hides, and slaves they carried south, and the silver and silks and slaves, the dinars and danegelds they bore back north, it is beyond our commission to tell; and they are mentioned only that we may see the Atlantic voyages against a backcloth of cause and effect, need and desire, ambition and action, characteristic of the Viking Age at home and the Viking Movement abroad.

We return to the Norwegians, the *Norðmenn* (Nordmanni), the men of the North Way (*Norðweg*). It was they who initiated and whose descendants sustained the Atlantic sea-routes, and this for a number of reasons. We begin with the obvious and essential observation that the Scandinavian lands belong to the north of Europe, and that Norway is the most northerly of them. Their physical axis lies from north-east to south-west; but in terms of human geography it lies north-south, with most of the fertile and level areas in the south. The northern half of the peninsula is largely mountainous, often inhospitable, and cold. North of Uppsala, say, good farming land was in short supply, with resultant pressure both north and south. Distances are formidable. I have remarked on an earlier occasion how astonishing it is to learn in Malmö that one is nearer as the crow flies to Turkey than to the North Cape, and in Oslo that Rome is more

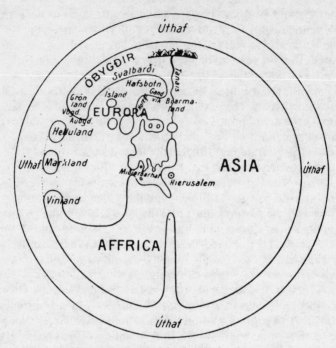

2. THE WORLD CIRCLE OF THE NORSEMEN
After A. A. Bjørnbo

accessible than Kirkenes. The coastline of Norway, not counting the indentations, is some 1,600 miles long, and an appreci-
able length of it lies north of the Arctic Circle. Providentially,
the circumstance that it is warmed by the waters of the Gulf
Stream and the mainland protected by its mighty *skærgaard* or
defensive wall of some 16,000 islands, skerries and the like,
keeps it navigable throughout all save the most hostile days of
the year. Similarly, many-islanded Denmark and the archipel-
agos of Sweden had encouraged the habit of travel and transport by water from the Bronze Age onwards.

The ordering of society in these sea-girt and mountain-
shackled lands was entirely of its own day and age, circumscribed
and not given to change. From the literary and archaeological
remains we can observe at close quarters a society with

three broadly defined classes: a ruling warrior-élite, the free-born user of land or comparable free-born person, and the slave. Kings and court poets, priests and law-givers, the makers of story, legend, and myth, were agreed upon this hierarchical and warlike principle. As the tenth-century mythological poem *Rígsþula* explained, the three orders of society were god-ordained and god-begotten for their separate fortunes. The slave did the world's dirty work, without pay and without legal or moral safeguards.[2] The freeman discharged honourable tasks and had the right to bear arms. The warrior-élite waged war in pursuit of riches and glory.

The retardive effect of high latitudes, long winters, severing distances, and a barriered landscape upon the emergence and development of the northern kingdoms and their society was considerable. Harsh mountains, dense forests, and sundering waterways ensured the persistence of the old enclosed farmer-communities and the Viking aristocracy, blessed with estates, privileges, weapons of war, and stiff-necked in its pride. A kingdom in the Northlands was what belonged to a king, and no king could maintain himself except by force of arms. The felt shortage of cultivable land, and the permanent need for ships and fighting-men to defend one's own goods and rights and to usurp those of other people, were powerfully contributory to the strife-torn internal and external history of the Viking Age.[3]

II. SHIPS AND SEAFARING

BUT whatever the struggle for land and aggrandizement at home, and whatever the local constrictions of climate, land shortage, and an increasing population, little of the Viking Movement overseas, including the seaborne assaults on the British Isles and the Continent which began in the last decades

[2] The practice of slavery among Viking peoples has received less attention than it deserves. In part this is due to the odd circumstance that the word 'thrall' (*þræll*) some two hundred years ago acquired romantic and attractive connotations: the thrall of love, to be enthralled, the adjective enthralling, and the like. The reality was, as always and everywhere, an abomination deodorized (but not sweetened) by usage.

[3] For an ampler statement see Gwyn Jones, *A History of the Vikings* (1984), pp. 59–77.

of the eighth century, and the North Atlantic voyages of discovery and colonization which distinguished the ninth, tenth, and early eleventh centuries—little of this could take place until northern shipwrights had brought the sailing-ship to some such state of excellence as we observe in the vessels found at Gokstad in Norway and Skuldelev in Denmark. From all the evidence, pictorial and archaeological, the necessary command of techniques was attained about the middle of the eighth century. Thereafter for some four hundred years the Vikings had the best ships of their time in northern and north-western European waters.

If we take the Gokstad ship as our prototype (a fine vessel of the mid ninth century), we might sum up the situation at the time of the early Viking raids thus: around the year 800 a leader of rank and means could have at his command for ventures overseas a seaworthy and manœuvrable sailing-ship, some $76\frac{1}{2}$ feet long from stem to stern, with a beam of $17\frac{1}{2}$ feet, and a little over 6 feet 4 inches from the bottom of the keel to the gunwale amidships. The Gokstad ship had a keel of 57 feet 9 inches, made from a single oak timber, and was clinker built of sixteen strakes of differing but carefully calculated thickness. The strakes were joined together by round-headed iron rivets driven through from the outside and secured inside by means of small square iron plates. The caulking was of tarred animal hair or wool. The hull was kept in shape by nineteen frames and crossbeams. The decking of pine, in this case loose so that the space beneath could be used for storage, was laid over these beams. The strakes below the waterline were tied to the frames with spruce root lashings (in the Oseberg ship with narrow strips of whale-bristle, in the Tune ship with bast), a device which contributed much to the ship's flexibility. This was still further increased by a carefully systematized treenailing of the above-water strakes to wooden knees and cross-beams or, in the case of the top two, to half-ribs secured to the strakes below and butted into the underside of the gunwale. The elasticity of this part of the ship was such that the replica of the Gokstad ship sailed across the Atlantic in 1893 by Magnus Andersen (a twenty-eight-day passage from Bergen to Newfoundland) showed a gunwale twisting out of true by as much as 6 inches, yet was safe, fast, and watertight. With her mighty keel and flexible frame and planking the Viking ship was an inspired combination of strength and elasticity.

The ship was constructed almost entirely of oak. The sixteen pairs of oars were of pine, so regulated in length that they struck the water in unison. They were operated not by means of rowlocks but by closable holes in the fourteenth strake. The mast, too, was of pine, probably about 35 feet tall, with a big square sail made of strips of heavy woollen cloth, strengthened, it would appear, by a rope network, and hoisted on a yard some 37 feet long. From the Gotland pictorial stones it appears that sail could be effectively shortened by the use of reefing lines, and recent opinion has inclined to the view that the Viking ship could be sailed across and even near the wind. This was largely due to the use of the *beitiáss*, a removable pole or tacking-boom whose heavy end was seated in a socket abeam of the mast while its lighter end was fitted to the forward leech of the sail to keep it taut and drawing when the ship was sailing on the wind.[4] She was steered by a side-rudder fastened to the starboard quarter, a singularly effective instrument pronounced by Magnus Andersen to be one of the clearest proofs of northern shipbuilding skills and seamanship. On his Atlantic crossing he found it satisfactory in every way, decidedly superior to a rudder on the sternpost, and manageable by a single member of the crew in any weather with just one small line to help him. Such ships would necessarily be furnished with a ship's boat, sometimes stowed on board, sometimes towed behind. It is unlikely that our sources' picturesque references to such exceed or even equal the dreadful and often fatal emergencies in which these were resorted to. Discomfort and squalor, especially on a colonizing voyage complete with families, animals, and extra gear abounding, were dire. But most things are made bearable by

[4] The *beitiáss* has been reported on favourably by Captain Magnus Andersen, who crossed the Atlantic in a replica of the Gokstad ship; Captain Folgar, who in 1932 took a replica of a 60–foot *knörr* across the Atlantic by one of Columbus's routes and returned to Norway by way of Newfoundland; and by Captain C. Sølver, after his experience of the *Hugin* in 1949. As the number of full-sized replicas of the Norse ocean-goer has increased during the last decade, with a resultant increase in voyages between the Scandinavian countries, to London and York, and even as I write (August 1984) the *Saga Siglar*, Captain Ragnar Thorseth, to West Greenland and Vinland, respect has grown, with good reason, for the sea-going qualities of the *hafskip* and *knörr*.

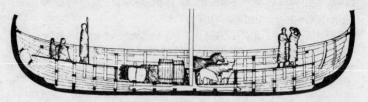

3. LENGTHWISE SECTION OF SKULDELEV WRECK I, A SEA-GOING
CARGO-SHIP WITH A HOLD AMIDSHIPS

usage and compulsion, and the general standards of northern
hygiene and cleanliness must have tamed the most queasy. Bail-
ing was by bucket and muscle-power; the anchor was of iron,
and in general was served by a rope and not an iron chain. The
ship could be tented for sleeping quarters by night. Finally it is
worth re-emphasizing that the ship which carried the Norsemen
overseas, whether to the British Isles, the Frankish Empire, or
(self-evidently) to the Atlantic Islands, Iceland, Greenland, and
America, was a *sailing-ship*: her oars were an auxiliary form of
power for use when she was becalmed, in some state of emer-
gency, or required manœuvring in narrow waters, fjords, for
example, or rivers. This was true of raiding ships and carriers
alike, though the ratio of men to space would naturally be
higher in the raider.

The ship of all work, the true ocean-goer, the *hafskip* or
knörr, was in its general construction similar to the Gokstad
ship, but broader in the beam, deeper in the water, and of a
higher freeboard. This has always seemed clear from saga evidence, and was confirmed by the raising of Wrecks 1 and 3 from
the waters of Peberrenden–Skuldelev in Roskilde Fjord, Denmark, in 1962. The five Skuldelev ships were sunk in the channel there c.1000, to prevent a sea-borne incursion. Wreck 2 is a
longship, some 95 feet long and 13 feet 9 inches wide, fully
capable of moving fifty to sixty men over to England; Wreck 5 is
a small warship, 59 feet by 8½. But the real finds proved to be
Wreck 3, oak-built, 43½ feet long and almost 11 feet wide, and
Wreck 1, built mainly of pine, some 54½ feet by 15. In these we
discern a coaster and a deep-sea carrier respectively—the first
of their indispensable kind to yield up their secrets to the ship-
wright and archaeologist. Students of the western voyages may

well hold Wreck 1 in esteem as representative of the *knerrir* which maintained the Iceland–Greenland–Vinland routes, even if their beginning was with the Gokstad ship. With her open carrying-space or hold amidships, her half-decks fore and aft protective of further freight, she is estimated to have been able to carry a cargo of 15–20 tons in a carrying-space of 30–35 cubic metres. With her good design, sound construction, tractable sail, and shallow draught, this northern-type clinker-built, double-ended keel boat could carry her cargo to all marts, all coasts, and put it safely ashore.

It is to the sturdy *knörr* (pl. *knerrir*) that we must turn when we seek to understand the haven-finding art of the Norse navigators. It is generally accepted that when the great Atlantic voyages of discovery and exploration took place in the ninth and tenth centuries the North had neither compass nor chart. How then could a Norwegian, Icelandic, or Greenland skipper in the year 1020 make his way confidently and accurately from, let us say, Bergen in Norway to the Eastern and Western Settlements of Greenland? Clearly he had his sailing directions, and some of these have been preserved in the passage from *Landnámabók* quoted on p. 157 below. First and foremost he would commit himself to a latitude sailing. This was no haphazard affair. To begin with he would move thirty miles or so north of Bergen to the landmark of Stad, because this had the same degree of latitude as his landfall in Greenland. If now he sailed due west he would find himself after the right count of days passing north of the Shetlands, and thereafter south of the Faeroes at a recognizable and prescribed distance from them. On the same course he would next traverse the ocean well to the south of Iceland and know where he was, not by the later measurement in miles, but by observing the birds and sea-creatures associated with those waters. On a good passage, in clear weather, and with a following wind, this part of the voyage would have taken about seven to ten days. It would take him almost as long again to sight the east coast of Greenland about eighty miles north of Cape Farewell. Now he must head southwest and reach the west coast of Greenland either by rounding the Cape or by threading Prins Christians Sund. From here on he would be following a well-described coastal route till he reached Herjolfsnes (the modern Ikigait), with its Norse farms and haven. Ahead lay the landmark of Hvarf, and thereafter many ports of call in the Eastern Settlement, in the region of the modern Julianehaab. He was now in the warm northward-setting coastal current of West Greenland and would progress with comparative ease and plenty of directions to the Western Settlement, in the neighbourhood of the modern Godthaab. He would have sailed the best part of 1,700 miles and taken the best part of a month to do so.

A voyage from Greenland (and we know of none from any-where else) to the Promontorium Winlandiæ would be of com-parable length and duration. The distance from Cape Farewell to northern Newfoundland as the crow flies is about 500 miles, but there is no evidence that any such flight or sea-voyage was ever attempted. Unable to determine longitude, the Norseman had no navigational aids to make such a crossing thinkable, much less possible. And even if he had he must contend with the heavy eastward tilt of the Canadian coast, with the conse-quence that southern Labrador is in the same longitude as Disco Bay back in Greenland, and the out-thrust peninsula of Nova Scotia in today's standard time is a full time-zone ahead of Boston. So the Vinland voyages of which we read in the docu-mentary sources, with the possible exception of Thorstein Eiriksson's storm-tossed meanderings (see p. 218 below), fol-lowed the 'classic' route north, west, and then the south- and south-east-running coast of Labrador. That means that our skipper would continue north from the Settlements by the well-attested route to the northern hunting-grounds, to the modern Holsteinsborg or the huge island of Disco. If from Disco he turned south-west for the eastern coast of Canada he would be conforming to a classic principle of Norse navigation, to make the shortest practicable ocean passage and use the clearest land-marks. He would also stand to benefit by the frequent northerly winds of the Davis Strait. From Disco or Holsteinsborg he would reach the southerly part of Baffin Island and know what kind of coast to expect there. He must now follow the land south, for an estimated number of days, passing the big inlet of Frobisher Bay and the entrance to Hudson Bay, till he sighted the forest land of Labrador, south of modern Nain. South of Hamilton Inlet he would be looking for the white beaches of the Strand and the distinctive keel-shaped Cape Porcupine (the

Furdustrandir and Kjalarnes of the sagas), and so down past Battle Harbour till in time he sighted Belle Isle and thereafter the northernmost tip of Newfoundland and Cape Bauld. From here to Épaves Bay and the Norse houses by Black Duck Brook was a defined route without navigational problems—though not, of course, without the formidable problems and perils of a rocky, ragged, and in its southern reaches notoriously fog-bound coast.

This, inevitably, is a crude simplification of the sailing directions a skipper and his crew must carry in their heads as they sailed the coasts of West Greenland and Labrador. The knowledge of landmarks could be hardly less demanding on a sailor through the Norwegian skærgaard, or a newcomer threading the western islands of Scotland, though there the use of local skills might generally be relied on. An immense sea-lore was indispensable, the lessons to be learned from cloud formations and the colour of water, marine creatures and birds,[5] ice-blink, currents, driftwood and weed, the feel of a wind. These sailors knew the sun and stars, the arts of rough and dead reckoning, and the use of a line to search the ocean's floor. In a good day's sailing of twenty-four hours they could cover 120 miles and more.[6]

[5] The use of birds for navigation goes back far beyond Floki Vilgerdarson's voyage to Iceland (see p. 158 below). The daily and seasonal flights of different birds would be closely marked by the mariner. It may have been the annual flights of geese migrating to their Icelandic breeding grounds which first convinced men in Ireland that somewhere north or north-west of them lay the land they would eventually discover and use for hermitages.

[6] The problems connected with the term *dægr sigling*, 'a day's sailing', are many and have been much discussed, notably by G. M. Gathorne-Hardy, *The Norse Discoverers of America* (1921), and Almar Næss, *Hvor lå Vinland?* (1956). For the early coasting voyages it seems to have meant a not too rigidly calculated twelve hours' sailing. When the Norwegian Óttar (Ohthere) tells us that it was over a month's journey from his home in Halogaland down the coast of Norway to Skiringssalir he makes it clear that he sailed with a following wind by day but went ashore every night. But Wulfstan, the second sea-captain whose narrative was incorporated by King Alfred in his translation of Orosius, tells us how he sailed the unobstructed course from Hedeby to Truso in seven days and nights, and that 'the ship was the whole way running under sail'. There is what appears to be an unequivocal statement to the same effect in *Heimskringla* (*Ólafs Saga Helga*, cap. 125), telling how Thorarin Nefjolfsson put to sea from Mœr in Norway on an urgent royal errand and enjoyed such a speedy following wind that he sailed to Eyrar (Eyrabakki) in Iceland in eight days (*á átta dægrum*) and could inform the Icelanders there that 'four nights ago I left King

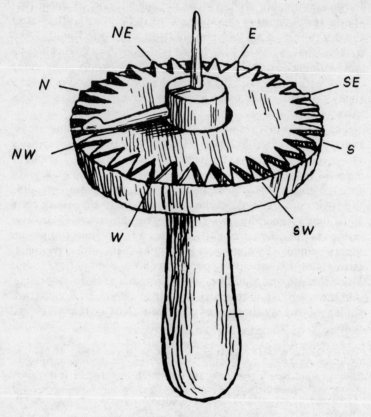

4. A NORSE BEARING-DIAL

But for the long Atlantic voyages between Norway, Faeroes, Iceland, Greenland, America, the first requisite was the mariner's ability to fix his latitude. That the Norseman could do this

Olaf Haraldsson . . . '. A day's sailing would thus appear to be half the diurnal round, a twelve-hour stint, and on sea-crossings in the long northern hours of summer light two such stints meant the full use of ship, crew, and the elements. But the sagas often leave the matter unresolved, like our own 'a day's outing' or 'a day's work', and *dægr sigling* seems at times to convey nothing more precise than that 'it takes a day to get there'. There is an excellent discussion of these matters by Paul Adam in 'Problèmes de navigation dans l'Atlantique Nord', in R. Boyer, *Les Vikings et leur civilisation. Problèmes actuels* (Paris, 1978), pp. 49–60.

is certain, though there is still doubt as to his method and instruments. We read, for example, of a detailed set of tables attributed to the Icelander Star-Oddi, which gave the sun's midday latitude week by week throughout the year, as he observed this in northern Iceland towards the end of the tenth century. This or similar information recorded on so simple an object as a marked stick would give the mariner an indication of his then latitude as compared with a known place. Any observation of the midday sun, or if need be of the Pole Star, even by so crude a method as the measurement of a shadow cast at noon or the calculation of the Star's height above the horizon expressed in terms of one's own arm, hand, or thumb, was a fair guide to latitude, which on the western voyages was much more important than longitude. Because if a storm-driven mariner (and there were many such during the early voyages of discovery and the ensuing period of trade) could get himself back to his correct latitude and sail in the desired direction he must, accidents and disasters apart, reach the place he was aiming for.[7] The extreme casualness of thirteenth-century saga sources relating to sea-voyages is possibly thus explained. A ship leaves the Oslofjord for Breidafjord in Iceland, or Breidafjord for the Eastern Settlement in Greenland, or the Eastern Settlement for Leifsbudir in Vinland, or makes any such voyage in reverse, and the full extent of our information may be that it had a following wind, an easy passage, was much delayed, or blown about, and then arrived at its destination. The casualness would be still more understandable if we could be sure that in the Viking Age the Norsemen had learned to make use of the light polarizing qualities of calcite or Iceland spar (*sólarsteinn*, sunstone), and could thus make an observation of the sun even when it was hidden from view. It is reasonable to assume that they had bearing-dials of a simple but effective kind, though the only indication of this is the half of a round disc of wood marked

---

[7] In effect, this meant the mariner's ability to determine where he was by observation of the sun or stars on that 360-mile-wide belt of ocean about 58° to 63° N., whose eastern (i.e. Norwegian) extremities were Jaeren or Lindesnes in the south and Trondheim in the north, and which gave access in the west to the Orkneys, Shetlands, and Faeroes, and to Iceland, south-west Greenland, and the North American coast from southern Baffin Island to northern Newfoundland.

with equidistant notches discovered by C. L. Vebæk in 1948 at Siglufjord in the Eastern Settlement of Greenland. Had it been whole the notches would number thirty-two, offering a sophisticated division of the horizon reminiscent of the late Middle Ages rather than Viking times, when an eight-point dial conforming to the eight named points of the Old Norse horizon would appear more natural.

III. HISTORY AND HISTORIOGRAPHY

WE turn now to those other enablers of our subject of study, the written sources relating to the Western Voyages, and more particularly those translated on pp. 143–248 below, some textual information about which will be found in Appendix VIII. It is by now widely known that during the last hundred years or more the documentary bases of our knowledge of the entire Viking Age have come in for a sustained and severely critical examination of their historical value, and as a result (and the conclusion is both irresistible and irreversible) there has been a marked decline of belief in their trustworthiness. Once-valued chronicles, annals, poems, inscriptions, and genealogies have all been examined and in varying degree found wanting—and maybe the Icelandic sagas, including the once confidently styled historical compendia like *Flateyarbók*, *Heimskringla*, and the King's Sagas generally, most wanting of all. Their every statement has been tested, and much of what was long accepted as a bedrock of fact is now seen as a crumbling cellarage of unverifiable tradition, skilled invention, tendentious evidence, and the vast and variegated book-learned lumber of antiquarian heads. Occasionally this has produced its own new gullibility of disbelief, but the overall gain can fairly be seen as enormous. Fortunately, the particular sagas and histories which tell of or bear upon the Atlantic voyages have never presented their students with a crude choice of all or nothing. It has always been the practice of their more informed critics to reject the impossible, question the improbable, sift the suspicious, and bring the residue to the bar of knowledge and judgement—a task made easier over the last twenty-five years or so by the skills of the archaeologist and his colleagues in the allied sciences.

The Atlantic voyages of the Vikings were not hare-brained adventures, forlorn hopes, or lucky throws of the dice. They were forward-looking and purposeful. They were not shipborne invasions leading to conquest, but planned attempts to colonize, develop and usefully exploit empty or sparsely inhabited living-space. It was only in Vinland-America that the first waves of explorers found a native population numerous enough and warlike enough to bar their way. The Viking Movement west may even appear less noxious than it was because, unlike the incursus into Europe, which was chronicled by its victims and had a well-deserved bad press, the western voyages were recorded almost exclusively by sympathetic and admiring northern historians and saga-men. The resulting documents are not pot-pourris of blood and destruction, but appear (for Vikings) restrained and reasonable. When we make, as we must, such self-inviting discards as the accretions of classical legend, Germanic folk-tale, biblical reminiscence, superstition and mythology, travellers' tales, romantic borrowings, and the many muddles attendant upon an over-long and far from disinterested oral tradition (and all these things are to be found in profusion, and usually under protective native colouring, in the Icelandic records)—once these are disposed of, the documents look more reasonable still.

It is therefore advisable for us to approach the voyages and assess the documents in a commensurately reasonable way. Like all human endeavour, the voyages were subject to miscalculation and good and bad fortune; but essentially they were safeguarded and hopeful ventures, requiring preparation, resolution and endurance, discipline and comradeship, and high qualities of leadership; and without good ships and skilled seamanship they could hardly have begun, much less proved successful. The men who sailed the sea-routes and beheld new terrains were full-fledged in the same hard school of precept and experience as Ohthere of Halogaland, and saw matters quite another way from that of Adam of Bremen and Saxo Grammaticus.[8]

Also, the Norse Atlantic saga, like the historical and family sagas themselves, is a subject where historiography, whether as

---

[8] For these two points of view see Appendixes I(*a*) and I(*b*).

the history of tradition or the tradition of history, is part of the whole cloth. For this is a context where history, by virtue of our limited knowledge, is of necessity the more or less chronological, more or less narrative, more or less accurate account of more or less identifiable persons and more or less verifiable events. The errors and misunderstandings of the written sources, like the long process of archaeological trial and error—to say nothing of at least a hundred displays of innocent self-deception or deliberate falsification (the so-called North American 'Viking relics' or 'remains')—these things are for study and assessment, and the first two categories for eventual enlightenment. Further, it seems to many that for any student, or general reader, to be left unversed in such engrossing topics as *Landnámabók*'s variable narrative of the threefold discovery and its anthologized account of the settlement of Iceland, and probably over-confident account of the first exploration of south-west Greenland (p. 209), and the exploits in Vinland of Eirik the Red's altogether too remarkable daughter Freydis (pp. 204 and 228), is to have real loss inflicted on him, with no attendant gain. That our written sources are embellished and likewise disfigured after the fashion of their time and kind is not a suspicious circumstance. The absence of these characteristics would be much more worrying. The more so inasmuch as the essentials of their story—the successive discoveries of new lands and the location and duration of the Norse Atlantic settlements—are beyond dispute, though surely open to improvement, as recent research work in Greenland and Canada seems to make certain.

IV. THE NORTHERN WORLD-PICTURE

IT would be presumptuous to say we have finished with the home truths, but the farthest horizons of our chapter-heading still await attention. What was the world-picture, the *imago mundi* of the Norseman? What was his view of the nature, demarcation, and geographical disposition of the physical, visible, and palpable world he knew he lived in? We are straightway confronted with two seemingly contradictory but in effect not irreconcilable concepts, one provided by the learned and loquacious bookmen of the North, the other pieced

5. THE DEVOURING WHIRLPOOL (OLAUS MAGNUS)

together by men who did not speculate over-nicely, but saw the northern seas and lands for themselves, and saw them not as the bookmen described them, but as they were—yet again the contrast between Adam of Bremen or Saxo Grammaticus and the good Ohthere. Wherever there was an attempted fusion of these views, it shows the expected mixture of fantasy and fact, mythology and early geographical science, fond arbitrary deduction and the checks of observation and common sense. No man illustrates this better than the learned and well-intentioned author of the *Historia Norwegiæ* (*c.*1170):

We have no knowledge as to what people dwell beyond these [Norway's northerly neighbours, including the Kirjals, Kvens, Finnas, and Permians]. But certain voyagers by sea, when seeking to make their way home from Iceland to Norway, were driven by violent and adverse winds into the Wintry Zone and fetched up between Greenland and Bjarmaland where, as they have testified, they encountered fantastically big men and a land inhabited by virgins who are said to become pregnant by drinking water. Separated from these regions by frozen bergs (*congelatis scopulis*) is Greenland, which country, discovered and settled and fortified with the Catholic Faith by the Icelanders, is the westernmost bound of Europe, extending almost as far as the Isles of Africa, where the refluent streams of Ocean [Mare Oceanum?]

flood in and over (*ubi inundant oceani refluenta*). Beyond Greenland, still farther to the north, hunters have come across people of small stature (*homunciones*), who are called *Scrælinga*. When they are struck [i.e. by a weapon] their wounds turn white and they do not bleed, but if they are hurt to death they bleed and bleed almost endlessly. They do not know the use of iron, but employ walrus tusks as missiles and sharpened stones in place of knives.[9]

The northern world-picture of the antiquaries had a good deal in common with that of the remote Classical world, though we are uninformed as to their transmission or degree of influence one upon the other, if any. Thus the Greek geographers (and poets) knew that there was a habitable world of men, the *Oikumene*, set loosely around an Inner Sea, and growing ever more barbarous and monster-ridden as it receded outwards from the known centres of culture and civilization, till at last the entire land-area, both known and conjecturable, was itself enclosed within the impassable confines of a Mare Oceanum which flowed around and occupied what was left of the world, and was inimical to life as human beings know it. Just so, thousands of years later, northern scholars would write of an Inner Sea, enclosed by a 'land-ring' beyond whose vague and perilous circumference lay *their* Mare Oceanum, from whose extravagant horrors no traveller-too-far could hope to return.

---

[9] *Hist. Norw.*, p. 119 in G. Storm, *Monumenta Historica Norvegiæ* (Kristiania, 1880). The *Historia* exists only in a manuscript of the mid fifteenth century, but Scandinavian scholarship accepts that the work, or part of it, is of much earlier date. Thorkil Damsgaard Olsen's summarizing chapter on 'Kongekrøniker og Kongesagær' in *Norrøn Fortællekunst* (Copenhagen, 1965) considers that it was written down before *c.*1266, and in part composed before the end of the twelfth century. The passage quoted here appears to relate to the period 1160–70, and there is general agreement (for a summary see Jansen, *Critical Account*, pp. 33–4) that it was written between then and the end of the century. The author, be it noted (his identity can only be guessed at), is sound on the discovery, settlement, and conversion of Greenland, and right about the northerly location, stature, and weapons of the Eskimo. He makes no reference to Helluland, Markland, or Vinland by name, but these may well be his African islands. Otherwise (and who among commentators shall cast the first stone?) he was the happy prisoner of the book-learning of his day.

His ocean-bestiary for northern waters might have been compiled with the unborn Olaus Magnus in view: whales which crunch ships like shrimps, and swallow down sailors; the one-eyed walrus with waving mane; the kraken and the wolf-fish; and a kind of marine uniped, the *hafstrambus* (merman?) sans head or tail, and looking like a tree-trunk as it hops up and down.

This Ocean was a development of the Norse pagan notion of the original Emptiness—which yet contained within itself every element necessary for the world's emergence into being. This was Ginnungagap, the Phantasmal Void, the Old Chaos of northern mythology, the expectant, magic-charged, in today's phrase 'cosmic soup' preceding the generation of life and order. Only now, instead of its being the beginning of everything, it was by virtue of its defining role around the rim of the world's flat or saucer-shaped disc the end of everything.[10]

But, we may well ask ourselves, had these cosmic adumbrations, from the Eddas to Adam of Bremen, from the synoptic historians to the *Natural History* of Pontoppidan, any discernible influence upon the course of Norse seamanship, discovery, and colonization? The answer is a cautious 'yes'. A belief in an Inner Sea or *Hafsbotn* (bay or gulf of ocean), easily identified with the North Atlantic Ocean and its contiguous waterways, was as reassuring to the Norse mariner as an awareness of the Mediterranean Sea's centrality was to his Greek, Roman, Phoenician and Massaliote counterpart. Not least because of the protective land-ring which separated it from the Mare Oceanum. The North Atlantic, true, 'that old grey Widow-Maker', was a formidable haunt for sailors, with its storms and winds and fogs, its immense rollers and baleful mirages, its tides and maelstroms, sea-hedges and whirlpools, and all such 'navels of the sea', but its accepted (though erroneous) geographical limits ensured in homely phrase that though you might fall into its waters, you couldn't fall off its edge.[11]

[10] This seems the place to record two important negatives. (1) There is no evidence that Strabo's concept of a global world ('The inhabited world forms a complete circle, itself meeting itself, so that if the immensity of the Atlantic Sea did not prevent, we could sail from Iberia to India along one and the same parallel over the remainder of the circle', *The Geography of Strabo*, trans. H. L. Jones (Loeb, 1917), was known to the West before the fifteenth century. For a summarizing article see T. E. Goldstein, 'Geography in Fifteenth-Century Florence', in *Merchants and Scholars* (Minneapolis, 1965). (2) We know of no document or map from southern Europe throughout the entire Middle Ages which makes mention of the Norse discovery of North America.

[11] But the Hydra of Error would continue to put forth new heads. Ginnungagap would appear in treatises and on maps not only as the surrounding Mare Oceanum, but as a kind of entry into or re-entry from that Ocean, to be found either between Vinland and Markland (Newfoundland and Labrador), Vinland and Greenland, or (by interpretation) between northern Labrador and Green-

The general state of knowledge in respect of the northern and westernmost reaches of the Norse world, with its accuracies, approximations, and echoing errors, is conveyed, suitably enough, by manuscripts of unknown or uncertain authorship and arguable dates lying between the mid twelfth and late fourteenth centuries. However, for all their uncertainties, they long pre-date the voyages of Columbus. The first is the so-called Geographical Treatise, MS AM 736, I, 4to (*c.*1300):

North of Norway lies Finnmark; from there the land veers north-east and east to Bjarmaland, which pays tribute to the king of Russia. From Bjarmaland there is uninhabited land extending the whole way north until Greenland begins. To the south of Greenland lies Helluland, and then Markland, and from there it is not far to Vinland, which some people consider extends from Africa. England and Scotland are one island, but each is a separate kingdom. Ireland is a large island. Iceland is likewise a large island, to the north of Ireland. These islands are all in that part of the world which is called Europe.

Konungs Skuggsjá, the 'King's Mirror', of *c.*1250, likewise sees Greenland as part of the Eurasian land mass, and considers that beyond Greenland no further land will be found, 'only the great ocean which runs around the world; and it is said . . . that the strait through which the empty ocean flows comes in by Greenland, and into the gap between the lands [i.e. Helluland, Markland, Vinland], and thereafter with fjords and gulfs it divides all countries, where it runs into the circle of the world.' A passage attributed to the lost compendium *Gripla*, but preserved in the *Grænlands annál*, a collection of great though irregular value of 1623, offers some amplification:

land, localities which bring the Strait of Belle Isle, Hudson Strait, and Davis Strait into the picture. Wherever sited, Ginnungagap was recognizable by the volume and fury of its tides and whirlpools and its strong whiff of Niflheim. Hence Adam of Bremen's account of certain mariners who north of Iceland 'fell into that numbing ocean's dark mist which could hardly be penetrated with the eyes [i.e. the *Dumbshaf* or Foggy Sea]'. Here they found to their terror that the 'current of the fluctuating ocean whirled back to its mysterious fountainhead and with utmost impetuosity drew the unhappy sailors . . . on to . . . the abysmal chasm—that deep in which the back flow of the sea . . . is absorbed and in turn revomited'. These particular mariners, by rowing with all their might, were fortunate enough to have escaped the 'peril of darkness and the land of frost' (trans. Tschann). I owe the excerpt to V. H. de P. Cassidy, 'The Location of Ginnungagap', in *Scandinavian Studies, Essays Presented to H. G. Leach*, ed. C. F. Bayerschmidt and Erik J. Friis (1965).

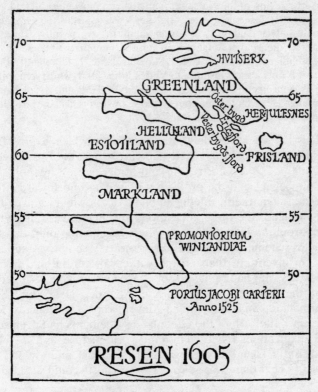

6. POUL RESEN'S MAP, 1605

'Relevant features' redrawn by G. M. Gathorne-Hardy to show its correspondences with the Stefánsson map of 1590, showing among other things the northern land-bridge, the non-existent Frisland, and a series of geographical approximations from Davis Strait to the Gulf of St. Lawrence

North of Norway lies Finnmark. Then the land veers north-east and east until it comes to Bjarmaland . . . There are uninhabited wastes extending the whole way north as far as the land which is called Greenland. . . In front of these lie the gulfs of ocean. Then the land veers south-west, and there are glaciers and fjords there, and islands lie off the glaciers. One glacier cannot be explored. To the second it is a half-month's voyage, and to the third a week's voyage. That is the one nearest the settlement, and is called Hvitserk [White-Sark]. Then the land veers north [here follows a brief account of the west coast of Greenland, the region of the Norse settlements] . . . Now must be told what lies opposite Greenland [i.e. what lies west opposite the Greenland colonies]. That land is called Furdustrandir [Marvelstrands]. There the cold is so intense that so far as men know it is uninhabitable. South of it lies Helluland, which is called Skrælingaland [Eskimoland]. From there it is only a short distance to Vinland the Good, which some maintain is a projection of Africa. Between Vinland and Greenland is Ginnungagap, which comes out of the sea which is called Mare Oceanum and surrounds the entire world.[12]

This, if we set aside those statements which express the unknown authors' (and their audience's) inevitably erroneous notions of the northern land-bridge, the mythological Ginnungagap, and the projection of Vinland northwards from Africa, is a markedly intelligent blend of knowledge and deduction. Indeed, the three aberrations are themselves fair deductions from *the facts as known*. There can be no doubt that the general scheme depends less on arbitrary assumption, and still less on invention, than on the witness of careful and honest observers who had rendered sober accounts of voyages over all save the remoter reaches of the Atlantic. The White Sea, Bjarmaland, Spitzbergen, Jan Mayen, capes, wastelands, and glaciers well north of the Greenland settlements had been seen and talked about and fitted into the world-picture, as had Helluland (Baffin Island), Skrælingaland (Labrador), and Vinland the Good.[13] That there was a Frozen Sea up north could surprise no

[12] Ginnungagap, so named and situated between Greenland and Markland, is a prominent feature of Guðbrandur Thorláksson's map of the North, 1606, preserved in the Royal Library, Copenhagen.

[13] H. L. Sawatzky and W. H. Lehn in 'The Arctic Mirage and the Early North Atlantic', *Science*, 192 (1976), pp. 1300–5, offer not only an entirely convincing explanation of the *hafgerðingar* of *Grænlendinga Saga* as an instance of the Arctic mirage (see p. 189 below), and an exposition of the power of refraction in certain climatic conditions (including the sighting and identification on 17 July 1939, by Capt. John Bartlett of the *Effie M. Morrissey*, of Snæfells Jökull (1,430 metres), then more than 500 kilometres to the north-east on the west coast of Iceland), but present a persuasive argument that 'information gleaned from these mirages was vital to Norse navigation and exploration in the North Atlantic'.

I append here the Sawatzky–Lehn explanation of the *hafgerðingar*: 'At sea, in the absence of normal terrestrial aids to orientation, the visual impact of the arctic mirage is much more profound than on land, and the observer has an overwhelming impression of being already below the lip of a genuine, if shallow, vortex. This impression, caused by the foreshortening of the refraction-induced slope in all directions, in effect 'staircases' the visible motion of the

one, least of all a sealer or walrus-hunter. Where else could it
be? And the circumambient land-ring, complete with fjords and
islands, was a guarantee (if only until called upon) that the
Norse discoverer would have a coast to follow, and at the right
time an ocean-crossing, at best back home, but at worst to some
known or guessable shore. The Norse world-picture at the very
least provided a sensible framework for a man to work in.

Postscript

Historiography, like History, is a continuing process, and Bor-
ealic historiography has proved no exception to the rule. When
with the benefit of hindsight we ponder man's devious and
ingenious nature we can feel no surprise at the sensational by-
products of his knowledge and mis-knowledge of his furthest
wests and farthest norths. It is unlikely that they deceived the
men who sailed and saw—men like Ohthere and the resourceful
explorers of Iceland, south-west Greenland, and the east Canadian coastline. Fantasy and science fiction thrive best in
studies, studios, and armchairs. Thus the notion of a continuous
land-ring, breached or unbreached by the horrendous outpourings of Ginnungagap, bedevilled medieval scholarly concepts of
Greenland, its inhabitants, and environs, and in novel ways
would seriously deform Atlantic cartography into the sixteenth
and even the seventeenth century. In a reputable sort of way it
affected the Icelandic map-makers, like Sigurður Stefánsson in
1590 (see his map on p. 118 below) and Guðbrandur Thorláksson in 1606 (see p. 89 below). In a disreputable way it may be
observed in the mendacious map of the Zeno brothers, 1558,
and all the ills that flowed from it: non-existent or misplaced
countries and islands that just weren't there, as practical
voyagers knew. With the fifteenth century's rediscovery of the
New World and the subsequent flowering of transatlantic

water in such a way as to exaggerate the perceived upward angle by a factor of
many times its actual magnitude, causing the waters to appear to be poised as if
to engulf the observer. Careful attempts made by us to determine the angle of
rise in the presence of this phenomenon resulted in an estimate of 2°. Precise
measurement from a shore position under equivalent conditions yielded a reading of 2'. The perceived angle, due to the effects and influence described, was 60
times as great as the actual angle. The presence of another vessel within the
range of view would only strengthen the impression of being within the tunnel
of a vortex.'

imperial politics, fantasy and forgery were put to practical use, and the power of myth sedulously exploited. So it was with that unseizable will-o'-the-wisp, the well-named *Inventio Fortunata* of the elusive fourteenth-century Oxford friar Nicholas of Lynn, an account (reported lost) of his high Arctic travels and observations, and the skilful use made of its abstract (reported found) by men as diversely significant as Richard Hakluyt the Younger, Gerard Mercator, and above all Queen Elizabeth of England's Welsh wizard and imperial claim-faker, John Dee.[14]

[14] For the *Inventio* see E. G. R. Taylor, 'A Letter Dated 1577 from Mercator to John Dee', *Imago Mundi*, 13 (1956), pp. 56–68. Whether a 'meer fable' or a mere muddle, its importance belongs with the seventeenth century and not the fourteenth. Dee, of course, was no less devoted to Prince Madoc and his legendary discovery of America in the eleventh century. He was likewise a listener to William Lambard's *Archaionomia* (1568) with its list of the British Arthur's northern conquests; and patriotism and policy alike disposed him to endorse Geoffrey of Monmouth's twelfth-century farrago of King Arthur subduing Scandinavia and Iceland, and welcome the even more flagrant extravaganzas of the (lost) *Gesta Arthuri*, which half a millennium later credited him with an empire extending from Lapland to the North Pole. For the ramifications and transformations of these oft-shattered and oft-renewed illusions see Gwyn A. Williams, *Madoc. The Making of a Legend*, 1979, and *Welsh Wizard and British Empire. Dr John Dee and a Welsh Identity*, Cardiff, 1980.

Part One

THE STORY

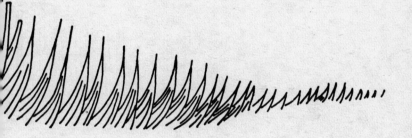

1

Iceland

I. BEFORE THE NORSEMEN

W HO first saw Iceland, and whether god-impelled, mirage-led, wind-whipt and storm-belted, or on a tin-and-amber course laid north to roll back trade horizons, we do not know. But he was a brave man, or an unlucky, and it was a long time ago.

The dragon prow of a Norse adventurer made the first recorded circumnavigation of the island about 860; the currachs of Irish anchorites had reached its south-eastern shore in the last years of the eighth century; but it is probable that Iceland's story starts in a remoter past than this. We have learned in the last seventy years that man's early knowledge of the sea and willingness to venture out upon it resulted in voyages undreamt of by nineteenth-century historians; and that this is as true of the northern as the southern hemisphere, of the Atlantic as the Pacific. By 2500 BC, and maybe much earlier, the sea was man's highway, and already the funerary ritual of the megalith builders of Spain, Portugal, and France was being spread by sea throughout the islands and peninsulas of the west, and from these northwards through the Irish Sea and Pentland Firth. The western sea-routes have been frequented ways ever since, for though profit and policy have often led peoples to stow knowledge under hatches, as did the Phoenicians in respect of Africa and the Cassiterides, or the merchants of Bristol in respect of their illegal fifteenth-century trade with Greenland, such mind-cargo is rarely lost to human memory. Someone knows, or confusedly recalls, that far out on the ocean's bosom lies a Land of Promise, Eternal Youth, silent refuge, stockfish profit. There is therefore nothing improbable in the notion that the Greek astronomer, mathematician, and geographer Pytheas of Massalia acquired in the purlieus of Britain as much news of Thule as he is thought to have bequeathed to it.

Unfortunately Pytheas's account of his voyage of exploration

to Britain and further north in 330–300 BC has not survived. We
have to rely instead on pieces of not always consistent information, at times derived from careless intermediaries, embedded in the writings of later and often derisory Greek
geographers. In this shadowed way we first meet the name
Thule, though it is far from certain that by Thule Pytheas
meant the country we now know as Iceland. It lay six days' sail
north of Britain (Strabo and Pliny), and one day's sail beyond it
lay a congealed, curdled, or frozen ocean (Pliny). At the time
of the summer solstice the sun was visible there for twenty-four
hours of the day (Cleomedis), or at least the night was very
short, lasting in some places two hours, in others three (Gemi-
nos), all of which is consonant with Iceland. But Pytheas speaks
of Thule as a country inhabited by barbarians, of whom he
offers credible intelligence. They have little in the way of domestic animals, he says, but live on millet and herbs, together
with fruit and roots. Those who have grain and honey make
drink from them. This grain, when it was cut, they brought into
large covered barns and threshed indoors, because the sunless-
ness of the climate and its downpours of rain made threshing
floors in the open impracticable. Of any such habitation the
archaeological record of Iceland is bare, while the little we
know of the cold recession in the climate of the northern hemisphere in Pytheas's day makes the identification still less likely.
The west coast of Norway has stronger claims to be this early
'farthest north', and those of Shetland and even Orkney are not
easily dismissed. If we can trust Strabo, Pytheas said of these
high latitudes that here was a region where earth, sea, and air
existed not as distinguishable elements, but inchoately as a con-
gelation of all three, a 'sea lung' heaving with the rhythmic
breath of Demogorgon, not to be journeyed on or sailed
through. This he saw for himself. But what it was that he saw,
whether fog-bank and slush-ice, or some legitimately powerful
effect of the imagination upon the massed phenomena of a bad
sub-arctic day, we fail to see it after him, our recognition of
Thule is stayed, and Iceland does not enter the historical
record.[1]

[1] For Pytheas see Gaston-E. Broche, *Pythéas le Massaliote* (Paris, 1935); V.
Stefánsson, *Ultima Thule* (1941); and *Pytheas Von Massalia*, Collegit Hans
Joachim Mette (Berlin, 1952) (contains the literary remains, pp. 17–35).

If not the Phoenicians and Greeks, were the Romans able to reach Iceland? The likeliest time for such an exploit would be during the bull-necked Carausius's control of the Classis Britannica, whether as admiral in the Low Countries or emperor of Britain (*c*.AD 286–93); but there is no literary evidence, and that of archaeology is slight and inconclusive: just three well-preserved Roman copper coins from the period 270–305 (these dates embrace the entire reigns of the emperors whose effigies they bear) discovered this present century, two at Bragðarvellir in Hamarsfjord, the other in the Hvalnes district of Lon, all in the south-eastern corner of Iceland. This area is the likeliest landfall of ships from the south. But we need not believe that so few and such low-valued coins came north with their first owners whether Roman or Scottish; it is likelier that they were brought to Iceland by a Norseman who had picked them up abroad, as part of a plundered hoard, as keepsake or curio, or for any of the thousand and one arbitrary reasons why a man has such things in his possession. Certainly, if a Roman vessel came so far north, by design or accident, there is no record of her return; the three copper coins are the sole memorial of her voyage, and when we weigh the hazards of the ocean and the land's inclemency we incline to add, of her crew.[2]

Meantime the western sea-routes were endlessly busy. When the day of the megalith builders was over, Celtic invaders of the Bronze Age took their place as voyagers by sea as well as land. For a further thousand years there was a continuous movement of peoples and cultures between the Continent and the islands and promontories of western Britain, till finally in the early Christian period the missionary fervour of the Celtic saints united Ireland and Brittany, Cornwall, Wales, and Strathclyde in a close cultural unity.[3] By the fifth and sixth centuries AD it was along these western routes alone that the peoples of Britain

[2] Kristján Eldjárn, *Gengið á Reka* (Reykjavík, 1948), pp. 10–24; *Kuml og Haugfé úr Heiðnum Sið í Íslandi* (1956), pp. 13–24; *Viking Archaeology in Iceland*, Þriðji Víkingafundur (1956), pp. 27–8; Einar Ól. Sveinsson, *Landnám í Skaftafellsþingi* (1948), pp. 2–3.

[3] For an attempt to set this 'Celtic thalassocracy' in a European context, see A. R. Lewis, *The Northern Seas* (Princeton, 1958), Chapter II, 'The Invasion Period' *passim*, and particularly p. 64, and see E. G. Bowen, *Britain and the Western Seaways* (1972).

and Ireland could maintain contact with the shrunken Roman civilization in Gaul and the western Mediterranean. Sea-going activity was unending, so that when the Irish saints and pere-grini sought for ever more distant isles and hermitages they had in aid an almost immemorial habit of ocean travel in addition to well-found ships and a rich navigational lore. These ships were currachs, made of hides (*coria*) over a wooden frame, some small as that constructed of two and a half hides in which three Irish pilgrims came to England to visit king Alfred in 891, others vessels of a good size and burden, able to transport at least a score of men with their gear and provisions. In these currachs, from monasteries such as Aran, Bangor, Clonfert, and Clonmacnoise, Irishmen by oar and sail reached every British coast (the famed Columba was in Iona by 563, and the obscure Govan (Welsh *Gofan*, Irish *Gobhan*) in his dramati-cally isolated cell in south-west Wales at the same time), then turned their prows to the northern ocean. Between Scotland and Orkney lies a narrow sound whose frequent storms and sudden changes from smooth water to a broken sea did nothing to daunt, though sometimes they drowned, early seafarers. From Orkney it is a bare 50 miles to Shetland, and from Shet-land less than 200 to the Faeroes. Here, to Iceland, the ocean gulf is wider, 240 miles; while from Malin Head in the north of Ireland the direct sailing distance is some 600; but the con-tinued northward progress of the peregrini seems inevitable, particularly when we allow for the well-attested effects of the northern *hillingar* or *fata morgana*, which may easily double the distance at which land grows visible to the hopeful travel-ler. Even the unhopeful was into soundings 400 miles from the Butt of Lewis.

It is often difficult to distinguish truth from fiction in the lives of Celtic saints, and never more so than when the saints are Irish. Which is a pity, because in their *Imrama* or travel-tales are to be found passages which seem to record, or rather reflect, experiences in high latitudes, with blowing whales and belching volcanoes. No pains were too severe for those who like Cormac ua Liathain sought their desert in the ocean, though for most who found it, in caves and huts on lonely islands, there remained only prayer and worship, solitude and self-mortifi-cation:

Eager wailings to cloudy heaven, sincere and truly devout con-
fession, fervent showers of tears.

A cold anxious bed, like the lying-down of the doomed, a brief
apprehensive sleep, cries frequent and early. . . .

Alone in my little hut, all alone so, alone I came into the world,
alone I shall go from it.

Others, true, sound a happier note, as in the anonymous
twelfth-century poem on St Columba's island hermitage:

Delightful I think it to be in the bosom of an isle, on the peak of a
rock, that I might often see there the calm of the sea. . . .

That I might see its splendid flocks of birds over the full-watered
ocean; that I might see its mighty whales, greatest of wonders.

That I might see its ebb and its flood-tide in their flow; that this
may be my name, a secret I tell, 'He who turned his back on Ireland.'

For most of these God-committed men *peregrinari pro
Christo* permitted no return. Starvation or violent death, all
terrors of earth and ocean were for God's sake welcome. The
peregrini had embraced the white martyrdom of a heroic
renunciation.[4]

The best known of the Irish *Imrama*, and the most relevant to
the story of Iceland, records the travels of St Brendan. On one
occasion, at no great distance north of them in the ocean, the
saint and his companions beheld a high mountain, its summit
wreathed in cloud and smoke; and as their ship was borne closer
to the island it was to find a coast so immensely towering that
they could hardly see the top of it, steep as a wall, and glowing
like coals. Ashore they lost one of their number to the devils
who dwelt here, and when by divine favour they were enabled
to sail away, they saw as they looked back the mountain now

---

[4] The two verse translations, the first of an eighth–ninth century original, are
from K. H. Jackson, *A Celtic Miscellany* (1951), pp. 307–10. For the peregrinus
see J. F. Kenney, *The Sources for the Early History of Ireland* (New York,
1929), vol. i, Ecclesiastical, p. 488: ' "peregrinus" as used in Ireland of the early
Middle Ages (Irish *deórad*) meant not one who goes on pilgrimage to a shrine
and then returns home, but one who departs his homeland to dwell for a space
of years or for the rest of his life in strange countries.' For *baanmartre* see Thur-
neysen, *Old Irish Reader* (trans. Binchy and Bergin) (Dublin, 1949), p. 36. The
OE *Guthlac* has a moving passage (lines 81 ff.) on those who 'dwell in deserts,
seek and inhabit of their own will homes in dark places, await their heavenly
mansion'.

freed from smoke, first spewing its flames into the heavens, then sucking them back again, so that the entire mountain down to the sea's edge had the appearance of a blazing pyre.[5] This certainly looks like the description of an erupting volcano near the southerly shore of a mountainous island, and one is tempted to think it not so much a new location of hell as a word-picture of a flaming Hekla, Katla, or some crater in Oræfi, with its attendant lava flow; but the Mediterranean had its volcanoes too, and classical literature many references to such, so we are still short of a full assurance. In fact, for reliable literary evidence that the Irish religious not only knew of Iceland but actually lived there for sixty to seventy years before its discovery by Norsemen, we must look not to the wonder-tales of the hagiographers, nor yet to the witness of Bede[6] (reminiscent as this last is of the Pytheas fragments, and readily adopted by the Icelandic authors or redactors of *Landnámabók*), that six days' sailing north of Britain lay the island whose name was Thule where for a few days in summer the sun was never lost to view below the horizon—not to these, for all their tantalizing interest, but to the sober testimony of the *Liber de Mensura Orbis Terræ* of the Irish monk Dicuil, written in AD 825, in which he sets down information about the islands that lie north of Britain taken by word of mouth from priests who in their turn spoke not by hearsay but from an exact and first-hand knowledge:

All round our island of Hibernia [says Dicuil] there are islands, some small, some tiny. Off the coast of the island of Britain are many islands, some big, some small, some middling; some lie in the sea to the south of Britain, others to the west; but they are most numerous in the northwestern sphere and the north. On some of these islands I have lived, on others set foot, of some had a sight, of others read. . . .

It is now thirty years since priests [*clerici*] who lived in that island [i.e. Thule] from the first day of February to the first day of August told me that not only at the summer solstice, but in the days on either side of it, the setting sun hides itself at the evening hour as if behind a little hill, so that no darkness occurs during that very brief period of time,

---

[5] O. O. Selmer, *Navigatio Sancti Brendani* (Notre Dame, 1959), p. 64; Plummer, *Vitæ Sanctorum Hiberniæ* (1910), i. 130; Kenney, op. cit., pp. 409–12.

[6] In his *De Ratione Temporum: In Libros Regum Quæstionum xxx liber.*

but whatever task a man wishes to perform, even to picking the lice out
of his shirt, he can manage it precisely as in broad daylight. And had
they been on a high mountain, the sun would at no time have been hidden from them. . . .

They deal in fallacies who have written that the sea around the island
is frozen, and that there is continuous day without night from the vernal to the autumnal equinox, and vice versa, perpetual night from the
autumnal equinox to the vernal; for those sailing at an expected time of
great cold have made their way thereto, and dwelling on the island
enjoyed always alternate night and day save at the time of the solstice.
But after one day's sailing from there to the north they found the frozen sea.[7]

Some of the puzzles inherent in these fascinating sentences
could not have been puzzles to Dicuil. Were these priests on a
first and isolated voyage of exploration, confirmatory of
Pytheas and Pliny? Or were they part of an established, if occa-
sional, traffic of Irish anchorites to Thule, as we may believe in
the light of the *De Ratione Temporum* (if we further believe
Bede's Thule and Dicuil's to be the same)? How many were
they, these anchorites, and with what resources? And how
account for the precise dating of their stay from the first day of
the Irish spring to the first day of the Irish autumn? Whatever
our answers, or even our cavils, they can hardly cast doubt on a
conclusion that towards the end of the eighth century Irishmen,
priests among them, reached Iceland where they spent the more
clement part of the year and observed the midnight sun. Which
is conclusion enough for the pre-Norse stage of Icelandic history.

[7] Ed. Walkenaer (Paris, 1807), pp. 27–30. Dicuil continues: 'There are many
other islands in the ocean to the north of Britain which can be reached from the
northernmost British isles in two days' and nights' direct sailing, with full sails
and an undropping fair wind. A certain holy man [*presbyter religiosus*]
informed me that in two summer days and the night between, sailing in a little
boat of two thwarts, he came to land on one of them. Some of these islands are
very small; nearly all of them are separated one from the other by narrow
sounds. On these islands hermits who have sailed from our Scotia [Ireland]
have lived for roughly a hundred years. But, even as they have been constantly
uninhabited since the world's beginning, so now, because of Norse pirates, they
are empty of anchorites, but full of innumerable sheep and a great many different kinds of seafowl. I have never found these islands mentioned in the books
of scholars.'

It is generally accepted that Dicuil is here speaking of the Faeroes, the Færey-
jar or Sheep Islands. For Dicuil in general see Kenney, op. cit., pp. 545–8.

From now on our concern is with Icelandic and Norwegian sources of information. *Íslendingabók* and *Landnámabók*, as well as the Norwegian History of Theodoricus, record that when the first Norse settlers arrived in Iceland there were already Irishmen resident there, Christians who refused to live with heathens, so betook themselves off, leaving behind them Irish books (that is to say, devotional books in the Latin tongue but written in Irish script), bells, and croziers, by which their nationality and character were established. These were the *papar* (sing. *papi*, Irish *pab(b)a*, *pob(b)a*, from Latin *papa*), monks and anchorites. From the evidence of place-names it is clear that there was a sprinkling of these *papar* over much of south-eastern Iceland, especially between the island of Papey and Papos in Lon. Much further west, beyond the ice-spurs of the Vatnajokul and the desolate sands of Skeidara, in the beautiful and fertile countryside of Sida, there was a cluster of *papar* at Kirkjubær; and such was the sanctity of the site that it was not granted to heathen men ever to dwell there. The first settler was Ketil the Fool (so styled because he was a Christian), a Hebridean Norseman and grandson of the great Ketil Flat-nose, and life sped well for him. After his day Hildir Eysteins-son presumed to show that a heathen *could* dwell at Kirkjubær; but as he reached the boundary of the homefield God's wrath was visited upon him, there he bowed, he fell, and where he bowed he fell down dead.

Of the economy of these *papar* we know nothing. The caves, byres, cells, and houses at various times ascribed to their habitation have all proved to be the work of later comers. Whether they succeeded in raising any variety of corn is not known, but it is likely that from no farther afield than the Faeroes they shipped flocks to provide them with milk and wool. They were certainly fishermen, and their numbers would be tiny, hardly a hundred all told. But this little said, we have said our all. We do not even know how this thin and temporary Christian occupation ended. Were the *papar* solitaries? Or does the place-name Pap(p)yli point to a cell or cloister? Did the same fate whelm them all, and what fate was it? 'Later they went away (*Þeir fóru síðan á braut*)': a laconic, unrevealing epitaph. And how came they to leave behind their precious books, their church- or hand-bells, crooks and croziers? Either their going was sudden and

bare, in the same currachs which had fetched them to Iceland;
or maybe these treasures came into Norse possession after their
flight into the inhospitable and deathly abodes of lava, rock,
and ice so plentiful in Iceland. Not that one normally associates
priests and Irishmen with flight. In any case, wherever they
went in Iceland, a male community vowed to chastity, their
days were numbered.

In one way only they and their like were to influence Icelandic history. They had discovered the Faeroes by about the year
700 and lived there till perhaps 820. The first Norse settler Grim
Kamban arrived about that time and maybe dispossessed them
of Sudero. Since his nickname appears to be cognate with Irish
camm, bent or crooked, he is more likely, despite the witness of
Færeyinga Saga, to have come by way of Ireland or the
Hebrides than direct from Norway, and may even have been a
Christian. The Norse pirates who followed him must quickly
have gained control of all the islands, but despite Dicuil's statement that the Faeroes were thereafter empty of hermits, some
of them and something of their lore must have remained behind
and helped prepare men's minds for Iceland. Similarly, knowledge of the Iceland hermitages must have spread throughout
Ireland and Scotland, Orkney and Shetland, and every wind-
swept corner of the Hebrides, so that Norse immigrants,
traders, pirates, and adventurers—all and everything implied
by the word 'Viking'—would receive intelligence, even of distance and direction, as to new land for the taking this side the
Frozen Sea.

II. THE NORSE DISCOVERY AND FIRST
SETTLEMENT

THE papar went away when the Norsemen came, and the
Norsemen came about 860. We need not suppose that the papar
took themselves off immediately after the discovery. It was the
wave of settlement rising fourteen years later which loosed
them from their rock-holes in the south-east, then swept them
to oblivion.

Our main source of information about the Norse discoverers
is *Landnámabók*, the Book of the Landtakings or Settlements.
According to one of its recensions, *Sturlubók*, the first of them

was Naddod the Viking. According to another, *Hauksbók*, it
was a Swede named Gardar Svavarsson, and to this we may
incline for three reasons: that *Hauksbók* seems here to rest
upon the authority of the original text of *Landnámabók*; that it
is supported by the two earliest Norse sources (written in Latin)
which treat of the subject, the anonymous *Historia Norwegiæ*,
of uncertain date but appearing to derive in part from an original of about 1170, and the *Historia de Antiquitate Regum Nor-
wagiensium* of Theodoricus Monachus, of about 1180,[8] and
third, if we can trust to the story (and its disparate versions
agree in this particular), that it was Gardar's son Uni whom
King Harald Fairhair hoped to use as a catspaw to bring Iceland
into subjection to Norway, presumably on the ground of his
right to inherit the entire country after his first-come-first-
served father. He was a true explorer, this Swedish Gardar, and
having reached land east of the Eastern Horn he sailed on past
the ice-mountains and bursting rivers of the Vatnajokul and the
long, flat, melancholy reaches of the harbourless south coast.
To a mariner under sail the prospect here is uninviting and he
would stand right out from the land, till at last the purple tusks
of the Vestmannaeyjar and the long sweep of the Landeyjar
conducted him to the inhospitable peninsula of Reykjanes, past
Skagi its northern extremity, where there would open up before
him the noble expanse of Faxafloi, shining-watered, mountain-
rimmed, and northwards, sixty miles away, the perfect cone of
the Snæfellsjokul. Past Snæfellsnes a second wide entry would
appear before him, Breidafjord, Broadfjord, with its uncoun-
table islands, reefs, and skerries, and the white snail-tracks of
its quick-drowning currents. Then the Vestfirthir, their glim-
mering waters webbed between the bony fingers of that contorted hand whose wrist lies back in Laxardal and Haukadal.
He would pass Isafjardardjup, Icefjord Deep, with the seven
axe-clefts in its southern shore backed by the desolation of
snow-pocked Glama, and at the northern end of the Deep, Kalda-
lon, where the ice-falls of the Drangajokul meet the sea. The

---

[8] Both published in G. Storm, *Monumenta Historica Norvegiæ* (1880). The
fact, or tradition, of Gardar's circumnavigation was indirectly confirmed, or
kept alive, in connection with Gunnbjorn Ulf-Krakuson's discovery of Greenland. See the reference to *Um Íslands aðskiljanlegar náttúrur*, p. 74 below, and
GríM, pp. 58 and 190.

man-rejecting wall of Snæfjallastrand comes next, and then the bitter entries of the Jokulfirthir. Soon now Gardar would round Hornbjarg, the North Cape, and along a rocky coast sail south and a little east into Hunafloi. Here he would find lands flatter and richer, long valleys running inland, but behind them always peaks, bluffs, broken ranges, and sometimes the glint of ice. He must have been tempted to put ashore here, or in the neighbouring fjords eastward, Skagafjord and Eyjafjord, and since the end of summer was at hand he would have done well to beach his ship and build winter quarters in the kindly head-reaches of this last. But he pressed his luck round one more promontory and came into Skjalfandi, the Trembler, where he built a house at the place called Husavik, House Bay, on a steep cliff face, by a bad harbour, open to invasion of the Arctic ice. When he put out the following spring he was forced to leave behind one of his crew, Nattfari, with a thrall and bondwoman. Just how this happened we do not know, but Gardar's need to get away when the chance presented itself may well have seemed imperative, and get away he did. Certainly Nattfari survived his abandonment, if such it was, for his name makes a modest appearance later in *Landnámabók*'s account of the North Quarter settlement.

So there is Gardar now, look on him as we will, as a man well attested and deservedly honoured for his remembered pioneering voyage, or if we prefer, as an acceptable prototype of the first circumnavigator (or circumnavigators), sailing north-east to the Arctic Circle and the headlands of Melrakkasletta, and on across Thistilfjord to the narrow peninsula of Langanes, where he must wait for a more northerly wind to carry him south to Vapnafjord. Soon thereafter he would be back in fjord country, this time the Austfirthir, the arms of water penetrating less deeply the riven plateau behind, and the spurs of land somewhat less formidable, but from Berufjord southwards the interior most daunting, as Gardar came back within sight of the Vatnajokul. Past Berufjord, too, he would be sailing off the papar country, and who can doubt with what dismay the anchorites of Papey and Papafjord beheld his high prow and striped sail before their eyes again, a grievous token that the decades of their seclusion were for ever over. When he reached the Eastern Horn again Gardar knew that he had

circumnavigated an island, so called it Gardarsholm after himself, and when he returned home spoke warmly of it.

The second arrival, the Viking Naddod, was not in search of
Iceland, and stayed no longer than he had to. As he sailed out
of Reydarfjord a heavy snowstorm enveloped the land, so he
renamed it Snæland, Snowland.

The third, Floki, is a more intriguing character, with his sacrifices and ravens. Presumably he had settlement in mind, for he
took livestock with him. From his landfall at Horn he followed
Gardar's course westward off the surfy southern shore, crossed
Faxafloi, which he named after one of his shipmates, and built a
hall at Brjanslœk on the far side of Breidafjord. From this
favoured spot he and his crew surveyed their blessings, fine pastures on land, islands for summer grazing, a fjord teeming with
fish and seals, and myriads of seabirds. Sheltered by natural
ramparts from cold northern winds, they were misled like many
who followed them by the blue skies and pricking sun of summer, and spent their time at the easy harvest of waters never
fished since the world began save by gulls and puffins and
salmon-hunting seals. For as a colonizer Floki was a greenhorn.
Suddenly winter was upon him, with snow and frost; the pastures vanished, and while the men need not go short their livestock perished. Spring, when it came, was cold, and when Floki
got himself up on a hill to the north his reward was the cheerless
sight of a southerly arm of Arnarfjord choked with drift ice. So
to Thule, Gardarsholm, Snæland, he added yet another name,
Ísland, Iceland, the name the land has borne ever since. The
bad season lasted long, they were late getting to sea, and their
troubles, had they known it, were far from over. Gales from the
south-west stopped them rounding Reykjanes, they were driven
back into Faxafloi, to the Borgarfjord area, where they spent an
unwilling second winter. Home in Norway, Floki, having given
the land a bad name, did his best to hang it; his shipmate Herjolf, who must have made a hair-raising passage over Faxafloi in
his parted tow-boat, found both good and bad to report; while
another shipmate, Thorolf, whom the Icelanders would have
needed to invent had he never existed, swore that butter
dripped from every blade of grass in the island, for which
reason he was nicknamed and has been known as Thorolf
Butter ever since.

In the stories of these three men, Gardar, Naddod, and Floki, as in *Landnámabók*'s account of the settlement by the foster-brothers Ingolf and Leif (Hjorleif) which follows, there is much to doubt and not a little to discard. Indeed, Ari Thorgilsson, the 'Father of Icelandic History', in his *Íslendingabók*, completed in the 1120–30s, makes no mention of the three discoverers, or of Hjorleif, and disposes of the revered figure of Ingolf in a bare sixty words. Even so, everything compels us to believe that there *were* Norse exploratory voyages to Iceland in the decade or so preceding the settlement, and that they cannot be dissociated from the Vikings in the West, that is, in the British Isles and the Faeroes.

By the late 860s Iceland would be a word in many men's mouths in Norway. It must have fallen joyfully enough on the ears of the foster-brothers Ingolf and Leif, who by virtue of their feud with earl Atli of Gaular, two of whose sons they had slain and thereafter paid for out of their estates, were in need of land and sanctuary. They promptly set off on a well-prepared reconnoitring expedition, reached the classic area of landfall in the south-east, sailed past Papey, then nosed their way through sand-reefs into the protected waters of the southern Alptafjord, on whose shores they spent the winter prospecting, and then returned to Norway in order to wind up affairs at home. Ingolf laid out what money they still had on goods useful for their voyage and settlement, while Leif took warshields aboard for a last raid on Ireland. He returned with a sword from which he was to get his nickname Hjorleif (Sword-Leif) and ten captives from whom he was to get his death. But Ingolf's auguries said nothing of this last—Hjorleif was no concern of Thor's—and away they sailed, each in command of his ship. As soon as Ingolf sighted land he flung his high-seat pillars overboard, a god-fearing man seeking a god's direction where he should make his new home. Like Hjorleif and his crew the pillars were borne west, but Ingolf brought his ship in by Ingolfshofdi, and somewhere near the Head spent his first winter. The Head is so compelling a landmark on this dangerous coast, so dramatically situated where the land after a long run south-west from the Horns bends abruptly west, and by reason of some violent disruption in distant times is so lonely and commanding a fortress promontory, that it is tempting to believe that the ancient remains on its eastern side are the remains of Ingolf's house there. But this is unlikely. All probability favours the notion that so canny and resourceful a leader would have looked for a kindlier site back in Oræfi, where still today, after many cruel convulsions of nature, there are delightful and sheltered farmsteads thriving between the talons of the jokul.

It was on another such head or land-isle, sixty-odd miles further west, that Hjorleif built his home. Hjorleifshofdi today stands up on the seaward edge of the black Myrdal Sands, perpendicular, green-topped, its sides eroded since 894 by nine deluges of ice and water from the ice-capped volcano Katla; but when the first settlers saw it it must have looked a safe and genial home amidst its plenitude of pastures and birch woods. Hjorleif set to build in earnest, to clear the ground and plough. But his Irish thralls, all fighting men with a hot brew of hate in their breasts, detested these menial tasks, and with their tale of a forest-bear contrived to destroy their masters.[9] They then made off with the womenfolk, movable goods, and necessarily the ship's boat, to certain precipitous islands they had observed from the brow of the Head, about fifty miles to the south-west, where they lived in their fools' paradise till Ingolf hunted them down and slew them in their turn. Their prodigious leaps to death still shadow a sunny passage through the Vestmannaeyjar, the Isles of the Irishmen. If the Settlement required an inaugural sacrifice (and man's imagination feeds on myth before history, legend before fact), Hjorleif and his Celtic slaves provided it. Iceland had been blooded.[10]

Ingolf had still not found his pillars. He spent his second winter at his dead brother's, then moved west, exploring coast and countryside as far as the river Olfus. So far it had not been too difficult for his thralls Vifil and Karli to hug the water's edge, keeping a look-out for the sea's rejections; but past the Olfus are wide lavafields, mud springs, and much desolation, so

[9] Hjorleif was not to know that the only bears ever found in Iceland are polar bears, drifted over on floes from Greenland, normally to the north coast.

[10] Vestmannaeyjar: the Isles of the Westmen, i.e. men of, or from, the British Isles, and more especially Irishmen. *Landnámabók*'s account of Hjorleif, in whom it is hard to have any belief whatsoever, reads like a triple-branched onomastic tale designed to explain a place-name likely to have an altogether more natural origin.

Ingolf, a practical man, turned inland with his main party, got himself across the river, and lay up for the winter under the benign flank of Ingolfsfell. Meantime his two thralls were making a progress round Reykjanes, west, then north, then east, till by luck or good judgement, or Thor helping, before the end of summer they found his high-seat pillars where Reykjavik stands today. So in the spring Ingolf made his third journey west, climbed up on to the heath, and one imagines not without misgiving skirted the crater-studded, lava-strewn, ash-littered hinterland of Reykjavik. But Thor had not misled his worshipper. He had brought him west to the well-spring of Icelandic history, of her law and constitution, and there endowed him with a patrimony ample as a homeland kingdom. With Ingolf in his high-seat at Reykjavik, the settlement of Iceland was auspiciously under way.

III. THE STRIPLING REPUBLIC

THE process of settlement begun with such vicissitude by Ingolf in the south-west was completed throughout the island some sixty years later. There would still be latecomers seeking Iceland's coasts, among them men as famous as Eirik the Red and Ketil Gufa with his death-dealing thralls; far-reaching estates would be hewn or refashioned, and residences splendid as those at Helgafell, Hjardarholt, and Reykholt were still to arise at a chieftain's bidding, but by *c*.930 all the habitable land had been formally taken into possession.[11] The lifeless sands, the lava-fields, the wastes and moraines would remain for ever empty; the sculptured mountains and glittering jokuls would be left to trolls and giants; of mortal men only lone-going outlaws, deathly and sterile, would attempt the central desolation, break out again, be hunted down, and perish. Some five-sixths of the country offered no support to human life. But wherever there was grass, the glint of leaf and berry, there would be found a farm. Along leagues of the sea's edge, lining the fjords,

---

[11] The word *landnám*, literally 'land-taking', was used in two related senses. It signified the claim to land, the taking of land into one's personal possession, and it thereafter denoted the land so taken, the settler's holding or estate.

softening the long valleys that penetrate inland, in nooks and hollows everywhere, there was pasture and birchwood, and it was with an eye to these, fresh water, freedom from snow and shelter from wild weather, a creek or ship's haven or land-route manageable by the small, tough, gallant, handsome Icelandic pony,[12] that the first settlers planned their homes. Often too with an eye to the beauty, splendour, or oddness of the site, so frequently reflected in Icelandic place-names: Ale-force River, Angelica Bank, Smoky Bay, Clearwater Pass, Glassriver Shaw and Cold Cheek, Red Dunes and Holy Mountain. Some felt the land breeze sweeter than the sea's, some smelled honey in the grass; and to some a god said, 'Leave here. Go there.'

The nation-to-be was notably fortunate in its founding families. They had ambition, independence, energy, an aristocratic tradition, and an aesthetic appreciation of character, of conduct, and good utterance, with all their consequences, and the dominant Norse strain was generously leavened with Celtic blood. The literary and historical sources play down the Swedish and Danish share in the settlement, whereas the grave-findings tend to exaggerate it, particularly the high proportion of chapes (which may point to Sweden) and the absence of any evidence for cremation (which possibly points to Denmark); and it is reasonable to think that there was a bigger infiltration of Swedes and Danes into Iceland by way of south-west Norway than native writings allow. Still, the Icelandic homeland was Norway, more particularly the south-west, Sogn, Hordaland, and Rogaland, though there were immigrants from the entire coastal area between Agdir and southern Halogaland. Iceland took not only men but law and language from the Norwegian west, and of all Scandinavia it was for Sogn and Hordaland that Icelanders of later generations felt the strongest emotional attachment. Also it was this area which most actively opposed Harald Fairhair's attempt to make one kingdom of Norway, and it was from ports and anchorages between Hafrsfjord and the Sognsjo that Vikings first sailed west-over-sea to Scotland

[12] The horse in Iceland should have a saga to himself. More than two-thirds of Icelandic Viking graves contain the remains of horses buried with their masters, often in a separate chamber. (See the Sílastaðir grave p. 45 and plate 16.)

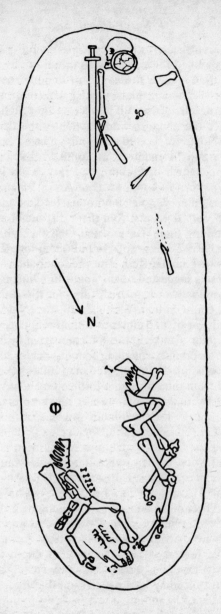

7. MAN'S GRAVE, SÍLASTAÐIR, KRÆKLINGAHLÍD, ICELAND

A man with his axe, sword, shield boss, knife, weights, and the skeleton of a horse

and her adjacent isles, to the Orkneys, Faeroes, and Ireland, with all this signified for Iceland in its turn.

Landnámabók records the names of roughly 400 settlement-men, and of these maybe one-seventh had a connection with the Celtic countries. Effective Viking action there dates from the last decade of the eighth century, when in the three ominous years 793–5 Norse freebooters not only pillaged Lindisfarne in Northumbria and Morgannwg in South Wales, but struck at Lambey Island north of Dublin, and the sacred isle of Iona. After 830 a pattern of conquest emerges in Ireland, Scotland, and the Isles, and various ambitious leaders from Norway hacked temporary domains from these distraught and mangled kingdoms, among them Turgeis and Olaf the White, Ivar the Boneless and Ketil Flatnose, Onund Treefoot, Eyvind East-man, and Thorstein the Red. The predominance of men from the south-west is suggested by the linguistic evidence too: ninth-century Norse loanwords in Irish came mostly from that area. Finngail and Gall-Gaidhill, White Foreigners (Norwegians) and Foreign Gaels (at first Irishmen who had renounced their faith and nation, later a mixed Norse–Celtic strain in both Ireland and western Scotland) roamed, fought, made and dissolved alliances, commanded, served, wed, and bred throughout these Celtic lands, from time to time reinforced by new Viking crews from home, by malcontents, rebels, adventurers, and great lords grown hungry for fresh lands in place of those they had forfeited to King Harald back in Norway.

But during the last third of the century the times grew less propitious for Norse adventurers not only in Ireland but in Eng-land and the rest of western Christendom. Harald Fairhair's vic-tory over the Vikings at Hafrsfjord in 885 ushered in a bad thirty years abroad. In 890 the Bretons heavily defeated the Viking army then plundering the Western Empire, and the fol-lowing year King Arnulf smote them anew on the Dyle near Louvain. The forces of Hastein and the Great Horde then moved over to England, but in a four-year campaign were so hammered by Alfred and his martial son that their army fell to pieces. In Ireland the initiative was back again in the hands of the native kings, and the capture of Dublin in 902 by Cearbhall king of Leinster gave the country comparative peace for twenty years. In Scotland Thorstein the Red was killed by guile or treachery about the year 900, and earl Sigurd of Orkney, by now master of Caithness and Sutherland, Ross and Moray, fulfilled his strange destiny of being destroyed by a dead man. He had killed the Scottish earl Melbrigdi and set his head to dangle at his saddle; but Melbrigdi had a protruding tooth, or tusk, which punctured the skin of his leg, the leg festered, and the earl sickened and died. At much the same time Onund Treefoot was prised out of the Hebrides. Ingimund who after the loss of Dublin in 902 thought to find land and wealth in Wales was promptly dispatched from Anglesey. Odo and Arnulf, Alfred and Edward and Ethelfleda lady of the Mercians, Cearbhall king of Leinster and the Welsh of North Wales and Anglesey, without knowing it were all making a contribution to the settlement of Iceland, which stood ready and waiting for adventurous but dispossessed men. And in Norway, most formidable contributor of all, there ruled Harald Fairhair.

To the Icelandic historians of the Middle Ages there was one over-riding reason why men sought homes and estates in Iceland. They came *fyrir ofríki Haralds konungs*, because of the tyranny of king Harald. It was this which drove Thorolf Mostrarskegg from Most to Thorsnes, uprooted Kveldulf and Skallagrim from the Firthafylki and sped them to Borgarfjord, brought Baug to Hlidarendi, and Geirmund Heljarskin from a prince's seat in Rogaland to a lord's estate in north-western Iceland. Some of the settlers had opposed Harald's attempt to unify (or as they saw it, seize) all Norway, some had fought against him at Hafrsfjord and suffered the bitterness of unrelieved defeat; others had merely held aloof from the struggle and so incurred the royal displeasure. They resented the loss of their titles, saw no reason why they should hold their estates of the king, regarded taxes as robbery and oaths of allegiance as the diminution of a free man's dignity. Some chose of their own accord to leave, while some among them were forcibly driven out:

Once he had established possession of these territories which were newly come into his power, King Harald paid close attention to the landed men and leading farmers, and all those from whom he suspected some rebellion might be looked for. He made everyone do one thing or the other, become his retainers or quit the country, or, for a third choice, suffer hardship or forfeit their lives; while some were maimed hand or foot. King Harald seized possession in every district of all odal rights [i.e., rights in land hitherto inalienable from the owner-family] and the entire land, settled and unsettled, and equally the sea and the waters, and all husbandmen must become his tenants, and those too who worked in the forests, and saltmen, and all hunters and fishers by sea and land—all these were now made subject to him. But many a man fled the land from this servitude, and it was now that many desert places were settled far and wide, both east in Jamtaland and Helsingjaland, and in the western lands, the Hebrides and Dublin district, Ireland, and Normandy in France, Caithness in Scotland, the Orkneys and Shetland, and the Faeroes. And it was now that Iceland was discovered.

This picture presented by Snorri Sturluson in *Egils Saga* of Harald's oppressive measures and personal ruthlessness even before the battle of Hafrsfjord is overdrawn, but it was the picture accepted by most informed persons in Iceland. In Norwegian tradition Harald appears as a wise, paternal ruler who gave Norway the peace and order she so badly needed, but to small nations struggling for their independence an external tyrant is an emotional necessity, and an unjust, relentless Harald was the most impressive of the many Norwegian candidates. That some chieftains left Norway because of him is not to be doubted. That their number was exaggerated, and the manner of their going dramatized, is certain.

Among them would be some of the Vikings whose lairs enlivened the south-west coast. These were men to whom the warlike pursuit of wealth and glory was an established way of life, forced on them by personal desire, family tradition, their social and economic system, and the geographical compulsions which made the sea the highway of a coast-dwelling aristocracy. For a century before the battle of Hafrsfjord they had been raiding east in the Baltic, west in the British Isles, and sailing the protected leads and water-alleys of Norway, then a land of petty kingdoms and jealous lordships. The Vikings of Sogn and Hordaland were well placed for voyages abroad and for intercepting the southern traffic in hides and furs and sea-ivory with Halogaland and Finnmark, and their subjugation was a necessity to a strong ruler like Harald Fairhair or earl Hakon. Many Vikings though were not just pirates. They did not despise the profits of trade, and their innumerable sea-crossings opened up much-needed routes and widened Norse horizons. Their sub-sequent conquests and piracy owed much to their created needs. The merchant-venturers who first brought cargoes of wine, honey, malt, and wheat, and English clothes and weapons from the west roused demanding appetites at home. Likewise these fjord-dwellers of the south-west were more vulnerable than most to the increase of population in Norway and the shortage of land which this increase made more and more pinching. So their main outpourings, whether from Norway direct to the Celtic lands or to Iceland, or to Iceland by way of the Celtic lands, were an inevitable phase of the great Viking Movement itself. There were compulsions other than Harald's real or fancied tyranny. Ingolf and Hjorleif had made the land too hot to hold them and left for Iceland twelve years before Hafrsfjord, and among those who travelled there soon after the battle were friends and loyal supporters of the king, like Ingimund the Old who settled Vatnsdal in the north and Hrol-laug, son of earl Rognvald of Mœr, who controlled all Horna-fjord in the east.

Among the settlers of Iceland was a high proportion of land-hungry, wealth-hungry, fame-hungry men, their native vigour and inventiveness quickened by their sojourn in the Celtic countries. There were three main sources of Celtic, and more specifically Irish, influence upon early Iceland. First there was the importance of settlers like Helgi the Lean, born of the mar-riage between a Norse nobleman and a princess of Ireland, and reared in the Hebrides. He did not stand alone. As late as the fourth generation in Iceland one of its foremost chieftains was Olaf Peacock of Hjardarholt, the son of Hoskuld Dalakollsson (of the line of Aud the Deep-minded) and Melkorka (Mael-Curcaigh) daughter of the Irish king Muircertagh. There seems to have been no bar to Norse–Irish and Norse–Pictish marriages at any social level. In addition there must have been a great deal of concubinage, for the Norsemen abroad (and for that matter at home) were notoriously addicted to the use of women. Con-sequently among the immigrants into Iceland from the lands west-over-sea there were many of mixed Norse and Celtic des-cent, including some who by blood were predominantly Celtic. Second there were the Celtic slaves brought out by Norse war-riors—often warriors themselves, prone to revolt and violence,

and some of them great men in their own country. There were
women slaves too, though their number is not known. Third
there was the influence of Irish civilization, its literature and
religion. One of the most famous of all settlers, Aud the Deep-
minded, was so devout a Christian that she gave orders for her
burial in the salty no-man's-land between high and low water,
so that she might not lie in unconsecrated ground like any
heathen. There were even more like Helgi the Lean, Christians
who reached for Thor in a tight corner. Soon the faith of their
kinsfolk went awry, their chapels and crosses grew derelict; but
they probably helped produce the climate of tolerance which
made the conversion of Iceland in the year 1000 the comparatively bloodless and worldly affair it proved to be. Among saga
heroes stand the Irish-named Njal, Kormak, and Kjartan; there
are Irish place-names in most parts of Iceland; there have been
attempts to relate Icelandic literary forms to those of Ireland;
and while the thesis is in its nature unprovable it is hard not to
believe that it was the Irish blood flowing in Norse veins which
distinguished the Icelanders from all other Scandinavian
peoples ethnographically and contributed in large measure to
their literary achievement in the twelfth and thirteenth
centuries.

Even so, the colonization of Iceland was a Norse Viking
undertaking. They sailed round the nesses, threaded the
islands, penetrated the fjords as far as their ships would carry
them, those sturdy *knerrir* with twenty or thirty men aboard,
women and children, animals, food, and timber. Some, we are
told, left their landing to fate or a god, threw their high-seat pillars over the side, and made their homes where these came
drifting in. They hallowed land to themselves with fire, with the
flighting of spears and arrows, by setting up peeled wands and
weapons, by marking the trees. It was probably the sheer arbitrariness of the settlers' methods, and the certainty that there
would be counter-claims and quarrels, that made the very men
who were said to have fled King Harald Fairhair's tyranny
resort to him for a ruling on the extent and demarcation of
estates (see p. 183 below).

Naturally, once he was ashore and with some sort of roof
over his head the would-be land-taker must begin to explore.
Skallagrim Kveldulfsson's land-taking in Borgarfjord, as

recounted in *Landnámabók* and amplified in *Egils Saga*, was typical of many. He came ashore, we are told, at the headland of Knarrarnes in the west, carried his cargo to land, and at once began to acquaint himself with the countryside. 'There was extensive marshland there and spacious forest, with plenty of room between mountains and sea, ample seal-hunting and good fishing.' Keeping close to the shore they moved southwards to Borgarfjord itself, and found there their comrades who had sailed in a second ship, who led Skallagrim to where his dead father's body had come to land in its coffin—as the prophetic old shape-changer had said it would:

Then Skallagrim took land in settlement between mountains and sea, the entire Myrar out to Selalon and inland to Borgarhraun, also south to Hafnarfjall—the whole area marked out by its rivers falling seawards. The following spring he brought his ship south to the fjord and into the inlet nearest to the spot where Kveldulf had come ashore. Here he established house and home, calling it Borg and the fjord Borgarfjord; and the countryside inland from there, that too they named after the fjord.

Much of this immense estate he distributed among his shipmates and kinsmen-at-law, so that in a year or two a dozen homesteads starred this delectable river-veined wilderness. And now they explored further afield, proceeding inland along Borgarfjord till the fjord became a river white with glacial silt, then still onwards through the virgin territory traversed by Nordra and Thvera, and found every river, stream, and lake filled with trout and salmon. He was a master of work, this big, black-visaged, bald-headed manslayer from the Firthafylki, a skilled raiser of crops and beasts, fisherman, sailor, and boat-builder, and a resourceful worker in iron. In short, a born pioneer:

He always kept a lot of men on hand, and sought busily after such supplies as might be found thereabouts which could prove useful to them; for at first they had little livestock in comparison with what was needed for the number of men they had with them. However, what livestock there was found its own food in the forest throughout the winter. Skallagrim was a fine shipbuilder, nor was there any shortage of driftwood west off the Myrar. He had a farm built at Alptanes, and had a second home there, from which he had men go out rowing for fish and seal-hunting and egg-collecting, for there was abundance of all these provisions, and also driftwood to be fetched back home. At that time too there were numerous whale-strandings, and harpooning them was free for all. And all creatures were at their ease in the hunting-grounds, for men were unknown to them.[13]

All in all the settlement of Iceland and the development of the infant Republic is the best-documented of medieval *Völkerwan-derungen*. There are the recorders of history like Ari Thorgilsson and in part measure the redactors of *Landnámabók*, and there are also those reworkers of tradition, the saga-men. And other interested parties, avouchers of a forefather's fame and grazing-rights, a church's eld and a bishop's leechcraft or zeal against the Devil, observers of men and beasts, ponderers and remem-brancers. Between them, with some truth and some invention, and much reinterpretation and cross-fertilization, and consider-able picturesque embellishment, they offer a fairly coherent and manageable version of events from 870 to 1262, from the arrival of the first settlers to the end of the independent Republic; and to history and saga we may now briefly address ourselves.

When the settlement men reached Iceland the country was theirs to do as they liked with. There was no need to subjugate a native population: the land was empty; nor were they in fear of attack 'from kings or criminals' abroad. They had the oppor-tunity for a unique experiment in nationhood, and after two generations during which they came to terms with the physical problems of colonization they set to work at it. They were intensely self-reliant and conservative, and for a while were content to live on their estates, distribute land, exact obedience, dispense justice, defend their own and their fol-lowers' interests in patriarchal aristocratic fashion. From the first they were devoted to their feuds. They met as friends and clashed as enemies, and soon the strategy of living among men as resolute as themselves made them feel the need for a form of government and the institutions that go with it. Their approach to these, as with much else in Iceland, was distinctive. Secular power and religious authority, united in the person of one and the same man, were to dictate the growth of the nation.

It is hard to know just how religious the Icelanders were. What Christianity there was soon came to an end, and though Njord, Tyr, and Balder, even Odin, had their followers, the

---

[13] *Egil's Saga*, trans. Gwyn Jones (1960), pp. 79–82.

gods who counted most in Iceland were Thor with his hammer and the phallused Frey. The worship of a god requires ceremonial and festive seasons, and a place to worship him. This usually entails the presence of a sacerdotal person at a sacred site or edifice, and it was long held on the evidence of the written sources that the old Norse religion conformed to this rule. But the findings of northern archaeology no longer permit us to think so. Thus *Eyrbyggja Saga*'s account of Thorolf Mostrarskegg's great temple at Hofstadir in Breidafjord[14] is as much an exercise of a thirteenth-century antiquarian's fancy as Adam of Bremen's eleventh-century description, with its attendant scholia, of the *nobilissimum templum* at Uppsala in his *Gesta Hammaburgensis*. That there was no purely priestly caste in ninth- and tenth-century Iceland has long been recognized, and that there were no exclusively ecclesiastical edifices there would seem to follow. The Germanic tradition was that of worship in the open air, or where the climate made this difficult, especially in winter, inside a building with a room big enough to hold a not-too-large assembly of men. In Iceland the *goði* was the man rich enough and authoritative enough to own such a building (*hof*) and provide the sacrifice and sacrificial feast. Not surprisingly the *goðar* (pl.) of Iceland were the corporate rulers of the land and its people.[15]

[14] 'He had a temple built—and a mighty edifice it was. There was a doorway in the side wall, nearer to the one end, and inside stood the pillars of the high-seat, with nails in them which were called the gods'-nails. The area inside was a great sanctuary. Further in was a room of the same shape and order as the choir in churches today, where in the middle of the floor, like an altar, stood a pedestal, with an arm-ring without a join lying on it, twenty ounces in weight, on which men must swear all their oaths. The temple-priest was required to wear this ring on his arm at all public assemblies. On the pedestal too must stand the sacrificial bowl, and in it a sacrificial twig, like an aspergillum, by means of which the blood, which was called *blaut*, shall be sprinkled from the bowl. The blood, that is, which was shed when animals were slaughtered as a sacrifice to the gods. Around the pedestal in this same room were set the images of the gods.' For more of Thorolf and his religion see pp. 164–5 below.

[15] 'Place-names provide the most valuable source for interpreting "*hof*". In Norway the names of 22 farms begin with the name of a god, followed by the word *hof*. Apart from these two-part *hof* names, no fewer than 85 farms are simply called *Hof*, a name also considered a vestige of paganism . . . The very nature of the names indicates that the word *hof* also incorporated the farm itself as the centre for ritual celebrations, and we will therefore venture to define *hof* as *a farm where cult meetings were regularly held for more people than those living on the farm*. The word was presumably first interpreted as "temple" after

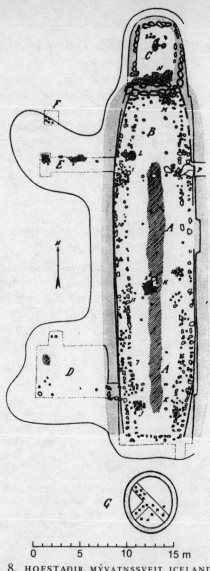

8. HOFSTAÐIR, MÝVATNSSVEIT, ICELAND

A large farmstead in northern Iceland, often called a temple-site. The large hall (A + B), is 36.3 metres long, 8.25 metres at its broadest, and narrowing at the gable ends. The outhouse (C) to the north is 6.2 by c.4 metres, and is unlikely to be of any religious significance. The large hall was a banqueting-hall on occasions, and the oval pit to the south (G) may have been used for sacral cooking

This meant that of the four hundred chief settlers and their families less than one-tenth were the real rulers of Iceland. *Landnámabók* is a shade prodigal of royal genealogies, but among the godar were men of royal descent, both Norse and Celtic, lords and lordlings, captains of ships and leaders of men. When in 927–30 legislative and judicial power was placed in the hands of thirty-six godar it was the descendants of such as these who inherited. The chosen thirty-six constituted the Althing or General Assembly of Iceland. The law administered there applied to the whole of the country, and had been adapted by Ulfljot of Lon from the Gulathing law of south-west Norway.[16] The godar elected a President or Lawspeaker for a renewable term of three years, whose duty it was to recite one-third of the law to the assembled congregation every year. Many, perhaps all, of the godar had been long accustomed to hold Things or gatherings for law in their own districts. Thorolf Mostrarskegg had established such a Thing at Thorsnes, and Thorstein Ingolfsson one at Kjalarnes. Under Ulfljot's law there would be twelve such throughout Iceland, each managed by three godar. The system was less democratic than it sounds. The Althing was unquestionably an assembly for law of all free men who chose to attend it; it was an excellent place to meet your friends, buy a sword, sell land, marry off a daughter, wear your best clothes, and share the excitement of a national occasion; but all power lay with the godar. The Constitution was anti-State. The Althing did not control the godar, but they it; and within their home-districts their rule was absolute. Going to law was a chancy business, and success in it impossible without the backing of one or more godar. Many of the famous lawsuits described in the sagas were a deployment of strength rather than a

the advent of Christianity . . . The *hofs* were permanent centres for local cult in Norway and Iceland. We may assume that the free population gathered on particular days of the year at certain farms which were *hof* in order to worship their gods by sacrifice and ritual feast, perhaps in continuation of cult celebrations at holy places in the open. No special building was needed for the ritual meal: the big room at the farm could be used.' Olaf Olsen, *Hørg, Hov og Kirk* (Copenhagen, 1966), pp. 280–1 (English Summary).

[16] 'Ulfljot's Law' has been preserved in snatches only, and no great faith can be placed even in those. The code's provisions are best regarded as antiquarian reconstructions by learned men of the twelfth or thirteenth centuries of what they judged such pre-Christian laws would be.

submittal to justice. Still it was better than nothing, and there were attempts to make the system more workable in 965, by establishing an apparently useless Quarter Thing and very successful Spring Thing for each quarter of the land and increasing the number of godar to thirty-nine, and in 1005 by instituting a Court of Appeal, the so-called Fifth Court, and increasing the number of godar to forty-eight. It was a Fifth Court because as part of the reform of 965 the legislature and the judicature had been separated, and instead of one court or *Alþingisdómr* there were four courts corresponding to the four Quarters of the country. All power remained with the godar, and no further reforms were attempted before the capitulation of the Republic in 1262.

And yet with all its imperfections Iceland owed much to the Althing. Its site was magnificent, the huge sunken plain of Thingvellir in south-west Iceland, lying between bold rifts and chasms and the biggest and second loveliest lake of the island, surrounded in the further distance by mountains of differing shape but constant beauty. It was created by fire, by earthquake and volcanic action, and a more impressive setting for national ceremony is hardly to be imagined. During the debate which established Christianity as the religion of Iceland men were dividing into two hostile camps there, when a man came running to the Althing to announce that fire was coming up out of the earth in Olfus. Said the heathens, with the Christians' argument in mind: 'No wonder the gods are angry at such talk!' But, 'At what were the gods angry, pray,' asked Snorri Godi in reply, 'when the lava we now stand on burned here?' Even in Iceland there are few more striking demonstrations of divine (or infernal) power than the riving of Thingvellir. It quickly established itself as a meeting-place for the nation. Indeed for part of every June it *was* the nation. Here from 930 on a man could know himself an Icelander and not a Norwegian at one or two removes. To travel the long, hard, but hospitable roads to the Althing, to share for a fortnight the bustle and business there, was to be at the hub of the wheel, the heart of the body legal, economic, political and social.

The strength of the godar as a ruling class ensured that medieval Iceland was never in any acceptable sense of the word a democracy. It would have been highly unnatural if it were. Still less was it a theocracy, for the authority of the godar even in heathen times and still more emphatically after the adoption of Christianity rested less and less on their religious office. Its enduring basis was secular strength, without which it was nothing. Normally the office descended from father to son, but it could be disposed of by gift, sale, or loan. It could also be divided and shared. By this possibility of transfer and acquisition, and an absence of controlling power above and over the godar, the peculiar Icelandic form of autocracy bore within itself from the beginning the seeds of its decay, and the political disasters of the thirteenth century followed logically from the constitutional advances of the tenth.

IV. LIFE AND LITERATURE

IN other respects too the Icelanders did not show themselves the most prudent of colonists. Many of them, for example, started off in Iceland by building big long-houses of the kind they were used to at home, but whose construction and upkeep required more timber and heating than their riven, barren, cold, wet island could supply. There was no native oak or beech or conifer, and in this land of 'stones, more stones, and all stones' by cosmic irony there is practically no stone suitable for building. Even a man's gravestone must be shipped in from abroad. So the houses were turf-built, with walls three to six feet thick, or thicker, and roofs on which a springy ewe could graze. But their inner construction and sometimes their inner lining was of timber, and the big hall of the Viking age, sixty or even a hundred feet long, required big pillars and cross-beams. So already by the eleventh century the Icelandic house was changing shape, with the big hall divided into two parts, sometimes with the addition of other rooms at right-angles to the main structure, and by the end of the Commonwealth the smaller passage-house (*gangahús*) was a belated recognition of cold reality. Again, the Icelanders never learned how to clothe themselves against cold and rain. Their foot-gear was particularly ill suited to their climate and terrain, and it is the witness of their foremost modern geographer that 'In times of starvation they did not even learn to eat several of the edible things found in the country, and their fishing tackle was not anything to boast of.'[17] Worst of all, they were improvident farmers. In a country where the balance between soil erosion through the rapid alternations of cold and thaw and soil building by glacial and volcanic action was at best precarious, they lived like prodigals, destroying the protective birch-scrub by intensive grazing, fire-wood felling and accidental forest fires. Without realizing it, they were living on their soil's capital; it lasted them for the best part of three centuries before its decline became disastrous and led to the denudation of whole districts. Except for his home-field the Icelandic farmer, primarily an animal husbandman, was something of a despoiler. For one reason or another, bad siting or a tale of bad seasons, about a quarter of the 600 farms named in *Landnámabók* were subsequently abandoned; but the index to spoliation is clearest in the farm register for 1703, when farms occupied numbered 4,059 and farms abandoned 3,200. It would, however, be unfair to argue that all of these were lost through human mismanagement. The land and later the climate were formidable.

And in justice there is much to be said too for that truest of the sons of Adam, the farmer. The men who came out to settle Iceland from Norway sought in the nature of things to live their lives after the Norwegian fashion, even as the men who went out to settle Greenland from Iceland expected to live their lives after the Icelandic. Of necessity the North Atlantic communities were based on agriculture, and more especially on the raising and use of cattle. They were farmer societies, chieftains, lawmen, bishops, and all. Their farms varied greatly in size and wealth. The facts are hard to come by. The more important settlers brought some animals with them, and more were thereafter imported. The richest surviving inventories are of late date. The church estate at Kirkjubær south in Sida in 1218 consisted of 30 cows, 7 *kúgildi* (a *kúgildi* representing the value of one cow in barren cattle), 180 ewes, 60 wethers, 60 castrated yearling rams, and 30 horses. In 1250, after a division of property, the expelled farmer still had 30 cows, 12 *kúgildi* in barren cattle, 120 ewes, 50 wethers, 70 yearling rams, 20 horses, 25 pigs and 50 domesticated geese. Byres big enough to stall four-

---

[17] Sigurður Thórarinsson, *Iceland in the Saga Period*, Þriðji Víkingafundur, p. 23.

teen to twenty beasts have been excavated on various old farms,
and during the severe winter of 1226–7 a hundred head of cattle
starved to death on the historian Snorri Sturluson's farm at
Svignaskard in Borgarfjord.[18] These like the commonalty of
barren cattle had undoubedly been kept out of doors the whole
year through. A considerable number of animals were killed off
before each winter to save keep, then jointed, salted, dried, or
otherwise preserved. A complement of horses was needed on a
farm, and they were essential for travel and transport. In
heathen times their flesh was eaten, and right down to the
seventeenth century stallions were bred and trained for the
national pastime of horse-fighting. The habitable parts of
the country were fairly well off for pasture; grass and hay were
precious commodities, and the law treated them as such. A
modest quantity of barley was grown, often on a strip system,
with labour-consuming windbreaks to protect the crop, but it
was always an uphill task, made worse and eventually more or
less brought to an end by the changes in climate. Certainly
home-grown grain was in short supply and costly, and it contributed little or nothing to the country's exports. Meat, including
that of sea-mammals and birds, dairy produce, and fish supplied
the Icelander's staple diet. For export the country had wool and
woollens, dressed sheepskins and hides, fats in forms as diverse
as cheese and tallow, and such indigenous novelties as falcons
for the sport of Europe's monarchies (the white falcon was the
most prized); stallions for horse-fighting; and after the Third
Crusade, 1187–92, sulphur for 'Greek fire'. As the art of war
developed, sulphur won a new importance in the manufacture
of 'thunder-flashes' (*herbrest*) made of fire, sulphur, vellum,
and a hemp fuse, on which *Lárentíus Saga*, the Saga of Lawrence, bishop of Holar, d. 1331, offers a very modern-sounding
note: 'In wars men often make thunder-flashes in order that
those caught unawares by the din will scatter in all directions.'
Somewhat unexpectedly, during the Commonwealth period

[18] All these figures are taken from Jón Jóhannesson, *A History of the Old
Icelandic Commonwealth* (1974), p. 289, as is the quotation from *Lárentíus
Saga* (from p. 316) later. Jón's chapter on 'Economic History and Material Culture', ibid., pp. 288–358, is the best account of all these matters for the English-
language reader.

Iceland seems not to have exported stockfish to Europe, though of all Icelandic exports it would later become the best known. In return for these exports Iceland imported timber (a prime necessity), tar, tools, weapons and metals in general, grain and flour, malt and honey, wine and church vestments, and fine linen.

Concurrently with all these activities the sixty thousand inhabitants of Iceland were preparing for an almost miraculous triumph in the art and practice of literature. The first generations were the fortunate inheritors, sustainers, and transmitters of a strong and distinctive culture, whose literary remains back home in Scandinavia have largely disappeared, but whose ships, tools, weapons, sculptures, carvings, inscriptions, buildings, and patterns, as they are displayed in the museums of Oslo, Stockholm, and Copenhagen, provide overwhelming evidence of Norse craftsmanship and artistic power. But for the Icelanders limitations were at once imposed upon that culture. The visual arts had flourished in both Ireland and Scandinavia, but in Iceland there was practically no stone to hew, no native wood to carve (though a number of splendid things like the door from the church at Valthjofsstadir show how the craft persisted), and little metal to mould; architecture and illumination were in the nature of things beyond their reach; and there is small evidence that they were a musical people. Their distinctive artistic expression must be in words, and by a singular stroke of fortune many of these words could be preserved. The long dark winters and certain quirks in the developing national character provided all the time in the world, the need to kill off most of their cattle ensured a large supply of week-old calves' skins for vellum, and the coming of Christianity and an acquaintance with books provided a practicable alphabet and a conventional format. Beginning on the estates of the wealthy chieftains and bishops and in the monasteries south and north, but spreading later among the farmers over the whole island, transcription took place on an unprecedented scale. There still exist in European libraries some 700 Icelandic manuscripts or fragments of manuscripts on vellum, and these, in Sigurður Nordal's words, are 'like the poor wreckage from a proud fleet', which on a cautious estimate must have been many times as numerous.

The substance of many of them is known far beyond Iceland's

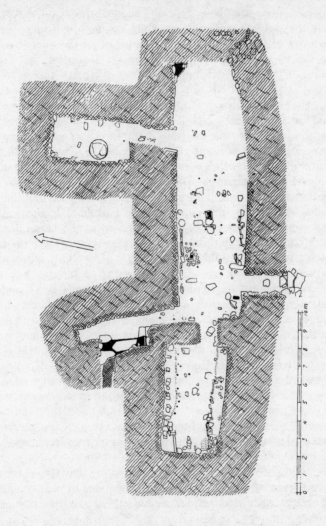

9. EARLY ELEVENTH-CENTURY FARM, GJÁSKÓGAR, THJÓRSÁRDALUR, ICELAND

The farm consists of four houses or sections; a hall 15 metres long, with a fire-place in the middle of the floor and sleeping-berths along both walls; a living-room with sitting-benches and a hearth; a dairy with an impression of a large vessel for milk or *skyr* sunk into the floor; and a privy with a groove running along one wall and opening out at the farther end

shores. There are those precious repositories, Codex Regius 2365 4to supreme among them, which contain the Eddic poems, the Lays of Gods and Men, a treasure of all Germania; there are the two undisputed works of Snorri Sturluson, the Prose Edda, in which a consummate artist recreates the heathen Norse mythology, tells how the gods have lived and how they shall die, and *Heimskringla*, those creatively narrative 'Lives of the Norse Kings' of which it has been said that they presented Norway with her national traditions; and there are the family sagas and *þættir*, perhaps 120 of them in all, together with the skaldic verses and other poems they preserve embedded in their prose. Less familiar but still blessed with northward-looking readers are such foundations of Icelandic history as the *Libellus Islandorum* of Ari the Learned, the 'Father of Icelandic history', and *Landnámabók*, with its record of the land-takings, the settlers and their sons and grandsons; the mythical and legendary Sagas of Old Time, the *Fornaldarsögur*, laden with marvels and adventures, the glory of the Skjoldungs and the sorrows of Sigurd and Gudrun; the Bishops' sagas, and that dramatic sequence of twelfth- and thirteenth-century history whose title is *Sturlunga Saga*. But there is an immense literature besides, much of it hardly to be discerned in the shadow of these works of native, national impulse. The Icelanders were earnest translators and adapters of foreign works. They rendered into their own tongue histories from Sallust to Geoffrey of Monmouth; there exist voluminous collections of story and lore concerning Our Lady, the Saints, and the Apostles; there is a full homiletic literature in Icelandic; and the treasuries of southern Romance were ransacked for 'sagas' of Tristan and Yvain, Erec and Blancheflor. The general impression is one of intense and unending activity, a broad, strong river of words, creative, informative, derivative, flowing from eager and acquisitive minds to the haven of the vellums.[19]

[19] As historians and preservers of the northern past the Men of Thule (*Tylenses*) had no greater admirer than Saxo Grammaticus. 'The diligence of the men of Iceland must not be shrouded in silence; since the barrenness of their native soil offers no means of self-indulgence, they pursue a steady routine of temperance and devote all their time to improving our knowledge of others' deeds, compensating for poverty by their intelligence. They regard

The sagas, then, are written literature. Conditions in medieval Iceland, it is true, were unusually favourable for the development of story-telling and oral tradition, and we hear a good deal about the practice of reciting stories before kings abroad and at entertainments, marriages, and all kinds of gatherings at home. But the sagas as we have them, and know them, are written. It is certain that oral tales, oral tradition, including old verses, form a considerable part of the raw material of the saga-writers, but it would be misleading to consider the sagas as the mere writing down of such tales or tradition. Modern scholarship is making us more and more aware of written sources for the sagas, both native and foreign, historical, legendary, homiletic, and exemplary. Among the sources drawn on by the author of *Eiríks Saga Rauða*, a singularly well-informed man, were not only the oral traditions of Thorfinn Karlsefni's descendants, but possibly *Grænlendinga Saga*,[20] and certainly *Sturlubók* and the Life of Olaf Tryggvason written by Gunnlaug Leifsson the Monk; while the influence of ecclesiastical and geographical writings and, in the case of *Hauksbók* especially, of family pride and genealogy are easily discernible.[21] The saga-men were in general of serious purpose and well-stored mind; they were organizers of material, both oral and written; and to think of them as mere transcribers by ear does them scant justice.

The word *saga* (plur. *sögur*) means something said, something recorded in words, and hence by easy transition a prose story or narrative. Specifically it is the term used to describe, or rather distinguish, the prose narratives which were Iceland's main contribution to the medieval literature of Europe, above all the *Íslendingasögur* or Sagas of Icelanders, which relate the

it a real pleasure to discover and commemorate the achievements of every nation; in their judgement it is as elevating to discourse on the prowess of others as to display their own. Thus I have scrutinized their store of historical treasures and composed a considerable part of this present work by copying their narratives, not scorning where I recognized such skill in ancient lore to take these men as witness' (*Gesta Danorum*, Preface).

[20] As argued by Jón Jóhannesson, 'Aldur Grænlendinga Sögu', in *Nordæla*, (1956), pp. 149–58. Ólafur Halldórsson, *GríM* (1978), thinks the two sagas are independent.

[21] The point is illustrated in Appendix VI, 'Of Spies and Unipeds'.

lives and feuds of individuals and families during the so-called
Saga Age, which lasted from 930 to 1030. That they were deliberately rooted in the values of a much mutated and anachronistic heroic age had consequences for both life and literature.
Judged by his secular literary memorials the Icelander was wedded to the principles of feud. This could be conducted by law or
the manipulation of law, or could proceed along well-charted
channels to private or public arbitration; but ideally feud was
blood-feud, and its solution (or more often its progression) was
by blood-vengeance. An unappreciative (and unacceptable)
summary of the Icelandic sagas is 'peasants at loggerheads'.
'Franklins at feud' would be harder to rebut. For more than
anything the sagas tell of the quarrels, killings, counter-killings,
victories, defeats, reconciliations, and general manœuvres of
individuals or families in a state of feud with a neighbour. The
medieval Icelander was blood-brother to the Normans, and the
energy and insight which they in their European context
devoted to architecture, war, and statecraft, he in his stonier
province gave to the arts of literature and feud. Admittedly the
sagas include much more than feud. Together they provide not
only a composite history of Iceland's heroic age; they are its
epic, and the fullest expression of the nation's soul. Without
them the Icelandic ethos is not to be comprehended, neither the
complex of ideals and beliefs nor the qualities of mind which led
to the best years of the Republic, the Greenland–Vinland
adventure, and to Icelandic literature, and on the other hand to
blood-feud, civil war, the loss of independence, and the disasters that ensued. The greatest of sagas is *Brennu-Njáls Saga*, the
Saga of the Burning of Njal, composed about 1280 by an
unknown master in the south-west of Iceland. To reduce its narrative riches to a sentence, it tells how the hero Gunnar of
Hlidarendi was brought to his death by fate and his own character; how the sage Njal was in the same fashion brought to destruction with his entire family; and how the man who burned
him and the man who avenged him grew reconciled. *Njála*, to
give it its title of affection, is one of the supreme works of European thirteenth-century literature.

But if *Njála* is the greatest of sagas it is not a lonely giant, and
it is permissible to have a favourite elsewhere. The chivalric and
sentimental reader may respond more warmly to the fine feeling

and noble situations of *Laxdæla Saga*; those who love high poetry and fierce adventure must always find *Egils Saga* irresistible; while the passionate regard of many Icelanders for the saga of the crossed and outlawed Grettir is a moving revelation of how a people may find its soul mirrored and its past expressed in the tale of one man. Among shorter pieces the saga of Hrafnkel Priest of Frey is almost flawless, a magnificent study of chieftainship in action, while the endearing tale of the simple-seeming Authun the Westfirther who bought a bear in Greenland and gave it to King Svein in Denmark achieves a full artistic perfection.[22] So too the skilful amalgamation of history, historical tradition, folk-tale, and Snorri Sturluson's thirteenth-century knowledge of the vicissitudes of the Greenland voyage, presented under the title 'The Only King who Rests in Iceland' (Appendix II), is one of a hundred examples that might be given of Icelandic narrative 'realism' and the resultant problem of belief.

At the cost of some slight repetition, and with a reference back to the section on 'History and Historiography' of the Introduction (pp. 14–16 above), and a directive ahead to parts of the Vinland story and Appendixes II and VI (pp. 121–2, 232–6, 283–5 below), we may now briefly conclude that for most of the good family sagas, those whose compilation and writing down was undertaken in a serious and responsible way, there was a beginning in family and general history and its attendant traditions. Remembering always that we are dealing with history as it was known to the medieval and not the modern mind, and remembering too that the saga-men were dealing with events which had taken place some two or three hundred years before. It follows further that the historicity of every saga must be established in a positive way by checking it with every known source of information, where possible with the archaeological record, and in a negative safeguarding way by distinguishing between the reasonable and the incredible elements in its narrative. Remembering further that though fiction or the recasting of material in the crucible of the creative imagination was an

---

[22] Both stories, *Hrafnkels Saga Freysgoða* and *Auðunar þáttr Vestfirzka*, appear in an English translation in Gwyn Jones, *Eirik the Red and Other Icelandic Sagas* (World's Classics, OUP, 1980).

essential element of all the best family sagas, there would be no sagas but for the saga-men's interest in history and regard for contemporary historical method. Of all this the numerous sagas whose opening chapters interact with *Landnámabók* or whose substance is permeated with historical or would-be historical events, like the sagas of Eirik the Red and the Greenlanders, are excellent examples. Underlying them is a sound historical tradition about the discovery and settlement of Greenland and the attempted colonization of a coastal area in North America. In the course of centuries this tradition has collected various accretions and confusions, but its core of truth has always been discernible, and in the last two decades investigation of the complex at Brattahlid invites disbelief in *Eiríks Saga*'s account of the genesis of 'Thjodhild's Church', but the existence of the church and Christian burial-ground is certain. We have convincing evidence that the northern extremity of Newfoundland and the area of Sacred Bay were the scene of early Norse habitation in the ancient Promontorium Winlandiæ.

V. THE REPUBLIC ENDS

THE first Icelandic Republic lasted for almost 400 years, if we date its inception from the arrival of Ingolf Arnarson; and no fewer than 330 if we regard the Age of Settlement, 870–930, as its preliminaries rather than its first chapter. As to its last, no nation worked harder at its own destruction, or was worse served by those to whom it had a right to look for leadership and example, and consequently, of all the periods of Iceland's history the Age of the Sturlungs, the last century of independence, has come in for most polemic, most abuse. It was an age of greed for wealth and power, of selfishness and pride, leading to civil war and national exhaustion, and its many betrayals ended in the greatest betrayal of all: the handing over of the nation to a foreign power. Even so we must guard against an over-righteous verdict and an over-simplified picture. The so-called 'betrayers' were as much the victims of history and circumstance as those they betrayed, and among their number were some of the most gifted and famous men the island has ever known.

No one cause, still less one event or person, led to the loss of

Iceland's independence in 1262–4, and the slackening of national life that ensued. The Icelanders' heritage of independence and individualism was in its nature perilous to political unity; but even had that unity been attained Iceland would have found it hard to remain a nation on her own. The settlers and their sons' sons were fine seamen whose ships carried them viking, trading, poetizing, exploring, to known and unknown lands. But already in the eleventh century fewer and fewer chieftains owned their own ships. Those belonging to their forefathers were by now lost or grown unseaworthy, and there was no native timber, no strong oak, with which to lay down the keels of new. In trustworthy sources of the twelfth century there are surprisingly few references to Icelandic-owned sea-going vessels; in the thirteenth century they are hardly to be found at all. A native-owned ship was becoming a rarity.[23] For a people inhabiting a mostly infertile island far out in the North Atlantic this was at best a dangerous development. Overseas trade and travel were now becoming possible only by the grace of others, which in the thirteenth century meant the Norwegians. This was the greatest danger of all, for in Norway both monarchy and church had plans of their own for Iceland, and these postulated the loss of her independence.

These plans were much helped by changing conditions in the island, where while personal (which means excessive) individualism remained constant, family ambition intensified. During the twelfth century power came increasingly into fewer sets of hands, as a small number of energetic and unscrupulous chieftains acquired the ownership of many godords or were allowed in return for reward and protection to exercise the privileges and controls that went with them. It followed that the old relationship between godi and thingman, chieftain and retainer, changed: it became less personal, more feudal. In theory a thingman could still transfer his allegiance, and so express his opinion of old master and new; but in fact his freedom of action had become circumscribed. Even in quarrels which did not touch him close he was forced to take sides. There had been noteworthy trials of strength between chieftains in the old days:

[23] See in particular the sub-chapters on ships and seagoing in Jón Jóhannesson, *Íslendinga Saga*, I and II.

armies of three or four hundred men twice confronted each other in the 960s after the burning to death of Blund-Ketil, and in 1012 almost the entire congregation for law was locked in battle on the sacred Thingfield after the burning to death of Njal; by 1121 Haflidi Masson (in whose home, ironically enough, the civil law of Iceland had four years earlier been amended and for the first time written down) could prosecute his quarrel against Thorgils Oddsson with a force of almost 1,500 men. A pattern was now established whereby levies drawn from entire Quarters replaced those bands of kinsmen and friends who rode out with the old-time protagonists of feud. Lesser men, and many chieftains with them, must throw in their lot with the Sturlungs, who controlled the Dales, Borgarfjord, and Eyjafjord, or with the Asbirnings of Skagafjord; with the Vatnsfirthings of the north-west or the Svinfellings of the east; with the Oddaverjar of the south whose star was setting, or the Haukadalers whose delayed and murky triumph would precede and ensure that of the Norwegian king. Loyalties drained away like water on sand, for the rending feuds and quasi-dynastic wars of the thirteenth century were made worse by struggles for supremacy within the contending groups, by disconcerting shifts of alignment, and by the ambiguous relationship of so many Icelandic chieftains to the Norwegian king. Many of Iceland's leading men who visited the court of King Hakon Hakonsson became his liegemen and promised him obedience; but of all the king's chosen instruments, Snorri Sturluson, Sturla Sighvatsson, Thord Kakali, Thorgils Skardi, and Gizur Thorvaldsson, only Thorgils wholeheartedly served the royal cause. Snorri, wise beyond his time and not enough the man of action, brooded and procrastinated and zealously accumulated estates and wealth and worries till Hakon wearied of him and he was murdered in a night raid on Reykholt in 1241. Sturla, too much the man of action and abusing the king's authority in order to square private accounts and forward personal ambitions, had already perished in 1238, cut down with two of his brothers after the battle of Orlygsstadir, in which his father, old Sighvat, died grim and reluctant of seventeen bloody wounds. Sturla's brother Thord Kakali by a skilled use of force and diplomacy became overlord of all Iceland, and might have become its king,[24] but his personal ambition showed so nakedly that King Hakon had him recalled in 1250, and he never set foot in his homeland again. Thorgils Skardi (another Sturlung), whose unquestioned loyalty to the king was enhanced by his intelligence and magnanimity, was treacherously murdered in 1258, while still a young man of thirty-two. Gizur alone survived the royal commission, to emerge as the most important man in Iceland and an earl. But the price he paid hardly bears thinking on. His wife and three sons and more than twenty of his household and friends died when his enemies burned Flugumyr, and his heart died with them. All that was good in his nature grew corrupted in those faithless times, and a man sensitive, intelligent, and deep-rooted in his country's past, grew cunning and merciless, and destroyed his country's freedom. The coldest reading in *Sturlunga Saga* is his reply to Thord Andresson whom he seized in 1264 while under a pledge of safe conduct. The wretched Thord asked Gizur to forgive him. 'I will', said Gizur, 'the minute you are dead.' No wonder Thord Kakali told King Hakon, when the king had asked him whether he would consent to live in heaven if Gizur were there too: 'Gladly, sire—so long as we might be far apart.'[25] Hatred pursued him at home, and suspicion abroad, and though the only earl in Iceland he died lonely and desperate as a fox in a stone trap. To Norway's king all these men were expendable. The more so because Hakon knew how divided were their loyalties and how enigmatic their purpose.

But his success was inevitable. Time, the spirit of the age, and the church were all on his side. By definition the Republic was an anachronism, pagan and anti-monarchic. The Icelanders *must* give allegiance to King Hakon, pronounced Cardinal William of Sabina, 'for he thought it against all reason that this country should not serve a king even as all other countries in the world'. Not only Norwegian bishops like the arch-intriguer Heinrek, but Icelanders like Brand, Arni, and Jorund were among the most determined underminers of the old Constitution. They stood for the monarchy because the monarchy stood for the church, and both before and after the loss of national

[24] See Appendix II, 'The Only King who Rests in Iceland'.
[25] Einar Ól. Sveinsson, *The Age of the Sturlungs*, p. 94.

independence they fought for the ecclesiastical control of church property, including church buildings and their revenues, which had always been, like the heathen places of worship which preceded them, the personal property of the chieftains who built them. Their success in securing these rights impoverished families as wealthy as the Oddaverjar and beggared beyond recovery many lesser godar. By these and other means the old way of life was being broken in pieces, and the old culture destroyed in its foundations. Also the Icelandic farmer, who more than any chieftain was the nation's prop and stay, grew sick to death of war and disorder. He wanted peace, and after 1250 and the recall of Thord Kakali saw no hope of it save by favour of the Norwegian king. When Thorgils Skardi offered himself as chieftain over Skagafjord after his victory at Thvera in 1255, it was a farmer, Broddi Thorleifsson, who made answer not only for himself, but for all his kind. If one must serve a chieftain, he said, very well, let it be Thorgils. 'But it would be better to serve none, if only a man could be left in peace.' Rule by chieftains was in discredit and men's minds were open to the only alternative: rule by a king. So it came about that between 1262 and 1264 the four Quarters of Iceland made submission to King Hakon. Soon they had a new civil and constitutional law from Norway, and a new church law. Within a decade they had peace and thereafter stagnation. For by an unforeseeable misfortune they had committed their future into the hands of Norway just as Norway entered upon a period of rapid decline. From now on the parent country would have more than enough to do to help herself, much less Iceland, which after enjoying a brief increase in her exports of fish was to suffer cruelly from lack of trade and communications. The number of independent farmers declined, householders became tenants and cottars, and, as always in hard times, the poor grew ever poorer. Many turned beggar and tramped the countryside. But much of Iceland's misery was not man-made. It came from the forbidding nature of the land. Geologically Iceland was still in the making, and its people shared in its growing-pains. For a start, the climate was becoming colder and bad ice-years increased in number after 1270, blocking the coasts and prolonging the already long winter. But worse tribulation was in store. The year 1283 ushered in a period of plague and famine: seven of the next ten years saw men and cattle die of cold, epidemic, or starvation. The turn of the century was marked by the eruption of the volcano Hekla, with violent earthquakes, and in 1301 as many as 500 people died by epidemic in the north. Between 1306 and 1314 only two years were free of volcanic action, earthquake, or plague, with their resultant loss of life and destruction of the means of existence. Periodically throughout the rest of the century the fire-mountains of the south would explode with terrifying force and devastate wide areas of the countryside. Farms vanished, pasture was erased, man and his beasts alike perished of blast, avalanche, flood, and fire, and wherever the pall of ash and pumice blackened Iceland's skies the birds as they flew fell dead to the poisoned ground. The eruption of Oræfajokul in 1362 with its attendant *jökulhlaup* or glacier-burst was 'in all probability the biggest explosive eruption in Europe since Pompeii was destroyed in AD 79.'[26] The whole area of Oræfi was temporarily abandoned, and two parishes were extinguished for ever. Even more notorious was Hekla, *mons perpetuo ardens*, recognized by an awed Europe as the Mouth of Hell itself. Here in time of eruption might be heard the gnashing of teeth and shrill lamentation, while the souls of the damned fluttered round like black ravens. It was Iceland's bitter distinction that it fulfilled the requirements of both the Viking and the Christian hells, the first cold and icy, the second endlessly aflame. And when at last these conceptions were combined, Hell's worst horror was seen to be Iceland's too, where the doomed alternate hopelessly between Tartarean fire and numbing glaciers and drift ice.

With it all, Iceland survived, though necessarily in herself and for herself. Her political dependence and maritime impoverishment, her natural catastrophes and the mere stark act of endurance would make it impossible for her to succour her neighbour Greenland when Greenland in turn felt the remorseless pressures of geography and history. There the Norsemen would be

---

[26] Sigurður Thórarinsson, *The Thousand Years Struggle against Ice and Fire* (Reykjavik, 1956), p. 46. The glacier-burst from Katla in 1918 may serve as an illustration of the destructive power of this phenomenon. Its discharge has been estimated as 200,000 cubic metres of water a second, roughly three times the discharge of the Amazon. The lifeless waste of the black Myrdal sands is Katla's enduring memorial.

lost beyond knowledge or redemption in a dark, impenetrable night; but Iceland would come safely through the fourteenth century, and however distant, however obscured, a fresh dawn lay ahead.

2

Greenland

I. DISCOVERY AND SETTLEMENT

THE early history of Norse Greenland is the life-story of Eirik
the Red. He was its first explorer and settler; he gave it a name
and took out shiploads of Icelanders to make their home there;
he brought its western coast firmly within the confines of late
tenth-century Norse geography. Yet he was not the first to
sight it.

About the Norse discovery of Iceland blew the winds of story
and chance. Ships blown off course and storm-driven about the
western ocean made landfalls unknown or unexpected. So with
Greenland. Late in the period of settlement, between 900 and
930, a man named Gunnbjorn Ulf-Krakuson, either when sailing from Norway to Iceland or on a circumnavigatory survey
designed to improve on Gardar's voyage of *c*.860, was storm-
driven into the ocean west of Iceland where he sighted a new
land and its attendant islands in the west. These islands, or skerries, were henceforth known by his name, Gunnbjarnarsker,
but it is a very long time since they were last satisfactorily identified. In the middle of the fourteenth century Ivar Bardarson
said the skerries lie half-way between Iceland and Greenland;
and since by Greenland he presumably meant the Norse settlements on its south-western coast, it seems reasonable to identify
them with islands east of Sermiligaq, near Angmagssalik, due
west of Snæfellsnes.[1] In any case, the land Gunnbjorn saw was
Greenland. He made no descent upon its shores, undertook no
survey, but his news was to bear good fruit back in Isafjord and

---

[1] So Gustav Holm, *MGr* 56 (1918). But nothing is certain, for their number,
nature, and position were the subject of speculation rather than geographical
knowledge. Thus in the *Grænlandsannáll* of Björn Jónsson of Skardsa (*c*.1625)
we read of the Gunnbjarnareyjar which lie off the mouth of the Isafjord, to the
north-west. A decade or so later Joris Carolus's map shows 'I. Gouberman' as
eight islands due west of the Vestfirthir, but Joris was a congenital inventor of
islands. The learned Arngrímur Jónsson at different times, in his *Gronlandia*

under Snæfellsnes, where his sons and his brother had earlier taken land in settlement.

Eirik the Red, a red-headed, red-bearded, and on occasion red-handed man, was by some accounts born on a farm in Jaeren, some thirty miles south of Stavanger in Norway, but in his middle teens was forced to leave the country along with his father Thorvald, by reason of a feud which ended in manslaughter. The Age of Settlement was over, the good land taken, and father and son could do no better for themselves than a farm on the harsh, rocky coast which runs south from Hornbjarg, Cape Horn. This ice-prone area must have struck young Eirik as a hard exchange for the green fields and early harvests of his boyhood home, so when his father died, and he himself was married and collecting a father's responsibilities, he abandoned Drangar and cleared land south in Haukadal, then as now an area of gnarled birchwood and pleasant grazing. Soon he was involved in heavy blood-feuds, thrown out of Haukadal by men with more bone in their fist than he, drawn into new manslayings in the islands of Breidafjord, and finally banished overseas for a period of three years. Still, he had a gift for friendship, and his friends stood by him manfully, but they were probably relieved to hear his resolution to rediscover the land Gunnbjorn

and *Specimen Islandiæ*, thought of them as west, north-west, and north of Iceland. They were inhabited and uninhabited. Jón lærði Guðmundsson attempted a summary in his *Um Íslands aðskiljanlegar náttúrur*, shortly after 1637: 'Gunnbiarnareyjar. Gunnbjorn Ulf-Krakuson, a Norwegian, who sailed the whole way round Iceland after Gardar in order to discover what lands would lie most adjacent to Iceland, first lighted on these islands, which appeared to him to be as it were skerries off Gardarsholm, full of birds and herbage and amply endowed with produce of the sea. Of these it would be too long to give an account. Master Juris tréfótur Hollendski [= Joris Carolus] is now the latest claimant to have landed there, and saw two churches. These [islands] will be six in number and all of them of a good size. Whether the English and Dutch ply their trade there I cannot say. They lie in the sea to the north-west off Ísafjardardjup and Adalvikur-rytabjarg, as the old poem recounts' (ed. Hermansson, Islandica, xv, p. 3). This old poem would appear to be Styrbjorn's prophetic verse about the fate of Snæbjorn Galti (see p. 171 below), in which case we are back where we started, and little the wiser. A legend on a map by Ruysch in the 1507 edition of Ptolemy reads '*Insula hæc anno Domini 1456 fuit totaliter combusta*' (O'Dell, *The Scandinavian World*, p. 359), which would dispose of island(s) and problem alike if we could accept it—which we cannot. *Gunnbiarne Skær, Goubar Schoer*, and the like, persist on maps till well into the eighteenth century.

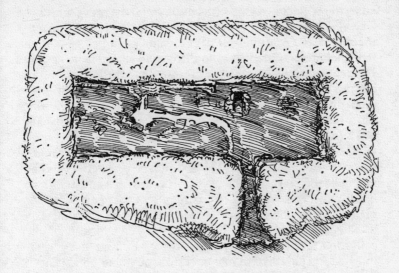

10. BRATTAHLID, THE GREAT HALL

The interior measures 14.7 × 4.5 metres. The walls, part stone, part turf, were between a metre and two metres thick. The entrance faces south-east, with a commanding view of the fjord. Opposite it, indoors, is the main fireplace, and a stone-covered channel conveyed fresh water through the house

Ulf-Krakuson had sighted the time he was storm-driven into the western ocean and discovered Gunnbjarnarsker. This need not have been a sudden resolution: Gunnbjorn's family had lived in Eirik's corner of Iceland, and the notion of new land for those venturesome enough to take it must have been often canvassed in the Vestfirthir. What now could be more natural than that the twin compulsions of banishment and ambition should make Eirik that man? In Norway as in Iceland the avengers of blood stood waiting. Ever a man of action, he sailed west through the islands, west past the Snæfell jokul, west for the glimpsed cloud-hackles and ice-shirted mountains of Greenland.[2]

From his hideout in Breidafjord he had the best part of 450

[2] That the retailers of tradition and 'history' made free with Eirik's scanty story is certain. In *Ætt Eiríks Rauða* (*Gripla*, 4 (1980), pp. 81–91) Ólafur Halldórsson presents reasons for doubting his outlawry from Norway and the details of his life and residences in Iceland, and suggests that we accept *Íslendingabók*'s statement that he was a Breidafjord man, born and bred.

miles to go. Sailing on the 65th parallel with the prevailing east-
erly of early summer behind him, he would be near enough to
the Greenland coast in four days (assuming that he hove to in
the brief hours of darkness) to discern its inhospitable nature.
He would then head south-south-west along the land, still con-
ning an iron landscape of mountain, nunatak, and the glittering
desolation of the ice-cap, till after long sailing he would start
threading the southern fjords and by way of Prins Christians
Sund feel his way to the western coast, then follow the bent of
the land north-west.[3] Soon thereafter he would know his hunch
had been right and that his hopes would be gratified. For as he
sailed in the warm bright days northwards beyond Hvarf he
quickly reached the southern extremity of the most habitable
region of Greenland. Inland, as ever, was the daunting majesty
of the ice-cap, but here it was hidden, and instead of the
contorted face of the eastern coast, rock-browed and glacier-
tongued, medusa-like to man and ship, he found himself navi-
gating an archipelago of bird-haunted islands, with a shore to
starboard fissured with deep, life-teeming fjords. The country
was most beautiful, and to a seaman's eye the fjords and island-
channels, with their good sailing and innumerable anchorages
and harbours, were altogether more attractive than the exposed
coasts of Iceland. While best of all for a man who, whatever else
he was, was still a farmer, he found at the inner extremities of
these fjords emerald grass, flowery hill-slopes, dwarf willow,
birch, and juniper. Edible berries grew there in profusion,
angelica, bog-cotton, and the mosses of home. Above all, the
land was empty of inhabitants, though various house-ruins,
fragments of boats and stone implements bore witness to an
earlier, and as they judged, non-European occupation. And as
he probed these fjords and explored the islands during the three
summers of his exile, for the first time in his life Eirik was free

---

[3] It was Otto Pettersson's view that Eirik would sail through Prins Christians
Sund and not need to round Cape Farewell, and he is likely to be right. If so,
this would support the notion sometimes expressed that during his third summer
Eirik explored the *east* coast of Greenland as far north as the latitude of the
head of Eiriksfjord, and that it was on this coast that he found relics of the
Eskimo. The Dorset Culture Eskimo had disappeared from the south-west
coast some 800 years before the Norsemen arrived there. But the detail of
Eirik's movements is quite uncertain.

of constrictive neighbours. We cannot doubt that his ideas expanded accordingly, for when he returned to Iceland it was to sing the praises of his new-found land, named not too unfairly, when we think of the luxuriant pastures of the southern fjords, *Grænaland*, The Green Land, or *Grænland*, Greenland.[4] The connotations of this happy title, *green*, *grass*, and *grow*, were a joyous augury to land-hungry men, and richly redolent of pastures new. He prepared at once for its permanent colonization. He would have returned too with a cargo of bearskins, reindeer, seal and walrus hides, and sea-ivory, as an earnest of the country's riches, and with a full crew to witness to its clemency.

At home he found many ready to listen to him. Ten years earlier Iceland had suffered the worst famine of her history, so terrible that some killed the old and helpless out of the way, and many starved.[5] So there were plenty with nothing to hope for at home, great householders fallen on evil times like Thorbjorn Vifilsson, and poor farmers overshadowed by such new-rich upstarts as the hateful Hen-Thorir. Even so, the response to Eirik's preaching must have surprised him. When he returned to Greenland early in the summer of 986 it was as leader of an armada of twenty-five ships, of which fourteen arrived safely. Some perished, more were forced back, but the effective colonization of Greenland must have begun with hardly less than four hundred people taking possession of land after the Icelandic fashion in the inner reaches of the hundred and twenty miles of fjord country extending north from Herjolfsnes to Isafjord.[6] Practically all these people were Icelanders.

Eventually the so-called Eastern Settlement of the modern

[4] Adam of Bremen, ever credulous, believed that the people there were of a greenish hue from the salt water, 'whence too that region gets its name'.

[5] 976 was a famine year throughout north and north-western Europe. After Iceland, Norway and England were among the worst sufferers.

[6] The locations of settlement were as follows. Herjolf took in settlement Herjolfsnes (the modern Ikigait) and Herjolfsfjord (Amitsuarssuk). Ketil took Ketilsfjord (Tasermiut). Hrafn took Hrafnsfjord (Agdluitsoq, or possibly its inner northern arm, up to Foss). Solvi took Solvadal (probably a valley running up from Kangikitsoq). Helgi Thorbrandsson took Alptafjord (Sermilik), named after his home fjord in Iceland. Thorbjorn Glora took Siglufjord (Unartoq), which according to Ivar Bardarson had the home comfort of hot springs. Einar took Einarsfjord (Igaliko). Hafgrim took Hafgrimsfjord (Eqaluit) and Vatnahverfi (the inner half of the peninsula between Igaliko and Agdluitsoq, and the

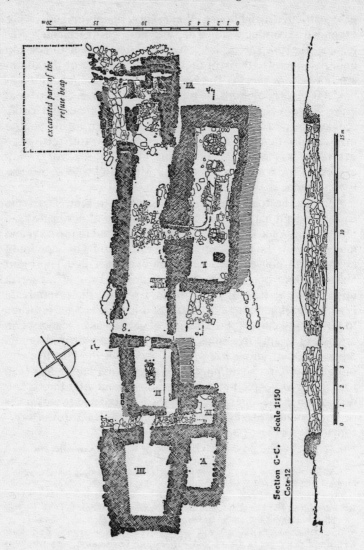

II. BRATTAHLID, THE NORTH FARM DWELLING

I, the oldest part of the complex, probably the site of Eirik the Red's great hall;
II–V, later extensions northwards, by way of a fire-house, sleeping-house, and
store-rooms; VI, the roofed well-house. Outside were byres, store-houses, and
other buildings

Julianehaab district would number by contemporary record 190
farms, a cathedral at Gardar, on the neck between Eiriksfjord
and Einarsfjord, an Augustine monastery and Benedictine nun-
nery, and twelve parish churches. Concurrently there were
hardy spirits pressing further north three hundred miles and
more to found the Western Settlement, Vestribyggd, in the district where Godthaab stands today. This was smaller but still
substantial, with its ninety farms and four churches.[7] That the
twenty or more farms round Ivigtut (with no church) should be
regarded as a Middle Settlement is doubtful; they seem rather
to belong to the Eastern Settlement. Between Eystribyggd and
Vestribyggd (we should probably describe them today as the
Southern and Northern Settlements, for their bearing one from
the other is north-west and south-east) the coastal strip was too
narrow for animal husbandry, and inland of the mountains lay
nothing but ice. 'Men', says the author of the *King's Mirror*, in
his mid-thirteenth-century description of Greenland, 'have
often tried to go up into the country and climb the highest
mountains in various places to look about and learn whether
any land could be found that was free from ice and habitable.
But nowhere have they found such a place, except what is now
occupied, which is a little strip along the water's edge.' Where
that strip failed them, they had nothing.

The uninhabited and uninhabitable parts of Greenland were
the Obyggdir, most of them good for little or nothing, but some
providing the two settlements with excellent hunting- and fishing-
grounds and with their best supply of driftwood. In these last,
hunters and skippers like the ogreish Thorhall in *Eiríks*

largest area of inland settlement in the Norse colonies). Arnlaug took Arnlaugsfjord (not entirely identifiable, but in the northern reaches of Eystribyggd). Eirik himself first lived on Eiriksey (Igdlutalik) off the mouth of
Eiriksfjord (Tunugdliarfik), and thereafter at Brattahlid (Qagssiarssuk), near
the northern inner extremity of the fjord, west across the water from the
modern airstrip at Narssarssuaq.

[7] *Det gamle Grønlands beskrivelse* (1930); *GHM*, iii. 228. In all some 400
Norse ruins have been discovered in Greenland, almost 300 of which are farms
of varying size and different periods. See Aage Roussell, *Farms and Churches in
the Mediaeval Norse Settlements of Greenland*, *MGr* 89 (1941); Michael Wolfe,
'Norse Archaeology in Greenland since World War II', in the *American-Scandinavian Review*, 49. 4 (1961–2), pp. 380–92; J. Meldgaard, *Nordboerne i
Grønland*, (1965); Finn Gad, *History of Greenland*, vol. i, (1970); H. M. Jansen, *A Critical Account . . . of the Norse Settlements in Greenland* (1972).

Saga or the gallant Sigurd Njalsson in *Einars Tháttr* reaped a rich and recurrent harvest by land and sea. The best hunting-grounds lay well to the north of Vestribyggd: Disco and its environs in latitude 70° N. was a favourite resort for men whose skill matched their hardihood, and here they built huts to serve them on their far thrusts north. Most journeyed in six-oared boats ('Oft was I weary when I tugged at thee!'), and completed their task during the months of summer. From today's Holsteinsborg northwards to the Nugssuaq peninsula lay the *Norðr-setr*, *-seta*, the Northern Hunting-Ground(s), and men who came sojourning here were said to 'go on, or into, Nordseta (*fara í norðsetu)*' for narwhal, walrus, and the esteemed white bear of Greenland. Nor was this their northern limit. In 1824 the Eskimo Pelimut discovered in one of three cairns on the island of Kingigtorssuaq, just north of Upernavik, and a little short of latitude 73° N., a small stone inscribed with runes which recorded that 'Erling Sighvatsson and Bjarni Thordarson and Eindridi Oddsson on the Saturday before the minor Rogation Day [25 April] piled these cairns and . . . '. The inscription, whose ending is unclear, dates from the mid fourteenth century (1333?), and presumably these men, voluntarily or involuntarily, had spent the winter on Kingigtorssuaq. We read too of a party who in 1266 returned to Eystribyggd from the Nordseta, after pushing farther north than had ever been heard tell of before. They had not seen any Eskimo dwellings save those in Kroksfjardarheidi in the Disco area. The church authorities promptly sent off an expedition of their own which got still further north into Melville Bay, almost to the 76th parallel. Its members saw many islands and all kinds of game, seals, whales, and so many bears that they dare not venture ashore. They saw Eskimo dwellings too, returned to Kroksfjardarheidi after seventy-two hours' sailing and a twenty-four-hour spell at the oars, this last on the Feast of St James (25 July), which experienced a frost by night. Síra Halldor's account of all this concludes with two picturesque meteorological observations which, like the famous *eykt* observation in Vinland (see pp. 124–5 below), leave us more or less where we decide to place ourselves. Then they returned to Gardar.[8]

---

[8] *Grœnlandsannál eitt eftir Hauksbók*, in *GríM*, pp. 53–4.

That men died of cold and hunger, sickness and shipwreck, and all the accidents attendant on high-latitude exploration, is as certain of these half-glimpsed expeditions of the Middle Ages as of the elaborately documented expeditions of the last two hundred and fifty years. The fate of Arnbjorn's crew in the later 1120s, as recorded in *Einars Tháttr*, is one example. There are others. We read of a shipwreck on the east coast in *Flóamanna Saga*, followed by Thorgils Orrabeinsfostri's desperate journey to safety in the south-west. This is not without its trappings of magic, mutiny, and murder most foul; but the account of the survivors dragging their boat over the glaciers and ice-floes, and when possible rowing through the open leads; the wounded bear at the water-hole with Thorgils hanging on to its lugs that it might not sink; the dead men covered by fallen snow; these look like the white bone of truth for many besides Thorgils.[9] The saga of Gudmund the Good (*Resenbók*) has a grim little anecdote of a ship's crew fighting over provisions and the last three survivors dying a day's journey short of safety. In 1189 a ship named *Stangarfoli* was wrecked in the Obyggdir with the priest Ingimund on board: the bodies of seven men were recovered fourteen years later. From the shaky evidence of *Tósta Tháttr* it would seem that such mishaps were common

---

[9] At the end of his travels Thorgils wound up with Eirik the Red at Bratta-hlid. From the first his welcome was a cool one (Thorgils was a Christian), and his chief exploit that winter did nothing to warm it. 'It happened there that winter that a bear made inroads on men's stock and did severe injury to many. Meetings were held about this, whether some remedy might be found, and what emerged was that a price was set on the bear's head. The people of both settlements agreed to this, but Eirik did not like it one bit. Then as winter drew to a close men came to trade with Thorgils and his foster-father Thorstein. There were a lot of men in the storehouse which contained their goods, and the boy Thorfinn Thorgilsson was there too, and this is what he said to his father: "There is such a lovely dog come outside here, father. I never saw one like him before, he is so big." "Leave it be," said Thorgils, "and don't be going out-side." Even so the boy went running out. It was the bear who had come there, strolling down off the glacier. It caught up the boy, who cried out. Thorgils rushed outside, and had his drawn sword in his hand. The bear was playing with the boy. Thorgils smote it between the ears with all his strength and passion, splitting the beast's skull right through, so that it fell down dead. He picked up the boy, who was hardly hurt at all . . . Eirik was not overjoyed at this deed . . . Some maintained that Eirik was displeased that Thorgils had the good fortune to achieve this deed, because he himself put an evil trust in the creature' (Cap. 25).

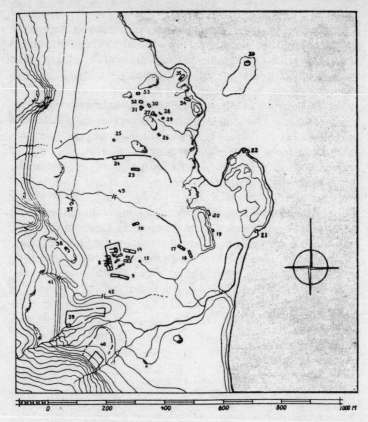

12. GARDAR, EASTERN SETTLEMENT, GREENLAND

The place is now called Igaliko (the deserted cooking-place). Survey map 1:10,000.
1: cathedral with churchyard; 8: episcopal residence; 9, 14: byres; 15: spring;
16: byre; 17–18: sheep-cotes; 19–22: storehouses; 23: enclosed garden; 24: byre
and barn; 25: horse paddock; 26–33: 'Thing booths'; 34–5, sheep-cotes; 36: storehouse; 38: sheep-pen; 39–40: large enclosures for domestic animals

enough for one Lika-Lodinn, Corpse-Lodinn, to find employ-
ment ransacking the northern Obyggdir for the dead bodies of
shipwrecked mariners which he would bring back south for
church burial.

But to return to the Settlements. The men who sold their
homes in Iceland and brought their families, wealth, or merely
their services out to Greenland, were most of them not hunters
or explorers, but solid settlement-men, and in everything save

13. THE CATHEDRAL AND BISHOP'S RESIDENCE AT GARDAR
(A PICTORIAL RECONSTRUCTION)

This sketch of the episcopal residence at Gardar was made by Aage Roussell immediately after excavations were finished in 1926. The big building at the far left is the cathedral with a choir and side chapels. It is surrounded by a churchyard dyke. The long block in the foreground is the residence. To the right is the big byre, and the belfry may be seen above the house. The other buildings are storehouses, stables, smithy, etc. (Compare the ground plan, Fig. 12 opposite.)

their choice of a homeland strongly conservative. They were husbandmen, concerned to raise stock, and for that they required, as the canny Eirik had foreseen, good grazing lands. These were to be found in fair profusion not on the outer coast but well up the fjords, sometimes close to the permanent ice, and it was along these inner reaches, in magnificent and challenging situations, that they built their houses and byres of stone and turf, roofing them with driftwood, and in their structure following or redeveloping the changing fashions of Iceland, or at times ringing such changes on these as to produce a Greenland style of their own. The heart of Norse Greenland was the

thirty miles from the head of Eiriksfjord by way of the head of
Einarsfjord to Vatnahverfi, and it was here that living conditions were easiest. The summer though short was warm and
pleasant, and it is noticeable that the richest herbage in Greenland is still to be found on the sites of these old Norse farms.
The situation of the Hill Farm at Brattahlid is positively idyllic,
with its dark and sparkling stream, its luscious dark green pastures, and the low ramparts of hills which protect it on all sides.
'It is reported', says the author of the *King's Mirror*, 'that the
pasturage is good, and that there are large and fine farms in
Greenland.' And again, 'The earth yields good and fragrant
grass.' The North and River farms at Brattahlid could support
twenty-eight and twelve cattle respectively, and the Bishop's
establishment at Gardar no fewer than seventy-five; and in
addition there were the horses they brought with them from
Iceland, sheep, goats, and a few pigs. 'The farmers', says our
same source of information, 'raise cattle and sheep in large
numbers, and make butter and cheese in great quantities. The
people subsist chiefly on these foods and on beef; but they
also eat the flesh of various kinds of game, such as reindeer
[caribou], whales, seals, and bears. That is what people live
on in that country.' And fish, in great variety and avid of the
hook.

On favoured sunny slopes a little corn grew and ripened; later
in the colony's history a little iron was worked; but of neither
was there enough. Timber too was in short supply, with no
native growth worth mentioning and only scanty driftwood
brought on a long rounding course from Siberia. Trade was
therefore a necessity of life for the Greenlanders, and for a
while this prospered well enough. Among the early settlers
were men who owned their own ships and plied the seas as merchant-venturers. From Greenland they carried furs and hides,
ropes and cables so strong that the heaving of threescore men
could not part them, with walrus and narwhal ivory, and white
falcons of such exquisite rapacity that in 1396 'the Duke of Bur-
gundy sent to Bayezid as a ransom for his son twelve Greenland
falcons'.[10] There were bears too, the white ice-bears of Green-

---

[10] So Vilhjálmur Stefánsson, *The Three Voyages of Martin Frobisher* (1938),
p. xliv, with a footnote reference to E. Müller-Röder, *Die Beizjagd und der
Falkensport in alter und neuer Zeit* (Leipzig 1906), p. 15.

land, esteemed throughout Europe as gifts for prelates and princes, the most memorable account of which will be found in the Icelandic tale of Authun the Westfirther. Greenland woollen was in demand too. Leif Eiriksson, the first white man to set foot in America, thought a cloak of this, together with a belt of walrus ivory, a ring for her finger, and a baby for her cradle, a suitable gift at parting for his Hebridean sweetheart Thorgunna. In addition the Greenlanders had seal-oil and similar commodities for export. In return they needed, and needed badly, timber, iron for all purposes, made weapons, corn, clothes of Continental style, and such further amenities of existence as malt, wine, and church vestments. Timber, iron, and corn could not in the nature of things be obtained from Iceland. They came from Norway instead, and for a while came sufficiently. So long as this balance of trade could be maintained, in theory the life of the white man in Greenland could go on for ever. Like the Eskimo they had hunting and fishing with all their products, and in addition animal husbandry to provide them with meat, milk, and wool. They lived in a hard world, but a world filled with hope and promise, and time must have seemed their friend. So:

> They on that sunlit morning
> Heard not the ice-floe's warning.

Their lives were too busy for omens and foreboding. Hardly was the settlement completed at Eystribyggd than men were moving north, and before the last roof was sodded at Vestribyggd there was a new religion in the land.[11] Thereafter for

---

[11] The erroneous notion that Leif Eiriksson was responsible, under King Olaf Tryggvason (who perished at the battle of Svold in the year 1000), for the conversion of Greenland, goes back to Gunnlaug the Monk and his *Life* of that monarch. Early sources such as the *Historia Norwegiæ* and *Ágrip* do not name Greenland among the lands converted by Olaf. The *Historia* gives the credit of the conversion to the Icelanders.

The earliest reliable reference to Greenland by name occurs in a papal Bull dated 6 Jan. 1053 sent by Pope Leo IX in Rome to Adalbert, Archbishop of Bremen, confirming his jurisdiction and perpetual authority over the bishops '*in omnibus gentibus Sueonum seu Danorum, Noruuechorum, Islant, Scrideuuinnum, Gronlant et universarum septentrionalium nationum . . . tibi tuisque successoribus perpetualiter tenere censemus.*' Adalbert, a man of high-riding ambition, was reconfirmed in these privileges two years later by Pope Victor II. Twenty years later, in his *Gesta Hammaburgensis ecclesiæ pontificum*, 1073–6,

twenty-five years men's mouths were full of news from Vinland the Good. There was oral story-telling and a literature in prose and verse, with the 'Greenland Lay of Atli' as its most notable survival; and for a craftsman there was all the walrus ivory and whalebone his hands could hope to use. Also they had to shape a constitution under which to live, and a legal system by which they could live together. The part played by Eirik the Red and his sons in all this was considerable, and probably decisive. Eirik's exact position in the colony has not been defined for us, but that he was its patriarch and first citizen is clear, and probably the authority with which he is credited in the sagas rested on some office analogous to the *allsherjargoði*, or leader of the Congregation, or the *lögsögumaðr*, or lawspeaker, of Iceland. He was followed by his son Leif, and Leif by his son Thorkel; and a full hundred years after Eirik's death we read how Sokki Thorisson and his son Einar, who lived at Eirik's Brattahlid, 'had great authority in Greenland, and stood head and shoulders above other men'. Probably Sokki was a descendant of Eirik's by blood or marriage; according to Ivar Bardarson, Greenland's laugmader or lawman was always domiciled at Brattahlid; but we lack evidence to prove what in its nature seems unlikely, that the chief office of the colony was hereditary. Like so much else the constitution of Greenland was on the Icelandic model, with a national assembly through which it could function. So the Republic, like the white man in Greenland, could in theory go on for ever. In fact it lasted till 1261, when the Greenlanders accepted the sovereignty of the King of Norway, and in return for various unrealized trading con-

Adam of Bremen was saying of the Greenlanders: 'To these also it is reported that Christianity has recently (*nuper*) winged its way.' Greenland's first bishop, Arnald (see 'The Story of Einar Sokkason', pp. 236–48 below), was not consecrated until the year 1124. These facts added together have suggested to some historians that the Conversion of Greenland could not have taken place as early as has been supposed, though it appears unlikely that it would have been delayed much beyond 1015.

The first reference to Greenland in Icelandic sources is in Ari's *Íslendingabók*, which assigns Eirik the Red's settlement to fourteen or fifteen years before the Conversion of Iceland in 1000, that is, to 985–6. The tone of the papal Bulls and Adam's extraordinary notions of life in Greenland have led to a suspicion in some quarters that Ari's dates are too early, but no acceptable alternative has as yet been advanced.

cessions surrendered their independence one year ahead of their kinsmen in Iceland.

II. DECLINE AND FALL

THE Greenland colony, as distinct from the Greenland state or nation, survived till the beginning of the sixteenth century, and the nature of its passing has greatly exercised men's minds. The Greenland colony was the remotest northern outpost of European civilization, and its extinction on a far strand, in an almost forgotten country, in worsening conditions of cold, with much macabre circumstance, has been thought by many of its students the most poignant tragedy ever played out by a Northern people. And it remains one of the unsolved mysteries of history.

We see now, wise after the event, that everything about the Norse settlements in Greenland was marginal. They could survive only if nothing altered for the worse. In Iceland the medieval European had staked the furthest claim north he could without abandoning a Scandinavian mode of life. Iceland lay on the outer fringe of the habitable world. Greenland lay beyond it. 'The church at Gardar', wrote Pope Alexander VI in 1492, 'is situated at the world's end', and the way there was notoriously *per mare non minus tempestuosissimum quam longissimum*. It was therefore a first requisite of the Greenlanders, if they were to control their destiny, that they should have sea-going ships of their own. But soon they had at their disposal neither the wealth nor the materials for these; after their submission to Norway they were expressly forbidden to use such; and from there on the conditions for survival were not at their own dictation. Political and economic changes abroad, without fault or offence of their own, could destroy them, and neglect would prove as deadly as assault. Second, their numbers were dangerously small, probably never more than four thousand souls. The population of Iceland in the year 1100 was roughly 80,000. Fire, ice, pestilence, and neglect reduced this to 47,000 by 1800— a murderous wastage in a fast-breeding race. Greenland had no such reservoir of human sacrifice. And third, of all European communities they were the most vulnerable to climatic change. For the rest of European man a run of cold winters and bad summers is a grievance and vexation; for the Greenlanders they sounded a death knell.

Throughout the North Atlantic area the ninth to the twelfth centuries were a comparatively warm period.[12] Had they not been, we should be troubled to account for the Greenland voyages of Gunnbjorn and Eirik the Red, and to a lesser extent the Vinland voyages of Bjarni Herjolfsson, Leif Eiriksson, and Thorfinn Karlsefni. In modern conditions of ice (by no means the severest on record), it would, for example, have been impossible for Eirik to make the journeys we hear he made, at the time of year and in the directions in which we are told he made them. He *must* now meet with ice, both off Greenland's east coast and off Eystribyggd on the west. He seems, however, to have moved about with complete freedom, and though only fourteen of the twenty-five settlement ships of the 986 armada reached Greenland, there is no mention of ice turning the

---

[12] The immense and deserved authority of Fridtjof Nansen (see especially *Klimatsvekslinger in Nordens Historie* (Oslo 1925); *Klimatsvekslinger i historisk og postglacial Tid* (Oslo, 1926)) and Vilhjálmur Stefánsson long helped inhibit many students of literature and history from accepting the picture of climatic change here set forth. On the other hand, archaeologists, geographers, oceanographers, zoologists, palaeobotanists, and, most important of all, climatologists are overwhelmingly (though sometimes in individual cases diffidently) in its favour. My own convictions I owe primarily to the writings, though not always to the conclusions, of Otto Pettersson, 'Climatic Variations in Historic and Prehistoric Time', *Svenska Hydrografisk-Biologiska Kommissionens, Skrifter V* (Göteborg 1914); Lauge Koch, *The East Greenland Ice, MGr* 130, (1945) (Koch sums up: 'Thus it seems that the Norsemen were troubled by the deterioration of the climate in the 13th century . . . however, before the extermination of the Norsemen an amelioration of the climate set in [after 1400 (p. 354)], so the Norsemen did not die out owing to a fall in the temperature, but more probably on account of a failing communication with Europe and the advance of the Eskimos from the north' (p. 349)); C. E. P. Brooks, *Climate Through the Ages*, revised edn. (1949); H. H. Lamb, 'Climatic Variation' (1960); 'On the Nature of Certain Climatic Epochs which differed from the Modern (1900–39) Normal', Rome Symposium on Changes of Climate with Special Reference to the Arid Zones, (1961). The writings, comments, or summaries of Poul Nørlund, Jón Jóhannesson, Hans Ahlman, E. Bull, Andreas Holmsen, G. Manley, William Hovgaard, Maads Lidegaard, C. L. Vebæk (Data presented to the Conference on the Climate of the 11th and 16th Centuries, Aspen, Colorado; Anthropological Section: 'The Climate of Greenland in the 11th and 16th Centuries (and the Time in Between)' (1962), typescript privately communicated by C.L.V.), Johannes Iverson, Knut Fægri, Jørgen Meldgaard, and Sigurður Thórarinsson have fortified them, as have, more recently, the pollen-analysts and the ice-core researchers.

others back. The Icelandic Annals (*Konungsannáll*) for 1126 have a short entry, *Steingrímr í ísum*, 'Steingrim in the ice', and no doubt this Icelander is the Isa-Steingrim who threw in his lot with the Norwegian merchants up in the Western Settlement in the year 1130 (see p. 241 below). *Einars Tháttr* also records how in this same summer of 1130 ice drove into the south-western fjords and prevented the Norwegians getting away. However, their beleaguering was a brief one, for the ice soon swept out again. Apart from this, saga accounts of the Greenland and Vinland voyages make no mention of ice at sea. In the case of Thorgils Orrabeinsfostri's shipwreck on the east coast already mentioned, it is worth noting that it was a shipwreck on the coast itself, *í vík nökkuri við sandmöl*, in a certain bay on a sand-dune or hillock, and it happened just one week before winter. Without pressing for too favourable a conclusion, it would appear from the saga evidence that around the year 1000 a latitude-sailing west from Snæfellsnes to the region of Ang-magssalik presented no problem to seamen, either because there was no drift ice off the east coast in early summer or, more likely, because such ice as there was was not formidable in quantity. In other words, East Greenland had nothing like the drift ice of later centuries. This is confirmed by the sailing directions preserved in *Landnámabók*, by Ivar Bardarson, and by the *Navigatio Vetus* of the Holar map of bishop Guðbrandur Thorláksson.

It is confirmed too by modern research into the history of European climate. There is a wealth of evidence of various kinds which allows modern scientists to conclude that during the 'Climatic Optimum' *c*.800 to 1200 the mean summer temperature of western and middle Europe was higher by at least 1 °C than it is at present; that in southern Greenland annual mean temperatures were 1 °C to 3–4 °C higher than now, and that sea temperatures in the northernmost Atlantic were of the same order of increase, with all that this must mean for the Canadian Archipelago and the area of Baffin Bay. The area of permanent ice lay north of 80° N., drift ice must have been rare south of 70° N., and very rare indeed in troublesome quantities south of the Arctic Circle. There is therefore no reason rooted in climate for disbelieving the Norse voyages to Greenland and the mainland of North America.

But in terms of the Greenland settlement the important thing to establish is not that the Climatic Optimum was somewhat warmer than our own warm period, but that it was succeeded by a period decidedly, and in the event fatally, colder. Here too literary, historical, archaeological, and (in the widest sense) meteorological and climatic evidence leads to the same conclusion: that after 1200 the climate of the northern hemisphere fell progressively for two hundred years or more, and that by c.1430 Europe had entered a 'Little Ice Age'. Over much of Europe the glaciers were beginning to advance, the tree-line fell lower, vegetation and harvests were diminished by the cold; and worst of all for the Greenlanders (though Iceland was a fellow sufferer) the sea temperatures sank, causing an immense increase in the drift ice which comes south with the East Greenland Current to Cape Farewell and then swings north-west so as to enclose first the Eastern and then the Western Settlement. For ice conditions by the middle of the thirteenth century we have the testimony of *Konungs Skuggsjá*, the *King's Mirror*:

As soon as one has passed over the deepest part of the ocean, he will encounter such masses of ice in the sea, that I know no equal of it anywhere else in all the earth. Sometimes these ice fields are as flat as if they were frozen on the sea itself. They are about four or five ells thick and extend so far out from the land that it may mean a journey of four days or more to travel across them. There is more ice to the north-east and north of the land than to the south, south-west and west; consequently, whoever wishes to make the land should sail around it to the south-west and west, till he has come past all those places where ice may be looked for, and approach the land on that side. It has frequently happened that men have sought to make the land too soon and, as a result, have been caught in the ice floes. Some of those who have been caught have perished; but others have got out again, and we have met some of these and have heard their accounts and tales. But all those who have been caught in these ice-drifts have adopted the same plan: they have taken their small boats and have dragged them up on the ice with them, and in this way have sought to reach land; but the ship and everything else of value had to be abandoned and was lost. Some have had to spend four or five days upon the ice before reaching land, and some even longer.

These ice floes have peculiar habits. Sometimes they lie as quiet as can be, though cut apart by creeks or large fjords; at other times they travel with a speed so swift and violent that a ship with a fair wind behind is not more speedy; and when once in motion, they travel as often against the wind as with it. There is also ice of a different shape which the Greenlanders call icebergs. In appearance these resemble high mountains rising out of the sea; they never mingle with other ice but stand by themselves.[13]

The more obvious consequences of these ice conditions for the mariner are set out in Ivar Bardarson's sailing directions a hundred years later (*c*.1360):

Item from Snæfellsnes in Iceland, where there is the shortest crossing to Greenland, the course is two days' and two nights' sailing due west, and there lie the Gunnbjarnarsker, half-way between Greenland and Iceland. This was the old course, but nowadays ice has come down from the north-east out of the gulf of the sea[14] so close to the aforesaid skerries that without risk to life no one can sail the old course and be heard of again. . . . Item when one sails from Iceland one must take one's course from Snæfellsnes. . . . and then sail due west one day and one night, then slightly south-west [*variant* then steer south-west] to avoid the aforesaid ice which lies off Gunnbjarnarsker; and then one day and one night due north-west, and so one comes right under the aforesaid elevation, Hvarf in Greenland, under which lie the aforesaid Herjolfsnes and Sandhavn.[15]

[13] L. M. Larsen (translator), *The King's Mirror* (New York, 1917), pp. 138–9. The brief quotations from the *King's Mirror* on pp. 79 and 82 are also from Larsen.

[14] We have noticed in our Introduction (pp. 20–2 above) the persistent belief in a land-bridge between Greenland and the north of Europe whose eastern conjunction was with Bjarmaland, beyond the White Sea. This continuous land, sometimes with a Giant-home legend, is to be observed on many maps, including those of Skalholt and Holar, and it must have figured prominently on the two maps of the world sent in 1551 by Burgomaster Grip of Kiel to King Christian III of Denmark—'from which your majesty may see that your majesty's land of Greenland extends on both maps towards the new world and the islands which the Portuguese and Spaniards have discovered, so that these countries may be reached overland from Greenland. Likewise that they may be reached overland from Lapland, from the castle of Vardöhus'. The existence of this well-charted un-land in the minds of men led to notable fantasies, not least that the Hafsbotn or Polar Gulf extended from longitude 20° W. to beyond 40° E. The land-bridge, happily, was not impassable for man or beast. One Halldor is reputed to have crossed it with a goat. The goat fed on pockets of grass, and Halldor on the goat's milk. Inevitably he became known as Goat-Halldor.

[15] *Det gamle Grønlands beskrivelse*, p. 19. The *King's Mirror* and Ivar accord well with Abbot Arngrim Brandsson's description of Iceland and her surrounding waters, written some time before 1350. See *Guðmundar Saga Arasonar*, cap. 2 (ed. Guðni Jönsson, *Byskupa Sögur* III, Íslendingasagnaútgáfan, 1948).

14. DE NAUFRAGIIS GRUNTLANDIÆ
Wreckage and driftwood off the Greenland coast (Olaus Magnus)

We are not asked to believe that there were no bitter spells during the good centuries, and no genial ones during the bad. That is not the way of the world's weather. But, reverting to the marginal position of the Greenland settlements, we may remember that conditions decidedly less severe than those that eventually obtained would quickly maim and finally destroy them. In high latitudes the formation of sea ice in falling temperatures is an ineluctable process, by nature's law. The calculated fall of temperatures in all waters north of 50° N. in the 'Little Ice Age' is from 1° to 3° below those of our own century, whose climate is generally comparable with that of Norse discovery and colonization. The most conservative of these figures will explain the deadly mantle of drift ice off the east Greenland coast, as the *King's Mirror* describes it, the subsequent choking of the fjords of the Eastern Settlement, and the reappearance on the west coast of the Eskimo or Skræling.[16]

[16] The name *Skrælingar* was applied by the Norsemen to the natives (Eskimo: Greenlandic *Kaláleq*, plur. *Kalátdlit*) they encountered in Greenland and (Eskimo or Indian) in Markland and Vinland. It is not certain what it means. 'It may be related to modern Norwegian *skræla* "scream", or to

When Eirik the Red and his fellow colonists established the Eastern and Western Settlements towards the end of the tenth century, they found traces of earlier occupants at both places. These were Eskimos of the Dorset culture who by now had either perished or migrated elsewhere. When the Norsemen came into direct contact with Skrælings in the second half of the thirteenth century, well north of the Western Settlement, these were a new wave of Eskimos, people of the Thule culture, who moving across Canada from Alaska entered Greenland some-time after 1100, and then, as the Inugsuk folk, proceeded to occupy its habitable areas. Some moved down the west coast, reaching Disco Bay by the thirteenth century and Vestribyggd a century later. They were off Eystribyggd's seaward limits by 1350–1400,[17] so pressed on to Cape Farewell, leaving Eystri-byggd as a lonely and anxious Norse outpost far behind them. Others, journeying north out of the environs of Thule, with the passing of the generations reached the regions now known as Nansen Land and Peary Land, whence they headed south in the direction of Scoresby Sound. But with this twofold saga of exploration and endurance we are concerned only in so far as it affected the Norse colonies on the west coast, and the Skræling inheritors of the east coast affected them not at all.[18]

Icelandic *skrælna*, "shrink". In modern Icelandic *skræling* means "churl", "coarse fellow", in modern Norwegian "weakling". Connexion with *skræla*, "scream" seems more natural, but the modern forms point rather to the other etymology' (*An Introduction to Old Norse*, revised by A. R. Taylor, (Oxford 1982, p. 218). The Eskimos' name for themselves was *Inuit* (sing *Inuk*)), 'human beings' or 'men'.

[17] The basic studies of these movements were those of Therkel Mathiassen, Erik Holtved, and Lauge Koch, all published in *MGr* at various dates since 1927. In general they place the Eskimo re-entry into Greenland some two cen-turies earlier, while Koch, *The East Greenland Ice*, p. 310, thinks 1350 too early a date for Eskimo encroachment on the fjords of the Eastern Settlement, per-haps by as much as a hundred years. For more recent work see Helge Larsen, J. Meldgaard, Kaj Birket-Smith, Finn Gad, H. C. Gullov, R. H. Jordan, R. McGhee, and T. H. McGovern.

[18] It is likely almost to the point of certainty that the Icelanders had some acquaintance with those parts of the east coast of Greenland which lay handiest to them, but it cannot have been continuous or extensive. It is even possible that Svalbard belongs in the region of Scoresby Sound. But a more likely candidate for the name is Jan Mayen island, which more or less conforms to the not always clear sailing directions of *Landnámabók* (see p. 157 below). For a note on the 'New Land' of the Icelandic Annals for 1194 and 1285 see p. 137 below. By acci-dent or design the Icelanders probably had more knowledge of their surround-ing waters than we credit them with.

15. POLAR ICE AND POLAR BEARS (OLAUS MAGNUS)

Presumably the growing cold and drier conditions after 1200 helped draw the Eskimo south. As the ice spread further and further down the west Greenland coast the seals followed it, and in their turn the Skrælings followed the seals, for their whole way of life depended on this creature. Walrus and whale, caribou and bear, ptarmigan and char, all were welcome in their season, but to the seal the Skræling was tied as with a birthcord. So what with the Norsemen drawn north for good hunting and driftwood, and the Eskimos drawn south after seals, encounters between them were inevitable. How many of these left blood on the snow we cannot say, for both Norseman and Eskimo had much at stake, and must have known it. Yet the changing climate would ensure that the future lay with that people which could best come to terms with it. The Eskimo, made self-sufficient by the seal, warmly clothed against the cold, mobile without being nomadic, with his summer tent and winter house and flashing kayak, was admirably equipped for survival. The Norseman, conservatively European in his dress to the end of the settlement, dependent upon iron, wedded to his flocks and herds and his wasting pastures, could not survive his *fimbulvetr*, that long and awful unremitting winter whose present onset, had he but known it, heralded the ending of his world.

It must have taken the white Greenlander some time to realize this truth. His natural reaction towards the short, dark, fur-enclosed bundles of humanity he encountered in the northern hunting-grounds would be not unlike that displayed towards the Skrælings of Vinland by the Greenland explorers of America. He would judge himself their superior, treat them as 'natives', and seek to exploit them. It would seem natural for him to covet their agreeable little women, but so far no trace has been found of a mingling of Norse and Eskimo stock anywhere or at any time during the settlement. Emphatically he would start by thinking himself top dog here as in so many other lands. But (to continue the metaphor) he was the wrong breed of dog for the country, and when the cold came to pinch him he must learn new tricks, cross-breed for a heavier coat, or die out.

The Western Settlement was at an end by 1342. Contemporary documentary evidence as to how this came about is both scanty and troublesome. Under that year the Annals of Bishop Gisli Oddsson record that

The inhabitants of Greenland of their own will abandoned the true faith and the Chrisitan religion, having already forsaken all good ways and true virtues, and joined themselves with the folk of America (*ad Americæ populos se converterunt*). Some consider too that Greenland lies closely adjacent to the western regions of the world. From this it came about that the Christians gave up their voyaging to Greenland.[19]

Unfortunately, even if we explain away *Americæ populos* as a centuries-late gloss on *Skrælingar*, we remain uncertain what its user meant by the phrase in which it is incorporated. Were these Skrælings the Indians and Dorset Eskimos encountered as early as *c*.AD 1000 in Markland and Vinland, where the Norse

---

[19] The 'American entry' is to be found in the so-called *Annalium Farrago* (*Islandica* 10, p. 2). The Annals were written in Latin *c*.1637, and it has been suggested that they were based on documents lost in the fire which destroyed the Cathedral at Skalholt in 1630. The 'parallel' lines in Lyschander's *Grönlandske Chronica* of 1608, themselves inviting a wary approach, have been invoked as a confirmation of sorts of this annal, but in view of its unproven authorship, unreliable provenance, uncertain transmission, and ambiguous meaning, one judges that no conclusion should be drawn from it in respect of Greenland's history in the fourteenth century.

Greenlanders in our informant's mistaken view had by 1342 gone off to join them? Or were they the Thule Eskimos of Greenland with whom in his equally mistaken view the Norse Greenlanders had by 1342 thrown in their lot in respect of race, culture, and religion? Presumably it was to investigate some such rumour of miscegenation and apostasy that a year earlier, in 1341, Bishop Hakon of Bergen had dispatched the priest Ivar Bardarson on his celebrated expedition to Greenland. It is a pity that Ivar's account of his subsequent visit to the Western Settlement is preserved in late manuscripts, at second or third hand, and in translation, and is couched in terms which have lent themselves to unending argument:

Item from the Eastern Settlement to the Western is twelve sea-leagues and all uninhabited. Up there in the Western Settlement stands a big church which is called Stensnes [= Sandnes] Church. This church was for a while a cathedral and the see of a bishop [*sic*]. At present the Skrælings hold the entire Western Settlement. There are indeed horses, goats, cattle, and sheep, but all wild, and no people, either Christian or heathen.

Item all this that is recorded above was told us by Iffuer bort [Ivar Bardarson], a Greenlander who for many years was steward of the bishop's household at Gardar in Greenland: how he had seen all this, and was one of those who were chosen by the Laugmader [*Lögmaðr*, lawman, chief officer] to go to the Western Settlement against the Skrælings, in order to expel them from the Settlement. But when they arrived there they found never a man, either Christian or heathen, merely some wild cattle and sheep. They made use of these cattle and sheep for provisions, as much as the ships could carry, and with this sailed back, and the aforesaid Iffuer was of their party.[20]

These seeming-simple sentences have been interpreted in various ways: as meaning that the Western Settlement had been forcibly exterminated by Skrælings; that the white population, man, woman, and child, had gone off fishing or hunting, with the grisly consequence that their would-be rescuers from Eystribyggd by carrying off their stock ensured their death by starvation the following winter; that the whites had become so blended with the Eskimos as to have abandoned animal hus-

---

[20] *Det gamle Grønlands beskrivelse*, ed. Finnur Jónsson (Copenhagen), pp. 8 and 29; Ólafur Halldórsson, *Grænlandslýsing Ivars Barðarsonar*, *GríM*, pp. 136–7 and 407–8.

bandry and a fixed settlement; that the whites either by themselves or in company with the Eskimos had migrated to Baffin Island or Labrador, so giving a literal meaning to Bishop Gisli Oddsson's words, *ad Americæ populos se converterunt;*[21] that Ivar Bardarson was a coward, a liar, or an ass, who took one perfunctory glance at one western fjord, or even one homestead, then sped home 'by sail and oar' to the safety of Eystribyggd, where with the connivance of the entire expedition he maintained for over twenty years his easily disprovable story.

Some of its details are troublesome enough. If Sandnes Church was ever the see of a bishop this is as much as we hear of it: it appears a most unlikely circumstance. The presence of domestic animals in a settlement devoid of human beings has been held inexplicable: yet it is probable that they could survive for a year or two without human aid. But if we allow for garbling and inaccuracy in the existing unsatisfactory versions of Ivar's report we are left with a conclusion which there is nothing to disprove and a good deal to support: that by the time of his visit the Western Settlement was extinct. For we know that the pastures of the Western Settlement had been affected before this time by an invasion of the pest *Agrotis occulta*, and so reduced in quality and extent as to make animal husbandry much more difficult. Again, in the early fourteenth century Greenland trade was seriously injured by the development of the trade in

---

[21] This view has been developed forcibly by Vilhjálmur Stefánsson in many of his writings and by Helge Ingstad, *Landet under Polarstjernen*, pp. 356–61, and has received the cautious approval of C. Gini, 'On the Extinction of the Norse Settlements in Greenland', The Institute of Economics, Bergen, Paper 10 (1958). Gini stresses the marked disequilibrium of the sexes in Vestribyggd graves, argues from that a similar disequilibrium in life, and puts forward the curious and untenable suggestion that it was mainly on the initiative of the Norse women that the whites went over to the Skrælings. This too is perhaps the place to mention the extensive collections of material and sometimes reckless speculations on the Norse Atlantic settlements of Jón Dúason, *Landkönnun og Landnám Íslendinga í Vesturheim*, (Reykjavik, 1941–48). The migration theory has its merits and disposes of various harassing difficulties; unfortunately it creates others, and the evidence for it is both thin and strongly debatable. The natural place of refuge for the hard-pressed Norsemen of the Western Settlement was with their fellow countrymen and kinsmen back in Eystribyggd. See Jørgen Meldgaard, 'Om de gamle Nordboer og deres Skæbne (Betragtinger over Helge Ingstads bog *Landet under Polarstjernen*)', in *Tidsskriftet Grønland* (1961), pp. 93–102. And see Appendix V. 'The Norse Greenlanders and Arctic Canada'.

furs and hides out of Russia, the growth of the English and Dutch cloth trade as against Greenland woollens, and the preference of French workshops for ivory from Africa or Asia over the inferior walrus tusk. The Western Settlement was no longer a viable economy. And as the climate grew colder its effects were more serious up there than in Eystribyggd. The colony must have been considerably weakened for decades before its end, and the arrival of the Skrælings was decisive. First the outlying farms were abandoned; the colony drew in upon itself; small groups would depart for Eystribyggd laden not only with their wordly goods but with grim news of the relentlessly advancing little men who were making life impossible for the people of the northern hunting-grounds first, and then for the cruelly tried homesteaders from Lodinsfjord to Lysufjord. Some of this news, not always understood and often darkly embroidered, would filter back to Iceland, Norway, and remoter Europe, and convince its hearers that something very queer and unpleasant was taking place out in Greenland, that the Norsemen were 'going over to' the Eskimos and abandoning the Christian faith, and that something must be done about it. But by the time Ivar Bardarson arrived in Greenland one of two things had happened: either the last survivors of the Western Settlement had drawn back south to safety, or they had been overrun and exterminated by the Skrælings. In either case, 'At present the Skrælings hold the entire Western Settlement', and Ivar's expedition did little more than confirm the fact. The distinctive culture of Scandinavia disappeared everywhere beyond latitude 62° N. After *c*.1350 the record of the Norse colonies is confined to Eystribyggd.

The documentary and archaeological record shows that the Eastern Settlement fought for its life tenaciously. Most of the Norse population lived there, and there too was most of the good land. Yet the loss of the Western Settlement was an irreparable affliction. For one thing it affected their use of the Nordseta, the best hunting-grounds of Greenland, which lay beyond it; and though the trade demand for Nordseta products was falling off this was a sharp diminution of the colonists' resources. Still worse would be the feeling that a similar fate threatened them too. Certainly the Eskimos were reacting strongly to the white man's presence in the south, and under the year 1379 we read in the Icelandic Annals (*Gottskálksannáll*) that 'The Skrælings attacked the Greenlanders, killed eighteen of them, and carried off two boys, whom they made slaves.'[22] Yet strangely enough, there was no compelling reason for head-on clashes between the south-moving Eskimos and the stationary Norsemen. The middens of the Eastern, and still more the Western, Settlement show that the Norsemen relied greatly on the seal for meat, but they were equally farmers and their homes lay far back in the fjords, for the sufficient reason that there was the best grazing. Eirik's splendid and extensive farm at Brattahlid, with its heavy concentration of neighbours, lay sixty miles from the outer limits of the *skærgaard*; the strong settlement in Einarsfjord and the numerous farms of the Vatnahverfi some forty to fifty. But these inner extremities of the fjords were of little interest to the Eskimo; they froze comparatively late in the year, and their ice was rarely safe. They were thus less attractive to hunters than the headlands, islands, and sea-ice outside where seals and other marine animals were more abundant. Encounters between the two peoples could in any case not be entirely avoided. Contemporary pieces of Eskimo sculpture and carving show with what curiosity the Skrælings observed their huge white neighbours, and some of the folk-tales collected by Rink record other than peaceful meetings. Yet such there must have been. There were advantages to be gained by both sides from peaceful trading, the evidence for which is sparse but of late increasing. The story of Bjorn Einarsson Jorsalafari (Jerusalem-farer) has often been invoked, but too much should not be made of it. Bjorn rescued a young Eskimo brother and sister from a rock in the sea, and they repaid him with the utmost devotion. Such was the girl's love for Bjorn's infant son that brother and sister threw themselves from a rock into the sea and perished when Bjorn took his family back home to Iceland.[23] It

---

[22] We do not know where this clash took place. Somewhere on the northern edge of the Eastern Settlement, as is commonly assumed, or were the victims a hunting party trying their luck in the Nordseta? The reference to slavery is unreal in an Eskimo context, but perhaps the Norsemen were not to know this. Direct evidence of strife between Norsemen and Eskimos is slight, whether documentary (as here) or archaeological.

[23] *Grænlands annál* (*GríM*, p. 53).

is a saving grace of humanity under all conditions that friendship and kindness keep breaking in. So long as the Norsemen
could keep to themselves (and this could eventually entail the
loss of the Northern Hunting-Grounds), the two races in theory
had elbow-room enough and need not prove deadly to each
other's way of life. We say 'in theory', for who can doubt the
stress and dismay under which the Eastern Settlement
laboured, with the Western Settlement gone, its own northern
spur around Ivigtut (the 'Middle Settlement') subsequently
abandoned, and the Skrælings in kayaks and umiaks plying the
fjord-mouths down to Herjolfsnes.[24]

Nor did they fear for their physical survival only. The Eastern
Settlement was now the sole custodian of the Christian faith in
the farther reaches of the West Atlantic. Helluland, Markland,
Vinland still languished under their blight of heathendom; and
now at home men of Norse stock, Christian for three and a half
centuries, were under suspicion of having abandoned themselves to the pains of hell-fire. Shafts of uncertain light pierce

[24] For the most relevant of the Eskimo folk-tales collected by Rink, 'Ungor-
tok Chief of Kakortok', see Appendix III, where it is reproduced. There is a
parallel story from the Norse point of view, written in Icelandic and printed in
Íslenzkar þjóðsögur og Æventyri, safnar hefur Jón Árnason, IV, edited anew by
Arni Boðvarsson and Bjarni Vilhjálmsson, (Reykjavík, 1956), under the title
Afdrif Íslendinga á Grænlandi (The Fate of the Icelanders in Greenland), and in
Jón Thorkelsson's *þjóðsögur og Munnmæli* (Reykjavík, 1956), under the title
Frá Íslendingum og Skrælingjum á Grænlandi (Concerning the Icelanders and
Skrælings in Greenland). It is very much a Norse variation on the Ungortok
theme of dissension between the two peoples: of a young Eskimo sportively, or
at best wantonly, killing a young Icelander from a kayak, and the revengeful
massacre of Eskimo men, women, and children by the Norse Greenlanders
under their leader Ingjaldur ('The Skrælings say Ingilli'). One man alone
escapes, to Nabaitsok (?), where the Skrælings plan vengeance in return. They
embark in a huge boat disguised as an iceberg, and descend on Veidifjord with
200 men when the entire population is in the church at Mass and weaponless.
The slaughter is complete. The only known source of the *sögubrot* or 'narrative
fragment' is a single sheet, folded in two, possibly part of a letter, and complete
in itself. Its handwriting is probably of 1830–40, and it has not been possible so
far to elaborate its provenance or identify its author. I owe my knowledge of it
to Magnús Einarsson of the National Museum of Man, Ottawa, and Ólafur
Halldórsson of Stofnun Árna Magnússonar, Reykjavík. The story has now been
translated by Magnús Einarsson, 'The Fate of the Icelanders in Greenland', and
has appeared as part of an article 'Greenlandic Eskimos and Norse: A Parallel
Tradition from Greenland and Iceland?' by Robert McGhee and Magnús
Einarsson, in *Folk*, 25 (Copenhagen, 1983), pp. 51–61.

the descending darkness. In 1355 King Magnus Smek commands Poul Knudsson to sail his ship to Greenland (there is no evidence that Poul did so): 'We do this for the glory of God and our soul's salvation, and for those forefathers of ours who brought Christianity to Greenland and have upheld it to this present time, and which we will not let perish in our day.'[25] In 1407 Church and Law joined hands to burn one Kolgrim at the stake for having carnal knowledge of Steinunn, daughter of lawman Hrafn the Icelander, by means of his black art (*með svarta-konstur*).[26] The often-quoted 'papal' letter of 1448 from Nicholas V to the self-appointing pair of Iceland bishops, Marcellus and Mathæus, looks like a forgery, but the pleas of the impudent are notoriously drafted for the maximum of appeal and effect, and the letter speaks with sad and anxious heart of the doleful situation of the Greenland Christians.[27] Clearly the fifteenth century was not lacking in pious prayers and heartfelt ejaculations for Greenland: what will be found wanting is any readiness to back these with action. The record of the Church in all this was deplorable. After the death of Bishop Alf in 1377 no bishop set foot in Greenland.

Even before 1261 a European and Christian way of life in the colonies depended on the maintenance of pasture, a putative balance of trade, and on hunting. As to the first, there was a native improvidence in both Iceland and Greenland.[28] As to the second, this meant trade with Norway. The precise terms of the

---

[25] *GHM* iii.122. Nørlund, *Viking Settlers in Greenland* (1936) p. 134.

[26] *Nyji Annáll*, sub. 1407. There appears to have been something other than morals or theology behind this brutal, and in Iceland and Greenland rare, punishment. So Jón Jóhannesson, 'Í Grænlandshrakningum' in *Íslendinga Saga*, ii. 246–7. The unhappy Steinunn went out of her mind and died soon after the burning.

[27] *The Flatey Book and Recently Discovered Vatican Manuscripts Concerning America as Early as the Tenth Century* (Norroena Society, 1906), pp. 167–9.

[28] In the summer of 1962 the remains of an extensive irrigation system were discovered at Brattahlid, designed to conduct lake water to pastures much nearer the fjord—pastures which still tend to dry up after a warm summer. The dykes served both the North and River Farms, and are probably of the four-teenth century. Similar but lesser systems have been reported from the Western Settlement, the most recent in 1984, and there is a very long man-made channel serving one of the farms in Sermilik-Isafjord. Further discoveries of a similar or related kind would invite a gentler consideration of the efficiency of farming methods in Greenland until the climate grew too cruel.

treaty between the two countries (if Greenland ever was a
sovereign state: the Hague Court in 1933 went no further than
to describe its medieval status as 'independent') have not been
preserved, but we may assume that the compensating benefit
expected by the Greenlanders for the surrender of their independence in 1261 was a guarantee of regular communications
with the adoptive parent country. The Norway–Iceland agreement of 1262 stipulated that six ships should sail from Norway
to Iceland during each of the next two years, whereupon the
situation should be fairly reviewed. In the long run, as we
know, the Icelanders were much deceived. And so was Greenland. At the end of the century the Crown made the Greenland
trade the monopoly of the Norwegian merchants of Bergen. We
can trace the consequences for Iceland with fair exactitude: in
the years 1326, 1350, 1355, 1374, and 1390 no ship reached Iceland from Norway, and in 1324, 1333, 1357, 1362, 1367, and
1392 one ship only. The consequences for Greenland would be
even more severe, as trading developments in Norway erased so
remote, perilous, and unprofitable a route from the merchant's
portolan. Bergen had become glutted with cheaper furs and
hides and walrus tusks raked from nearer hunting grounds;
Martin IV in Rome and the Archbishop of Nidaros wag sad
heads at each other over the resultant devaluation of the Greenland tithe, payable in such commodities. Oh, for gold and silver
for one more Crusade! And this as early as 1282, before the bottom fell out of the market. Besides, Norway was distraught with
political and economic troubles of her own. After 1261 too her
maritime glory was fast passing away. The Viking ship, so vic-
tory-fraught, so shapely, was being run out of business by the
commodious and economic German cog, and Norwegian
designers and shipwrights were failing completely to meet their
challenge. Concurrently the kingdom's strength was sapped;
foreign-born or incompetent rulers sacrificed her interests to
their own; and in 1349 the Black Death, ship-borne from England, slew one in three of her population, then crossed the seas
to ravage the Hebrides, Orkney, and Shetland, and the helpless
Faeroes. At home Bergen was particularly hard hit. Savaged
now by pestilence, the town would be sacked and burned in
1393 by the Victual Brethren, and in 1428–29 by Bartolomæus
Voet, while the Bryggen three times suffered almost total des-

truction in the fires of 1322, 1413, and 1476. Worst of all was the rising power of the Hansa merchants of Germany, whose growth during the thirteenth and fourteenth centuries was sensational. They were a harsh problem for Bergen well before 1300; in 1343 they established their kontor there, and as the century progressed secured a stranglehold on its carrying trade—and by 1400 on that of all Norway. Strangely enough, they appear never to have dispatched a ship to Greenland, and to have left Iceland to her own resources till the English started fishing the banks in 1408–09. Probably they felt no urge to exert themselves; till that date all exports from both countries fell into their hands at Bergen. Possibly in the case of Greenland the Crown-implemented monopoly was still respected. In the light of Icelandic experience we can assume that after 1382 the Crown levied a tax of one-twentieth on all business done with Greenland too, that this sackgeld (*sekkjagjald*) was payable in advance, and that without the royal consent no one might sail there to buy or sell. The Crown had its commissioner in Greenland to enforce these regulations. And we know that the royal prerogative was so strongly enforced that a hapless mariner storm-driven to Greenland's western shore incurred the royal wrath by the mere process of supplying his necessities. Such blinkered cupidity brought profit to no one and cruelly harassed the contracting colony. The indifference of Danish or half-German monarchs to their more distant dependencies after the Union of Kalmar in 1397 could be expected. Indeed, one could argue that the extinction of Norse Greenland was an inevitable consequence of the new European maritime and expansionist economy.

Evidence for communication between Greenland and the outside world after the middle of the fourteenth century may be summarized thus. For the first few decades one ship, safe-guarded by royal monopoly, made the Greenland run at frequent intervals, though apparently not every year. This was the *Grœnlands knörr*, the Greenland carrier; but she seems not to have been replaced after her loss in 1367 or 1369. Thereafter communications were scanty. What records we have of visits to Greenland relate to a strange assortment of men: Bjorn Einarsson Jorsalafari or Jerusalem-farer was cast away there in 1385 for two years; a party of Icelanders was driven off course to

arrive there in 1406 and remain for four years; a somewhat shadowy pair, Pining and Pothorst, made a shadowy voyage to
Greenland and perhaps more widely about the western ocean,
and even to Labrador, soon after 1470, thereby adding fresh
shades of fantasy to Renaissance cartography and as much
cloud as daylight to sixteenth-century adumbrations of the
remoter North.[29] In addition we may conclude that an occa-

---

[29] Didrik Pining must have been a remarkable man, a Norwegian admiral in
the Danish navy under Christian I and King Hans, a 'matchless freebooter'
against the English and the Hansa, and sea-raider upon the Spanish, Portuguese, and Dutch. He was also governor of Iceland for a while, and later of Vardöhus, though it is not easy to distinguish parts of his career from that of his
young kinsman of the same name. According to *Purchas his Pilgrimes*: 'Item,
Punnus and Potharse, have inhabited Island certayne yeeres, and sometimes
have gone to Sea, and have had their trade in Groneland' (Glasgow edn. (1906),
xiii. 168). New light, though in part but darkness visible, was shed upon their
activities by Bobé's discovery in 1909 at Copenhagen of a letter dated 3 March
1551 from Carsten Grip, Burgomaster of Kiel, to King Christian III (part of
which has been quoted above, p. 91): 'The two admirals (*sceppere*) Pyningk and
Poidthorsth, who were sent out by your majesty's royal grandfather, King
Christian the First, at the request of his majesty of Portugal, with certain ships
to explore new countries and islands in the north, have raised on the rock
Wydthszerck [Hvitserk], lying off Greenland and towards Sniefeldsiekel
[Snæfellsjokul] in Iceland on the sea, a great sea-mark [a recognizable cairn] on
account of the Greenland pirates, who with many small ships without keels fall
in large numbers upon other ships.'
   Four comments: (i) Pining and Pothorst appear to have met with Eskimos,
not Norse Greenlanders, and provoked them to a scuffle. This suggests that
they did not reach the west coast. (ii) Possibly the obscure John Scolvus was
with them as pilot, and debatably João Vaz Cortereal was of their company.
(iii) By transposing Hvitserk to the open sea our *piratæ* continued a process
which would end by littering the Atlantic with Hvitramannaland, Friesland,
Estland, *et al.* (iv) It is sad to learn that Pining and Pothorst by land or water,
tempest, rope, or the knife of a smiler, came after all to a bad end (Nansen, *In
Northern Mists* (1911), ii.129).
   Further to John Scolvus: His name is to be found in a legend on the Gemma
Frisius globe of *c.*1595 as Johannes Scolvus Danus, and the argument for his
Danish provenance was deployed at length by Sofus Larsen in his *The Discovery
of North America Twenty Years before Columbus* (1925). But Charlevoix in his
Histoire . . . de la Nouvelle France, (1744) prefers the form Jean Scalve . . .
Voyageur Polonois, modulated and improved to Jan of Kodno by modern
espousers of his claim. Luis Ulloa, starting from a Catalan, Joan Baptista
Colom and his presumed alias Cristobal Colón, made the philological equation
Colom = Scolvus and the personal equation Johannes Scolom = Christopher
Columbus. Admiral Samuel Eliot Morison keel-hauled all these candidates and
their commentators in *The European Discovery of America: The Northern*

sional ship was storm-driven to Greenland of whose fate we
hear nothing, and that resolute and high-handed English skippers in the fifteenth century sailed into Greenland waters for
fish and sea-beasts, for honest trade where it offered, and for
plunder where it lay to hand.[30] Of Bjorn Jorsalafari we hear
specifically that it was the polar ice which prevented his getting
away; and probably it was for the same reason that the visitors
of 1406 had to spend four years in Eystribyggd. During their
stay they witnessed two Christian ceremonies, the burning of
Kolgrim, to which we have already referred, and a wedding in

Voyages, (1971). Halldór Hermansson had more or less dismissed them the
Service in *The Problems of Wineland* (1936). Latterly, Arthur Davies ('Prince
Madoc and the Discovery of America in 1477', *The Geographical Journal*,
150. 3 (1984), pp. 363–72) has precariously identified John Scolvus (Germ.
scholfuss, skilful) with the Welshman John Lloyd, or Llwyd, the 'Thylde'
praised by William of Worcester in 1480 as 'the most expert shipmaster of all
England', but his case lacks proof, and our pilot stays lost to view in tricky
waters.

[30] There was a swarming of English ships in Icelandic waters in the fifteenth
century, a hundred a year come from Bristol and other ports 'unto the costes
colde'. Their skippers and crews were hard men plying a hard trade in a hard
age; they included among their number adventurers and (some) rascals, and
abduction, robbery, ill-treatment, and murder were among the islanders' occa-
sional hazards. If anything, matters grew worse when the Scots and Germans
came seeking their cut of northern profit. That a number of Icelanders, including children, found their way to England is certain, but whether they were purchased, stolen away, or simply transported, is not always clear. But taking the
worst view of the English–Icelandic venture, we should not accept such partisan
charges as Hannes Palsson's in 1425 or forget that the English were frequently
blamed for the wrongdoing of others. Also, English trade with Iceland was
indispensable to the Icelanders and helped them through a very bad time. For a
general review see E. M. Carus-Wilson, 'The Iceland Venture', in *Medieval
Merchant Venturers* (1954), pp. 98–142, and Björn Thorsteinsson, 'Henry VII
and Iceland', in *Saga-Book*, 15 (1957–9), pp. 67–101. As for Greenland, direct
evidence for English piracy is slight, but clauses in successive treaties between
Denmark and England allow us to assume trespass in Greenland waters. For
Bristol ventures north and north-west see J. A. Williamson, *The Cabot Voyages
and Bristol Discovery under Henry VII*, Hakluyt Society, Second Series, no. 120
(1962), and with respect to Greenland, pp. 13–14 and 18. There is the papal letter of 1448 already referred to (see p. 101 above), which suffers from the double
disability that it is probably a forgery and that its exhortatory style hides rather
than reveals the identity of the barbarians who 'gathering together in a fleet on
the neighbouring shores of the Pagans, attacked the entire people in a cruel
invasion', and carried off the natives of both sexes into slavery. There is also the
testimony of Niels Egede's *Beskrivelse over Grønland* (ed. H. Ostermann, *MGr*
120 (1939), p. 268) but this is of the late eighteenth century, which is late
indeed. See Gad, chapters 4–5.

the church at Hvalseyjarfjord, at which Síra Eindridi Andresson, then acting as officialis pending the appointment of a new
bishop of Greenland, and Síra Pal Hallvardsson officiated. This
last was no maimed ceremony, but was marked by the calling of
the banns on the three preceding Sundays, and the nuptial mass
was read at the altar. Everything was done in form and with its
proper dignity, and neither then nor at any point of this
astonishingly well-documented sojourn do we hear anything to
imply a weakening of the Christian faith in the settlement. The
circumstance is important, for when these Icelanders got safely
away in the late summer of 1410, waved hands and called their
last farewells, silence and the dark enfold the Greenland Settlements, and the last act of the tragedy at Eystribyggd was to be
played out without a spectator from the outside world.

There are many prepared to say nothing could be more
appropriate than that our last unclouded sight of the Greenland
colonists should be of them in Hvalsey church. For the Church
as such, the Establishment, is coming to stand in a less than
wholly favourable light to researchers into the long, slow, and
painful decline to which they were now condemned. What looks
like the unalert conservatism of the Greenlanders has been
remarked on by various students, and of late much of the blame
for it has been laid like an unwanted child at the church-door.
The new trend towards palæo-ecological investigation and the
synthesis of archaeological and anthropological knowledge, and
more specifically the multi-faceted work on Western Settlement
middens and cognate repositories of the discards and droppings
of man and man's fellow-travellers, from Sister Cow to Brother
Louse—these have helped particularize the problem in three of
its phases.[31]

First there is the Norseman's unwillingness over a period of
three centuries to learn from the Eskimo's superior seal-hunting

[31] My next three paragraphs are heavily indebted to a series of articles by
Thomas H. McGovern of Hunter College, New York: 'The Economics of
Extinction in Norse Greenland', in *Climate and History*, ed. Wigley *et al.* (Cam-
bridge, 1981); 'The Lost Norse Colony of Greenland', in *Vikings in the West*,
ed. Guralnick, (Chicago, 1982) (from which the quotation is taken by permission); 'The Arctic Frontier of Norse Greenland', in *Archaeology of Frontiers
and Boundaries*, ed. Green and Perlman (Academy Press, NY, 1985),
pp. 275–323; 'Contributions to the Paleoeconomy of Norse Greenland', in *Acta
Archaeologica*, (to appear, 1985–6) and see Appendix IV below.

techniques. He exploited the migratory concentrations of harp, hooded, and common seals, which lent themselves to communal boat-drives, but has left no sign that he adopted the Eskimo practice of taking the ringed seal at breathing-holes with a toggled harpoon. Those effective aids to Arctic living, the harpoon, the skin-boat or kayak, and well-designed fur-clothing, he left to their inventors. Equally surprising is the lack of evidence that he made effective use of the extensive Greenland fisheries; nor does he seem to have possessed equipment for hunting the baleen whale. The comparative paucity of fish remains in and about the old Norse farmsteads is in sharp contrast to its abundant presence in the other Norse Atlantic colonies. That Greenland was too remote and too ill-equipped with ships to share in the common market for fish might be expected; but it remains an extraordinary fact that the settlers culled so little of the abundant harvest of edible fish that haunted local waters. Instead, their staple diet was the meat and animal products of cattle, sheep, goats, and caribou, walrus and seal. Incidentally, Greenland domestic animals were of small size even by medieval standards.

Second, and related to these failures or shortcomings, was the Norse persistence in the annual Nordseta hunt, though this was probably forced upon them if they were to get their hands on the wherewithal with which to pay their burdensome tithes at home and abroad, and so maintain that desired balance of trade which in fact proved to be unmaintainable. The Northern Hunting-Grounds were the source of such luxuries as polar-bear skins and walrus ivory and hides, and unless the resident bishop till 1377 and his resident deputy thereafter were to lose credit in Nidaros and home-comforts at Gardar, these were luxuries the Greenlanders must keep on producing. Every informed visitor of our own day to south-west Greenland, one imagines, has been surprised by the number of Norse church ruins to be found there, and may well have reflected on the disproportionate demand made on a small community by their erection and never-ending need of maintenance and restitution, even in the colony's heyday. Worse, by the mid fourteenth century the Church would hold two-thirds of the best grazing-land, and present investigation is all too surely revealing the discrepant standards of living known on the big rich farms and the small poor ones.[32] A burdensome ecclesiastical superstructure with a Europe-fixated administrative policy was no guard against darkness and cold:

> Although we are still a long way from understanding all of the causes of the demise of Norse Greenland, one factor we cannot overlook is the failure of the colonists actively to pursue economic alternatives, to seek out and adopt new technologies, and to retain the innovative flexibility of the *landnám* years. In the long run, too much cultural stability may be as deadly as too little. A society led by court-appointed bishops, lonely for the comforts of the European homeland, may have found itself a poor match for a society led by accomplished hunters whose ancestors had conquered the High Arctic in their long trek from Alaska.

Then, third and again related, the Norse Greenlander, whatever else he was, was in some degree a farmer. When the climate worsened he was at once in jeopardy. Maybe not even wise governance and Norwegian help could have saved him— and he got neither in good measure. The seasonal round must grow too hard, and its components too demanding. The main sealing season ran through late May and early June; the main caribou hunt probably took place between late August and early October. The haymaking season began in late July and ended in early September. The byred cattle would start calving in the spring, and this would be followed by their short spell out of doors. Sheep and goats would not fare much better. The entire processes of farm husbandry would be squeezed together for the summer, at just the time when men must fare in their six-oared boats up to the northern hunting-grounds, a thirty-day round trip from the Western Settlement, and taking a full fifty from the Eastern, in addition to three or seven weeks in the hunting-grounds. How could any economy cope with such demands? Whoever lost out, the farmer was sure to, with too small a labour force, too many things to see to, and a worsening climate. Eight months a year spent in byre gave his cattle no chance of healthy renewal; cold and wet impoverished his harvests. The fluctuating of sea-ice upset the seal migrations; hares were half bone and the ptarmigan all feathers. Beggars cannot

[32] For a glimpse of terminal or near-terminal desperation and squalor, see Appendix IV, 'A Winter too Many: Nipaitsoq V54', below.

be choosers. The Norse Greenlander must eventually slaughter his precious calves and milch-cows and eat them. And when they were gone, then what? The wonder is not that the Norse Greenlanders disappeared from sight, but that they survived so long.

Eighty years after the Hvalsey wedding the long memory of the Roman Church stirred with regard to Greenland. No action followed stronger than a letter from Pope Alexander VI favouring the proposal of Matthias bishop-elect of Gardar to sail to Greenland in person and lead the souls of the strayed and the apostate to the path of eternal salvation:

Since, as we have been informed, the church at Gardar is situated at the world's end in the country of Greenland, where the inhabitants for lack of bread, wine, and oil, are accustomed to feed on dried fish and milk, by reason of which and because of the very infrequent sailings which were wont to be made to the aforesaid country due to the severe freezing of the seas, no ship is believed to have put in to land there for eighty years, or if such sailings happen to have been made they could not have been made, it is considered, save in the month of August when the ice had melted; and whereas it is likewise reported that for eighty years or thereabouts no bishop or priest whatsoever has in personal residence been in charge of that church; because of which and because too of the absence of orthodox priests it has come about that a great many of that diocese who were formerly believers have, alas, renounced their sacred baptismal vows; and in as much as the inhabitants of that country have no relic of the Christian faith save for a certain corporal [the small square linen cloth on which the chalice and the host are placed during Mass] which is displayed once a year, upon which a hundred years earlier the Body of Christ was consecrated by the priest last in residence there:—for these, then, and other considerations. . . . [33]

This is a grim picture, not correct in all its details (as to diet, it is certain that the settlers ate more meat than dried fish), and in its account of the spiritual life of Eystribyggd contradictory of the evidence of the Icelanders who sailed from there in 1410,

[33] The letter was printed in *Norsk Historisk Tidsskrift* (1892), p. 407, and with an English translation (not used here) in *The Flatey Book and Recently Discovered Vatican Manuscripts Concerning America as Early as the Tenth Century*, (Norroena Society, 1906), pp. 175 ff.

and to whose eighty-year-old voyage it seems specifically to refer. One suspects that the letter is not based on fresh intelligence, but on oppressive rumour and garbled recollection, in which the black art of Kolgrim hung like a cloud over the bright ceremony in Hvalseyjarfjord church. After all, the cry of apostasy in Greenland had by now been sounded for a century and a half. And the increase in polar ice off Greenland was a fact known to every mariner who sailed the northern seas, and to every merchant prince from the Tyskebryggen of Bergen to Canynges' wharves in Bristol, and from Bristol to the counters of the Portingales.

Yet some sailing after 1410 there must have been, at least to Herjolfsnes in the south of the Eastern Settlement, and for the incoming traveller his first port of call. Here for long centuries the sea has been fingering the bones and coffin shards of the old Norse burial ground on the point, pawing them into the light of day, then scrabbling them off to their fresh oblivion. And there in 1921 Poul Nørlund found dead Greenlanders buried in exactly such costumes as were current in continental Europe throughout the fourteenth century, and even a few examples of the latest fashions of the second half of the fifteenth.[34] But to

---

[34] Most of the garments from Herjolfsnes, including the liripipe hoods, says Nørlund, 'may without hesitation be placed in the latter half of the fourteenth century and the period round about 1400' (*Viking Settlers*, p. 126). These present no problem, in view of the recorded sailings of the Greenland *knörr* till 1367–9 and the Annal entries concerning ships driven to Greenland in 1381, 1382, 1385, and 1406. The pieces from the second half of the fifteenth century are less numerous than some commentators assume. Nørlund speaks of three children's caps. 'Two caps are very simple, round with a flat crown, the sides fairly high. Any period might have designed them, but we recognize them as a head covering that was very popular in the fifteenth century, whereas caps from earlier times are different, mostly rounded or conical in the crown. Now if any doubts should be entertained that these small caps can be given a fairly exact dating, there remains one about which there cannot be much discussion. It is 25 to 30 cm high, rather conical, standing steeply up from the forehead but widening out at the back of the neck. It is one of the high caps shown us on the paintings of Dirk Bout, Memling and other Flemish painters, worn in the time of Louix XI and Charles the Bold, in the latter half of the fifteenth century. This makes our cap a very important document in Greenland's medieval history, testimony that as late as towards the sixteenth century there must have been ships going to Greenland from Europe. It is not a solitary witness either. There are fragments of dresses with quite close folds sewn at the waist, one of them also with a V-shaped neck opening, and these two are fashion details belonging to

erect on this a theory of regular visits and trade is to force the evidence. One ship and a single voyage, planned or involuntary, could account for it all. Though this, no doubt, is to force the evidence in the opposite direction, and the truth will lie in between. It has been clear too for a good while that the gloomy deductions of physical decline, early death, and crippling malformation drawn by their first examiners from the Herjolfsnes skeletons, especially those of the women, cannot be sustained, and that these remains are in any case untypical of Norse Greenlanders elsewhere in the Settlements.

But they died Christians and received Christian burial. True, the Herjolfsnes dead speak only for themselves, but theirs was an entirely uncontaminated Norse enclave in an Eskimo subcontinent. There is still not the slightest trace of assimilation to the Eskimo in any of the graves—those tell-tale graves which grew progressively shallower as more of the ground became permanently frozen. And there is a second respect in which they speak only for themselves, for the other skeletons of Eystribyggd and those of Vestribyggd are eloquent against them. These are the bones of normal men and women, wellnourished, bothered a good deal by rheumatism (who in the medieval world was not?), but untouched by chronic disease, and free of morbidity.[35]

When and how the Eastern Settlement was extinguished we may never know. Most probably it was soon after the year 1500. There must have been a prolonged weakening of the colony in

the later part of the fifteenth century' (p. 125). 'Among the other objects found during the excavations are some which presumably are imported fifteenth-century wares, a knife from the episcopal kitchen, a fragment of a Rhenish stone jug, which lay at the foundation of the banqueting hall at Herjolfsnes' (p. 126).

[35] The argument may be followed in Fr. C. C. Hansen, *Anthropologia Medico-Historica Grænlandiæ Antiquæ*, MGr 67, no. 3 (1924); K. Fischer-Möller, *Skeletons from Ancient Greenland Graves*, MGr 119, no. 4'(1938); *The Medieval Norse Settlements in Greenland*, MGr 89, no. 2 (1942); K. Bröste and K. Fischer-Möller, *The Medieval Norsemen at Gardar*, MGr 89, no. 3 (1944); J. Balslev-Jørgensen, *The Eskimo Skeleton*, MGr 146, no. 2 (1953); Jón Steffensen, *Stature as a Criterion of the Nutritional Level of Viking Age Icelanders*, þriðji Víkingafundur (1958); Jørgen Meldgaard, *Nordboerne i Grønland* (1965); Helge Ingstad, *Land under the Pole Star* (1966) (contains a summary on pp. 306–9 with an opinion on the evidence from Professor dr. med. Johan Torgersen and Prosektor dr. med. Bernard Getz).

readiness for the final act. Possibly at Herjolfsnes, more probably at Unartoq, there is evidence of mass burial which points to the ravages of an epidemic, maybe the Black Death, though this is without confirmation from historical sources. As had happened at Vestribyggd, we must imagine the colony contracting under Eskimo pressure, outlying families falling back upon the main areas of habitation, and some (and these not necessarily the weaker spirits) seizing their opportunity to get away to Iceland and Norway. Others were carried off forcibly by rough-dealing marauders from Europe, among whom it is to be feared that the English held a bad pre-eminence; and it is reasonable to believe that their deep-felt isolation, in addition to these other troubles, bred a moral and mental debility which affected their will to survive. On the whole, the old theory of the Greenland colony dying out in increasing isolation from an indifferent world must still hold the field.[36]

The archaeological evidence has not been without its bizarreries. In 1950 the Danes excavated the remains of a remarkably long longhouse in Vatnahverfi, consisting of a byre and the house proper, of six or seven rooms. It had a kitchen and a pantry, and in the pantry floor, which had been dug down a little to receive them, were the remains of three wooden barrels. These had been used to store milk, probably in the form of *skýr*. In one of the barrels were the tiny bones of almost a hundred mice—remarkable, since till that moment no one knew that mice had existed in the Greenland settlements.[37] They must have climbed in when the farm went derelict, eaten the last food they could find, failed to get out, and so perished. Nearby, in another big farm of the Vatnahverfi, were found fragments of two small crucifixes carved in steatite, various artefacts of iron, including knives, and in a passage-way some human bones,

---

[36] Ingstad suggests that the people of the Eastern Settlement went off to join their compatriots of Vestribyggd on the North American mainland, or that they transferred wholesale to England (p. 371). But there is no weighable evidence for either alternative. From Vestribyggd the natural asylum was Eystribyggd; from Eystribyggd it was Iceland and Norway. But whether in their few and poor ships they reached it, whether they perished on the way, or whether they ever made the attempt, these are things we do not know.

[37] But since those early days the Greenlandic house-mouse has come into his archaeological own—and the own is just about everywhere.

16. GREENLAND ESKIMO

including the badly decomposed pieces of a skull. Anthropology tells us that its owner in life was white and a Norseman. It would seem then that he was the last inhabitant of the farm, and therefore unburied. It is possible that he was the last man left alive in the settlement.[38]

What trust we should place in the story of Jon Greenlander who claimed to have sailed into a deep fjord near Cape Farewell somewhere about 1540, is hard to determine. He had been blown off course when sailing from Hamburg to Iceland. On both mainland and islands they saw houses; and on one island there were many sheds and booths and stone houses for drying fish. Here too they discovered 'a dead man lying face downwards on the ground. On his head he wore a well-made hood, and in addition clothes both of frieze and of sealskin. Near him was a sheath-knife, bent and much worn and wasted away. This knife they took with them as a keepsake.'[39] *Se non é vero, é ben trovato*. Whether in this wretched place or another the last

---

[38] C. L. Vebæk, 'Topographical and Archaeological Investigations in the Norse Settlements in Greenland', pp. 116–19 (in Þriðji Víkingafundur).

[39] *GHM*, iii. 513–14. Jon was called Greenlander because he had been blown off course thither no less than three times.

Norseman in Greenland lay dead, and the Iron Age was all wasted away.

When in 1586 the Englishman John Davis escaped from the loathsome desolation of Greenland's south-eastern coast and beheld with relief the 'plain champaign country, with earth and grass' within the fjords of the west, he found no white men nor traces of them, 'nor saw anything save only gripes, ravens, and small birds, as larks and linnets'. These were the fjords of the ancient Western Settlement, but it was the same in the Eastern Settlement too. Land and water and all they contained belonged to the cheerful, enduring Eskimo. The Norse story of Greenland was ended.

3

Vinland the Good

VENTURE AND WITHDRAWAL

ABOUT the Norse discovery of Iceland and Greenland, we have
seen, blew the winds of story and chance, which were the winds
of destiny too. In the late summer of 986, a month or so after
Eirik the Red stood out past Snæfellsnes with his Greenland-
bound armada of twenty-five ships, they would blow again,
triumphantly, to fill the sails of a young Icelander named Bjarni
Herjolfsson, and after three days' sailing drive him south to an
unknown fogbound region of ocean. It was some days before
the fog lifted and he was able to determine the quarters of the
heavens. One day's sailing more and his eyes beheld the shores
and forests of the New World. In his own lifetime this young
man was to win the reproaches of the Norwegians for not going
ashore and spying out the land; and during ours he has taken
rough handling from scholars disgruntled at his presumption in
sighting America before Leif the Lucky. It is therefore worth
recalling to mind the purpose of his epoch-making journey and
the qualities of seamanship which brought it against all probability to its fortunate ending. Bjarni had spent the winter of
985–6 in Norway. In the summer he sailed to Iceland with a full
cargo, intending to spend the winter with his father. But when
he reached Eyrar (i.e., Eyrarbakki), near the mouth of Olfus
river, it was to hear the startling news that Herjolf had sold his
estates and departed for Greenland. We discern a certain stub-
bornness in our saga's view of Bjarni: he had set out for home,
and home he meant to go. So with the consent of his crew he set
off on what they all knew would be a risky journey, pilotless,
chartless, compassless, for the south-western fjords of Greenland. Three days out, and the mountains and glaciers of Iceland
whelmed under the horizon, they fell a prey to north winds
and then to fog, and for many days had no notion which way
they were going. Then the sun broke through, they took fresh

ings, hoisted sail, and journeyed for a whole day before sighting a land which was not mountainous, but well forested, with low hills. His crew, metaphorically speaking, were still all at sea, but Bjarni, if he didn't know where he was, at least knew where he was not. This could not be Greenland—and it was for Greenland he was headed. Too single-minded, perhaps too prudent, to go ashore, he held north along the coast for two days' sailing. The land here, they saw, was still well forested but flat. Again he refused to put in, and sailed with a south-west wind for three more days till they came to a land which was high, mountainous, and glaciered. A land in Bjarni's opinion good for nothing. So yet again he turned his prow from the land, and after four days' sailing before a strong wind he reached Herjolfsnes in Greenland. Without unduly imperilling his ship and crew he had done what he set out to do, and *Grænlendinga Saga* by drawing on oral tradition and later geographical and navigational lore has compiled his log-book—the plain if not unvarnished record of a practical man.

Tenth- and twentieth-century criticism of Bjarni amounts to little more than that he was not another Gardar, Ohthere or Eirik the Red. He was a trader and later a farmer, not an explorer. But the entire pattern of life and thought in the Viking North made it certain that his discovery would not be forgotten or neglected by people as endlessly daring as they were incurably land-hungry. It was not even necessary to put to sea to know that Bjarni spoke truth about new lands to the west. Medieval geographical thinking, the Norse *imago mundi*, favoured the notion of more land to be found beyond Greenland, and, more practically, when men climbed the high mountains behind the settlement areas of Greenland (as the *King's Mirror* informs us they did) they would see far in the distance either land itself or the cloud formations they associated with land. At the narrowest point of Davis Strait just two hundred miles separate Cumberland Peninsula from Greenland. It is unthinkable that during the great age of Norse exploration men would not have undertaken so short and challenging a passage.[1]

In the light of the record speculation is unnecessary. There

---

[1] See too the Introduction, pp. 9–14 and 17–24, for some thoughts on practical seamanship and both practical and chairborne geographical knowledge.

was considerable discussion of Bjarni's voyage down in the Eastern Settlement, and the sons of Eirik the Red were quick to act upon it. There was a suggestion that Eirik himself should undertake a new voyage of glory into the west, but this was not in his destiny; he fell off his horse on his way to the ship, and various broken bones kept him at home. The ship was Bjarni's, purchased from him by Eirik's son Leif, a tremendous sailor, and the first skipper reported to have made direct voyages between Greenland, Scotland, Norway, and back again. He would certainly get every scrap of information he could from Bjarni, and it is reasonable to assume that he enlisted some of his crew. He sought to follow Bjarni's course in reverse, and did so with precision. First they reached the land which Bjarni had reached last, mountainous and glaciered, grassless and barren. One look ashore was enough. Bjarni had been right: there was nothing here to tempt a husbandman, and having named it Helluland, Flatstone Land, they sailed on their way to the south.

When next they stood in to the land and put out their ship's boat they were in the flat and forested country where Bjarni's crew had vainly hoped to go ashore for wood and water. We learn rather more about it on this second visit. There were extensive white sands there, and the coast itself was level and cliffless. Here too Leif bestowed a name in accordance with the land's main feature: Markland, Wood or Forest Land. But he was still anxious to be on his way and probe these new lands further. After two days' sailing with a north-east wind they came to an island lying north of what appeared to be a mainland with a cape projecting northwards from it. This was that region of the New World which Leif was to name Vinland, the Promontorium Winlandiæ of the maps which would be prepared by Sigurður Stefánsson about 1590 and Hans Poulson Resen in 1605.[2] Leif

---

[2] Sigurður's map survives only in a copy made by Thórður Thorláksson in 1670 (Ny kgl. Saml. 2881 4to, f. 10 v., in the Royal Library, Copenhagen). The map is there wrongly dated 1570, roughly the date of Sigurður's birth. Whether Resen's map was based on Sigurður's or whether both were copied from a common original, has been much debated. When allowance is made for the fact that Sigurður's lines of latitude are consistently rated too high over the whole western Atlantic (note the correspondence of northern Newfoundland and southern Ireland), both maps indicate northern Newfoundland with exactitude as the Promontorium Winlandiæ.

17. THE
SKÁLHOLT MAP OF
THE NORTH
ATLANTIC
REGION, BY
SIGURÐUR
STEFÁNSSON, 1590

wintered in Vinland, and his booths and big houses at Leifsbudir mark the first area of European habitation of the American continent. The following spring they made ready to sail away, had a good wind, and came to Greenland safe and sound.

Back home in Greenland Leif's western voyage came in for the same close scrutiny as Bjarni's. He had done much, admittedly; yet there was a sense in which he merely whetted the curiosity of his fellow colonists. His brother Thorvald for one (we are still following *Grænlendinga Saga*'s version of events) wanted to know more, and so far as Leif was concerned he was welcome to learn the hard way and go to Vinland to know it. Which is what Thorvald did. By this time he was traversing a known route and reached Leifsbudir without incident, to spend a quiet winter there. In the spring he proceeded to act on his expressed notion that Vinland needed an altogether more extensive exploration. He sent his ship's boat to examine its western coast, and throughout the summer they explored a beautiful and well-wooded country without coming across any sign of human habitation other than a solitary wooden grain-holder. The following summer Thorvald took his ship first east and then north in the general direction of Markland. He gave the name Kjalarnes, Keelness, to a certain cape, repaired his ship there, and shortly afterwards headed into a beautiful, well-forested fjord. Here they encountered their first Skrælings, killed those they could lay their hands on, and in a retaliatory raid Thorvald was killed by an arrow which whipped into him from between gunwale and shield. His crew got back to Leifs-budir without more damage; they wintered there, and the following spring sailed away and reached Eiriksfjord with a freight of heavy but exciting news.

Thorvald's well-conducted though fatal expedition, with its considerable additions to Norse geographical knowledge, was to be followed by the abortive voyage of his brother Thorstein, who wanted to bring his body home to rest among his kinsmen, but who in fact spent a trying summer storm-tossed on the immense triangle of ocean between Iceland, Ireland, and Cape Farewell. This in its turn was followed by Thorfinn Karlsefni's attempt to establish a permanent colony in Vinland. This was an elaborate and well-planned venture consisting of three ships with no fewer than a hundred and sixty men, some of them accompanied by their wives, and taking 'all sorts of livestock' with them, including, one would guess, cows and a bull, mares and a stallion, ewes and a ram, and maybe goats and pigs. They began by moving up the coast with the warm north-setting coastal current as far as the Western Settlement, possibly because Karlsefni's wife had property there, but far more likely because this had already revealed itself to be the most promising route. From the Western Settlement they sailed still further north, to Bjarney(jar), Bear Isle(s), which we cannot identify with any certainty, but may be in the neighbourhood of the modern Holsteinsborg, or may be Disco. The arguments for the Holsteinsborg region is that here the current turns west towards the North American shore, and that the twentieth-century mariner would regard it as a waste of time and effort to sail north of there before heading for the south of Baffin Island. Both Holsteinsborg and Disco might lay claim to an argument that Karlsefni would seek to reduce his time on the open sea to a minimum for the sake of his animals. The 'northern digression' might also arise from a Norse sailor's need of a guiding coastline on extensive voyages north or south because of his difficulty with the problem of longitude.

So, sped by a wind from the north, Karlsefni reached Helluland, Baffin Island. But not necessarily the precise area of Baffin Island reached and named by his predecessors. Like Markland and presumably Vinland, Helluland was the name of an extensive stretch of coast and country. Which in its turn makes it enough for present purposes to say that when Karlsefni sailed before the same north wind for two days and reached Markland he was somewhere off the forested part of Labrador.[3] From there after a long while of coasting he came to a quite closely described area of what was still Labrador. Two of its features were unusual. There was a cape on which they found the keel of a ship and which they named Kjalarnes, Keelness, and beaches and sands of such remarkable length that they called them Furdustrandir, Marvelstrands, because 'it was such a long business sailing past them'. We are instantly reminded of events and places in the voyages of Leif and Thorvald. When Leif arrived in the land he named Markland he found the country 'flat and covered with forest, with extensive white sands wherever they went, and shelving gently to the sea'. Two days south they sighted Vinland. In turn, Thorvald sailing north along the land from Leifsbudir met heavy weather off a certain cape, they were driven ashore, and so damaged their keel that they had to fit a new. Studying the old and broken one—'Said Thorvald to his shipmates: "I should like us to erect the keel on the cape here, and call it Kjalarnes."' Clearly Thorvald's Kjalarnes and Karlsefni's are the same, and if we seek to identify it, whether we accept the sagas' accounts as literally true, read into

---

[3] AM 557 says that they sailed for two days before a north wind; *Hauksbók* that they sailed onwards from Helluland for two days and changed course from south to south-east. Thereafter the accounts deviate. AM 557 says that from their landfall in Markland they came to Kjalarnes after two days' sailing; *Hauksbók* that they sailed 'for a long while' before arriving there. Either we must emend the time of sailing from an unspecified place in Baffin Island to an unspecified place in Labrador (a shaky undertaking at best, though Finnur Jónsson's suggestion of v for ii is not too daunting), or accept *Hauksbók*'s *langa stund* for Karlsefni's coastal sailing from his landfall in Markland on down to Kjalarnes. This latter is much to be preferred. *Grænlendinga Saga* offers no details. Karlsefni left Greenland, and in an unspecified time and by an unspecified route reached Leifsbudir in Vinland.

them a common principle of place-naming in Iceland, Norway, and Denmark, or find in them a well-known type of onomastic story, is not all that important. What is important is the verifiable existence of remarkably long white sandy beaches and a keel-shaped cape two days' sailing north of Leifsbudir. They are to be found immediately south of Hamilton Inlet, on the southeastern coast of Labrador. These sandy beaches for sailors along the rocky and formidable coasts from Baffin Island south are indeed 'marvelstrands', over forty miles in length, with a low-lying background of grass and spruce and juniper. The sand, says Captain Munn, fine and hard, is 'fit for the old-fashioned hour-glass'. From the Strand, as these turf-backed fifty-yard-wide white beaches are called, Cape Porcupine extends two miles to sea, an impressive keel-shaped profile, still in our own day a main landmark for all who fish these waters.

Fortunately the discrepancies between our two literary sources, the *Flateyjarbók* version (*Grænlendinga Saga*), and the AM 557 and *Hauksbók* version (*Eiríks Saga Rauða*), whilst troublesome enough are not unmanageable. Both versions are the workings over of original material in accordance with the well-established facts of saga-making. Deviations, accretions, influences, reinterpretations, misunderstandings (especially as to the different places reached by the different explorers), changes of emphasis, and varying allocations of credit are to be expected; but the important thing to recognize is that these confirm rather than deny a sound underlying historical tradition. For a start *Grænlendinga Saga* is much less interested in Iceland and the Icelanders than is *Eiríks Saga Rauða*. *Grænlendinga Saga* is concerned with the family of Eirik the Red (which incidentally gives great weight to its account of Bjarni Herjolfsson); *Eiríks Saga Rauða* is more interested in the Icelanders Gudrid and Karlsefni, from whom Hauk Erlendsson, the owner and part-scribe of *Hauksbók*, claimed descent. *Grænlendinga Saga* makes all its voyagers, Leif, Thorvald, Karlsefni, and Freydis reach the same place, Leifsbudir, and with the exception of Thorvald there they stayed. In *Grænlendinga Saga* Leifsbudir and Vinland are more or less synonymous terms. But in *Eiríks Saga Rauða* we have two encampments described in detail, Straumfjord and Hop, and it is noticeable how closely the description of Leifsbudir corresponds with that of Hop: the shoals, the river, and the lake. Even the climate was the same. At Leifsbudir 'the nature of the land was so choice that it seemed to them that none of the cattle would require fodder for the winter. No frost came during the winter, and the grass was hardly withered.' At Hop 'no snow fell, and their entire stock found its food grazing in the open'. Yet the identification of Leifsbudir with Hop is highly improbable, the more so because Leifsbudir and Straumfjord also have features in common, and appear from the sailing directions and geographical evidence to be one and the same place in northern Newfoundland. Presumably the author of *Grænlendinga Saga* was conscious of his ignorance in these matters and worked up a description of Leifsbudir from tradition persistent in Skagafjord in Iceland, with the puzzling consequence for posterity that in his saga, to adopt Thórhallur Vilmundarson's equation, Straumfjord + Hop = Leifsbudir. Such correspondences and differences are all too typical of the saga accounts. Thus *Grænlendinga Saga* ascribes the first sighting of the North American coast to Bjarni Herjolfsson and the first exploration to Leif Eiriksson, whereas *Eiríks Saga Rauða* makes no mention of Bjarni and makes a perfunctory and even fatuous business of Leif's discovery of Vinland. *Grænlendinga Saga* tells of separate voyages by Leif's brother Thorvald and Thorfinn Karlsefni, while *Eiríks Saga* has them voyage together; *Eiríks Saga* as tendentiously as wrongly lets Leif introduce Christianity into Greenland at the instigation of Norway's King Olaf Tryggvason—a mistake avoided by its fellow-saga; *Grænlendinga Saga* tells of a melodramatic and bloody voyage to Vinland conducted by Leif's melodramatic and bloody sister Freydis, but *Eiríks Saga*, as though mindful of the family's credit, does not. There are, in addition, various self-announcing fictions from all the voyages, Leif's sweet dew, Haki and Hekja, Thorhall the Hunter's unknown species of whale, the second Gudrid, Thorvald's uniped, and the Ancestral Indian's impossible addiction to cow's milk among them.[4] Their dismissal neither affects the voyages themselves nor simplifies the real problems, but it does rid them of some clutter.

There has been much argument during the past hundred

---

[4] Something of Haki and Hekja and of the uniped will be found in Appendix VI.

years whether we should rid them of the grapes and the vines too. Vinland, however we interpret it, is a descriptive name, one of a long succession of such: Iceland, Greenland, Flatstone Land, Wood Land, as well as Sheep Isles, Bear Isles, Keelness, and Marvelstrands. We find the name first in the *Descriptio insularum aquilonis* or 'Description of the island countries of the North' which forms the fourth book of Adam of Bremen's *Gesta Hammaburgensis ecclesiæ pontificum*. Adam tells us that he derived his information about Vinland from Svein Estridsson, king of the Danes, who died in 1076:

> He told me too of yet another island, discovered by many in that ocean, which is called Wineland from the circumstance that vines grow there of their own accord, and produce the most excellent wine. While that there is abundance of unsown corn there we have learned not from fabulous conjecture but from the trustworthy report of the Danes.[5]

King Svein then, and Adam after him, had the same notion of Vinland as Thorhall the Hunter who in verses generally accepted as old and genuine lamented that all he had to drink for his undoubted pains was water from the well (see p. 225 below). In saga tradition Vinland was certainly *Vínland*, Wineland, or Wineland the Good, *Vínland hit góða*, because it was a place which produced grapes which in turn produced wine. Saga evidence as to this is overwhelming, which makes it difficult to accept recent theories that Vinland was not *Vínland* at all, but *Vinland* (*vin*, pl. *vinjar*, with a short vowel), Grass Land, Pasture Land, Land of Good Grazing.[6] Grass was as desirable, and

---

[5] 'Præterea unam adhuc insulam recitavit, a multis repertam in illo oceano, quæ dicitur Vinland, eo quod ibi vites sponte nascantur, vinum optimum ferentes. Nam et fruges ibi, non seminatas, abundare, non fabulosa opinione, sed certa Danorum comperimus relatione' (*Gesta*, IV. xxxix (38)).

[6] This view was advanced by the Swedish philologist Sven Söderberg in 1888 and published in the *Sydsvenska Dagbladet Snällposten* of 30 October 1910. He thought that the saga-writers uncritically accepted the ideas of Adam of Bremen, who was given to wild and whirling accounts of distant places. To adopt it, as has been done by the recent equaters of Vinland with the northern tip of Newfoundland, i.e. the Finn V. Tanner, the Norwegian Helge Ingstad (who, however, does not reject the possibility of vines and wild wheat growing in Vinland), and the Dane Jørgen Meldgaard, disposes of many problems, among them the need to fit Vinland within the northern limits of the wine-producing grape at the end of the tenth century, or, if that cannot be done, to provide evidence that to the Greenlanders and Icelanders grapes were not grapes and vines not vines, but squash-berries, cow-berries, red, white, black, and blue

essential, to the would-be colonizers of Vinland as to their fathers in the Faeroes, Iceland, and Greenland. Timber and pasture together would delight them. But grape-clusters might supply the headier flavour that Leif needed to incite the Greenlanders to fresh land-takings. In land-naming as in other ways Leif was his father's son, and Wineland out-tops Greenland as Grassland could never do. Besides, we can believe in the grapes. Their northern limit of growth today is about latitude 45° N., but in the 1530s Jacques Cartier, the discoverer of the St Lawrence, found abundance of grapes on both sides of the river, and wild corn rather like rye or oats at the Baie de Chaleur and on various islands in the Gulf. Champlain, Leigh, and Denys support him.[7] It may therefore be assumed (a shade optimistically) that in far more favourable climatic conditions, such as obtained at the time of the Vinland voyages, the northern limit of the wild grape included some part of Newfoundland's northern peninsula. Finally, it is not fatal to the credibility of the saga accounts of these voyages if we conclude that grapes were met with not in the northern tip of Newfoundland but when the Norsemen sailed somewhat further south, as we are explicitly told they did on at least two occasions. For we must at all times remember that there is no theory of the Vinland voyages of discovery reconcilable with *all* the evidence.

Probably the most difficult discard of all to make is the observation that at Leifsbudir 'The sun had there *eyktarstaðr* and

---

berries, or even birch trees (by no means a full list of the proffered substitutes). It also provides a rational and attractive sequence of lands proceeding south: stone, wood, grass. Perhaps, indeed, too rational. There is no doubt that *vin*, pasture, meadow, grazing, is a frequent element in early Norwegian local names, but it appears to have fallen into complete, or almost complete, disuse before the time of the Vinland voyages, and is not to be found in the place-names of the Faeroes, Iceland, or Greenland. It is certainly not impossible that the bookish saga-men of Iceland, unacquainted with the element (almost always a suffix) -*vin* and influenced by notions of the Insulæ Fortunatæ, too easily inclined to *vín-*. But on balance there seems no compulsive reason for setting aside the overwhelming saga tradition with respect to *Vinland*, Wineland, and with all doubts registered I retain it.

[7] The evidence has been many times presented, from Anspach, *A History of the Island of Newfoundland*, edn. of 1827, to Gathorne-Hardy, *The Norse Discoverers of America* (1921; new edn. 1970). And see Wahlgren, 'Fact and Fancy in the Vinland Sagas', in *Old Norse Literature and Mythology: A Symposium*, ed. E. C. Polomé (Univ. of Texas, 1969).

dagmálastaðr on the shortest day (*or* days)'. This looks the kind
of factual, unemotional statement which could determine the
latitude of this particular part of Vinland beyond any argument.
But there is no question on which the experts are more divided
and the layman more helpless. That those making the observation were impressed by the more even balance of day and
night in winter in Vinland than back home in Greenland and
Iceland is stated; and that on a particular day or days in winter
the sun was visible, though presumably then at point of rising
and setting, at a certain time in the morning and a certain time
in the afternoon. These could not be clock times, for the Norsemen had no clocks in the early eleventh century. Therefore
eyktarstaðr and *dagmálastaðr* are points on the horizon, such as
were used by the Icelanders to estimate the time of day by the
position of the sun, or, more positively, they are bearings of the
sun itself. From this, all other things being certain, for example,
the exact significant of *eykt* in Iceland in Leif's time, the exact
significance of *um skammdegi*, and all such corrections of calculation as are needed for the effects of refraction, changes of sea
level, the actual as well as the astronomical horizon, and a
knowledge of what a Norse sailor meant by sunrise and sunset
(i.e. the rise or descent of edge or centre)—all these things
established for the early eleventh century, if not beyond the
possibility of error at least within a negligible margin of error,
Vinland should stand revealed, at least in its northernmost
possibility. But of the three most distinguished students or part-
nerships of students who have tried to determine the northernmost limit at which the observation could have been made,
Storm and Geelmuyden, supported by Captain Phythian of the
United States Naval Observatory, settled for latitude *c*.49° 55′;
G. M. Gathorne-Hardy first for latitude *c*.49°, though 'in all
probability the words indicate a much more southerly latitude',
but later for south of latitude 37°; while Dr Almar Næss, re-
working and revising the calculations of M. M. Mjelde, thinks it
'very probable' that Vinland lay south of Chesapeake Bay (36°
54′ N.). In other words, while this famous sentence may help to
convince us that someone made a significant observation somewhere in America, it helps not at all to determine the site of
Leif's booths.

Our review of the documentary (which means primarily the

18. VINLAND

A sketch by Thórhallur Vilmundarson, redrawn by Halldór Pétursson, showing
The author of the sketch has not attempted a reconstruction of the ruins, but
(*left*) is the coast of Labrador, with Belle Isle (*centre*) at the entrance to the
Sacred Island (*left*), then Little Sacred

saga) evidence for Norse settlement site(s) in North America by
now affords us more or less the same opportunity for judgement
as that confronting both practical and theoretical inquirers in
the 1950s. It remains only to add with or without the benefit of
hindsight that *Eiríks Saga Rauða's* description of Markland–
Vinland topography fits south-eastern Labrador and northern
Newfoundland better than anywhere else. South of Furdustrandir, says the saga, the coast becomes indented with bays
(*vágskorit*), which is true of the coast of Labrador, with Sandwich Bay as its most impressive immediate example. Later it
became indented with fjords (*fjarðskorit*), or possibly as in

PANORAMA
Black Duck Brook flowing past Ingstad's 1962 excavation site into Épaves Bay.
offers a generalized picture of the presumed scene *c.*AD 1000. In the background
Strait. In the background (*right*) is Cape Bauld. Out in Sacred Bay is Great
Island (behind Warrens Island)

Hauksbók by one particular fjord. If fjords, these are the
entries from north of Battle Harbour to the Strait of Belle Isle;
if fjord, the entrance to the Strait of Belle Isle itself. On this
reading of the evidence Karlsefni's Straumfjord, Stream or Current Fjord, was the northern entrance of the Strait of Belle Isle,
which he had no reason to know was a passage to the south
rather than a penetration of the land. These were sailors with
experience of the immense fjords of Greenland, Iceland, and
Norway, and their error, if it can with propriety be called such,
was shared by a list of distinguished navigators till the 'discovery' by Jacques Cartier more than five centuries later.

Straumey, Stream Island, may have been Belle Isle, or even Great Sacred Island, lying in an arm of sea between Cape Bauld, the northern tip of Promontorium Winlandiæ, and Cape Onion. A few miles south are the grassy shores of Sacred Bay and in particular L'Anse aux Meadows (i.e. l'Anse-au-Medée: *Midi* or a ship's name *Médée*) and Épaves Bay, where Black Duck Brook curves to the sea round a bluff whose environs have been the scene of human settlement over a long period of history—the earliest traceable occupations being of *c*.4000 BC. The outlook over L'Anse aux Meadows and the adjacent countryside, and out over the island-dotted Strait of Belle Isle, with Cape Bauld to the right, and the coast of Labrador to the left, is a splendid one. *þar var fagrt landsleg.*[8] It offered the promise of good grazing, if not quite the 'tall *or* abundant grass' of *Eiríks Saga Rauða* (though it must be remarked that there is nothing among the Norse remains to show that their animals ever grazed it), with nearby forest for timber and game. The streams teemed with fish, and the sea's harvest was inexhaustible. There was a further advantage too. During the first two winters of Eirik's exploration of Greenland he made his home on islands outside the fjords, where supplies were good and he was in sight of the open sea. Similarly the explorers of Vinland found themselves a base which promised them the fullest possible freedom of movement and the clearest observation of the movement of others, should such there be. The climate was of less roseate hue than would be affirmed by saga-men two hundred or more years later, but on the whole a good country of the kind they were used to. And empty. Or seeming so.

Here, then, if we can accept the best-charted lines of saga evidence, lay not necessarily the legendary Vinland but the area of the first Norse settlement in North America. But for many the 'if' has always proved a big one, and Vinland has been sought and found at numerous points on the American coast between Hudson Bay and the state of Florida.[9] With the uncovering of

[8] Curiously enough, since Karlsefni was a Skagafjord man, it strongly reminds Icelandic observers of Skagafjord itself: a thought-provoking thought.

[9] To confine the illustration to Karlsefni's Straumfjord: this has been placed in Hudson Bay (Reman, *The Norse Discoveries and Explorations in America*, (Berkeley and Los Angeles, 1949)); Labrador (Fernald, 'The Plants of Wineland the Good', *Rhodora*, 12 (1910)); Labrador and Newfoundland

L'Anse aux Meadows in the early 1960s came a wonderful concentration of minds and a wondrous contraction of sites, but the
story remains a noble one, reaching back to the great names of
the Norwegian Fridtjof Nansen (1911), the American A. M.
Reeves (1895), and the Danes Gustav Storm (1887) and C.
Rafn (1837); but inasmuch as the long search has now homed in
on the Norse remains at L'Anse aux Meadows and firmly established the northern extremity of Newfoundland as the Promontorium Winlandiæ, it must suffice to mention with regard the
more recent names of the Canadian Captain W. A. Munn,[10] the
Finn Vaïno Tanner,[11] the Dane Jørgen Meldgaard,[12] and the
Norwegians Helge and Anne Stine Ingstad.[13]

Helge Ingstad, overtaking and improving on the work of his
predecessors, discovered the site at L'Anse aux Meadows,
Épaves Bay, at the northern tip of Newfoundland's Great
Northern Peninsula in the summer of 1960. During the next
eight years he and his wife not only established its authenticity
as a place of medieval Norse habitation, but carried out extensive excavations there, so that eight house-sites or building-sites
have come to light, with their expected assortment of hearths,
cooking-pits, a smithy, bog-iron and slag, a ring-headed bronze
pin and a soapstone spindle-whorl, and twoscore or more iron

(Straumfjord and Hop respectively: Hovgaard, *The Voyages of the Norsemen to
America* (New York, 1914)); the St Lawrence Estuary (Steensby, *The Norse-
men's Route from Greenland to Wineland, MGr* 56 (1918)); Baie de Chaleur
(Hermannsson, *The Problem of Wineland* (Ithaca, New York, 1936)); New
Brunswick (Matthias Thórðarson, *The Vinland Voyages* (New York, 1930), and
Íslenzk Fornrit, iv (1933)); Nova Scotia (Storm, *Studier over Vinlandsreiserne*
(Copenhagen, 1887)); southern New England (Haugen, *Voyages to Vinland*
(New York, 1942)); Massachusetts (Fiske, *The Discovery of America*, (Boston,
1892); Arbman, *The Vikings* (1961)); Rhode Island (Rafn, *Antiquitates Ameri-
canæ* (Boston, 1837)); Long Island Sound (Gathorne-Hardy, *The Norse Disco-
verers of America* (1921)); Virginia (Mjelde, followed by Næss, *Hvor lå
Vinland?* (Oslo, 1954)). Reuter's theory of Georgia and Florida (*Germanische
Himmelskunde* (München, 1934)) was never to be taken seriously.

[10] *Vinland Voyages* (St John's, Newfoundland, 1914; repr. 1946).
[11] *De gamla nordbornas Helluland, Markland och Vinland. Ett försök till lok-
alisering ar huvudetnpperna i de isländska Vinlandsagorna,* (Åbo, 1941) and
*Outlines of the Geography, Life and Customs of Newfoundland-Labrador (the
Eastern Part of the Labrador Peninsula)* (Helsinki, 1944).
[12] *Fra Brattahlid til Vinland* (Naturens Verden, Copenhagen, 1961).
[13] *The Discovery of a Norse Settlement in America*, vol. 1, A. S. Ingstad
(Oslo, 1977); vol. 2, H. Ingstad, to appear.

rivets. Three of the buildings were large ones.[14] The artefacts are few and not impressive; there are no human skeletons, no weapons, no conclusive evidence of farming or husbandry, not even a Thor's hammer or a Christian cross. The definitive report of Parks Canada is still awaited, but the whole complex has undergone intensive scrutiny by Canadian, American, and Scandinavian archaeologists and workers in the ancillary disciplines, Indian and Eskimo as well as Norse, and its genuineness is not to be doubted. Patently, such a demonstration of a Norse Viking presence, however sparse or disjointed, in a saga-signposted area of the Promontorium Winlandiæ has a significance far beyond any hoped-for but unrealized identification with any such site as those attributed to Leif Eiriksson or Thorfinn Karlsefni.

In Iceland the Norse settlers found a few papar, and the books, bells, and croziers they left behind them. In Greenland they found the habitations of men, fragments of boats and stone artefacts, but no people. So far in America they had come across a grain-holder when Thorvald's men explored the west coast of Newfoundland, and Thorvald had encountered and brutally handled some Skrælings on the voyage that led to his death. Who were these Skrælings? Indians or Eskimos? Recent investigations suggest that the Norsemen fell foul of both. By the time of the Norse incursion, coastal Labrador and the island of Newfoundland had a long and still not fully charted history of both Indian and Eskimo occupation. The Indians who were dominant throughout Newfoundland about the year AD 1000 were the Ancestral Indians, that is, the ancestors of the tribes known to later European explorers as the Micmacs of New Brunswick, the Montagnais of southern Labrador, and the Beothuks of Newfoundland itself, a people short on witness because they were exterminated by the white man in the early nineteenth century. With their bows and arrows, spears and harpoons, and light, deft birch-bark canoes, and their considerable hunting skills by land and water, they were well equipped to fend off a limited Norse incursion. All three groups spoke an

[14] For a fuller account of the site and the work done there by the Ingstads and later by Parks Canada, see Appendix VII, 'The L'Anse aux Meadows Site', by Birgitta Wallace.

Algonquian language, lived much the same kind of life in small tent-dwelling communities, had a sophisticated knowledge of stone tools, and are often referred to as the Point Revenge Indians because of the distinctive archaeological evidence presented by the site so named.

The other people encountered by the Norsemen, and more particularly along the coasts of northern Labrador, were the Palæo-Eskimos, more often called Dorset Eskimos. Their remoter antecedents, whether in Siberia or Alaska, are not fully clear, but by *c*.2000 BC they had entered large areas of Arctic Canada, and in the course of time would enter Greenland too and leave their traces for Eirik the Red's exploring party towards the end of the tenth century (see pp. 76 and 93 above and p. 148 below), though they had disappeared from the areas of Norse settlement a good while earlier. They had also pressed south to occupy the mountainous tundra of northern Labrador, and had taken over the Ungava coast of Hudson Bay and territories to the west of it. Slowly but surely they dispossessed the Indian inhabitants of most of the Labrador coast to the south, and entered Newfoundland, which remained in their hands till *c*.AD 500, when the Indians took over once more.

That the saga narratives under the general title of Skrælings speak of both Indians and Eskimos, sometimes leaving us in doubt as to which is which, is just what might be expected from saga-men in touch with remote but genuine tradition: there are parallels to this confusion in the journals of rediscovery from the end of the fifteenth century, and on maps of the sixteenth. The Strait of Belle Isle has been a cross-roads during the whole period of which we have record. Norse, Basque, French, English, all have been drawn here, Indian and Eskimo too. Meldgaard in 1954 and 1956 excavated ancient settlements of Dorset Culture Eskimos in Arctic Canada, Labrador, and Newfoundland, and in the latter year dwellings of their contemporary Indian neighbours in the Northwest River area of Lake Melville, with illuminating results for our assessment of Thorvald's and Karlsefni's northern expeditions from Leifsbudir-Straumfjord. Since then the scientists of Canada and the United States have advanced our general knowledge still further. According to *Grænlendinga Saga* Thorvald set off eastward then north from Leifsbudir, reached Kjalarnes, and then turned into the

mouth of the next fjord they came to, Hamilton Inlet, where he
was killed by an arrow. According to *Eiríks Saga Rauða* Thorvald and Karlsefni set off northwards from Straumfjord, passed
Kjalarnes, then bore away west (Hamilton Inlet offering the
only possible entrance), with a forest wilderness to port. When
they had been on their travels for a long time they lay at anchor
by the mouth of a river flowing from east to west, exactly as
English River flows into Lake Melville, where Thorvald was
killed by an arrow. The use of the bow and arrow was unknown
to the Eskimos of this culture and time, so Thorvald was killed
by an Indian arrow, bearing the same kind of arrowhead as was
found in 1930 by Aage Roussell at Sandnes in the Western
Settlement of Greenland, where it had lain in the north-west
corner of the churchyard, and the same kind of arrowhead as
Meldgaard found in the ancient Indian settlement by Northwest
River at the extremity of Lake Melville in 1956. The Sandnes
arrow is pure Indian, made of quartzite identical with the
quartzite of Labrador. It therefore may be regarded as the one
almost indisputable and clinching piece of archaeological evidence of Norse significance from the American continent
before the summer of 1962.[15] Likewise the boats found by

[15] The arrowhead has been newly examined and some refinement suggested
in respect of the quartzite from which it was manufactured (W. Fitzhugh, 'A
Review of Paleo-Eskimo Culture History in Southern Quebec–Labrador and
Newfoundland', *Études Inuit* (1980) 4, pp. 21–31), but it remains an Indian
arrowhead of the period AD 1000–1500. However, Fitzhugh's team of searchers
in the Hamilton Inlet and English River area (reports in the *Bulletin of the Canadian Archaeological Association*, 4 (1972) and 5 (1973)), found no evidence of
Thorvald's journeyings or resting-place in that region 'now heavily grown over
with spruce with a thick forest floor of moss, birch, and alders', a circumstance
in no way surprising, and a salutary reminder of the problems facing the seeker
after genuine Norse remains.
   The 'Maine penny' much in the news of late is a genuine Norwegian coin of
1065–80 found in reputable circumstances and an acceptable archaeological setting in an early Indian site at Goddard Point near the mouth of Penobscot Bay,
Maine. It has been drilled through, presumably for wear as an ornament. The
best opinion (Bourque and Cox, 'Maine State Museum Investigation of the
Goddard Site, 1979', in *Man in the Northeast*, (1981); McGhee, 'Norsemen and
Eskimos in Arctic Canada', in *Vikings in the West*, (1982), and 'Contact
Between Native North Americans, etc.', in *American Antiquity*, (1984)) con-
siders that the coin travelled south not in Norse hands but from the Dorset
Eskimos of northern Labrador by way of northern Indians to the Indians of
Maine.

Thorvald on this expedition were Indian boats. Though they are called 'skin-boats' (*hudkeipa*), they could hardly be Eskimo kayaks.[16] It is the Indians of whom we have plentiful evidence that they slept under their upturned birch-bark canoes. Additional though not over-reliable saga evidence of Indians living, as we suspect they did, inland of the Eskimo-held coastal strip of eastern Labrador will be found in *Eiríks Saga Rauða*'s reference to the white-clad inhabitants of Hvitramannaland, for if this has any meaning at all it must refer to the white chamois or buckskin dancing robes of the Naskaupi. Presumably the Skrælings with whom Karlsefni first traded and later fought at Hop, south of Straumfjord (if we can place any faith at all in the details of so fantasy-ridden an event), were Indians. There was a shower of missiles (*skothrið*), and the Skrælings had 'war-slings' too (*höfdu ok valslöngur, Skrælingar*), whose nature has been much debated. It may have been 'the formidable instrument to which the name of "balista" may be applied', described by Schoolcraft as an Algonquin (Algonquian) weapon in ancient times;[17] or it might be, as Meldgaard suggested, the Eskimo bladder-float harpoon, or harpoon with a blown-up bladder attached, unknown to the Indians, but a main device of

[16] There is no evidence that the Dorset Culture Eskimos had kayaks. Probably they had not. In any case, it is not to be expected that saga tradition two hundred and fifty years later would distinguish clearly, even scientifically, between what the Norsemen over so long a period saw of the Dorset Culture Eskimo in Vinland and the Thule Culture Eskimo in Greenland. Every Eskimo and every Indian was a Skræling.

[17] The following has been many times quoted: 'Algonquin tradition affirms that in ancient times, during the fierce wars which the Indians carried on, they constructed a very formidable instrument of attack, by sewing up a large boulder in a new skin. To this a long handle was tied. When the skin dried it became very tight round the stone, and after being painted with devices assumed the appearance and character of a solid globe upon a pole. This formidable instrument to which the name of 'balista' may be applied, is figured (Plate 15, fig. 2) from the description of an Algonquin chief. It was borne by several warriors who acted as balisteers. Plunged upon a boat or canoe it was capable of sinking it. Brought down upon a group of men on a sudden it produced consternation and death' (H. R. Schoolcraft, *Indian Tribes of the United States*, (1851), i. 85). (For a conflicting view see De Costa, *The Pre-Columbian Discovery of America by the Northmen* (1890), p. 130 n. 3.) The Montagnais and Naskaupi were of Algonquian origin and still speak dialects of the original Algonquian language (Tanner, *Newfoundland–Labrador*, p. 575).

the Dorset folk of the year 1000.[18] Or it may be held to belong
with the bull, the axe, and Freydis's valkyrie-bosom, among the
illusory decorations of a very odd encounter.

[18] *Fra Brattalid til Vinland*, p. 372. It would help here if we could be reasonably sure where Karlsefni's lodgement at Hop took place. It was certainly south
of Straumfjord. Thorhall the Hunter, according to both *Hauksbók* and AM 557,
wished to proceed north from there by way of Furdustrandir and look for Vinland. Straumfjord had not come up to his expectations, with its cold, hungry
winter and absence of wine. He was a skilled and resourceful explorer of empty
places who seems to have been impressed by a land of promise just north of
Kjalarnes—that very Hamilton Inlet which had attracted or was to attract Thorvald and Karlsefni in their turn. But for the present Karlsefni intended to
explore in a southern direction, and more specifically (*Hauksbók*) down the
eastern coast of Promontorium Winlandiæ (according to *Grænlendinga Saga*
Thorvald had already sponsored a probe down its western coast). And so he
did, and came after a good while (*lengi*) to a river mouth and landlocked bay so
protected by sandbars or islands that it was only at full flood they could enter
the river itself. Here they found wild wheat and vines, a hand-harvest of 'holy
fish', and an abundance of many kinds of animals in the forest. And here they
found Skrælings, aborigines, 'natives'. The information supplied by *Hauksbók*
as to where this new encampment might be is not easy to understand, but probably is intended to tell us that Hop lay as far south of Straumfjord as Thorvald's
death-scene (here embellished with rhetoric as derivative as it is pseudo-
heroic—cf. Thormod Coalbrow's-poet's dying words after the battle of Stikla-
stadir, as reported in *Heimskringla*, *Ólafs Saga Helga*, cap. 234) lay north of it.
AM 557, which we must regard as closer to the original than *Hauksbók* is, says
nothing under this head; while for the author of *Grænlendinga Saga* there was
no journey south, therefore no Hop, and Karlsefni's encounter with the Skrælings took place at Leifsbudir, which if we are to identify it with any place in *Eiríks Saga Rauða* should be Straumfjord. Relevant here is the intriguing and
possibly very important sentence in both versions of *Eiríks Saga Rauða* that 'It
is some men's report that Bjarni and Freydis [H. Gudrid] had remained behind
there [i.e. at Straumfjord], and a hundred men with them, and proceeded no
farther, while Karlsefni and Snorri had travelled south with forty men, yet spent
no longer at Hop than a bare two months, and got back again that same summer.' This could be taken as meaning that Karlsefni's expedition to Hop was a
summer voyage of exploration (on the face of it sensible enough), that the
Norsemen did not spend a winter there, and that, as in *Grænlendinga Saga* the
encounter with the Skrælings, including Freydis's folk-magical share in it, took
place at Leifsbudir-Straumfjord. Another seeming witness to confusion in *Eiríks Saga Rauða* is that Karlsefni decides twice to sail for the north, first for
Straumfjord, and then for Greenland, and on each occasion finds five Skrælings
near the coast.

From the many uncertainties two facts emerge, the first that by the time the
two Greenland–Vinland sagas were written down in the form in which we have
them, marked contradictions had developed in the topographical and geographical traditions associated with the areas of settlement, the second that we cannot place Hop on the map, and if we accept *Eiríks Saga Rauða*'s account of
Karlsefni's spending a winter there, it must be with misgiving.

Odd or not, this pitched battle with the warlike Skrælings was decisive for the fate of Karlsefni's attempt to establish a permanent European colony in North America. His numbers were small, and their weapons inadequate. They were unwilling to woo and unable to conquer. So for a start they pulled back from Hop and returned to their base at Straumfjord. Karlsefni, a right-thinking man where any save Skrælings were concerned, considered it his duty to try and find Thorhall the Hunter and his eight or nine comrades, who had gone off dissatisfied in the hope of finding the winy Vinland in the Hamilton Inlet–Lake Melville area. So he undertook the voyage north and west which brought him into fresh collision with the Skrælings. Not wishing to imperil his comrades any further he withdrew to Straumfjord for a third, unhappy winter. The presence of women in the camp led to sour quarrels and deep division, and it must have been with the taste of failure in their mouths that they sailed from Vinland next spring. In their company sailed the infant Snorri, Karlsefni's son, the first known white man to be born in that vast continent—and Bjarni Grimolfsson and his crew, half of whom were to perish miserably on that vast sea.[19]

There would be other voyages to Helluland, Markland, Vinland. Thus, the very next summer after Karlsefni's prudent

[19] The chronology of the Vinland voyages is not strictly determinable, chiefly because *Grænlendinga Saga* and *Eiríks Saga Rauða* tell different stories in a different order, and also because we lack a firm and detailed framework for the first two or three decades of Norse Greenlandic history (see pp. 85–6 above). If we accept the version of events proffered by Ari's *Íslendingabók* and by *Grænlendinga Saga*, then the sequence of voyages begins with Bjarni Herjolfsson's sighting of Labrador and Baffin Island in the summer of 986. It continues with Leif's exploratory voyage, which *Eiríks Saga Rauða* says took place (accidentally at that) in the year 1000, but the saga's evidence here is emphatically to be rejected. Where nothing is susceptible of proof, it would be best to set it five to ten years later, after Bjarni's voyage to Norway and return to Greenland and the subsequent airing of the subject in the Eastern Settlement. Thorvald's voyage, if he made it alone, would follow within a couple of years. Karlsefni's colonizing expedition, the crux of the Vinland venture, could hardly have taken place before 1020 (he was born, we judge, *c*.995), and his subsequent career and what we know of his family history suggest it could not have taken place much after 1025. If we consider that Ari's dating, for patriotic and family reasons, was too quickly off the mark, we would need to move Bjarni's voyage closer to the year 1000, but I express my personal feeling that there is no compelling reason for doing so. See Guðbrandur Vigfússon, *Origines Islandicae* (1905), vol. ii pp. 591–5; G. M. Gathorne-Hardy, *The Norse Discoverers of America* (1921; new edn. 1970), p. 137; and Ólafur Halldórsson, *GríM* (1978), pp. 376–82.

19. KAYAKS AND UMIAK

The nearer kayaker's dress is modern (nineteenth century). Both kayaks carry a
bladder-float harpoon and double-bladed paddle. Large skin-boat (*umiak*) in
the background

withdrawal Eirik's virago of a daughter, the redoubtable
Freydis, made a bloodstained and, one would judge, highly fictionalized journey to Leifsbudir. A century later, in 1121, the
Icelandic Annals record that 'Bishop Eirik of Greenland went
in search of Vinland' (*Konungsannáll*); 'Eirik the Greenlanders' bishop went to look for Vinland' (*Gottskálksannáll*); to
what end and with what success we do not know.[20] Nor do we
know whether he ever returned. The next, and last, reference
to the lands beyond Greenland is from the Annals for 1347.
'There came also a ship from Greenland, smaller in size than
the small Icelandic boats; she came into the outer Straumfjord
[near Budir, on Snæfellsnes], and had no anchor. There were
seventeen men on board. They had made a voyage to Markland, but were afterwards storm-driven here' (*Skálholtsannáll
hinn forni*); 'At this time came a ship from Greenland, which
had made a voyage to Markland, and had eighteen men on
board' (*Flateyjarannáll*). Presumably they had been to Markland to fetch timber, of which the Greenlanders at all times
stood in mortal need, and possibly furs, and but for the accident
of their being driven clean across the sea to Iceland the Annals
of that country would not have mentioned them. Which leaves

[20] The Greenlanders had no bishop before the consecration of Arnald in
1124 (see *Einars Tháttr*, p. 237). Was Eirik a bishop *in partibus infidelium*, sent
to convert the Skrælings?

us to speculate how many successful voyages were made between Greenland and Markland during the preceding three centuries, and whether after the loss of the Western Settlement and the Nordseta towards the middle of the fourteenth century such voyages could ever be undertaken again.

It is tempting to assume that such skilled and intrepid seamen as the Norsemen were till their glory dimmed towards the end of the thirteenth century would have pressed on south of the Promontorium and maybe north of the original landfalls in Baffin Island. Yet nothing we hear of the unsettled parts of Helluland in the 'lying sagas' invites a full trust. Southwards it could well be different, especially if we interpret the phrase 'Promontorium Winlandiæ' as indicating the northern extremity of an undefined area extending south. Maybe after all it was as a result of far-ranging voyages to coasts below the Promontorium that tales of grape-clusters and warm winters enriched the Norse tradition of Vinland; maybe longer voyages and later travellers blurred the outlines of Leif's landing and Karlsefni's settlement. A single archaeological discovery in New Brunswick, Nova Scotia, or the Gulf of St Lawrence (or, be it admitted, even New England) could yet convert theory into fact. For what good reason, one asks, must the area of Sacred Bay be *hið eina sanna Vínland*—'Vinland the one and only'? Yet at present there is no incontrovertible evidence that the Norsemen reached any of these places, much less sailed farther south.[21] Karlsefni had shown that there was nothing south but trouble, and so far as the record goes (and it may not go far enough) his countrymen respected the lesson. In any case, long journeys south would in course of time become impracticable, indeed impossible, if only because the Greenlanders had no ships good enough for the purpose. The ship that came to the outer Straumfjord in 1347 was small by even the degenerate Icelandic standard, and the heart had gone out of Norse seamanship.[22]

[21] But see Appendix VII, pp. 300–1 below, for the mouth of the St Lawrence River and north-east New Brunswick.

[22] The entries in the Icelandic Annals for 1285 concerning the discovery of New Land (*nýja land*) by the priests and brothers Adalbrand and Thorvald, the sons of Helgi; and for 1289, telling how King Eirik Magnusson of Norway sent Land-Rolf (*Landa-Rólfr*) to Iceland to seek New Land, with the confirmaton of 1290 that he did indeed solicit men for the journey; these I have not pursued. They most probably relate to somewhere on the east coast of Greenland.

And by force of circumstance—the unexpected presence or arrival of a native population, the Indian and the Dorset Eskimo in America, the Thule Eskimo in Greenland; the colonists' lack of manpower and a dominant weaponry; climatic change and their long and chancy lines of communication; the fated recession of Norse sea-power; the decline and extinction of their springboard, base, and refuge in Greenland, and the many problems of homeland Scandinavia—by virtue of these and lesser things, the drive had gone out of the Norse progress west. Thus, of the three major Atlantic ventures, Iceland, Greenland, and Vinland–America, only the settlement in Iceland took root and bore fruit. The Greenland colonies perished miserably, and in Wineland the Good the fabled grapes withered on the vine. But all the voyages stand high among the more peaceful Viking battle honours, and it is right for us to mark and honour them as an unforgettable contribution to our common European–American historical heritage, and more widely to the story of human endeavour.

Part Two

THE SOURCES

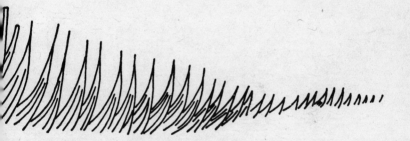

4

The Book of the Icelanders

Íslendingabók or *Libellus Islandorum*

Prologue

THE Book of the Icelanders I composed first for our bishops
Thorlak and Ketil, and showed it both to them and to Sæmund
the priest; and according as it pleased them to have it just as it
was, or augmented, I have written this too, covering the same
ground but omitting the Genealogies and the Lives of the
Kings, while adding to it what has since become better known
to me, and is now more fully related in this version than in that.
But anything that is set down wrongly in this history, it is our
duty to give preference to what is proved to be more correct.

In this book are contained chapters, 1, Of the Settlement of
Iceland; 2, Of the Settlers and Legislation; 3, Of the Establish-
ment of the Althing; 4, Of the Calendar; 5, Of the Division into
Quarters; 6, Of the Settlement of Greenland; 7, Of how Chris-
tianity came to Iceland; 8, Of Foreign Bishops; 9, Of Bishop
Isleif; 10, Of Bishop Gizur.

HERE BEGINS THE BOOK OF THE ICELANDERS

1. *Of the Settlement of Iceland*

Iceland was first settled from Norway in the days of Harald
Fairhair, son of Halfdan the Black, at the time (according to the
belief and count of Teit my tutor, son of bishop Isleif, and the
wisest man I have known; of Thorkel Gellisson, my father's
brother, whose recollection reached far back; and of Thurid
daughter of Snorri Godi, who was at once variously wise and a
trusty informant) when Ivar Ragnar Lodbrok's son had the
English king Saint Edmund put to death; and that was 870 years
after the birth of Christ, according to what is written in his,
Edmund's, saga.

A Norwegian named Ingolf is the man of whom it is reliably reported that he was the first to leave there for Iceland, when Harald Fairhair was sixteen years old, and a second time a few years later. He settled south in Reykjavik. The place is called Ingolfshofdi, east of Minnthakseyr, where he made his first landing, and Ingolfsfell, west of Olfus river, where he afterwards took land into his possession. At that time Iceland was covered with forest between mountain and seashore.

There were Christian men here then whom the Norsemen call 'papar'. But later they went away because they were not prepared to live here in company with heathen men. They left behind Irish books, bells, and croziers, from which it could be seen that they were Irishmen.

Then came a great movement of men out here from Norway, till King Harald set a ban on it, because he thought Norway would grow depopulated. They reached this agreement, that every man who was not exempted and should leave there for here must pay the king five ounces. It is said too that Harald was king for seventy years, and lived to be eighty years old. These were the origins of that tax which is now called land-ounces; at times more was paid, at times less, till Olaf Digri laid down that everyone who made the journey between Norway and Iceland should pay the king half a mark, except for women-folk and such men as he exempted. So Thorkel Gellisson informed us.

2.   Of the Settlers and Legislation

Hrollaug, son of earl Rognvald of Mœr, settled east in Sida; whence are come the Men of Sida.

Ketilbjorn Ketilsson, a Norwegian, settled south at the Upper Mosfell; whence are come the Men of Mosfell.

Aud, daughter of Ketil Flatnose, a lord in Norway, settled west in Breidafjord; whence are come the Men of Breidafjord.

Helgi Magri, a Norwegian, son of Eyvind Eastman, settled north in Eyjafjord; whence are come the Men of Eyjafjord.

And when Iceland had become settled far and wide a Norwegian named Ulfljot first brought law out here from Norway (so Teit told us); this was called Ulfljot's Law. He was the father of that Gunnar from whom the Djupadalers are descended in Eyjafjord. For the most part these laws were modelled upon the then Gulathing Law, on the advice of Thorleif the Wise, Horda-Kari's son, as to what should be added, taken away, or be differently set out. Ulfljot lived east in Lon. It is said that Grim Geitskor was his foster-brother, he who at Ulfljot's direction explored the whole of Iceland before the Althing was established. For this, every man in the land gave him a penny, which he later donated to the temples.

3. *The Establishment of the Althing*

The Althing was established where it now is at the instance of Ulfljot and all the people of Iceland; but before this there had been a Thing at Kjalarnes, which Thorstein, son of Ingolf the Settler, and father of Thorkel Mani the Lawspeaker, held there together with those chieftains who allied themselves with it. But a man who owned the land at Blaskogar had been outlawed for the murder of a thrall or freedman. His name is given as Thorir Cropbeard, and his daughter's son was called Thorvald Cropbeard, the one who later went to the Eastfirths and there burned his own brother Gunnar to death in his house (so Hall Orækjuson told us). The name of the murdered man was Kol, from whom that ravine gets its name which has ever since been called Kolsgja, where the corpse was discovered. The land thereafter became public domain, and the Icelandic people set it apart for the use of the Althing, for which reason wood can be cut free for the Althing in the forests there, and on the heath there is common pasture for the use of the horses. This Ulfhedin told us.

Wise men have said too that in the space of sixty years Iceland was fully occupied, so that after that there was no further taking of land. About then Hrafn, son of Hœng the Settler, took the lawspeakership next after Ulfljot and held it for twenty summers [930–49]. He was from Rangarhverfi. This was sixty years after the slaughter of king Edmund, and a winter or two before king Harald Fairhair died, according to the reckoning of well-informed men. Thorarin, brother of Ragi and son of Oleif Hjalti, took the lawspeakership next after Hrafn and held it a further twenty summers [950–69]. He was a Borgarfjord man.

4. *Of the Calendar*

It was at this same time, when the wisest men here in the land
had been counting 364 days in the two alternating seasons of the
year (which means 52 weeks, or twelve months of thirty days
apiece, plus four days over), that men noticed by the course of
the sun how the summer was moving backwards into the spring.
But no one could enlighten them how in a full year there is one
day over and beyond the full count of weeks—which was the
cause of this. There was, however, a man by the name of Thorstein Surt, a Breidafjord man, son of Hallstein the son of Thorolf Mostrarskegg the Settler and of Osk, daughter of Thorstein
the Red, who had a dream, and imagined he found himself at
the Law Rock when there was a great congregation there, and
he was awake, whereas all the rest, he imagined, were asleep;
but afterwards he imagined himself asleep, and all the rest, as
he thought, grew awake. This dream Osvif Helgason, the
maternal grandfather of Gellir Thorkelsson, interpreted thus,
that all men should be silent while he spoke at the Law Rock,
but once he himself fell silent they would all applaud what he
had said. These two were both very shrewd men. So later on,
when men came to the Thing, he proposed this motion at the
Law Rock, that every seventh summer a week should be added
on, and see how it worked. And exactly as Osvif had interpreted the dream, everybody woke up to the implications of
this, and it was immediately made law by the counsel of Thorkel
Mani and other wise men.

By true reckoning there are 365 days in each and every year,
if it is not leap-year, when there is one day more; but by our
reckoning there are 364. So when by our reckoning there is an
addition made of one week to every seventh year, but nothing
added by the other reckoning, then seven years will prove of
equal length by either reckoning. But should two leap-years
occur between the years which must be added to, then it
becomes necessary to make the addition to the sixth year.

5. *Of the Division into Quarters*

A great lawsuit arose at the Thing between Thord Gellir, son of
Oleif Feilan from Breidafjord, and that Odd who was known as

I. A VIKING

2. NORSE TOOLS
Anvil, tongs, rasp, shears, hammer-head, and nail-block of iron

3. NORSE WEAPONS
Swords, axe-heads, spears, shield, and helmet

4. THE OSEBERG SHIP IN ITS MOUND
The carved stern seen from the port side

5. THE VALTHJÓFSSTAÐIR DOOR

Probably the door of a chieftain's hall, later used as a church door. The lower circular field (not illustrated here) contains a device of four interlacing dragons. The upper circular field shows three scenes from the story of 'Le Chevalier au Lion': the knight on horseback saves the lion from a dragon (*below*); the lion accompanies the knight; the lion mourns on the knight's tomb. The runic inscription may be translated: '[Behold] the burial place of the mighty king who slew this dragon.'

6. HVALSEY, GREENLAND

The Church, c. 1300, is to the left, and the Great Hall right. In between are the farm buildings, and in the foreground is the enclosure.

7. HVALSEY: THE OLD HALL

Looking west to the Great Hall. On the right the gravel bench inside the rear wall, in the middle the long fire-trench and ember-pit, on the left the south row of post holes. Measurements: 14×4 metres

8. THE CATHEDRAL, GARDAR (IGALIKO)

The Cathedral ruins are in the foreground. Behind stand houses of modern Greenlanders, constructed in large measure of stones taken from the ruins.

9. DORSET ESKIMO

10. KAVDLUNAK (NORSE GREENLANDER)

I I . THE GOKSTAD SHIP

12. KJALARNES AND FURDUSTRANDIR
Cape Porcupine and the Strand on the coast of Labrador

13. THINGVELLIR, ICELAND

14. THE HOLY MAN OF FLATATUNGA
A mid-eleventh century representation of an Icelandic scholar, priest, or saint

15. THOR

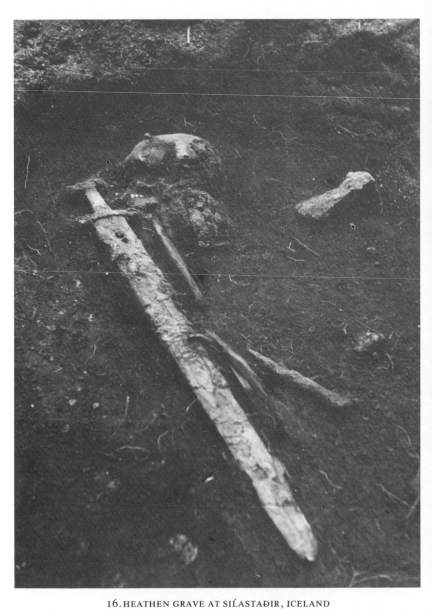

16. HEATHEN GRAVE AT SILASTAÐIR, ICELAND

A man's bones with axe, sword, shield boss (the shield had been placed to cover his head),
knife, weights, and (out of the picture) a spear and the skeletons of two horses

17. FLATEYJARBÓK

Part of col. 283. The passage begins with Leif's 'Is that the truth, foster-father . . .?', concerning Tyrkir's claim to have discovered vines and grapes, and ends with Thorvald's decision to go to Vinland

18. THE HEGGEN VANE
Before serving as a church
weather-vane, this arrow-
scarred, bronze-gilt
standard had adorned a
fighting ship at sea.
Karlsefni's wooden
húsasnotra was probably an
object of this kind

19. THE VINLAND VOYAGE, I

Leaving Brattahlid. View down Eiriksfjord (Tunugdliarfik)

20. THE VINLAND VOYAGE, 2

Promontorium Winlandiæ. Cape Bauld, the northern extremity of Newfoundland, seen from the Strait of Belle Isle. In the distance (*right*) may be glimpsed the first area of settlement. Leif, Thorvald, and Karlsefni all came this way

21. DRANGAR, EIRIK THE RED'S FIRST HOME IN ICELAND

22. BRATTAHLID, EIRIK THE RED'S HOME IN GREENLAND

The stone walls in the foreground are those of the third, early thirteenth-century church

23. CHRISTIAN GRAVE AT SANDNES, GREENLAND

The skeletons of a man, woman, and child, with a small wooden cross between them. Parts of a fourth, superimposed, skeleton are also visible

24. SWORDS

The Viking's chief weapon. *Left*, beautiful and deadly, the Lodingen sword, from Lofoten, Norway

25. THE SANDNES CHRIST

26. L'ANSE AUX MEADOWS. PICTORIAL VIEW

27. L'ANSE AUX MEADOWS. HOUSE D

28. L'ANSE AUX MEADOWS.
RECONSTRUCTED COMPLEX,
HOUSES A–B–C, AT THE
TIME OF THE NORSE
OCCUPATION

29. L'ANSE AUX MEADOWS.
MIDDEN. SPRUCE ROOT
ROPES

Tungu-Odd, a Borgarfjord man. Odd's son Thorvald had taken part with Hen-Thorir in the burning to death of Thorkel Blund-Ketilsson in Ornolfsdal. But Thord Gellir came to lead in the suit because Herstein, son of Thorkel Blund-Ketilsson, was married to his niece Thorunn, the daughter of Helga and Gunnar and sister to Jofrid, the wife of Thorstein Egilsson. They were prosecuted at the Thing which used to be in Borgarfjord, at the place since called Thingnes; for it was then the law that suits for manslaughter must be prosecuted at the Thing which was nearest to the spot where the manslaughter had taken place. But they came to blows there, and the Thing could not be carried on by law. Thorolf Fox, brother of Alf of Dalir, fell there from Thord Gellir's party. So later they carried their suits to the Althing, where once again they came to blows. This time men fell from Odd's party, and in addition Hen-Thorir was outlawed and later killed, together with others too who were at the burning.

Then Thord Gellir made a speech about this at the Law Rock, what a disadvantage it was for men to have to travel to strange Things to bring a case for manslaughter or for hurt to themselves; and he recounted what had happened to him before he could bring this case to law, arguing that many would run into trouble in their turn unless a remedy was found.

The land was then divided into Quarters, so that there were three Things in each Quarter, and men of the same Thing must hold their lawsuits together; save that in the Northerners' Quarter there were four, because they could not reach any other agreement (the men who lived north of Eyjafjord were not prepared to attend the Thing there, while those who lived to the west there would not attend at Skagafjord). Still, the nomination of judges and the constitution of the Logretta should be the same from this Quarter as from any other. But later the Quarter Things were established, as Ulfhedin Gunnarsson the Lawspeaker told us.

Thorkel Mani, son of Thorstein Ingolfsson, took the lawspeakership after Thorarin the brother of Ragi, and held it for fifteen summers [970–84]. Then Thorgeir Thorkelsson of Ljosavatn held it for seventeen summers [985–1001].

6. *Of the Settlement of Greenland*

The land which is called Greenland was discovered and settled from Iceland. Eirik the Red was the name of a Breidafjord man who went out there from here and took land in settlement at the place which has ever since been called Eiriksfjord. He gave the land a name, and called it Greenland, arguing that men would be drawn to go there if the land had a good name. Both east and west in the country [i.e. at both the Eastern and Western Settlements] they found the habitations of men, fragments of boats [? of skin, *keiplabrot*], and stone artefacts, from which it may be seen that the same kind of people had passed that way as those that inhabited Vinland, whom the Greenlanders call Skrælings. When he began to settle the land, that was fourteen or fifteen years before Christianity came to Iceland [i.e. 985 or 986], according to what a man who had himself gone out with Eirik the Red told Thorkel Gellisson in Greenland.

7. *Of how Christianity came to Iceland*

King Olaf Tryggvason (Tryggvi the son of Olaf, the son of Harald Fairhair) introduced Christianity into Norway and into Iceland. To this country he sent a priest whose name was Thangbrand, who taught men Christianity and baptized all who embraced the faith. For Hall Thorsteinsson of Sida had himself baptized early, and likewise Hjalti Skeggjason from Thjorsardal, and Gizur the White, the son of Teit, the son of Ketilbjorn of Mosfell, and many other chieftains. But they were the majority even so who opposed and rejected it. When he had been in Iceland a year or two he took himself off, having been the death of two or three men here who had lampooned him. And when he returned to Norway he informed king Olaf of all that had happened to him, declaring it a thing past hoping for that Christianity should be accepted here, at which the king grew very angry, and proposed as a consequence to have those of our countrymen who were over in Norway maimed or killed. But that same summer Gizur and Hjalti arrived there from Iceland and persuaded the king to let them off, promising him their help in a fresh attempt to get Christianity even yet adopted here, and affirming their conviction that it would be successful.

The following summer they left Norway, together with a priest by the name of Thormod, and arrived in the Vestmanna-eyjar when ten weeks of summer were past, having had an excellent passage. Teit said he was told this by a man who was present there himself. It had been made law the summer before this that people should come to the Althing when ten weeks of summer were past, whereas until then they used to come a week earlier. Gizur and his men proceeded to the mainland without delay, and then to the Althing, but they persuaded Hjalti to stay behind in Laugardal with eleven men, because he had already been convicted a lesser outlaw the summer before at the Althing for blasphemy. This came about because he spoke this little ditty at the Law Rock:

> The gods I'd not blaspheme:
> Yet bitch I Freyja deem.

Gizur and his men went on their way till they reached a place called Vellankatla, by Olfusvatn, and from there sent word to the Althing that all their supporters should come and meet them, for they had already heard tell how their adversaries meant to bar them from the Thingfield by force of arms. But before they moved off from there, Hjalti came riding in along with those who had stayed behind with him. They then rode on to the Thing, and their kinsmen and friends had already come to join them, just as they had requested. But the heathen men gathered together, armed to the teeth, and it came so near to a fight that there was just no saying how things would go.

The next day Gizur and Hjalti went to the Law Rock and made known their message, and report has it it was remarkable how well they spoke. And what followed from this was that one man after another, Christian and heathen, called witnesses, each swearing that he would not live under the same laws as the other, after which they left the Law Rock.

Then the Christians requested Hall of Sida that he should proclaim that law which was right and proper for Christians; but he got out of this, in that he made payment to Thorgeir the Lawspeaker that he should proclaim the law—even though he was still a heathen. And later when men had returned to their booths, Thorgeir lay down and spread his cloak over him, and lay quiet all that day and the night following, and spoke never a word. But the next morning he sat up and announced that men should proceed to the Law Rock. And once men had made their way there he began his speech. The affairs of the people, he said, would be in sorry plight if men were not to have one law, all of them, in this land; and he put this to men in many ways, how they must never let such a state of affairs come about, maintaining that strife would be the result, so that it could be taken as certain that such contention would arise among men that the land would be laid waste by reason of it. He related how the kings of Norway and Denmark had carried on war and battles between them for a long time till the people of those countries made peace between them, even though they themselves did not want it. And that policy answered so well that in no time at all they were sending each other precious gifts, and peace was maintained for the rest of their lives. 'And now,' he added, 'I think it policy that we do not let those prevail who are most anxious to be at each other's throats, but reach such a compromise in these matters that each shall win part of his case, and let all have one law and one faith. It will prove true, if we break the law in pieces, that we break the peace in pieces too.' And he so concluded his speech that both sides agreed that all should have that one law which he would proclaim.

Then it was made law that all men should be Christians, and be baptized, those who so far were unbaptized here in Iceland.[1] But as for the exposure of infants the old laws should stand, and for the eating of horse-flesh too. Men might sacrifice in secret if they so wished, but it would be a case for lesser outlawry should witnesses come forward. But a few years later this heathendom was abolished like the rest. This was the way, Teit told us, that Christianity came to Iceland.

And this summer, according to what Sæmund the priest relates, King Olaf Tryggvason fell. He was fighting then against Svein Haraldsson, king of the Danes, and Olaf the Swede, son of Eirik king of the Swedes at Uppsala, and Eirik Hakonarson who later was earl of Norway. That was 130 years after the

---

[1] *Kristni Saga* adds the pleasant detail that all men of the North and South Quarters, and most of the West Quarter men, were baptized at the hot springs, 'because they had no wish to enter cold water'.

slaughter of Edmund, and 1,000 after the birth of Christ, according to the general count.

8. *Of Foreign Bishops*

These are the names of the foreign bishops that have been in Iceland, according to Teit's account. Fridrek came here in heathen times, while these were here later: Bjarnhard the Bookwise, five years; Kol, a few years; Hrodolf, nineteen years; Johan the Irish, a few years; Bjarnhard, nineteen years; Heinrek, two years. And yet another five came here who styled themselves bishops: Ornolf and Godiskalk, and three Armenians [?*ermskir*], Petrus, Abraham, and Stephanus.

Grim Svertingson of Mosfell took the lawspeakership after Thorgeir and held it two summers [1002–3], when he got permission for his nephew Skapti Thoroddsson, his sister's son, to have it, because he himself was hoarse of speech. Skapti held the lawspeakership twenty-seven summers [1004–30]; it was he who established the constitution of the Fifth Court, and this in addition, that no manslayer should make legal declaration of a slaying against any person other than himself, whereas until then the same law in respect of that applied here as in Norway. In his day many chieftains and great men were outlawed or exiled for manslaying or assault by virtue of his power and authority. He died the same year Olaf Digri fell (the son of Harald, son of Gudrod, son of Bjorn, son of Harald Fairhair), thirty years after Olaf Tryggvason fell; whereupon Stein Thorgestsson took the lawspeakership and held it for three summers [1031–3]. Then Thorkel Tjorvason held it twenty summers [1034–53]; then Gellir Bolverksson for nine summers [1054–62].

9. *Of Bishop Isleif*

Isleif, son of Gizur the White, was consecrated bishop in the time of King Harald of Norway (the son of Sigurd, son of Halfdan, son of Sigurd Hrisi, son of Harald Fairhair). And once the chieftains and good men saw how Isleif was a man altogether more able than those other clerics who were to be found here in the land, many gave him their sons to teach, and had them ordained as priests; of whom two were afterwards consecrated bishops: Kol, who lived in Vik in Norway, and Jon of Holar.

Isleif had three sons, who were all able chieftains: bishop Gizur, Teit the priest, father of Hall, and Thorvald. Teit was brought up by Hall [Thorarinsson] in Haukadal, the man who by universal report was the most generous and magnanimous of lay-men here in Iceland. And I too came to Hall, when seven years old, the winter after Gellir Thorkelsson, my father's father and my fosterer, died; and there I lived for fourteen years.

Gunnar the Wise had taken the lawspeakership when Gellir [Bolverksson] relinquished it, and held it for three summers [1063–5]; then Kolbein Flosason held it for six [1066–71]; the summer he took the lawspeakership King Harald fell in Eng-land. Then Gellir held it a second time, for three summers [1072–4]; then Gunnar held it a second time, for one summer [1075]; whereupon Kolbein's nephew Sighvat Surtsson held it for eight [1076–83]. In those days Sæmund Sigfusson came to Iceland from down south, from France, and had himself ordained priest.

Isleif was consecrated bishop when he was fifty; Leo the Ninth was Pope at the time. The next winter he spent in Nor-way, and came out here thereafter. He died at Skalholt, after he had been bishop for twenty-four years (so Teit told us): this was on the Lord's Day, six nights after the Feast of Peter and Paul, and eighty years after the fall of Olaf Tryggvason [i.e. 6 July 1080]. I was there at the time with Teit my tutor, and was twelve years old.

But Hall, who was of good memory and truthful and remem-bered when he was baptized, told us this, that Thangbrand bap-tized him at the age of three—which was one year before Christianity was established here by law. He set up housekeep-ing at the age of thirty, lived at Haukadal for sixty-four years, and was ninety-four years old when he died—which was on the Feast of Bishop Martin, the tenth winter after the death of bishop Isleif [11 November 1089].

10. *Of Bishop Gizur*

Bishop Gizur, son of Isleif, was consecrated bishop at the prayer of his fellow-countrymen in the days of King Olaf

Haraldsson, two years after the death of bishop Isleif. One of these years he spent here in Iceland, the other in Gautland. And his right name then was Gisrod, so he told us.

Markus Skeggjasson held the lawspeakership next after Sighvat, taking it up that summer when bishop Gizur had been just one year here in the land, and holding office for twenty-four years [1084–1107]. From his relation are written in this book the periods of office of all the lawspeakers who lived too early for our own memory; but his brother Thorarin, and Skeggi their father, and other wise men informed him as to the periods of those who lived too early for his memory, in accordance with what their paternal grandfather Bjarni the Wise had told them, who remembered Thorarin the Lawspeaker together with six of his successors.

Bishop Gizur was better loved by the whole populace than any other man of whom we have knowledge here in Iceland. By reason of the affection he was held in, the persuasion of himself and Sæmund, and the counsel of Markus the Lawspeaker, it was made law that all men should count and evaluate their entire property, then swear that it was valued correctly, whether it was in land or chattels, and then give tithes thereof. It is a powerful token of how obedient the population was to this man that he could bring it about that all the property then existing in Iceland was valued under oath, tithes apportioned therefrom, and a law passed that this shall hold good as long as Iceland is inhabited.

Bishop Gizur also had it laid down as law that the see of the bishop that was in Iceland should be at Skalholt, whereas before it had been nowhere; and he endowed the see with the land at Skalholt and further riches of many kinds, both in land and chattels. And when he thought this establishment had prospered well in the matter of its wealth, he gave away more than one-fourth of his diocese to this end, that there might be two bishops' sees in the country, as the Northlanders requested of him, rather than one. But first he had a count made of all the franklins in Iceland. In the Eastfirthers' Quarter they were 840, and in the Rangriver Men's [Southern] Quarter 1,200; in the Breidafirthers' [Western] Quarter 1,080, and in the Eyjafirthers' [Northern] Quarter 1,440. But there was no count made of men who were not subject to Thingfaring tax throughout the whole of Iceland.

Ulfhedin, son of Gunnar the Wise, took the lawspeakership after Markus and held it nine summers [1108–16]; then Bergthor Hrafnsson held it for six [1117–22]; and then Gudmund Thorgeirsson held it for twelve summers [1123–34]. The first summer Bergthor recited the law there was this innovation made, that our law should be committed to writing at Haflidi Masson's house the following winter, at the dictation and under the surveillance of Haflidi and Bergthor and such other wise men as were appointed for the purpose. They were to make all such new provisions in the law as appeared to them to be improvements on the old, and these were to be announced the following summer in the Logretta, and all of them which were not then opposed by the majority should be adopted. So what happened was that the Manslaughter Section and many other portions of law were committed to writing and recited by clerics in the Logretta that following summer. And all were well pleased with it, and not a soul spoke against it.

It happened further, that first summer Bergthor recited the law, that bishop Gizur failed to attend the Thing because of an illness. He sent word to the Althing, to his friends and the chieftains, that they should pray Thorlak, son of Runolf, the son of Thorleik, the brother of Hall of Haukadal, to let himself be consecrated bishop. Without exception they acted upon his instruction, and the thing came about, because Gizur himself had pressed for it so strongly. Thorlak went abroad that summer, and returned the summer after, and was then consecrated bishop.

Gizur was consecrated bishop when he was forty. Gregory the Seventh was Pope at the time. He spent the winter after that in Denmark, and the following summer returned here to Iceland. When he had been bishop for twenty-four years, like his father before him, then Jon Ogmundarson was consecrated bishop, the first to the see of Holar. He was then fifty-four years old. Twelve years later, when Gizur had been a bishop for thirty-six years all told, Thorlak was consecrated bishop. Gizur had him consecrated to the see of Skalholt in his own lifetime. Thorlak was then twenty-eight years old. And bishop Gizur died thirty nights later at Skalholt, on the third day of the week, the fifth of the kalends of June [28 May 1118].

In that same year died Pope Paschalis the Second, earlier than bishop Gizur, and Baldwin king of Jerusalem, and Arnald patriarch of Jerusalem, and Philip king of the Swedes; and later that same summer Alexius king of the Greeks died, after he had occupied the throne of Constantinople for thirty-eight years. Two years later there was a change of lunar cycle. By then Eystein and Sigurd had been for seventeen years kings in Norway, in succession to their father Magnus, son of Olaf Haraldsson. This was 120 years after the fall of Olaf Tryggvason, 250 after the slaughter of Edmund king of the English, and 516 years after the death of Pope Gregory, who it is recorded introduced Christianity into England. He died in the second year of the reign of the emperor Phocas, 604 years after the birth of Christ, according to the general count. Which makes 1,120 years in all.

Here this book ends.

Appendix

This is the kindred and genealogy of the bishops of the Icelanders:

Ketilbjorn the settler who settled south at the Upper Mosfell was father of Teit, father of Gizur the White, father of Isleif who was the first bishop of Skalholt, father of bishop Gizur.

Hrollaug the settler who settled east in Sida, at Breidabolstad, was father of Ozur, father of Thordis, mother of Hall of Sida, father of Egil, father of Thorgerd, mother of Jon, who was the first bishop of Holar.

Aud the settler who settled west in Breidafjord, at Hvamm, was mother of Thorstein the Red, father of Olaf Feilan, father of Thord Gellir, father of Thorhild Rjupa, mother of Thord Horse-head, father of Karlsefni, father of Snorri, father of Hallfrid, mother of Thorlak, who is now bishop of Skalholt in succession to Gizur.

Helgi Magri the settler who settled north in Eyjafjord, at Kristnes, was father of Helga, mother of Einar, father of Eyjolf Valgerdarson, father of Gudmund, father of Eyjolf, father of Thorstein, father of Ketil, who is now bishop of Holar in succession to Jon.

5

The Book of the Settlements

Landnámabók

1. *Iceland*

[S. 1–2] In the book *De Ratione Temporum* which the Venerable Bede composed, there is mention of an island which is called Thile, of which books record that it lies six days' sail north of Britain. There, said he, there came no day in winter, and no night in summer when the day is at its longest. The reason scholars believe that Iceland is called Thile is because over much of the country the sun shines all night when the day is at its longest, and then again over much of it the sun is not seen by day when the night is at its longest.

Now according to what is written, Bede the priest died 735 years after the Incarnation of our Lord, and more than a hundred years before Iceland was settled by Norse men. But before Iceland was settled from Norway, there were men there whom the Norse men style 'papar'. These were Christians, and people consider that they must have been from the British Isles, because there were found left behind them Irish books, bells, and croziers, and other things besides, from which it might be deduced that they were Vestmenn, Irishmen. [H. *adds* These things were found east in Papey and in Papyli.] It is recorded in English books that at that time there was trafficking to and fro between those countries.

When Iceland was discovered and settled from Norway, Adrian was pope in Rome, and after him John, who was the fifth of that name in the apostolic seat; Louis son of Louis was emperor north of the Alps, and Leo and Alexander his son over Byzantium. Harald Fairhair was king of Norway; Eirik Eymundarson king of Sweden, and Bjorn his son; and Gorm the Old was king of Denmark. Alfred the Great was king of England, and Edward his son; Kjarval in Dublin, and earl Sigurd the Mighty in Orkney.

Learned men state that from Stad in Norway it is seven days' sail west to Horn in the east of Iceland; and from Snæfellsnes, where the distance is shortest, it is four days' sea west to Greenland. And it is said if one sails from Bergen due west to Hvarf in Greenland that one's course will lie some seventy or more miles south of Iceland. [H. From Hernar in Norway one must sail a direct course west to Hvarf in Greenland, in which case one sails north of Shetland so that one sights land in clear weather only, then south of the Faeroes so that the sea looks half-way up the mountainsides, then south of Iceland so that one gets sight of birds and whales from there.] From Reykjanes in the south of Iceland there is five days' sea to Jolduhlaup in Ireland [H. *adds* in the south; and from Langanes in the north of Iceland] it is four days' sea north to Svalbard in the Polar Gulf. [H. *adds* And it is a day's sail to the unlived-in parts of Greenland from Kolbeinsey (*i.e.* Mevenklint) in the north.]

2. *The Discoverers*

[*Sturlubók* version, 3–5] It is reported that men had a voyage to make from Norway to the Faeroes: some make mention in this connection of Naddod the Viking. But they were storm-driven into the western ocean and discovered a big country there. In the Eastfirths they walked up on to a high mountain and had a good look all round, whether they would be able to see smoke or some sign that the land was inhabited, but saw nothing. In the autumn they returned to the Faeroes. As they sailed away there was a heavy snowfall on the mountains, for which reason they called the land Snæland, Snowland. They praised the land highly. The place they had come to is now known as Reydarfjall in the Eastfirths. So said priest Sæmund the Learned.

There was a man named Gardar Svavarsson, a Swede by descent: he set off to find Snæland at the direction of his mother, a seeress. He reached land east of the Eastern Horn, where in those days there was a haven. Gardar sailed round the land and found that it was an island. He spent the winter north at Husavik in Skjalfandi, and built a house there. In the spring, when he was ready for sea, their boat was torn adrift with a man named Nattfari on board, together with a thrall and a bondwoman. He made a home at the place since called Nattfaravik, but Gardar returned to Norway and praised the land highly. He was the father of Uni, father of Hroar Tungu-godi. After this the land was called Gardarsholm: there was forest growing then between mountain and seashore.

There was a man named Floki Vilgerdarson, a great Viking. He set off to find Gardarsholm and sailed from the place now known as Flokavardi, at the junction of Hordaland and Roga-land. But first he made for Shetland, and lay at anchor there in Flokavag: his daughter Geirhild lost her life there in Geir-hildarvatn. On board ship with Floki was a franklin named Thorolf and another named Herjolf, while there was also a Hebridean on board by the name of Faxi. Floki had taken three ravens to sea with him. When he loosed the first, it flew aft astern; the second flew high into the air, then back to the ship; the third flew straight ahead in the direction in which they found land. They made Horn from the east and sailed along the south coast. As they sailed west round Reykjanes and the fjord opened out before them so that they could see Snæfellsnes, 'This must be a big country we have found,' said Faxi. 'There are big rivers here!' Ever since it has been called Faxaos, Faxi's Estuary. Floki and his crew sailed west across Breidafjord and made land at what is now called Vatnsfjord, by Bardarstrand. The fjord was full of fish and seals, and because of the fishing they overlooked the need to make hay, and all their livestock perished during the winter. The spring was very cold. Floki walked up on to a high mountain, and north beyond the mountain could see a fjord full of drift ice, so they called the country Ísland, Iceland, the name by which it has been known ever since. Floki and his followers were determined to get away that summer, but completed their preparations to leave only a short while before winter. They failed to make their way round Reykjanes, their boat was torn adrift with Herjolf on board, who got ashore at what is now called Herjolfshofn. Floki spent the winter in Borgarfjord, where they found Herjolf, and next summer they sailed for Norway. When men inquired about the country, Floki gave it a bad name, Herjolf had both good and bad to say of it, while Thorolf swore that butter dripped from every blade of grass in that land they had found, for which reason he was nicknamed Thorolf Butter.

[*Hauksbók* version, 3–5] There was a man named Gardar, son of Svavar the Swede; he owned estates in Seeland but had been born in Sweden. He made a journey to the Hebrides to claim his wife's inheritance from her father, but as he was sailing through the Pentland Firth a gale drove him off course, and he was carried into the western ocean. He reached land east of Horn. Gardar sailed round the land and found that it was an island. He came to a fjord which he called Skjalfandi, put out a boat there, and his thrall Nattfari went aboard. The mooring-line broke, and he came ashore at Nattfaravik, away beyond Skuggabjorg. Gardar, though, made land the other side of the fjord and spent the winter there, which was why he called it Husavik, House Bay. Nattfari stayed behind with his thrall and bondwoman, which is why the place is called Nattfaravik;[1] but Gardar sailed back east and praised the land highly and called it Gardarsholm.

There was a man named Naddod, the brother of Oxen-Thorir, and a relation by marriage of Olvir Barnakarl. He was a great Viking, who went off to make a home for himself in the Faeroes for the good reason that he had nowhere else where he would be safe. He left Norway with the Isles in mind, but was sea-tossed to Gardarsholm, where he arrived at Reydarfjord in the Eastfirths. They walked up on to a very high mountain to find whether they could see any human habitation or smoke, but saw never a sign. As they sailed away, there was a heavy snowfall, for which reason he called it Snæland, Snowland. They praised the land highly.

There was a great Viking by the name of Floki Vilgerdarson who set out from Rogaland to seek Snæland. They lay in Smjorsund. He offered up a big sacrifice and hallowed three ravens which were to guide him on his way, for in those days sailors in the Northlands had no loadstone. They built a cairn where the sacrifice had been made and called it Flokuvardi—it is at the junction of Hordaland and Rogaland. But first he made for Shetland, and lay at anchor there in Flokavag: his daughter Geirhild lost her life there in Geirhildarvatn. On board ship

---

[1] But *Landn*. S. 247 says further: 'Nattfari, who had come out with Gardar, owned Reykjadal earlier and had marked the trees; but Eyvind Askelsson drove him away and let him have Nattfaravik.'

with Floki was a franklin named Thorolf, another named Herjolf, and Faxi, a Hebridean. From Shetland Floki sailed to the
Faeroes, where he found a husband for that daughter of his
from whom Thrond of Gata is descended. From there he sailed
out to sea with the three ravens he had hallowed in Norway.
When he loosed the first, it flew aft astern; the second flew
high into the air, then back to the ship; the third flew straight
ahead in the direction in which they found land. They made
Horn from the east and sailed along the south coast. As they
sailed west round Reykjanes and the fjord opened out before
them so that they could see Snæfellsnes, 'This must be a big
country we have found,' said Faxi. 'There are big rivers here!'
Ever since it has been called Faxaos. Floki and his crew sailed
west across Breidafjord and made land at what is now called
Vatnsfjord, by Bardarstrand. The entire fjord was full of fish
and seals, and because of the fishing they overlooked the need
to make hay, and their livestock perished during the winter.
The spring was very cold. Floki walked north to a mountain
and saw a fjord full of drift ice, so they called the country Iceland. They went away that summer, but were late with their
preparations. The site of their hall is still to be seen east of
Brjanslœk, likewise their boat-house and fire-pit. They failed
to make their way round Reykjanes, their boat was torn adrift
with Herjolf on board, who got ashore at Herjolfshofn. Floki
got ashore in Borgarfjord; they found a whale on a bank west
of the fjord, so called it Hvaleyr; and there they found Herjolf.
Next summer they sailed for Norway. Floki gave the land a bad
name, Herjolf had both good and bad to say of it, while Thorolf swore that butter dripped from every blade of grass in that
land they had found, for which reason he was nicknamed Thorolf Butter.

3. *The Settlers*

Ingolf and Hjorleif

[S. 6–9] There was a man named Bjornolf, and another
Hroald: they were the sons of Hromund Gripsson. They left
Telemark because of some killings and made their home at
Dalsfjord in Fjalir. The son of Bjornolf was Orn, the father of

Ingolf and Helga, while the son of Hroald was Hrodmar, the father of Leif.

The foster-brothers Ingolf and Leif went on viking cruises with the sons of earl Atli the Slender of Gaular, Hastein, Herstein, and Holmstein. All their activities together turned out well, and when they returned home they arranged to make an expedition together the next summer. That winter the foster-brothers made a feast for the earl's sons, and at this feast Holmstein made a vow that he would marry Orn's daughter Helga or no woman at all. This vow of his got a poor reception; Leif turned red, and there was little love lost between him and Holmstein when they parted at the feast.

Next spring the foster-brothers made ready to go off harrying: they planned a meeting with earl Atli's sons. Their meeting-place was at Hisargafl, and Holmstein and his brothers promptly attacked Leif and his party. When they had been fighting a while, up came Olmod the Old, Horda-Kari's son and a kinsman of Leif's, and lent him and Ingolf a hand. In this fight Holmstein fell and Herstein fled, whereupon Leif and his foster-brother went off harrying. The following winter Herstein marched against them, meaning to kill them, but they got news of his movements and moved against him. Once again there was a big fight, and Herstein fell. Following this, their friends from Firthafylki came crowding in to join the foster-brothers; emissaries of theirs were sent to meet earl Atli and Hastein, to offer peace terms, and the terms they reached were that Ingolf and Leif should pay over their estates to that father and son.

Then the foster-brothers fitted out a big ship of theirs, and set off to find that land Raven-Floki had discovered—the one called Iceland. They found it, and made a stay in the Eastfirths, in the southern Alptafjord. The land looked to them more promising south than north. They spent one winter in the land and then returned to Norway.

After this Ingolf laid out their money for the Iceland voyage, while Leif went on a viking cruise to the British Isles. He went harrying in Ireland, where he found a big underground house, which he entered. All was dark till light shone from a sword which a man was holding. Leif killed this man, and took the sword from him and great riches too, and from there on was known as Hjorleif, Sword-Leif. Hjorleif harried far and wide in

Ireland, winning great riches there, and taking captive ten thralls, whose names are as follows: Dufthak and Geirrod, Skjaldbjorn, Halldor and Drafdrit (the rest are not named). After this Hjorleif returned to Norway to meet Ingolf his foster-brother. He had before this married Ingolf's sister, Helga Arnardottir. That winter Ingolf offered up extensive sacrifice and sought auguries of his destiny, but Hjorleif would never sacrifice. The auguries directed Ingolf to Iceland, so each brother-in-law fitted out his ship for the Iceland voyage, Hjorleif putting his booty on board, and Ingolf their common stock; and once they were ready they put to sea.

The summer Ingolf and Hjorleif went off to settle Iceland, Harald Fairhair had been twelve years king of Norway; there had passed since the beginning of the world 6,073 winters, and from the Incarnation of Our Lord 874 years. They sailed in company till they sighted Iceland, when they were parted. As soon as Ingolf sighted Iceland he cast his high-seat pillars over-board for an omen, vowing he would settle where the pillars came ashore. He reached land at the point now known as Ingolfshofdi, Ingolf's Head, but Hjorleif was carried west along the coast. He grew short of drinking water, so the Irish thralls tried a scheme of kneading meal and butter together; this, they claimed, was not a thirst-maker. They called it *minnþak*, but just as it was ready heavy rain came on, so they were able to catch water in the awnings. When the *minnþak* began to turn mouldy they threw it overboard, and it drifted ashore at the point now known as Minnthakseyr. Hjorleif reached land at Hjorleifshofdi, Hjorleif's Head. There was a fjord there in those days, and the end of the fjord turned in towards the head-land. There he had two halls built, the walls of one eighteen fathoms long, and of the other nineteen. Hjorleif stayed there that winter; then in the spring he wanted to sow. He had only the one ox, so made his thralls drag the plough. While Hjorleif was occupied about the house with his men, Dufthak evolved a scheme whereby they were to kill the ox and report that a for-est-bear had killed him, and afterwards set upon Hjorleif and the rest, if they went hunting the bear. So now they reported this to Hjorleif, and when they set off to hunt the bear and were scattered about the wood, the thralls attacked each his appointed prey and murdered them to the last man. Then they ran off with the women, the movable goods, and the boat. The thralls made their way out to the islands they could see in the sea to the south-west, where they continued living for a while.

There were two thralls of Ingolf's, Vifil and Karli by name, whom he sent west along the sea's edge looking for his seat-pillars. When they got as far as Hjorleifshofdi they found Hjorleif lying dead, so back they went to tell Ingolf what had happened. He was deeply moved by these killings, and after-wards set off west to Hjorleifshofdi, and when he saw Hjorleif lying dead, this is what he said. 'This was a sorry end for a brave man,' said he, 'that thralls should be the death of him; but so it goes, I see, with such as are not prepared to offer up sacrifice.' Ingolf had Hjorleif and his men buried and took charge of their ship and their share of the property. Ingolf then walked up to the headland and could see islands lying out to sea, to the south-west. It struck him that they would have run off there, because the boat had disappeared, so away they went to look for the thralls, and found them in the islands at the place now known as Eid. They were eating a meal when Ingolf surprised them. Panic whelmed them, and they ran each his own way. Ingolf killed them all. The place where Dufthak died is called Duf-thaksskor. Many of them jumped off the cliff which has since been known by their name. The islands where these thralls were killed have been known ever since as the Vestmannaeyjar, because they were Vestmenn, Irishmen. Ingolf and his men took the wives of their own men who had been murdered away with them; they returned to Hjorleifshofdi, and it was there they spent the second winter.

The following summer he travelled west along the sea's edge, and spent the third winter under Ingolfsfell, west of Olfus river. This same season Vifil and Karli found his high-seat pillars by Arnarhval, west of the heath. In the spring Ingolf came down over the heath, to site his home where his pillars had come ashore, and lived at Reykjavik, and the pillars are there to this day in the living-room. Ingolf took land in settlement between Olfus river and Hvalfjord west of Brynjudalsa, and between there and Oxara, and the whole of the land projecting west. Said Karli: 'We travelled past good country to bad purpose, if we must live on this stuck-out limb of land!' So he cleared out, taking a bondwoman with him; but Ingolf gave Vifil his freedom, he made his home at Vifilstoftir, and Vifilsfell is named after him. He lived many a long day, and was a trusty man. Ingolf had a house built at Skalafell, and from it observed smoke over at Olfusvatn, where he found Karli.

Ingolf was the most celebrated of all settlers, for he came here to an unlived-in country and was the first to settle down in it: the other settlers did so by his example.

He married Hallveig Frodadottir, the sister of Lopt the Old. Their son was Thorstein, who had the Thing instituted at Kjal- arnes before the Althing was established. Thorstein's son was Thorkel Mani the Lawspeaker, whose way of life was best of all those heathen men in Iceland of whom there is record. In his last illness he had himself carried out into the rays of the sun and committed himself into the hands of that God who had created the sun. Moreover he had lived as purely as those Chris- tian men whose way of life is best. His son was Thormod, who was godi over the whole congregation when Christianity came to Iceland.

Thorolf Mostrarskegg

[S. 85] Thorolf the son of Ornolf Fishdriver lived in Most—the reason why he was called Mostrarskegg. He was a great sacri- ficer who believed in Thor. He departed for Iceland because of the tyranny of King Harald Fairhair, sailing by way of the south coast; but when he arrived west off Breidafjord he cast overboard the pillars of his high-seat, on which the image of Thor was carved, supplicating Thor to come ashore wherever he would have Thorolf settle, with this undertaking, that he would dedicate his entire settlement to Thor and name it with his name. Thorolf sailed into the fjord and gave it a name, call- ing it Breidafjord, Broadfjord. He took land in settlement on its south shore, near the middle of the fjord, where he found Thor drifted on to a cape which is now known as Thorsnes. They landed further up in the bay which Thorolf named Hofs- vag, where he built himself a home and raised a great temple, which he dedicated to Thor. The place is now known as Hof- stadir. In those days there had been little or no settlement in Breidafjord.

Thorolf took possession of the land from Stafa in as far as Thorsa, and called the whole promontory Thorsnes. He had so

great a reverence for the mountain which stood on that promontory, and which he called Helgafell, Holy Mountain, that
no man should turn his unwashed face to it, and there was so
inviolate a sanctuary there that nothing, neither man nor beast,
should suffer harm there unless they left it of their own accord.
It was the belief of Thorolf and his kindred that they would all
die into this mountain.

There on the cape where Thor came ashore Thorolf had all
courts held, and it was there that the district Thing was established with the approval of all who lived in that countryside.
When men were in attendance at the Thing it was strictly forbidden for them to ease themselves on land, but a skerry known
as Dritsker was earmarked for the purpose, for they would not
defile so sacred a site as was there. But when Thorolf was dead,
and Thorstein his son still young, Thorgrim Kjallaksson and
Asgeir his brother-in-law were not prepared to walk to the
skerry to ease themselves. But the Thorsnes men would not put
up with this, the way they intended to defile so sacred a site, so
they came to blows, Thorstein Thorskabit and Thorgeir Keng
against Thorgrim and Asgeir; certain men fell and many were
wounded before they could be parted. Thord Gellir made peace
between them, and in as much as neither side would give way
the field was then unhallowed by reason of the blood shed
there. So now it was decided to remove the Thing from where it
used to stand and up into the ness where it stands today, which
consequently became a famous holy place. Thor's stone still
stands there, on which they broke those men whom they sacrificed; and close by is the ring of judgement where men were
sentenced to be sacrificed. There too Thord Gellir established
the Quarter Thing with the approval of all who lived in the
Quarter. . . .

[S. 123] Thorolf Mostrarskegg's son Hallstein took Thorska-
fjord in settlement and lived at Hallsteinsnes. He offered up a
sacrifice that Thor should send him pillars for a high-seat, whereupon a tree drifted ashore on his land which was sixty-three
ells long and two fathoms thick. This was used for high-seat pillars, and from it are made the high-seat pillars of practically
every homestead throughout that network of fjords. The place
is now called Grenitrenes, Pinetree Ness, where the tree came
ashore. Hallstein had been out harrying in Scotland, where he

captured those thralls he brought home with him. These he sent to the salt-workings on Svefneyjar.[2]

Helgi Magri

[H. 184] There was a nobleman in Gautland by the name of Bjorn, the son of Hrolf of the River; he was married to Hlif, daughter of Hrolf the son of Ingjald, son of King Frodi (Starkad the Old was court-poet to both these kings), and their son's name was Eyvind. Bjorn had a quarrel over land with Sigfast the father-in-law of Solvar king of the Gauts. Sigfast had married his daughter to earl Solvar, and the earl backed Sigfast so strongly that he laid forceful hands on all Bjorn's estates. So Bjorn made over all his goods in Gautland to Hlif his wife and Eyvind his son, and departed from the east with twelve horses laden with silver. But the night before he departed the country he burned Sigfast to death in his house, together with thirty men, then made for Norway.

He came west to Agdir, to Grim the Hersir at Hvinir . . . who made him most welcome. Bjorn and his comrades spent the winter with Grim, but one night in late spring Bjorn woke to find a man standing over him with a drawn sword and shaping to cut at him. He grabbed at his arm—he had been hired by Grim to cut off Bjorn's head. Bjorn did not kill him. Grim had intended to betray him for the sake of his money. So away went Bjorn to Ondott Kraka who had his home in Hvinisfjord . . . Bjorn went on viking cruises to the British Isles in the summers, but his winters he spent with Ondott. It was now that Hlif died back in Gautland, so Bjorn married Ondott's sister Helga; their son was Thrond the Far-sailer. Next, Hlif's son Eyvind came from the east to Bjorn his father, and when Bjorn grew tired of campaigning he took over his father's warships together with that profession he had followed. Later, in Ireland, Eyvind married Raforta daughter of King Kjarval. She gave birth to a boy in the Hebrides, and he was put out to foster there. Eyvind was called Eastman because he had come west across the sea from the kingdom of the Swedes back east. Two years later they

[2] According to tradition he found his thralls asleep upon Svefneyjar, Sleep Isles, when they should be making salt, and hanged them by the cliffs called Galgi, Gallows.

returned to the islands to see how the boy was doing, and saw a boy there with fine eyes but no flesh on his bones, for he was starved, which was why they nicknamed him Helgi Magri, Helgi the Lean. After this he was fostered in Ireland.

Bjorn died at Ondott his brother-in-law's. Grim argued that it was for the king to take over his entire inheritance, because he was a foreigner and his sons were west across the sea; but Ondott held on to that wealth on behalf of his nephew Thrond.

Helgi was brought up in Ireland; he married Thorunn Hyrna, the daughter of Ketil Flatnose of the Hebrides . . . they had a lot of children. In course of time Helgi went to Iceland with his wife and children, Hrolf and Ingjald and that Ingunn whom Hamund Heljarskin married (he too came out with Helgi). When Helgi sighted land he consulted Thor as to where he should go ashore; the oracle directed him to Eyjafjord, strongly enjoining him to hold neither east nor west of it. Before the fjord opened up ahead of them his son Hrolf asked whether, if Thor had directed them into the Arctic Ocean for winter quarters, he would have obeyed or not. [S. His son Hrolf asked whether Helgi would have held for the Arctic Ocean if Thor had directed him there, for it seemed to the crew high time to leave the sea now that summer was so far advanced.] Helgi made land beyond Hrisey and inwards of Svarfadardal, to spend his first winter at Hamundarstadir. They had so severe a winter that it was touch and go whether the livestock they brought with them would perish; but in the spring Helgi walked up on to Solarfjall and could see how the land looked much darker [i.e. freer from snow] up in the fjord [S. *adds* which they called Eyjafjord, Island Fjord, from the islands which lay off its mouth]. He carried everything he had back on board ship, and landed by Galtarhamar, where he put a couple of pigs ashore, a boar by the name of Solvi and a sow, and when they were found three years later in Solvadal, all told there were seventy of them.

That winter Helgi lived at Bildsa, then in the summer explored the entire countryside, taking in settlement the whole of Eyjafjord between Siglunes and Reynisnes, and building a big fire at every river mouth down by the sea, thus hallowing to himself the entire fjord between those nesses. One winter later Helgi moved his household to Kristnes, where he lived to the

end of his days. He was very mixed in his beliefs: he believed in
Christ, and yet made vows to Thor for sea-voyages and in tight
corners, and for everything which struck him as of real importance.

While Helgi was moving house Thorunn Hyrna was delivered
of a child on Thorunnarey in Eyjafjardararkvisl. This was when
Thorbjorg Holmasol, Island-sun, was born.

And afterwards Helgi distributed land among his sons and
sons-in-law.

Ketilbjorn the Old

[S. 385] There was a nobleman in Naumudal by the name of
Ketilbjorn, the son of Ketil and Æsa daughter of earl Hakon
Grjotgardsson; he was married to Helga, Thord Skeggi's
daughter. Ketilbjorn went out to Iceland at a time when the
land alongside the sea was already extensively settled. He had a
ship which bore the name Ellidi, and brought her into Ellida-
aros [the mouth of Ellidi river] below the heath, and spent his
first winter with his father-in-law Thord Skeggi. In the spring he
went up over the heath to look for some good land. They had a
place to sleep there and built themselves a hall: the place is now
known as Skalabrekka, Hall-slope. When they left there they
came to a river which they called Oxara, Axe river, because
they lost their axe there. They spent some time under the
mountain peak which they named Reydarmuli, Trout-peak,
because there they left behind the river-trout which they had
caught in the river. Ketilbjorn took all Grimsnes in settlement
north of Hoskuldslœk, the whole of Laugardal, and all
Byskupstunga up to Stakksa, and made his home at Mosfell . . .

Ketilbjorn was so rich in money that he ordered his sons to
forge a cross-beam of silver for the temple (*hof*) they were
building. This they refused to do. So with Haki his thrall and
Bot his bondwoman he hauled the silver up on to the mountain
with two oxen, and they buried the treasure so that it has never
been found from that day to this. Whereupon he did away with
Haki at Hakaskard and with Bot at Botarskard.

[His son] Teit married Alof the daughter of Bodvar of Vors,
the son of Vikinga-Kari: their son was Gizur the White, the
father of bishop Isleif, father of the bishop Gizur. Another son

of Teit was Ketilbjorn, the father of Kol, father of Thorkel, father of Kol the Vik Men's bishop. Many great men are descended from Ketilbjorn.

Geirrid and Thorolf

[S.86] Geirrod was the name of a man who left Halogaland for Iceland, and with him . . . Ulfar Kappi. Geirrod took land in settlement inwards from Thorsa to Langadalsa, and lived at Eyr. To Ulfar his shipmate he gave land on both sides of Ulfarsfell and inland from the mountain.

Geirrod had a sister by the name of Geirrid, whom Bjorn son of Bolverk Blindingatrjona, Gadfly Snout, married: their son's name was Thorolf. After Bjorn's death Geirrid went out to Iceland with her son, and they spent their first winter at Eyr. In the spring Geirrod gave his sister a homestead in Borgardal, while Thorolf went abroad and applied himself to viking cruises. Geirrid was not grudging of her food to men: she had her hall built straddling the highway, and would sit on a stool outside and invite guests in, and there was always a table standing indoors with food on it.

Thorolf returned to Iceland after Geirrod's death. He challenged Ulfar for his land and offered him holmgang [*i.e.* island-going, wager of battle]. Ulfar was old by this time and childless; he fell on the island, while Thorolf was wounded in the leg; he walked lame ever after, for which reason he was nicknamed Bægifot. Thorolf took some of Ulfar's land in succession to him, and some Thorfinn of Alptafjord took.

4. Strife and Feud

Murder on Gunnbjorn's Skerries

[S.151–2] Snæbjorn, the son of Eyvind Eastman and brother of Helgi Magri, took land in settlement between Mjovafjord and Langadalsa, and made a home in Vatnsfjord. His son was Holmstein, the father of Snæbjorn Galti. Snæbjorn Galti's mother was Kjalvor, so he and Tungu-Odd were first cousins. Snæbjorn was fostered at Thingnes with Thorodd, but at times would be staying with Tungu-Odd or his mother.

Hallbjorn the son of Odd of Kidjaberg (the son of Hallkel the brother of Ketilbjorn the Old) married Tungu-Odd's daughter

Hallgerd. They spent their first winter at Odd's, and Snæbjorn Galti was living there at the time. There was little love between husband and wife.

In the spring Hallbjorn made preparations for changing house at the moving-days in late May, and as he got ready Odd left home for the hot spring at Reykjaholt, where his sheep-houses stood. He had no wish to be present when Hallbjorn moved out, for he had a notion Hallgerd would be unwilling to go with him. Odd had always been a peace-maker between them.

When Hallbjorn had saddled their horses he walked into the women's bower, and there was Hallgerd, seated on the dais combing her hair. Her hair fell all about her and down to the floor, for she and Hallgerd Snuinbrok have had the loveliest hair of all the women of Iceland. Hallbjorn told her to stand up and be moving. She sat still and said nothing. Then he laid hands on her, but she did not stir. This happened three times. Then Hallbjorn stood in front of her and spoke this verse:

> 'My lady clad in linen
> Lets me stand and stare before her;
> Fair Goddess of the ale-cup,
> She turns her back and scorns me;
> Cold grows my love, and colder
> All hope such hate can alter;
> Pale on my cheek grief's pallor,
> And sorrow gnaws my heart-roots.'

After this he twisted her hair round his hand, intending to drag her off the dais, but she sat firm and unstirring. So at that he drew his sword and cut off her head, walked out and rode away, and they were three men together, with a couple of pack-horses.

There were only a few people at home, but they sent instantly to tell Odd. Snæbjorn was staying at Kjalvararstadir, and Odd dispatched a messenger to him, asking him to see to the pursuit, for he himself, he said, would be making no move. Snæbjorn gave chase with eleven men, and when Hallbjorn and his companions saw that they were pursued they begged him to ride off, but he refused. Snæbjorn and his men caught up with them at the hillocks which are now known as Hallbjarnarvordur, Hallbjorn's Cairns. Hallbjorn got up on to the hillocks with his men, and it was from there that they made their defence. Three men from Snæbjorn's party fell there and both Hallbjorn's companions. Next Snæbjorn sheared off Hallbjorn's foot at the ankle-joint; he hobbled off to the southernmost hillock, where he killed two more of Snæbjorn's men, and where he himself fell. That is why there are three cairns on that hillock, and five on the other. After this Snæbjorn returned home.

Snæbjorn owned a ship in Grimsaros, and Hrolf of Raudasand bought a half share in her. They were twelve in either party. With Snæbjorn were Thorkel and Sumarlid, the sons of Thorgeir the Red, son of Einar of Stafholt; and he further added to his company Thorodd of Thingnes, his foster-father, together with his wife; while Hrolf took Styrbjorn, who after a dream he had spoke this verse:

> 'I see the bane
> Of both us twain:
> Grim weird to dree
> North-west o'er sea.
> Frost there and cold,
> Horrors untold;
> By such revealed,
> Know Snæbjorn killed.'

They set off in search of Gunnbjarnarsker and found land. Snæbjorn was unwilling for them to go exploring by night. Styrbjorn left the ship and found a purse of money in a burial mound and hid it. Snæbjorn struck him with his axe, and the purse fell down. They built a hall which became buried under snow. Thorkel the son of Red discovered that there was water on a pole which protruded from the house window (this was in Goi [February and early March]), so they dug themselves out. Snæbjorn was mending the ship, while Thorodd and his wife stayed at the house on his behalf, along with Styrbjorn and his men on behalf of Hrolf. The others were fishing and hunting. Styrbjorn killed Thorodd, and he and Hrolf together killed Snæbjorn. The sons of Red and all the rest of them gave pledges, in order to save their lives.

They made Halogaland, and from there voyaged to Iceland, to Vadil. Thorkel Trefil had a shrewd idea how matters had

gone with the sons of Red. Hrolf built a fortress on Strandar-
heid, and Trefil sent Sveinung for his head. First he came to
Myr to Hermund, then to Olaf at Drangar, then to Gest at
Hagi, who sent him on to Hrolf his friend. Sveinung killed both
Hrolf and Styrbjorn, then went back to Hagi. Gest exchanged
sword and axe with him, and supplied him with two black-
maned horses; then had a man ride round Vadil right to Kollafjord, and got Thorbjorn the Strong to go and claim the horses;
and Thorbjorn killed him at Sveinungseyr because Sveinung's
sword snapped off below the hilt. Because of this Trefil would
boast against Gest, when their wits were matched together, that
he had so out-witted Gest that he himself sent a man to cut off
the head of his own friend.

Love the Destroyer

[S. 284] Uni the son of Gardar, who first discovered Iceland,
went out to Iceland at the bidding of King Harald Fairhair, proposing to subjugate the land, after which the king had promised
to make him his earl. Uni reached land at the point now known
as Unaos and set up house there; he took land in settlement
south of Lagarfljot, the entire countryside as far as Unaloek.
But once the Icelanders got wind of his purpose they treated
him very coolly, would sell him neither livestock nor provisions,
and he could not keep his footing there. Uni went off to the
southern Alptafjord, failed to make a lodgement, so left the
east with twelve men, and came in the winter to Leidolf Kappi
in Skogahverfi, who took them in. He became the lover of
Thorunn, Leidolf's daughter, and by spring she was carrying his
child. Uni now wanted to clear out with his men, but Leidolf
rode after him; they met by Flangastadir and fought there,
because Uni was not prepared to go back with Leidolf. Certain
of Uni's men fell there, and willy-nilly back he went, for Leidolf
wanted him to marry his daughter and settle down, then take
the inheritance after his day. Somewhat later Uni ran away
when Leidolf was absent from home; but once Leidolf knew of
it he rode after him and they met by Kalfagrafir. This time he
was so angry that he killed Uni and all his comrades.

[*Þórðarbók*. Uni the Dane the son of Gardar wished to make
Iceland subject to himself or to King Harald Fairhair. He lived
at Os, but knew no rest there, so set off to explore the land

more widely and found winter quarters with Leidolf. Uni became the lover of Thorunn his daughter and wanted to take her away with him, but Leidolf rode after him, they fought by Kalfagrafir, and men fell on either side. Then they parted, but Uni got only a short way before Leidolf came up in pursuit, they fought a second time, and Uni and his comrades fell.]

The son of Uni and Thorunn was Hroar Tungu-Godi; he took Leidolf's entire inheritance; he was an overpowering sort of man. He married a daughter of Hamund (a sister of Gunnar of Hlidarendi); their son was Hamund the Halt, a notable man-slayer. Tjorvi the Mocker and Gunnar were Hroar's nephews.

Tjorvi asked for Astrid Manvitsbrekka, the daughter of Modolf, but her brothers Ketil and Hrolf refused him the lady, and gave her to Thorir Ketilsson. So Tjorvi drew their like-nesses on the privy wall, and every evening when he and Hroar went to the privy he would spit in the face of Thorir's likeness and kiss hers, until Hroar scraped them off. After that he carved them on the handle of his knife, and spoke this verse:

> 'First, Wealth-Thrud and her Thorir
> Well-drawn I set on wall,
> Young bride as well as bridgegroom,
> So insolence matched insult!
> Now hold I carved on knife-hilt
> Her homage-laden image;
> Many's the word I've whispered
> In ear of that bright lady!'

From which arose the killing of Hroar and his sister's sons.

The Sons of Baug

[S. 348] There was a man named Baug, the foster-brother of Ketil Hœng, who went out to Iceland, to spend his first winter at Baugsstadir and his second with Hœng [at Hof in Rangar-vellir]. At Hœng's direction he took in settlement the whole of Fljotshlid down from Breidabolstad to meet with Hœng's own land, and made a home at Hlidarendi. His sons were Gunnar of Gunnarsholt, Eyvind of Eyvindarmuli, and, third, Stein the Swift; while his daughter was that Hild whom Orn of Vælugerdi married.

Stein the Swift and Sigmund, Sighvat the Red's son, had a

journey to make back home from Eyrar and they arrived all together at the Sandholar ferry (Sigmund, that is, and Stein's companions). Each party wanted to cross the river first. Sigmund and his men shoved Stein's housecarles out of their way, and sent them packing from the boat, but just then up came Stein and promptly struck Sigmund his deathblow. For this killing all Baug's sons were banished from Fljotshlid. Gunnar went off to Gunnarsholt, Eyvind east under Eyjafjall to Eyvindarhol, and Snjallstein [*i.e.* Stein the Swift] to Snjallsteinshofdi. Sigmund's daughter Thorgerd was far from pleased when her father's slayer came out there, and goaded Onund her husband into taking revenge for Sigmund. Onund made for Snjallshofdi with thirty men and set fire to the house there. Snjallstein came out and gave himself up; they led him up to the Head, where they killed him. Gunnar took up the bloodsuit for this killing. He was married to Hrafnhild Storolfsdottir, sister of Orm the Strong; their son was Hamund, and the pair of them, both father and son, were outstanding men for strength and fine appearance.

Onund was outlawed for killing Snjallstein; for two years he sat tight with a strong body of men about him, while Gunnar's brother-in-law Orn of Vælugerdi watched his every move. The third winter, after Yule, in the light of Orn's information, Gunnar fell upon Onund with thirty men as he was going from the games with eleven men to fetch his horses. They clashed in Orrustudal, Battle Dale; Onund fell with three of his men, and one man of Gunnar's. Gunnar was wearing a blue cloak. He rode up along Holt to Thjorsa, then just short of the river fell off his horse, dead of his wounds.

Once Onund's sons Sigmund Kleykir and Eilif the Rich grew up they pressed their kinsman Mord Fiddle to take up the bloodsuit. This was no easy matter, said Mord, in respect of an outlawed man. They stressed that they felt strongest of all about Orn, who lived closest to them, so Mord's advice was this, that they should contrive a suit for full outlawry against Orn and so run him out of the district. So Onund's sons prosecuted Orn for unlawful grazing, and he was outlawed to this extent, that he should fall unhallowed [*i.e.* without need for atonement] at the hands of the sons of Onund everywhere except at Vælugerdi and within arrow-shot range of his own land. Onund's sons lay

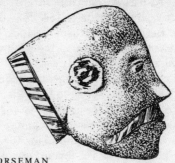

20. NINTH-CENTURY NORSEMAN
A carving in wood from the Oseberg
wagon

in wait for him endlessly, but he took good care of himself; even
so they got their chance at him one day when he was chasing
cattle off his land; they killed him, and everyone thought he
would have fallen unhallowed.

But Thorleif Gneisti, Orn's brother, paid Thormod Thjostar-
son (he had just put in to Eyrar from abroad) to hallow Orn. He
flighted so long a shot from his long-bow that Orn's death was
found to have taken place inside his arrow-shot-range sanctuary. So now Hamund Gunnarsson and Thorleif took up the
blood-suit for Orn, while Mord backed those brothers, who
paid no fine but were banished out of Floi. Then, on behalf of
Eilif, Mord asked for Thorkatla Ketilbjarnardottir, and Hordaland came with her from home by way of dowry, and it was
there Eilif made his home; and on behalf of Sigmund he asked
for Arngunn, Thorstein Drangakarl's daughter, so he left for
the east. Finally Mord gave his sister Rannveig to Hamund
Gunnarsson, who then returned to the Hlid, and their son was
Gunnar of Hlidarendi.

5. *Thralls*

Ketil Gufa's Irishmen

[S. 125] There was a man called Ketil Gufa Orlygsson . . .
[who] came out to Iceland when the period of settlement was
well advanced. He had been on viking cruises in the west, on

which he had captured Irish thralls, one called Thormod, a second Floki, a third Kori, a fourth Svart, and two by the name of Skorri. Ketil came to Rosmhvalanes, to spend the first winter at Gufuskalar, then in the spring went on to Nes and spent his second winter at Gufunes. It was now that Skorri the elder and Floki ran off with two women and a lot of goods; they went into hiding in Skorraholt, but were killed in Flokadal and Skorradal.

Ketil found no place to live in the Nesses, so went into Borgarfjord, to spend his third winter at Gufuskalar on Gufa river. Early in the spring he made a journey west to Breidafjord, looking for a place for himself. Here he stayed at Geirmundarstadir; he asked for Geirmund's daughter Yr and got her, whereupon Geirmund [Heljarskin] directed Ketil to territories west in the fjord. But while Ketil was out west his thralls ran off and came by night to Lambastadir. At this time Thord was living there, the son of Thorgeir Lambi and Thordis Yngvarsdottir, the aunt of Egil Skallagrimsson. The thralls set the house on fire, and burned Thord to death with all his household; they broke into a storehouse and seized a lot of goods and chattels, next drove in horses and loaded them, then headed off on the road to Alptanes. The morning they moved out Thord's son Lambi the Strong came home from the Thing; he set off in pursuit of them, and men flocked to him from the homesteads round about. When the thralls saw this they went running off, every one his own road. They caught Kori on Koranes, but some took to swimming. Svart they caught up with on Svartsker, Skorri on Skorrey off the Myrar, and Thormod out on Thormodssker, a mile from land.

And when Ketil Gufa came back he set off westward past the Myrar and spent his fourth winter on Snæfellsnes at Gufuskalar. Later he took in settlement Gufufjord and Skalanes out as far as Kollafjord.

Atli of Fljot

[S. 149] There was a nobleman in Sogn named Geir, who was known as Vegeir, Temple-Geir or Holy-Geir, he was such a great man for sacrifices. He had many children. Vebjorn Sygnakappi, the Sognmen's Champion, was his eldest son, and in addition Vestein, Vethorm, Vemund, Vegest, and Vethorn, while Vedis was his daughter. After the death of Vegeir, Vebjorn fell foul of earl Hakon, as was related earlier, so the brothers and their sister set off for Iceland. They had a hard passage and a long, but reached Hloduvik west of Horn in the autumn. Thereupon Vebjorn set about a mighty sacrifice: earl Hakon, he said, was that very day sacrificing in order that disaster might overtake them. But while he was about his sacrifice his brothers pressed him to get moving, he neglected his business, and they put to sea. That same day, in foul weather, they were shipwrecked under huge cliffs; with great difficulty they got themselves up, Vebjorn leading the way. That is now called Sygnakleif, the Sognmen's Cliff. Atli of Fljot, a thrall of Geirmund Heljarskin, took them all into shelter for the winter. And when Geirmund heard tell of this resourceful act of Atli's he gave him his freedom together with the farm he had charge of. [H. Atli . . . took them all into shelter for the winter, telling them there was nothing to pay for their keep. Geirmund, he assured them, was not skimped for provisions. When Atli met Geirmund, Geirmund asked him how he could be so bold as to entertain such men at his, Geirmund's, expense. 'Because', replied Atli, 'it will be remembered as long as Iceland is lived in how splendid was that man's way of life when a thrall of his dared do such a thing without asking his leave.' 'For this conduct of yours', announced Geirmund, 'you shall receive your freedom, along with the farm which was in your charge.'] In the days to come Atli became a man of mark and substance.

The following spring Vebjorn took land in settlement between Skotufjord and Hestfjord, Horsefjord, as far as he could walk round in a day, and that piece over and beyond which he called Folafot, Foalfoot. Vebjorn was a great man for fighting, and there is a big saga relating to him. He gave Vedis in marriage to Grimolf of Unadsdal; they quarrelled and Vebjorn killed him alongside Grimolfsvatn, in return for which Vebjorn was killed at the Quarter Thing at Thorsnes, and three others with him.

Rodrek and Rongud

[S. 194] Hrosskel was the name of a man who took in settlement the whole of Svartardal and all Yrarfellsland at the direction of Eirik [of Goddalir]; he took land into his possession down as far as Gilhagi and lived at Yrarfell. He had a thrall whose name was Rodrek, whom he sent up along Mælifellsdal looking for settleable land on the high ground to the south. He came upon that ghyll leading south from Mælifell which is now known as Rodreksgil, where he set up a new-peeled staff which they called Landkonnud, Land-prober, and after that made his way back . . .

[S. 196] There was a man named Vekel the Shape-changer who took land in settlement down from Gila to Mælifellsa and lived at Mælifell. He heard about Rodrek's journey, and a little later went south himself to that high ground looking for settleable land. He came upon the mounds which are now known as Vekelshaugar, shot an arrow [*or* spear] between them, and at that point turned back. And when Eirik of Goddalir heard of this, he sent a thrall of his, Rongud by name, south to the high ground; he too went looking for settleable land. He came south to Blondukvisl, then went up along the river which flows down from west of Vinverjadal, and west to the lava between Reykjavellir and the mountain Kjol, Keel, where he came across the tracks of a man. As he saw it, these must have come from the south. It was there he erected the cairn which is now known as Rangadarvarda, Rongud's Cairn. At that point he turned back, and Eirik gave him his freedom for this journey of his; and from then on a route was established over the high ground between the Southlanders' Quarter and the Northlanders'.

6. *Animals*

Seal-Thorir and Mare Skalm

[S. 68] There was a man named Grim, the son of Ingjald, son of Hroald of Haddingjadal, the brother of Asi the hersir. He went to Iceland to look for land, sailing the northern route, and spent the winter on Grimsey in Steingrimsfjord. His wife's name was Bergdis, and his son's Thorir.

In the autumn Grim rowed out fishing with his housecarles, and the lad Thorir lay in the prow in a sealskin bag which was drawn in at the neck. Grim pulled up a merman, and when he came up asked him: 'What do you prophesy of our fortune? And where shall we settle in Iceland?' 'No point in prophesying of you and your men,' the merman answered him, 'but for the lad who lies in the sealskin bag, why, yes. He shall settle and take land where Skalm your mare lies down under her load.' Not another word could they get from him, but later that winter Grim and his men rowed out fishing, whilst the lad was left ashore, and were drowned to the last man. [H. In the winter Grim rowed out fishing with his thralls, and his son was with him. And when the lad began to grow chilly they wrapped him in a sealskin bag which they drew in at the neck. Grim pulled up a merman. 'Tell us our lives and how long we shall live,' said Grim, 'or you shall never see your home again.' 'There is no point in your knowing, save for the lad in the sealskin bag, for before spring comes you will be dead, but your son shall settle and take land where Skalm your mare lies down under her load.' Not another word could they get from him, but later that winter Grim died and is buried in a mound there.]

In the spring Bergdis and Thorir left Grimsey and went west over the heath to Breidafjord. Skalm kept moving ahead and never once lay down, and they spent their second winter at Skalmarnes in Breidafjord. The following summer they turned off south, and still Skalm kept going till they came off the heath south into Borgarfjord, at a point where two red sandhills stood before them, and there she lay down under her load under the westernmost hill. And it was there that Thorir took land in settlement from south of Gnupa to Kalda, below Knappadal, between mountain and seashore. He lived at the outer Raudamel, and was a great chieftain.

When Thorir was old and blind he came out of doors late one evening and saw how a man was rowing from the sea into the mouth of Kalda river in an iron boat, a big, evil-looking creature who walked ashore and up to the farm called Hripi, where he started digging at the entrance to the milking-shed. During the night fire erupted out of the earth, and it was then that Borgarhraun was blasted and consumed. The farm stood where Eldborg, the Fire-Fortress, stands now . . . Skalm, Thorir's mare, came to her death in Skalmarkelda, Skalmsquag.

Dove-Beak and Mare Fly

[S. 202] Thorir Dufunef, Dove-beak, was a freedman of Oxen-Thorir's. He brought his ship into Gonguskardsaros at a time when the whole country west had already been settled, so off he went north over Jokulsa river to Landbrot and took land in settlement between Glodafeykisa and Djupa, and made a home at Flugumyr.

At that time a ship came here to Iceland into Kolbeinsaros with a cargo of livestock. They lost a young mare in the woods at Brimnesskogar, and Thorir Dufunef bought the reversion of her, and later found her: she was the fleetest of all horses, and was called Fluga, Fly.

There was a man named Orn who travelled the countryside and was a wizard. He waylaid Thorir in Vinverjadal, as he was making his way south past Kjol, and made a bet with him as to whose horse was the fleeter, for he had a fine stallion of his own. They bet a hundred in silver apiece. They rode south, the two of them, past Kjol, till they arrived at the course which has been known ever since as Dufunefsskeid, Dufunef's Course. The difference in their horses' speed was so marked that Thorir turned back to meet Orn half-way along the course. Orn took the loss of his wager so much to heart that he had no desire to live; he went up under the mountain now called Arnarfell and did away with himself. Fluga was left behind there, she was so exhausted, but when Thorir returned from the Thing he found a grey, black-maned stallion keeping her company, and she was in foal by him. From them sprang Eidfaxi, who was shipped abroad and caused the death of seven men at lake Mjor in one day, and perished there himself. Fluga was lost in a bog at Flugumyr, Fly-mire.

Buck-Bjorn

[S. 328–9] Living in Nordmœr in Norway at a place called Moldatun was a man known as Hrolf the Hewer. His sons were Vemund and Molda-Gnup, great manslayers and iron-smiths. Vemund recited this ditty while he was in the smithy working:

> 'I bore alone
> From eleven men
> A killer's name.
> Blow harder, man!'

Gnup departed for Iceland because of his own killings and his brother's, and took land in settlement between Kudafljot and

Eyjara and all Alptaver. There was a big mere there in those days, and wild swans for the catching. Molda-Gnup sold part of his settlement to numerous men, and the district grew thick with people before fire and lava over-ran it, and they fled away west to Hofdabrekka to build booths and tent them over at a place called Tjaldavoll. But Vemund the son of Sigmund Kleykir would not allow them quarters there, so now they went to Hrossagard where they built a long-house and spent the winter. Quarrels arose because of them, and killings, so next spring Molda-Gnup and the rest of them went west to Grindavik, where they settled down. They had hardly any livestock. By now Molda-Gnup's sons, Bjorn and Gnup, Thorstein Hrungnir and Thord Leggjaldi, were grown to man's estate.

One night Bjorn dreamed that a rock-dweller appeared before him, offering to go partners with him, and it seemed to him he said yes to it. After which a buck came to his she-goats, and his flocks multiplied so fast that soon he was rolling in money. Ever after he was known as Hafr-Bjorn, Buck-Bjorn. Men with second-sight saw how all the guardian spirits of the countryside accompanied Hafr-Bjorn to the Thing, and Thorstein and Thord when hunting and fishing.

Coalbiter and Bear

[S. 259] There was a man by the name of Arngeir who took in settlement the whole of Sletta between Havararlon and Sveinungsvik. His children were Thorgils, Odd, and that Thurid who married Steinolf of Thjorsardal. [H. *adds* Odd was for ever hanging about the fire when a lad; he was a sluggard and branded a 'coalbiter'.] Arngeir and Thorgils left home in a snowstorm looking for sheep and never came back. Odd set off to look for them and found them both dead. A white bear had killed them: he was devouring his prey when Odd arrived on the scene. He killed the bear, then hauled it back home, and men report that he ate the whole of it, claiming that he avenged his father when he killed the bear, and his brother when he ate it. From there on Odd proved a very awkward one indeed. He was such a shape-changer that he walked from home, from Hraunhofn, one evening and next morning arrived in Thjorsardal to give help to his sister when the Thjorsardalers were about to stone her to death. [H. to stone her for witchcraft and troll-dom].[3]

7. *Hungry Years*

[*Skarðsárbók*, Viðauki, 1–2] There was a great famine-winter in Iceland in heathen days at the time when King Harald Gray-cloak fell and earl Hakon seized power in Norway [975–6], the severest there has been in Iceland. Men ate ravens then and foxes, and many abominable things were eaten which ought not to be eaten, and some had the old and helpless killed and thrown over the cliffs. Many starved to death, while others took to theft and for that were convicted and slain. Even the outlaws killed each other, for at the instance of Eyjolf Valgerdarson it was made law that anyone who killed three outlaws should him-self go free.

Eighty years later came another year of dearth. It started that winter Isleif was consecrated as bishop by bishop Albertus of Bremen, in the days of King Harald Sigurdarson. And the first winter Isleif was in Iceland [1057–8] there was severe mortality here because of hunger. Everything was eaten then that tooth could fasten on.

During the summer the bishop had a vow taken at the Thing that men should fast on the twelfth day of Yule for three years, for that was the custom at Herford in Germany where he had been at school. There was such deep snow everywhere at this time that most men had to walk to the Thing [in June]. But as soon as this vow was taken the weather cleared immediately, it developed into a splendid summer, and the following winter was so clement that the earth was quite unfrozen, and men walked barefoot to service at Yule, and built houses and walls during January and February.

[*Kristni Saga, c*.14] In the year bishop Gizur died [1118] there was a great famine in Iceland. During Holy Week there came so great a snowstorm that in some districts in the north men could not hold services in the churches. On Good Friday itself a mer-chant ship was driven ashore under Eyjafjall, spun into the air, fifty-four-oared vessel as she was, and dashed down bottom up.

---

[3] A walk of about 220 miles over some of Iceland's worst country.

The first day of Easter few men could get to service to take the sacrament, and some perished out of doors.

A second storm came after his death, the day men rode to the Thing [19 or 20 June]. It was then that the church at Thingvellir for which King Harald Sigurdarson had had the timber cut was broken to pieces.

That summer thirty-five ships came out to Iceland; many were wrecked on the coast, some broke up at sea under their crews' feet, and only eight got away again, including those which had spent the previous winter here, while none of them got off the sea before Michaelmas. By reason of this host of men there was a great famine here . . .

One year after the death of bishop Gizur a notable person, Thorstein Hallvardsson, was killed. The year after that the Thing was very well attended. During those seasons the mortality had been so high that priest Sæmund the Learned made an announcement at the Thing that the men who had died of sickness could not be fewer in number than those who were then attending the Thing.

8. *Of the Settlement in General*

I

[H. 294] The Eastfirths were settled first in Iceland; but between Hornafjord and Reykjanes was the area last to be fully settled: there wind and surf stopped men getting ashore, what with the lack of harbours and the exposed nature of the coast.

Some of those who came out earliest lived close up to the mountains, remarking the quality of the land there, and how the livestock was keen to get away from the sea up to the high ground. Those who came out later thought that these first-comers had made over-extensive settlements; but King Harald Fairhair made peace between them on these terms, that no one should settle land more widely than he and his crew could carry fire round in one day.

They must light a fire when the sun showed in the east. They must light further smoke-fires, so that each might be observed from the other, and those fires which were lighted when the sun showed in the east must burn till nightfall. Afterwards they

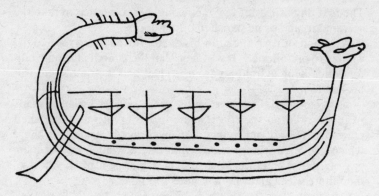

21. A NORSE SHIP
From Bergen, first half of the thirteenth century

must walk until the sun was in the west, and at that point light other fires.

II

[*Skarðsárbók* 313] It was the law that a woman should not take land in settlement more widely than a two-year-old heifer, a half stalled beast in good condition, might be led round on a spring day between the rising and setting of the sun.

III

[H. 268] This was the beginning of the heathen laws, that men should not have a ship with a figure-head at sea, but if they had, they must remove the head before coming in sight of land, and not sail to land with gaping heads and yawning jaws, so that the spirits of the land grow frightened of them.

IV

[S. 398] Learned men say that the land was fully settled in a space of sixty years, so that the settlements have not been more numerous ever since. At that time many of the original settlers and their sons were still alive.

V

[S. 399] Learned men say that some of the settlers who occupied Iceland were baptized men, mostly those who came from west across the sea. Under this head are named Helgi Magri and Orlyg the Old, Helgi Bjola, Jorund the Christian, Aud the Deep-minded, Ketil the Fool, and still more men who came from west across the sea. Some of them remained faithful to Christianity to the day of their death, but this rarely held good for their families, for the sons of some of them raised temples and sacrificed, and the land was altogether heathen for about a hundred years.

VI

[H. 354] Now the settlements which were made in Iceland have been rehearsed according to what learned men have written, first priest Ari the Learned, Thorgils' son, and Kolskegg the Learned. But I, Hauk Erlendsson, wrote this book after the book written by Herra Sturla Thordarson the Lawman, a most learned man, and after another book written by Styrmir the Learned. I took from each book whatever it contained over and above the other, though for the most part they had the same matter to relate; it is not surprising therefore that this *Landnámabók* is longer than any other.

6

The Greenlanders' Saga

Grænlendinga Saga

I

THERE was a man by the name of Thorvald, the son of Asvald, son of Ulf Oxen-Thorir's son. Thorvald and his son Eirik the Red left the Jaeder [in Norway] for Iceland because of some killings. Iceland was by this time extensively settled. They made their first home at Drangar, High Rocks, in the Hornstrandir, where Thorvald died. Eirik married Thjodhild, the daughter of Jorund and Thorbjorg Ship-bosom, who was by this time married to Thorbjorn the Haukadaler. Eirik now left the north and made his home at Eiriksstadir alongside Vatnshorn. Eirik and Thjodhild's son bore the name Leif.

After killing Eyjolf Saur and Holmgang-Hrafn, Eirik was driven out of Haukadal, moved west to Breidafjord, and made a home on Oxney at Eiriksstadir. He lent Thorgest his dais-beams, but failed to get them back when he asked for them, out of which arose the quarrels and strife with Thorgest and his people of which there is an account in Eirik's saga. Styr Thorgrimsson backed Eirik's case, as did Eyjolf from Sviney, the sons of Thorbrand from Alptafjord, and Thorbjorn Vifilsson; while backing Thorgest and his side were the sons of Thord Gellir together with Thorgeir from Hitardal.

Eirik was outlawed at the Thorsnes Thing. He fitted out his ship for sea in Eiriksvag, and when he was ready to leave, Styr and the others escorted him out past the islands. He told them he meant to look for that land Gunnbjorn Ulf-Krakuson sighted the time he was storm-driven west across the ocean, when he discovered Gunnbjarnarsker, Gunnbjorn's Skerries. He would be coming back, he said, to get in touch with his friends should he discover that land.

Eirik sailed by way of Snæfellsjokul. He found that country,

making his landfall at the place he called Midjokul, which is
nowadays known as Blaserk, Blacksark. From there he headed
south along the coast, to discover whether the land was habitable in that direction. He spent his first winter at Eiriksey, near
the middle of the Eastern Settlement, and the following spring
went on to Eiriksfjord where he sited his house. In the summer
he made his way into the western wilderness, bestowing place-
names far and wide. He spent his second winter at Holmar by
Hvarfsgnipa, but during the third summer pressed on north the
whole way to Snæfell and into Hrafnsfjord. He now reckoned
he had got as far as the head of Eiriksfjord, so turned back and
spent the third winter at Eiriksey off the mouth of Eiriksfjord.

The following summer he returned to Iceland and brought his
ship to Breidafjord. He called the country he had discovered
Greenland [AM 53 fol. Green Land], for he argued that men
would be drawn to go there if the land had an attractive name.
He spent the winter in Iceland, but the following summer went
off to colonize the land. He made his home at Brattahlid, Steep
Slope, in Eiriksfjord.

Learned men tell us that this same summer Eirik the Red
went off to colonize Greenland, thirty-five [AM 53 fol., 54 fol.,
61 fol., and Bergsbók: twenty-five] ships set sail from Breidafjord and Borgarfjord, but only fourteen of them succeeded in
getting there. Some were forced back and some perished. This
was fifteen years before the Christian faith became law in Iceland. It was this same summer bishop Fridrek and Thorvald
Kodransson returned to Norway from Iceland.

These men who went out with Eirik at this time took land in
settlement in Greenland: Herjolf took Herjolfsfjord (he lived at
Herjolfsnes); Ketil, Ketilsfjord; Hrafn, Hrafnsfjord; Solvi,
Solvadal; Helgi Thorbrandsson, Alptafjord; Thorbjorn Glora,
Siglufjord; Einar, Einarsfjord; Hafgrim, Hafgrimsfjord and
Vatnahverfi; Arnlaug, Arnlaugsfjord. While some went on to
the Western Settlement.

IA

When sixteen [AM 53 fol., 54 fol., 61 fol., and *Bergsbók*: four-
teen] years had elapsed from the time Eirik the Red went off to
settle Greenland, his son Leif made a voyage from Greenland

to Norway. He reached Thrandheim that same autumn King Olaf Tryggvason had departed from the north, out of Halogaland. Leif brought his ship to Nidaros and went immediately to see King Olaf, who preached the Faith to him as to those other heathen men who came to see him. The king found Leif no problem; he was baptized with all his shipmates, and spent the winter with the king, and was well entertained by him. [*Flateyjarbók*, col. 222.]

That same summer [*i.e.* the year 1000] King Olaf sent Gizur and Hjalti to Iceland, as was recorded earlier. And now he sent Leif to Greenland, to preach Christianity there. The king provided him with a priest and various other holy men to baptize folk there and instruct them in the true faith. Leif set sail for Greenland that summer, and while at sea picked up a ship's crew of men who lay helpless there on a wreck. He reached Greenland at the end of summer and went to lodge at Brattahlid with Eirik his father. From this time forward men called him Leif the Lucky, but his father contended that one thing cancelled out the other, in that Leif had rescued a ship's company and saved the men's lives, but had also introduced a shyster (for such he styled the priest) into Greenland. Even so by the advice and persuasion of Leif Eirik was baptized, and all the people of Greenland.[1] [*Flateyjarbók*, col. 233.]

II

Herjolf was the son of Bard Herjolfsson; he was a kinsman of Ingolf the Settler. Ingolf gave [the elder] Herjolf and his people land between Vag and Reykjanes. At first Herjolf [the younger]

---

[1] The statement of the saga, p. 197, that Eirik died in heathendom is to be preferred. His odour in tradition was certainly that of a heathen. One remembers his rumoured attachment to the white bear killed by Thorgils in *Flóamanna Saga* (see p. 81 above), and his shapestrong kinsman Farserk in *Landnámabók*. Yet when the news of the Conversion of Iceland blew over the intervening ocean, as it must have done soon after the year 1000, he may well have had himself primesigned in Viking fashion (i.e. signed with the cross, but not baptized, so that he might live in fellowship with Christian men and even be buried in the outer verges of a Christian churchyard, and all this without formally renouncing his heathen beliefs). *Prima signatio* would have had the important result of reconciling Eirik with his strong-willed wife Thjodhild and securing him domestic peace (see p. 217 below).

lived at Drepstokk. His wife's name was Thorgerd, and their son's Bjarni, a most promising young man. From his early days onwards he was a keen traveller abroad, and had prospered both in purse and general reputation. He spent his winters overseas or with his father alternately, and very soon had a ship of his own for voyaging. The last winter Bjarni spent in Norway, Herjolf went off to Greenland with Eirik and got rid of his farm. On board ship with Herjolf was a Christian from the Hebrides, he who composed the *Hafgerðingadrápa* or Lay of the Towering Waves,[2] which contains this verse:

> I pray the blameless monk-prover,
> Our Father, my journey to further;
> Heaven's lord, may he bless and let hover
> His hawk-perching hand my head over.

Herjolf made a home at Herjolfsnes, and a most admirable man he was. Eirik the Red lived at Brattahlid; his state was one of high distinction, and all recognized his authority. These were Eirik's children: Leif, Thorvald and Thorstein, and a daughter whose name was Freydis, who was married to a man named Thorvard. They lived at Gardar, where the bishop's seat is nowadays. She was very much the virago, while Thorvard was just a nobody. She had been married to him mainly for his money. The people in Greenland were heathen at this time.

Bjarni brought his ship to Eyrar that same summer his father had sailed away in the spring. He was taken heavily aback by the news, and had no mind to discharge his ship's cargo. His shipmates asked him what he proposed to do, and he replied that he meant to carry on as usual and enjoy winter quarters at

---

[2] The author of the *King's Mirror* in his account of the marvels of the Greenland seas has this to say of the Sea-Hedges or Towering Waves: 'Now there is still another marvel in the seas of Greenland, the facts of which I do not know precisely. It is called 'sea hedges', *hafgerðingar*, and it has the appearance as if all the waves and tempests of the ocean have been collected into three heaps, out of which three billows have formed. These hedge in the entire sea, so that no opening can be seen anywhere; they are higher than lofty mountains and resemble steep, overhanging cliffs. In a few cases only have the men been known to escape who were upon the seas when such a thing occurred' (trans. Larsen). Steenstrup's century-old explanations that these were the result of seaquakes (*Aarb. f. nord. Oldkynd. og Hist.* (1871)) has now yielded to the Sawatzky–Lehn thesis of the effect of the Arctic mirage (see pp. 22–3 above).

his father's home. 'I shall steer my ship for Greenland, if you are prepared to go along with me.' They all said they would abide by his decision. 'Our voyage will appear foolhardy,' said Bjarni, 'since no one of us has entered the Greenland Sea.' Even so they put out the moment they were ready, and sailed for three days before losing sight of land. Then their following wind died down, and north winds and fog overtook them, so that they had no idea which way they were going. This continued over many days, but eventually they saw the sun and could then get their bearings [*or* determine the quarters of the heavens]. They now hoisted sail, and sailed that day before sighting land, and debated among themselves what land this could be. To his way of thinking, said Bjarni, it could not be Greenland. They asked him whether he proposed to sail to this land or not. 'My intention', he replied, 'is to sail close in to the land.' Which they did, and could soon see that the land was not mountainous and was covered with forest, with low hills there, so they left the land to port of them and let their sheet turn towards the land.

After this they sailed for two days before sighting another land. They asked whether Bjarni thought this in its turn was Greenland. In his opinion, he said, this was no more Greenland than the first place—'For there are very big glaciers reported to be in Greenland.' They soon drew near to this land, and could see that it was flat country and covered with woods. Then their following wind died on them. The crew talked things over and said they thought it common sense to put ashore there; but this Bjarni would not allow. They reckoned they were in need of both wood and water. 'You lack for neither,' said Bjarni, and got some hard words for this from his crew.

He gave orders to hoist sail, which was done; they turned their prow from the land and sailed out to sea three days with a south-west wind, and then they saw the third land, and this land was high, mountainous, and glaciered. They asked whether Bjarni would put ashore there, but no, he said, he had no wish to. 'For to me this land looks good for nothing.' So without so much as lowering their sail they held on along the land, and came to see that it was an island.

Once more they turned their prow from the land and held out to sea with the same following wind. Soon the wind freshened, so Bjarni ordered them to reef, and not crowd more sail than was safe for their ship and tackle. This time they sailed for four days, and then saw the fourth land. They asked Bjarni whether he thought this was Greenland or not. 'This is very like what I am told about Greenland,' replied Bjarni, 'and here we will make for the land.'

So that is what they did, and came to land under a certain cape in the evening of the day. There was a boat on the cape, and there too on the cape lived Herjolf, Bjarni's father. It was for this reason the ness got its name, and has been known ever since as Herjolfsnes. Bjarni now went to his father's, gave over his sailing and stayed with him for the rest of Herjolf's life, and later lived there as his father's successor.

III

The next thing that happened[3] was that Bjarni Herjolfsson came over from Greenland to see earl Eirik, and the earl made him welcome. Bjarni gave an account of those travels of his on which he had seen these lands, and people thought how lacking in enterprise and curiosity he had been in that he had nothing to report of them, and he won some reproach for this. Bjarni became a retainer of the earl's, and next summer returned to Greenland.

There was now much talk about voyages of discovery. Leif, son of Eirik the Red of Brattahlid, went to see Bjarni Herjolfsson, bought his ship from him, and found her a crew, so that they were thirty-five all told. Leif invited Eirik his father to lead this expedition too, but Eirik begged off rather, reckoning he was now getting on in years, and was less able to stand the rigours of hard times at sea than he used to be. Leif argued that of all their family he would still command the best luck, so Eirik gave way to him, and once they were ready for their voyage came riding from home. When he had only a short way to cover to the ship, the horse he was riding on stumbled, Eirik fell off, and damaged his foot. 'It is not in my destiny', said Eirik then,

---

[3] The narrator means after the death of Olaf Tryggvason at the sea-fight at Svold, in the year 1000. Earl Eirik Hakonarson, one of his adversaries there, then became earl of Norway. See *Íslendingabók*, p. 150 above.

'to discover more lands than this we are now living in. Nor may we continue further this time all together.' Eirik returned home to Brattahlid, but Leif rode on to the ship and his comrades with him, thirty-five of them all told. There was a German on the expedition named Tyrkir.

They now prepared their ship and sailed out to sea once they were ready, and they lighted on that land first which Bjarni and his people had lighted on last. They sailed to land there, cast anchor and put off a boat, then went ashore, and could see no grass there. The background was all great glaciers, and right up to the glaciers from the sea as it were a single slab of rock. The land impressed them as barren and useless. 'At least', said Leif, 'it has not happened to us as to Bjarni over this land, that we failed to get ourselves ashore. I shall now give the land a name, and call it Helluland, Flatstone Land.' After which they returned to the ship.

After that they sailed out to sea and lighted on another land. This time too they sailed to land, cast anchor, then put off a boat and went ashore. The country was flat and covered with forest, with extensive white sands wherever they went, and shelving gently to the sea. 'This land', said Leif, 'shall be given a name in accordance with its nature, and be called Markland, Wood Land.' After which they got back down to the ship as fast as they could.

From there they now sailed out to sea with a north-east wind and were at sea two days before catching sight of land. They sailed to land, reaching an island which lay north of it, where they went ashore and looked about them in fine weather, and found that there was dew on the grass, whereupon it happened to them that they set their hands to the dew, then carried it to their mouths and thought they had never known anything so sweet as that was. After which they returned to their ship and sailed into the sound which lay between the island and the cape projecting north from the land itself. They made headway west round the cape. There were big shallows there at low water; their ship went aground, and it was a long way to look to get sight of the sea from the ship. But they were so curious to get ashore they had no mind to wait for the tide to rise under their ship, but went hurrying off to land where a river flowed out of a lake. Then, as soon as the tide rose under their ship, they took their boat, rowed back to her, and brought her up into the river, and so to the lake, where they cast anchor, carried their skin sleeping-bags off board, and built themselves booths. Later they decided to winter there and built big houses.

There was no lack of salmon there in river or lake, and salmon bigger than they had ever seen before. The nature of the land was so choice, it seemed to them that none of the cattle would require fodder for the winter. No frost came during the winter, and the grass was hardly withered. Day and night were of a more equal length there than in Greenland or Iceland. On the shortest day of winter the sun was visible in the middle of the afternoon as well as at breakfast time.[4]

Once they had finished their house-building Leif made an announcement to his comrades. 'I intend to have our company divided now in two, and get the land explored. Half our band shall remain here at the hall, and the other half reconnoitre the countryside—yet go no further than they can get back home in the evening, and not get separated.' So for a while that is what they did, Leif going off with them or remaining in camp by turns. Leif was big and strong, of striking appearance, shrewd, and in every respect a temperate, fair-dealing man.

One evening it turned out that a man of their company was missing. This was Tyrkir the German. Leif was greatly put out by this, for Tyrkir had lived a long while with him and his father, and had shown great affection for Leif as a child. He gave his shipmates the rough edge of his tongue, then turned out to go and look for him, taking a dozen men with him. But when they had got only a short way from the hall there was Tyrkir coming to meet them. His welcome was a joyous one. Leif could see at once that his foster-father was in fine fettle. He was a man with a bulging forehead, rolling eyes, and an insignificant little face, short and not much to look at, but handy at all sorts of crafts.

'Why are you so late, foster-father,' Leif asked him, 'and parted this way from your companions?'

---

[4] Literally: The sun had there *eyktarstaðr* and *dagmálastaðr* on the shortest day (*or* days). The Norsemen had no clock time in the early eleventh century, but the period indicated was more or less that extending three hours each side of noon.

By way of a start Tyrkir held forth a long while in German, rolling his eyes all ways, and pulling faces. They had no notion what he was talking about. Then after a while he spoke in Norse. 'I went no great way further than you, yet I have a real novelty to report. I have found vines and grapes.'

'Is that the truth, foster-father?' Leif asked.

'Of course it's the truth,' he replied. 'I was born where wine and grapes are no rarity.'

They slept overnight, then in the morning Leif made this announcement to his crew. 'We now have two jobs to get on with, and on alternate days must gather grapes or cut vines and fell timber, so as to provide a cargo of such things for my ship.' They acted upon these orders, and report has it that their tow-boat was filled with grapes [?raisins]. A full ship's cargo was cut, and in the spring they made ready and sailed away. Leif gave the land a name in accordance with the good things they found in it, calling it Vinland, Wineland; after which they sailed out to sea and had a good wind till they sighted Greenland and its mountains under their glaciers.

Then a man broke silence and said to Leif: 'Why do you steer the ship so near the wind?'

'My mind is on my steering,' Leif replied, 'but on other things as well. Do you notice anything out of the way?'

No, they said, they saw nothing unusual.

'I am not clear,' said Leif, 'whether I see a ship there or a reef.'

Now they could see it too and reckoned it was a reef. But Leif's sight was so much ahead of theirs that he could pick out men on the reef.

'What I am thinking is for us to beat up into the wind', said Leif, 'so that we can close them if they need a call from us, and we find ourselves obliged to go and help them. But if they are not peaceful men, we and not they will have control of the situation.'

So now they worked up to the reef, lowered their sail and dropped anchor, and put off the second small boat they had with them. Tyrkir asked who was in charge of their party.

His name was Thorir, their leader replied. He was a Norse man by descent. 'And what is your name?'

Leif told him.

'Are you a son of Eirik the Red of Brattahlid?' he asked him.

Leif said yes, he was. 'And what I want now is to invite you all aboard my ship with as much of your goods as she can take.'

They accepted the offer and afterwards sailed for Eiriksfjord with this load, till they reached Brattahlid, where they discharged their cargo. Then Leif invited Thorir to stay with him together with Gudrid his wife and three men besides, and found lodgings for the rest of the crews, Thorir's mates as well as his own. Leif lifted fifteen men off the reef. He was afterwards known as Leif the Lucky, and had prospered now in both purse and reputation.

That winter a severe sickness afflicted Thorir's company, and Thorir died, together with a great part of his crew. Eirik the Red died too that winter.

IV

There was now much discussion of Leif's expedition to Vinland. His brother Thorvald considered that the land had been explored in too restricted a fashion. So Leif said to Thorvald, 'If you want to, go you to Vinland, brother, in my ship; but first I want her to go for the timber which Thorir had on the reef.'

That was done, and now Thorvald made preparations for this voyage along with thirty men, under the guidance of Leif his brother. Later they put their ship ready and sailed out to sea, and nothing is recorded of their voyage till they came to Vinland, to Leifsbudir, where they saw to their ship and stayed quiet over the winter, catching fish for their food. But in the spring Thorvald ordered them to make their ship ready, and for the ship's boat and certain of the men to proceed westward along the coast and explore there during the summer. It looked to them a beautiful and well-wooded land, the woods scarcely any distance from the sea, with white sands, and a great many islands and shallows. Nowhere did they come across habitation of man or beast, but on an island in the west found a wooden grain-holder. They found no other work of man, so returned and reached Leifsbudir that autumn.

Next summer Thorvald set off eastwards with the merchant-ship and further north along the land. Off a certain cape they met with heavy weather, were driven ashore, and broke the

keel from under the ship. They made a long stay there, mending
their ship. Said Thorvald to his shipmates: 'I should like us to
erect the keel on the cape here, and call it Kjalarnes, Keelness.'
This they did, and afterwards sailed away and east along the
land, and then into the entrance to two adjoining fjords, and to
a headland jutting out there which was entirely covered with
forest. They brought the ship to where they could moor her,
thrust out a gangway to the shore, and Thorvald walked ashore
with his full ship's company. 'This is a lovely place,' he said,
'and here I should like to make my home.' Then they made for
the ship, and saw three mounds on the sands up inside the headland. They walked up to them and could see three skin-boats
there, and three men under each. So they divided forces and
laid hands on them all, except for one who got away with his
canoe. The other eight they killed, and afterwards walked back
to the headland, where they had a good look around and could
see various mounds on up the fjord which they judged to be
human habitations. Then after this so great a drowsiness overtook them that they could not keep awake, and all fell asleep.
Then a cry carried to them, so that they were all roused up, and
the words of the cry were these: 'Rouse ye, Thorvald, and all
your company, if you would stay alive. Back to your ship with
all your men, and leave this land as fast as you can!' With that
there came from inside the fjord a countless fleet of skin-boats
and attacked them. 'We must rig up our war-roof', ordered
Thorvald, 'each side of the ship, and defend ourselves to the
utmost, yet offer little by way of attack.' Which they did. The
Skrælings kept shooting at them for a while, but then fled away,
each one as fast as he could.

Thorvald now inquired among his men whether anyone was
wounded. Not a wound among them, they assured him. 'I have
got a wound under my arm,' he told them. 'An arrow flew in
between gunwale and shield, under my arm. Here is the arrow,
and it will be the death of me. I command you, make the fastest
preparations you can for your return. As for me, you shall carry
me to that headland where I thought I should so like to make
my home. Maybe it was truth that came into my mouth, that I
should dwell there awhile. For there you shall bury me, and set
crosses at my head and feet, and call it Krossanes for ever
more.'

Greenland was at that time Christian, though Eirik the Red had died before the coming of Christianity.

Now Thorvald died. They did everything he had asked of them, and afterwards set off and rejoined their comrades, and they told each other such tidings as they had to tell. They stayed there that winter and gathered grapes and vines for the ship. The following spring they prepared to leave for Greenland, and brought their ship into Eiriksfjord, and the news they had to tell Leif was big news indeed.

V

Meanwhile, what had happened in Greenland was that Thorstein of Eiriksfjord had taken a wife, and married Gudrid Thorbjarnardottir, who, as was recorded earlier, had been the wife of Thorir Eastman. But now Thorstein Eiriksson felt impelled to go to Vinland to fetch the body of his brother Thorvald; he put the same ship in readiness, choosing her crew for their size and strength, and taking with him twenty-five men and Gudrid his wife. As soon as they were ready they sailed to sea and out of sight of land. They were storm-tossed the whole summer, had no notion where they were going, but after one week of winter reached land at Lysufjord in Greenland in the Western Settlement. Thorstein looked round for lodgings for them, and found such for all his shipmates, but he and his wife were left stranded and had to remain a couple of nights on board ship.

Christianity was still in its infancy in Greenland at this time.

It happened early one morning that some men came to their tent on board ship, and their leader asked what people they might be in the tent.

'There are two of us,' replied Thorstein. 'Who is asking?'

'My name is Thorstein, but I am known as Thorstein the Black. My purpose in coming here is that I would like to ask both you and your wife to come and stay with me.'

Thorstein said he would have to consult his wife, who however left it to him, so he accepted.

'Then I will come for you tomorrow with a carthorse, for I lack nothing in the way of provision for you both. But is is very quiet staying with me, for there are just the two of us, my wife and myself, at home. I am not very sociable. Also I hold a different faith from yours, though I suspect you hold the better.'

He came for them next day with the carthorse, and they went to stay with Thorstein the Black, who looked after them well. Gudrid was a woman of handsome appearance, clever, and very good at getting on with strangers.

Early in the winter a sickness attacked Thorstein Eiriksson's company, and many of his shipmates died. He ordered coffins to be made for the bodies of those who perished, had them conveyed to the ship, and suitable arrangements made for them. 'For I mean to have all the bodies transferred to Eiriksfjord in the summer.' There was only a brief respite till the sickness attacked Thorstein the Black's household too. The first to fall ill was his wife, whose name was Grimhild. She was a great strapping woman, strong as a man, yet her illness brought her low, even so. Shortly afterwards Thorstein Eiriksson fell ill; they were both laid up at the same time; then Grimhild, Thorstein the Black's wife, died. Once she was dead Thorstein the Black went out of the room for a board to lay the corpse on. Said Gudrid: 'Don't be away long, my Thorstein!' So be it, he said. Then Thorstein Eiriksson spoke: 'Marvellous are the ways of our hostess now, for she is heaving herself up on her elbows, and swinging her feet over the bedstock, and feeling for her shoes.' At that same moment in came franklin Thorstein, and instantly Grimhild fell back, and every beam in the room gave out a groan. And now Thorstein made a coffin for Grimhild's body, and carried it out and made suitable arrangements for it. And though he was a man both big and strong, he needed all his powers before he succeeded in getting her out of the house.

Now Thorstein Eiriksson's illness grew worse, and he died. Gudrid his wife was quite distraught. They were all there in the living-room at the time. Gudrid had seated herself on a stool in front of the bench on which her husband Thorstein was lying, and now franklin Thorstein lifted her in his arms off the stool, and sat down with her on another bench opposite Thorstein's body, and spoke to her helpfully in many ways, comforting her, and promising that he would keep her company to Eiriksfjord with the bodies of Thorstein her husband and his shipmates. 'Also,' he told her, 'I will take on more people here, for your comfort and solace.'

She thanked him. But then Thorstein Eiriksson sat up, and—
'Where is Gudrid?' he asked.

Three times he asked this, but she stayed silent.

Then she asked franklin Thorstein: 'Shall I answer his question, or not?'

He told her not to answer. Then franklin Thorstein walked across the floor and sat on the stool, with Gudrid seated on his knees. 'What do you want,' he asked, 'namesake mine?'

There was a pause, then he answered: 'I am anxious to tell Gudrid what lies ahead of her, that she may bear my death more resignedly, for I have come to a good resting-place. What I have to tell you, Gudrid, is this, that you will be given in marriage to an Icelander, and long shall be your life together. Many descendants shall spring from you and him, vigorous, bright and noble, sweet and of good savour. You shall leave Greenland for Norway, and Norway for Iceland, and in Iceland make a home. There you will live, the two of you, for a long time, and you shall live longer than he. You shall go abroad, and make a pilgrimage south to Rome, and return home to Iceland to your own place, whereupon a church shall be raised there, where you will live and take the vows of a nun, and where you will die.'

Then Thorstein sank back, and his body was laid out and carried to the ship.

Franklin Thorstein made good all his promises to Gudrid. He disposed of his holdings and livestock in the spring, saw Gudrid to the ship together with everything they possessed, got the ship all ready and found her a crew, and afterwards made the journey to Eiriksfjord, where the bodies were laid to rest at the church. Gudrid went to Leif's at Brattahlid, while Thorstein the Black built himself a home in Eiriksfjord and lived there for the rest of his life, and was held to be a very fine man.

VI

That same summer a ship arrived in Greenland from Norway. Her captain was a man named Thorfinn Karlsefni, a son of Thord Horsehead, the son of Snorri Thordarson of Hofdi. Thorfinn Karlsefni was a very well-to-do man, and spent the winter at Brattahlid with Leif Eiriksson. It did not take him long to set his heart on Gudrid; he asked for her hand, and she left it to Leif to answer for her. So now she was betrothed to him and their wedding took place that winter.

There was the same talk and to-do over the Vinland voyages as before, and the people there, Gudrid as well as the rest, put strong pressure on Karlsefni to undertake an expedition. So his voyage was decided on, and he secured himself a ship's company of sixty men and five women. Karlsefni entered into this agreement with his shipmates, that they should receive equal shares of everything they made by way of profit. They took with them all sorts of livestock, for it was their intention to colonize the country if they could manage it. Karlsefni asked Leif for his houses in Vinland. He would lend the houses, he said, but not give them.

Next, then, they sailed their ship to sea and reached Leifs-budir all safe and sound, and carried their sleeping-bags ashore. They soon enjoyed a big and splendid catch, for a fine big whale was stranded there. They went and cut it up, and had no problem with regard to food. The livestock went on up ashore there, but it was soon found that the males grew unmanageable and played havoc all round. They had brought the one bull with them. Karlsefni had timber felled and dressed for his ship's cargo, laying the wood out on a rock to dry. They took every advantage of the resources the country had to offer, both in the way of grapes and all kinds of hunting and fishing and good things.

After that first winter came summer. It was now they made acquaintance with the Skrælings, when a big body of men appeared out of the forest there. Their cattle were close by; the bull began to bellow and bawl his head off, which so frightened the Skrælings that they ran off with their packs, which were of grey furs and sables and skins of all kinds, and headed for Karlsefni's house, hoping to get inside there, but Karlsefni had the doors guarded. Neither party could understand the other's language. Then the Skrælings unslung their bales, untied them, and proffered their wares, and above all wanted weapons in exchange. Karlsefni, though, forbade them the sale of weapons. And now he hit on this idea: he told the women to carry out milk to them, and the moment they saw the milk that was the one thing they wanted to buy, nothing else. So that was what came of the Skrælings' trading: they carried away what they bought in their bellies, while Karlsefni and his comrades kept their bales and their furs. And with that they went away.

The next thing to report is how Karlsefni had a formidable stockade built around his house and they put everything in good order. At this time too his wife Gudrid gave birth to a boy whom they named Snorri. Early in the second winter the Skrælings came to visit them; they were much more numerous than last time, but had the same wares as before. 'And now', Karlsefni ordered the women, 'you must fetch out food similar to what made such a hit before, and not a thing besides.' And once the Skrælings saw that they tossed their packs in over the palisade.

Gudrid was sitting inside in the doorway by the cradle of Snorri her son when a shadow fell across the door, and a woman walked indoors in a dark close-fitting kirtle [?*námkyrtill*]— rather short she was, and wearing a band around her head, her hair a light chestnut, pale of face, and with such big eyes that no one ever saw their equal in a human skull. She walked to where Gudrid was sitting.

'What is your name?' she asked.

'My name is Gudrid. And what is your name?'

'My name is Gudrid,' she replied.

At that Gudrid the housewife held out her hand to her, that she should sit down beside her, when all of a sudden Gudrid heard a loud crash and the woman disappeared. That very same moment one of the Skrælings was killed by a housecarle of Karlsefni's because he had tried to steal their weapons; and away they ran as fast as they could, leaving their clothes and their goods behind them. No one had noticed that woman except Gudrid.

'We had best lay our heads together now,' said Karlsefni, 'for I fancy they will be paying us a third and hostile visit in full force. So let us follow this plan, that ten men move forward on to the ness here, letting themselves be seen, while the rest of our company go into the forest to clear a place there for our cattle, against the time when their host advances from the wood. Also we must take our bull and let him march at our head.'

The ground where their clash was to take place was set out

after this fashion, that there was lake on one side and forest on the other, so they followed Karlsefni's plan. The Skrælings advanced to the spot Karlsefni had fixed on for battle, battle was joined, and many fell from among the Skrælings' host. There was one big, fine-looking man in the Skræling host who Karlsefni imagined must be their chief. One of the Skrælings had picked up an axe, he stared at it for a while, then swung at a comrade of his and cut at him. He fell dead on the instant, whereupon the big man caught hold of the axe, stared at it for a while, then flung it as far out over the water as he could. After which they fled to the forest, each as best he might, and that was the end of their encounter.

Karlsefni and his troop spent the entire winter there; but in the spring Karlsefni announced that he would be staying there no longer. He wanted to go to Greenland. They made ready for their journey, and fetched away with them many valuable commodities in the shape of vines, grapes, and furs. And now they sailed to sea, and reached Eiriksfjord safe with their ship, and it was there they spent the winter.

VII

There was now fresh talk of a Vinland voyage, for this appeared an enterprise at once profitable and honourable. The same summer that Karlsefni returned from Vinland a ship arrived in Greenland from Norway, commanded by two brothers, Helgi and Finnbogi, who stayed there in Greenland over the winter. These brothers were Icelanders by descent and from the East-firths. The next thing to report is that Freydis Eiriksdottir made a journey from her home at Gardar; she called to see the brothers Helgi and Finnbogi, and invited them to take their vessel on an expedition to Vinland, and have equal shares with her in all such profit as they might obtain there. They said they would, so from them she went on to see her brother Leif and asked him to give her the houses he had built in Vinland. He made his usual answer: he would lend the houses, he said, but not give them. The arrangement between Freydis and the brothers was this, that they should each take thirty able-bodied men on their ship, in addition to any womenfolk; but Freydis immediately showed her disregard for this, taking an extra five men and so concealing them that the brothers had no suspicion of it till they reached Vinland.

Now they put to sea, having arranged beforehand that so far as possible they would sail in company. There was, indeed, little between them, but even so the brothers arrived a shade ahead and carried their gear up to Leif's houses. But once Freydis arrived, they too unloaded ship and carried their gear up to the houses.

'Why have you carried your stuff in here?' Freydis demanded.

'Because we assumed', they said, 'the whole arrangement between us would be kept to.'

'Leif lent the houses to me,' she retorted, 'not to you.'

'We are no match for you in wickedness, we brothers', said Helgi. They moved their gear out and built their own hall, siting it further away from the sea by the lakeside, and making the necessary preparations, while Freydis had timber felled for her ship.

Now winter set in, and the brothers suggested starting games and holding entertainments to pass the time. That was the way of it for a while, till there was a turn for the worse between them, and deep division made, and the games ended, and no coming and going between the houses. This went on for much of the winter. Then early one morning Freydis got out of bed and put on her clothes (but not her shoes and stockings), and such was the weather that a heavy dew had fallen. She took her husband's cloak, wrapped it about her, then walked over to the brothers' house, to the door. A man had gone outside a little earlier and left the door ajar: she pushed it open, and stood in the entrance a while without saying a word.

Finnbogi was lying at the innermost end of the hall. He was awake. 'What do you want here, Freydis?'

'For you to get up and come outside with me. I want to talk to you.'

So that is what he did. They walked to a tree-trunk which lay under the wall of the house, and sat down on it.

'How are you liking things?' she asked him.

'I think the country a good and fruitful one,' he replied, 'but this cold wind blowing between us, I think that bad, for I swear there is no reason for it.'

'As you say,' said she. 'I think the same. But my business in coming to see you is that I should like to trade ships with you brothers, for you have a bigger one than mine, and I want to get away from here.'

'I can meet you on that,' he said, 'if it will please you.'

With that they parted, she went home, and Finnbogi back to bed. She climbed into bed with her cold feet, and at this Thorvard woke, and asked why she was so cold and wet. She anwered in a passion. 'I have been to those brothers,' she said, 'asking to buy their ship—I wanted to buy a bigger one. But they took it so badly that they beat me, maltreated me—and you, wretch that you are, will avenge neither my shame nor your own! I can see now that I am not back home in Greenland, but I shall separate from you unless you take vengeance for this.'

He could not endure this baiting of hers. He ordered his men to turn out immediately and take their weapons, which they did, and crossed straightway to the brothers' house and marched in on the sleeping men, seized them and bound them, then led them outside, each man as he was bound. And Freydis had each man killed as he came out.

Now all the men were killed, but the women were left, and no one would kill them.

'Hand me an axe,' said Freydis.

Which was done, and she turned upon the five women they had there, and left them dead.

After this wicked deed they returned to their own quarters, and it was only too clear that Freydis felt she had handled the situation very well. She had this to say to her companions. 'If it is our fate to return to Greenland, I shall be the death of any man who so much as mentions what has taken place. What we must say is that they stayed behind here when we sailed away.'

So early in the spring they made ready the ship the brothers had owned, with every valuable commodity they could lay their hands on and the ship carry. Then they sailed to sea, had a good passage, and brought their ship to Eiriksfjord early in the summer. Karlsefni was still there and had his ship ready and waiting to put to sea. He was waiting for a wind, and men maintain that a more richly freighted ship never left Greenland than this one he was captain of.

Freydis now went to her farm, for it had taken no harm all this while. She made lavish gifts to all the members of her crew, because she wanted to keep her misdeeds hidden. She now settled down at home. But they were not all so secretive by nature as to keep their mouths shut about their crimes and misdeeds, so that they did not come to light in the end; and eventually it came to the ears of Leif her brother, who thought it a sorry story indeed. He seized three of Freydis's crew and tortured them till they confessed to the whole thing together, and their stories tallied. 'I have not the heart', said Leif, 'to treat my sister Freydis as she deserves, but I predict this of her and her husband: no offspring of theirs will come to much good.' And such proved the case, that from there on no one thought anything but ill of them.

But what must now be recounted is how Karlsefni made his ship ready and sailed to sea. He had a good crossing, reached Norway safe and sound, stayed there over the winter and disposed of his wares. They were made much of, both he and his wife, by the most notable people in Norway; but the following spring he made his ship ready for Iceland. When all was in readiness, his ship lying off the jetty and waiting for a wind, a southerner came up to him, a man from Bremen in Germany, and asked him to sell him his figurehead.[5]

'I don't want to sell,' said Karlsefni.

'I will give you half a mark of gold for it,' said the southerner.

This struck Karlsefni as a handsome offer, so they closed the deal, and off went the German with the figure-head. Karlsefni had no idea what wood it was; but it was maple [birds-eye maple? paper birch? *mösurr*] fetched from Vinland.

Karlsefni now sailed to sea and brought his ship to the north of Iceland, to Skagafjord, where she was drawn ashore for the winter. In the spring he bought Glaumbæjarland, and built a home there in which he lived for the rest of his life. He was a man of great distinction and nobility, and from him and his wife Gudrid has sprung a numerous and splendid progeny.

[5] *húsasnotra*: the ornament of a ship's prow or stern, which could also serve as the weather-vane or gable-decoration of a house. See Plate 18.

And when Karlsefni was dead, Gudrid and her son Snorri (he who had been born in Vinland) took charge of the estate. But when Snorri got married Gudrid went abroad and made a pilgrimage south to Rome, and afterwards returned to the home of her son Snorri, who had by now had a church built at Glaumbær. In course of time Gudrid became a nun and recluse, and it was there she spent the rest of her days. Snorri had a son named Thorgeir, who was the father of Yngvild, the mother of bishop Brand. The daughter of Snorri Karlsefni's son was named Hallfrid, who was the wife of Runolf, father of bishop Thorlak. Another son of Karlsefni and Gudrid was named Bjorn, who was the father of Thorunn, mother of bishop Bjorn. A great many men are descended from Karlsefni, who has proved a man blest in his kin. And it is Karlsefni who of all men reported most succinctly what happened on all these voyages of which some account has now been given.

7

Eirik the Red's Saga

Eiríks Saga Rauða
also called
Þorfinns Saga Karlsefnis (Þórðarsonar)

I

THERE was a king named Olaf who was known as Olaf the White: he was a son of King Ingjald, son of Helgi, son of Olaf, son of Gudrod, son of Halfdan Whiteleg the Upplanders' king. Olaf went raiding in the west and conquered Dublin in Ireland along with the Dublin territory, and made himself its king. He married Aud the Deep-minded, the daughter of Ketil Flatnose, son of Bjorn Buna, a man of rank from Norway; and the name of their son was Thorstein the Red. Olaf fell in battle there in Ireland, after which Aud and Thorstein made their way to the Hebrides, where Thorstein married Thurid the daughter of Eyvind Eastman and sister of Helgi Magri. They had many children.

Thorstein became a warrior-king and allied himself with earl Sigurd the Mighty, the son of Eystein Glumra, and they conquered Caithness and Sutherland, Ross and Moray, and more than half Scotland. Thorstein made himself king there, till the Scots betrayed him and he fell there in battle. Aud was in Caithness when she heard tell of Thorstein's death. She had a merchant ship built secretly in the forest, and once she was ready hoisted sail for the Orkneys and found a husband there for Thorstein the Red's daughter Groa, the mother of that Grelod whom earl Thorfinn Skull-splitter married. After that she set off to seek Iceland and had twenty freemen on board her ship. She reached Iceland and spent the first winter in Bjarnarhofn with her brother Bjorn. Later Aud took in settlement all Dalelands between Dogurdara and Skraumuhlaupsa. She made her home at Hvamm and had a place for her devotions at Krossholar, where she had crosses erected, for she had been baptized and held strongly to the Christian faith.

Many notable men accompanied her to Iceland who had been taken prisoner during the raiding west and were, in a manner of speaking, slaves. One of these was called Vifil. He was a man of good family who had been taken prisoner over the western sea and was, nominally at least, a slave till Aud set him free. When Aud gave homes to her ship's crew, Vifil asked why she didn't give him one like the rest of them, but Aud said it would signify little. He would be counted a fine man, she said, whatever his position. Still, she gave him Vifilsdal and he made his home there. He married a wife, and their sons were Thorgeir and Thorbjorn. These were promising men and grew up with their father.

II

There was a man by the name of Thorvald who was the son of Asvald, son of Ulf Oxen-Thorir's son. Thorvald's son was called Eirik the Red, and both father and son left the Jaeder [in Norway] for Iceland because of some killings. They settled in the Hornstrandir and made a home at Drangar, where Thorvald died. Eirik then married Thjodhild, the daughter of Jorund Ulfsson and Thorbjorg Ship-bosom, who was by this time married to Thorbjorn the Haukadaler. Eirik now left the north and cleared land in Haukadal and made his home at Eiriksstadir alongside Vatnshorn. In time Eirik's thralls caused a landslide to crash down upon the farm of Valthjof at Valthjofsstadir, whereupon Valthjof's kinsman Eyjolf Saur killed the thralls by Skeidsbrekkur above Vatnshorn. For this offence Eirik killed Eyjolf Saur. He killed Holmgang-Hrafn too at Leikskalar. Gerstein and Odd of Jorvi, both kinsmen of Eyjolf's, took up his case, and Eirik was thrown out of Haukadal. He then took possession of Brokey and Oxney, and lived at Tradir in Sudrey that first winter. It was now that he lent Thorgest his dais-beams. Eirik made his home at Eiriksstadir. He asked for his beams, but failed to get them. Eirik went to Breidabolstad to fetch the beams away, but Thorgest gave chase, and they came to blows a short way from the house at

Drangar. Two of Thorgest's sons fell there as well as certain other men.

From now on both sides kept a large body of men under arms. Styr and Eyjolf from Sviney, Thorbjorn Vifilsson and the sons of Thorbrand from Alptafjord backed Eirik, while backing Thorgest were the sons of Thord Gellir together with Thorgeir from Hitardal, Aslak from Langadal, and Illugi his son.

Eirik and his following were outlawed at the Thorsnes Thing. He put his ship all ready in Eiriksvag, while Eyjolf kept him in hiding in Dimunarvag for as long as Thorgest and his men were combing the islands for him. Thorbjorn, Eyjolf, and Styr escorted Eirik out past the islands, and they parted on warm terms of friendship, Eirik promising that they should receive just such help themselves, should it lie in his power to provide it and the occasion arise that they had need of him. He told them he meant to look for that land Gunnbjorn Ulf-Krakuson sighted the time he was storm-driven west across the ocean, when he discovered Gunnbjarnarsker, Gunnbjorn's Skerries. He would be coming back, he said, to get in touch with his friends should he discover that land.

Eirik sailed to the open sea by way of Snæfellsjokul and made his landfall at the glacier which is called Blaserk, Blacksark [557 Hvitserk, Whitesark]. From there he headed south, to discover whether the land was habitable in that direction. He spent his first winter at Eiriksey, near the middle of the Eastern [H. and 557 *wrongly* Western] Settlement, and the following spring went on to Eiriksfjord where he sited his house. In the summer he made his way into the western wilderness [H. *adds* spending a good deal of time there], and bestowed place-names far and wide. He spent his second winter at Eiriksholmar off Hvarfs-gnipa, but during the third summer pressed on north the whole way to Snæfell and into Hrafnsfjord. He now considered he had got as far as the head of Eiriksfjord, so turned back and spent the third winter at Eiriksey off the mouth of Eiriksfjord.

The following summer he returned to Iceland and reached Breidafjord. He spent the winter with Ingolf at Holmlat. In the spring he came to blows with Thorgest, and Eirik got the worst of it, but later they reached peace terms between them. This same summer Eirik went off to colonize the land he had discovered, calling it Greenland, for he argued that men would be all the more drawn to go there if the land had an attractive name.

III

Thorgeir Vifilsson found himself a wife, marrying Arnora the daughter of Einar of Laugarbrekka, the son of Sigmund, the son of Ketil Thistle who had settled Thistilfjord. The second of Einar's daughters was called Hallveig, whom Thorbjorn Vifilsson married, getting land at Laugarbrekka, at Hellisvellir, along with her. Thorbjorn moved house there and became a man of great note. He was a good farmer [557 a godord-man] and had a fine estate. His daughter, Gudrid by name, was a most beautiful woman and distinguished in everything she did and was.

Living at Arnarstapi was a man by the name of Orm, who had a wife named Halldis. Orm was a good farmer and a close friend of Thorbjorn's, and Gudrid was there a good long time with him as his foster-child.

Living at Thorgeirsfell was a man by the name of Thorgeir. He was prosperous and in his day had been freed from bondage. He had a son named Einar, a handsome, accomplished sort of person, and a great dandy too. He made his living by trading overseas, and had done well at it. He spent his winters in Iceland and Norway alternately. It must now be told how one autumn when Einar was here in Iceland he set off with his wares out along Snæfellsnes, with the intention of selling them there. He came to Arnarstapi, where Orm offered him hospitality which he accepted, for they were on very friendly terms together. Einar's goods were carried into a certain storehouse there, after which he unpacked them, showed them to Orm and his household, and invited him to help himself to anything he liked. Orm accepted, vowing that Einar was a good trader and one of fortune's favourites.

As they were busying themselves with the wares a woman walked past the storehouse door. Who could she be, Einar asked Orm, that lovely woman who walked past the doorway there? 'I have not seen her here before.'

'That is my foster-child Gudrid,' replied Orm, 'franklin Thorbjorn's daughter from Laugarbrekka.'

'She must be a fine match,' said Einar. 'Have not quite a lot of men come asking for her?'

'Why yes, she has been asked for, friend, naturally,' Orm told him, 'but she is not just for the picking up. It is the general opinion that she will be rather particular in her choice of a husband, and her father too.'

'All the same,' said Einar, 'she is the woman I mean to try for, so I should like you to put a case for me to her father, and make an effort to see that it succeeds, for I shall repay you with the full weight of my friendship. Master Thorbjorn must surely see that such family ties would suit us both admirably. He is a man of high reputation and great estate, yet his means I am told are diminishing fast; whereas I and my father with me are short of neither land nor money, and it would do Thorbjorn a power of good if this marriage could be arranged.'

'Certainly I regard myself as your friend,' said Orm, 'but I am not at all eager to put forward this proposal, even so, for Thorbjorn is a proud man, and ambitious too.'

Einar was emphatic that nothing would satisfy him but for his proposal to be put to Thorbjorn, so Orm agreed he should have his way. Einar then travelled back east [MSS south] until he reached home again.

Some time later Thorbjorn held a harvest feast as was his custom, for he was a princely sort of man. Orm attended from Arnarstapi, together with a good many other friends of Thorbjorn's. Orm found an opportunity to talk to Thorbjorn. He told him how Einar from Thorgeirsfell had visited him recently, and what a promising sort of man he was turning out to be, then went on to raise the question of marriage on Einar's behalf, claiming it would prove a good thing for more persons and reasons than one. 'It could well prove of great assistance to you, franklin, from the money point of view.'

'I did not expect such words from you', replied Thorbjorn, 'as that I should marry a daughter of mine to the son of a slave. You must be convinced my money is running out, and she shall not go back home with you, since you consider her worth so poor a match.'

After this Orm returned home, and all the other guests to their respective households. But Gudrid stayed behind with her father and spent the winter in her own home.

Then in the spring Thorbjorn sent out invitations to his friends, and a fine feast was prepared. A lot of people attended. In the course of the feast Thorbjorn called for silence, then spoke as follows: 'I have lived here a long while and had strong proof of men's goodwill and affection for me. And I believe we have got on well together, you and I. But now my affairs are taking a turn for the worse, though so far my estate has been held a not dishonourable one. Now I prefer to uproot my home rather than destroy my good name, and will sooner depart the country than bring shame on my family. I plan to fall back on the promise of my friend Eirik the Red, which he made when we parted from each other in Breidafjord, and if things go as I would have them, I mean to go to Greenland this summer.'

[H. This change of plan of his dumbfounded his hearers, for Thorbjorn was a very popular man; yet they felt sure that Thorbjorn had committed himself so deeply in speaking of this that there could be no question of dissuading him.] Thorbjorn gave presents to his guests, the feast came to an end, and with that everyone returned home. Thorbjorn sold his lands and bought himself a ship which had been laid up in Hraunhafnaros. Thirty men decided to undertake this voyage with him, among whom were Orm from Arnarstapi, together with his wife, and those of Thorbjorn's friends who could not bring themselves to part from him. In due course they put to sea. As they set off the weather was fine, but once they were out at sea the good wind dropped; they were caught in severe storms, and made slow progress the whole summer through. Next, sickness broke out in their company, and Orm died, as did Halldis his wife, and half their ship's company. A big sea got up, and they suffered great hardship and misery of all kinds, yet with it all reached Herjolfsnes in Greenland right at the start of winter. Living there at Herjolfsnes was a man by the name of Thorkel, a man of many skills and an excellent farmer. He took Thorbjorn into his house for the winter with his entire crew, and right royally he entertained them. Thorbjorn and all his shipmates had a very good time there.

At this same time there was a great famine in Greenland; men who had gone out fishing and hunting made poor catches, and some never came back. There was a woman there in the Settlement whose name was Thorbjorg; she was a seeress and was called the Little Sibyl. She had had nine sisters [H. *adds* all of them were seeresses], but now only she was left alive. It was Thorbjorg's practice of a winter to attend feasts, and those men in particular invited her to their homes who were curious to know their future or the season's prospects. Because Thorkel was the leading householder there it was considered his responsibility to find out when these hard times which now troubled them would come to an end, so he invited her to his home, and a good reception was prepared for her, as was the custom when a woman of this kind should be received. A high-seat was prepared for her, and a cushion laid down, in which there must be hen's feathers.

When she arrived in the evening, along with the man who had been sent to escort her, this is how she was attired: she was wearing a blue cloak with straps which was set with stones right down to the hem; she had glass beads about her neck, and on her head a black lambskin hood lined inside with white catskin. She had a staff in her hand, with a knob on it; it was ornamented with brass and set around with stones just below the knob. Round her middle she wore a belt made of touchwood, and on this was a big skin pouch in which she kept those charms she needed for her magic. On her feet she had hairy calf-skin shoes with lengthy, strong-looking thongs to them, and on the thong-ends big knobs of lateen. She had on her hands catskin gloves which were white inside and furry.

Now when she came inside everyone felt bound to offer her fit and proper greetings, which she received according as their donors found favour with her. Master Thorkel took the prophetess by the hand and led her to the seat which had been made ready for her. Thorkel then asked her to run her eyes over the household and herd and the home too. She had little comment to make about anything. During the evening tables were brought in, and what food was prepared for the seeress must now be told of. There was porridge made for her of goat's beestings, and for her meat the hearts of all living creatures that were available there. She had a brass spoon and a walrus-ivory-handled knife mounted with a double ring of copper, with its point broken off. Then when the tables were cleared away franklin Thorkel walked up to Thorbjorg and asked what she thought of the household there and men's state and condition, and how soon he [H. she] would be informed as to the things he had asked her and which men wanted to know. She replied that she would have nothing to announce till the following morning, when she had slept there the night through.

But on the morrow, in the latter part of the day, she was fitted out with the apparatus she needed to perform her spells. She asked too to procure her such women as knew the lore which was necessary for performing the spell, and bore the name Varðlokur [H. Varðlokkur], Spirit-locks. But no such women were to be found, so there was a search made right through the house to find whether anyone was versed in these matters.

'I am unversed in magic,' was Gudrid's reply, 'neither am I a prophetess, yet Halldis my foster-mother taught me in Iceland the lore [H. chant] which she called Varðlokur.'

'Then you are wiser than I dared hope,' said Thorbjorg.

'But this is a kind of lore and proceeding I feel I cannot assist in,' said Gudrid, 'for I am a Christian woman.'

'Yet it might happen', said Thorbjorg, 'that you could prove helpful to people in this affair, and still be no worse a woman than before. Still, I leave it to Thorkel to procure me the things I need here.'

Thorkel now pressed Gudrid hard, till she said she would do as he wished. The women now formed a circle all round, while Thorbjorg took her seat up on the spell-platform. Gudrid recited the chant so beautifully and well that no one present could say he had ever hear the chant recited by a lovelier voice. The seeress thanked her for the chant, saying that she had attracted many spirits there who thought it lovely to lend ear to the chant—spirits 'who before wished to hold aloof from us, and pay us no heed. And now many things stand revealed to me which earlier were hidden from me as from others. And I can tell you that this famine will not last longer [H. *adds* than this winter], and that the season will mend when spring comes. The sickness which has long afflicted us, that too will mend sooner than was expected. As for you, Gudrid, I shall repay you here and now for the help we have derived from you, for your future is now an open book to me. You will make a match here in Greenland, the most distinguished there is, yet it will not prove of long duration; for your ways lie out to Iceland, where there will spring from you a great and goodly progeny, and over this progeny of yours shall a bright ray shine. And so, my daughter, farewell now, and happiness go with you.'

After this men approached the prophetess and inquired one by one about what they were most concerned to know. She was free with her information, and small part indeed of what she said failed to come true. Next she was sent for from another house, and off she went, and then Thorbjorn was sent for, because he was not prepared to stay in the house while such heathendom was practised. The weather quickly improved with the advent of spring, just as Thorbjorg had announced. Thorbjorn put his ship in readiness and journeyed on till he reached Brattahlid. Eirik welcomed him with open arms, expressing warm satisfaction that he had come there. Thorbjorn spent the winter with him together with his family [H. *adds* but they found lodgings for the crew among the farmers]. Later in the spring Eirik gave Thorbjorn land at Stokkaness, a fine house was built there, and there he lived from that time forward.

IV

Eirik had a wife whose name was Thjodhild, and two sons, one called Thorstein and the other Leif, both of them promising men. Thorstein was living at home with his father, and no man then in Greenland was held as promising as he. Leif had sailed to Norway, where he was resident with King Olaf Tryggvason.

But when Leif sailed from Greenland in the summer, they were driven off course to the Hebrides. They were a long time getting a good wind thence, and had to remain there for much of the summer. Leif took a fancy to a woman by the name of Thorgunna. She was a lady of good birth, and Leif had an idea she saw farther into things than most. As he made ready to sail away Thorgunna asked to come with him. Leif wanted to know whether her people were likely to approve of this, to which she answered that that was of no importance. Leif replied that he thought it imprudent to carry off so high-born a lady in a strange country. 'We are too few for it.'

'Don't assume', said Thorgunna, 'you will necessarily find you have chosen the wiser course.'

'That is a risk I must take,' said Leif.

'Then let me tell you,' said Thorgunna, 'that it is not just a question of me alone. I am carrying a child, and that, let me tell you, is your doing. I believe too that when this child is born it will be a boy, and for all your indifference now, I shall still raise the boy and send him to you in Greenland once he can take his place among other men. I believe too that having this son will prove just such an asset to you as your present abandonment of me deserves. And I am thinking I may come to Greenland myself before the game is played out.'

Leif gave her a gold ring for her finger, a cloak of Greenland woollen, and a walrus-ivory belt. This boy came to Greenland, declaring that his name was Thorgils, and Leif admitted his paternity. It is some men's tale that this same Thorgils came to Iceland the summer before the Froda-marvels.[1] He certainly came to Greenland thereafter, and there was thought to be something rather queer about him before the finish.

Leif and his men set sail from the Hebrides and reached Norway in the autumn, where he proceeded into the court of King Olaf Tryggvason. The king paid him many honours, feeling sure he was a man of great ability.

Then came the day when the king found occasion to speak with Leif. 'Are you proposing to sail to Greenland this summer?' he asked him.

'I am,' said Leif, 'if such is your will.'

'I think it will be a good thing,' replied the King. 'You shall carry out a mission for me there and preach Christianity in Greenland.'

Leif said it was for the king to command, but added that he thought this mission would be a hard one to carry out in Greenland.

The king said the had never seen a man better fitted for it than he. 'You will bring it luck.'

'That will be the case', said Leif, 'only if I enjoy your luck too.'

Leif put to sea as soon as he was ready, was storm-tossed a long time, and lighted on those lands whose existence he had not so much as dreamt of before. There were wheatfields grow-

---

[1] The hauntings at Froda are recorded in *Eyrbyggja Saga*, chapters 50–5.

ing wild [*lit.* self-sown] there and vines too. There were also those trees which are called maple [*mösurr*, see p. 205], and they fetched away with them samples of all these things [H. *adds* some trees so big that they were used in housebuilding. Leif found men on a wreck and] carried them home with him, and provided them all with lodgings for the winter, showing great magnanimity and gallantry in this as in so much else, since it was he who introduced Christianity into the country, besides rescuing these men; and ever afterwards he was called Leif the Lucky.

Leif landed in Eiriksfjord and went home to Brattahlid, where everybody welcomed him with open arms. He soon preached Christianity and the Catholic Faith throughout the country, unfolding to men the message of King Olaf Tryggvason, and telling how much excellence and what great glory went with this religion. Eirik took coldly to the notion of abandoning his faith, but Thjodhild embraced it at once and had a church built, though not over near the farm. This church was called Thjodhild's Church, and it was there that she offered up her prayers, along with those men who adopted Christianity, who were many. Thjodhild would not live with Eirik as man and wife once she had taken the faith, a circumstance which vexed him very much.

There was now a lot of talk to this end that men [557 he] should go and find this land which Leif had discovered. Thorstein Eiriksson was the leader in this, a good man, and shrewd and popular too. Eirik likewise was invited along, for men felt that his luck and good management would prove their best asset. He took his time over it, but did not refuse when his friends pressed him. So now they fitted out that ship Thorbjorn had brought to Greenland, and twenty men were chosen as her crew. They had few goods with them, weapons for the most part, and provisions. The morning Eirik rode from home he took with him a little box which had gold and silver in it. He hid this treasure, then went on his way, but when he was still hardly any distance from home he fell off his horse, broke some ribs, damaged his shoulder joint, and cried aloud 'A iai!' Because of this mishap he sent word to his wife Thjodhild that she must remove the money he had hidden, for he reckoned he had paid this price for concealing it. Later they sailed out of Eiriksfjord

22. 'THJODHILD'S CHURCH,' BRATTAHLID, GREENLAND

A pictorial reconstruction by Jens Rosing. Eirik's North Farm is seen to the left. Thorbjorn Vifilsson's farm at Stokkanes stood a little to the north on the far side of the fjord

as merry as can be, for they had high hopes of their venture. But for a long time they were storm-tossed on the ocean and could not hold to the course they intended. They came in sight of Iceland and encountered birds from Ireland likewise. Then their ship was driven to and fro about the North Atlantic,[2] and in the autumn they turned back very battered and worn, and made Eiriksfjord at the beginning of winter.

'You were merrier in the summer sailing out of the fjord than you are now,' said Eirik. 'And yet you have much to be thankful for.'

'Be that as it may,' replied Thorstein, 'a leader's business just now is to hit on some plan for these men who are on their beam ends here, and make provision for them.'

Eirik agreed. 'It is true enough what they say, it is easy to be wise after the event, and such will be the case here. You shall have your way in this.'

So all those who had nowhere else to go went along with that father and son. Later [H. they went home to Brattahlid and spent the winter there].

The story now goes on to tell how Thorstein Eiriksson asked for Gudrid Thorbjarnardottir in marriage, and his proposal

[2] *um haf innan.* For the Inner Sea, see pp. 18–23 above.

found favour with both her and her father. So that was what
they settled on, that Thorstein should mary Gudrid, and the
wedding took place at Brattahlid in the autumn. The festivities
went off well and there was a big gathering present. Thorstein
owned an estate in the Western Settlement on a holding known
as Lysufjord. Another man, also named Thorstein, owned a
half share in this estate. His wife's name was Sigrid. Thorstein
and Gudrid with him went to Lysufjord in the autumn, to his
namesake's, where they got a warm welcome and stayed on
over the winter. What happened now was that sickness attacked
the homestead quite early in the winter. The foreman there was
called Gardar, and very unpopular he was too. He was the first
to fall ill and die, and after that it was not long till they were falling ill and dying one after the other. Next Thorstein Eiriksson
fell ill, and Sigrid too, the wife of his namesake. One evening
Sigrid wanted to go to the privy which stood opposite the outer
door. Gudrid went with her, and they were seated there facing
this door when 'Oh,' cried Sigrid, 'oh!'

'We have acted rashly,' said Gudrid, 'and you are in no fit
state to be about in the cold, so let us get back in as quickly as
we can.'

'I cannot go as things are now,' replied Sigrid. 'Here is the
entire host of the dead before the door, and in their company I
recognize Thorstein your husband, and I recognize myself there
too. How dreadful it is to see such a thing!' And when this
passed off, [H. *adds* 'Let us go now, Gudrid,'] she said, 'I do
not see the host any longer.' The foreman too had disappeared,
who she thought earlier had had a whip in his hand and was trying to scourge the company.

After this they went back indoors, and before morning came
she was dead, and a coffin was made for her body.

This same day men were planning to row out fishing, and
Thorstein saw them down to the waterside. At twilight he went
down to see what they had caught. Then Thorstein Eiriksson
sent word to his namesake that he should come and see him,
saying that things looked far from healthy there, and that the
lady of the house was trying to get on her feet and under the
clothes with him. And by the time he arrived back indoors she
had worked her way up to the edge of the bed alongside him.
He seized hold of her and laid a pole-axe to her breast.

Thorstein Eiriksson died towards nightfall. The other Thorstein told Gudrid to lie down and sleep, promising that he would himself keep watch over the bodies throughout the night. She did so, and soon fell asleep, but when only a little of the night was past Thorstein Eiriksson raised himself up and said it was his wish that Gudrid should be summoned to him, for he desired to speak to her. 'God wills that this hour is granted me by way of remission and for the amendment of my state.' Franklin Thorstein went to find Gudrid and woke her, bidding her cross herself and pray God to help her. 'Thorstein Eiriksson has spoken to me, that he wants to see you, but it is for you to decide what course you will take, for I cannot direct you one way or the other.' 'It may be', she replied, 'that this wondrous event is intended as one of those things which are to be stored in our hearts for ever; yet I trust that God's keeping will stand over me. And under God's mercy I will risk speaking with him; for I cannot escape, if I am fated to suffer hurt. I have no wish for him to haunt us further—and that, I suspect, is the alternative.'

So Gudrid went now and found her Thorstein, and it seemed to her that he was weeping. He spoke certain words quietly in her ear, so that she alone heard them; but what he did say [H. *adds* so that everyone heard] was that those men would be truly blest who kept their faith well, for salvation and mercy attended upon it; though many, he added, kept their faith ill. 'Nor is that a good usage which has obtained here in Greenland since the coming of Christianity, to lay men down in unconsecrated [557 consecrated] ground with only a brief service sung over them. I want to be borne to church, and those others likewise who have died here; but I want Gardar to be burnt on a pyre as soon as possible, for he is the cause of all the hauntings which have taken place here this winter.' He spoke to her further of her own affairs, declaring that her future would be a notable one. He bade her beware of marrying a Greenlander, and urged her too to bestow their money upon the church, or give it to the poor; and then he sank back for the second time.

It had been the custom in Greenland, ever since the coming of Christianity, that men were buried on the farms where they died, in unconsecrated [557 consecrated] ground. A stake would be set up, leading from the breast [H. *adds* of the dead], and in due course, when clergy came that way, the stake would be pulled up and holy water poured into the place, and a service sung over them, even though this might be a good while later.

The bodies [H. *adds* of Thorstein Eiriksson and the rest] were borne to the church at Eiriksfjord, and services sung over them by the clergy. Later Thorstein died, and his entire estate passed to Gudrid. Eirik took her into his own home, and looked after her and hers well.

V

Living in the north of Iceland, at Reynisnes in Skagafjord (the place is now called [Stad]), was a man known as Thorfinn Karlsefni, the son of Thord Horse-head. He was a man of good family and very well-to-do. His mother's name was Thorunn. Thorfinn was a trader overseas, and had the name of a good merchant. One summer Karlsefni fitted out his ship with Greenland in mind. Snorri Thorbrandsson from Alptafjord decided to go with him, and they had forty men with them. A man by the name of Bjarni Grimolfsson, a Breidafjord man, and another named Thorhall Gamlason, an Eastfirther, made their ship ready the same summer as Karlsefni, proposing to sail to Greenland, and they too had forty men aboard. They put to sea with these two ships as soon as they were fitted out. There is no record of how long they were at sea, but this can be said, that both ships made Eiriksfjord in the autumn. Eirik and other of the settlers rode to the ships, and they promptly started a brisk buying and selling. The skippers invited Eirik [557 Gudrid] to help himself to anything he liked from among their wares; and Eirik showed himself no less generous in return, for he invited the two ships' crews to come and spend the winter with him at Brattahlid. The merchants accepted this offer, off they went with Eirik, and their goods were now transferred to Brattahlid, where there was no lack of fine big storehouses to keep them in. [H. *adds* Nor was there a noticeable lack of anything else they needed]. The merchants had a very good time at Eirik's over the winter.

But as the time wore on towards Yule Eirik came to look less cheerful than was his habit. So one day Karlsefni came and had a word with him. 'Is something the matter, Eirik? I can't help thinking you are rather more silent than you were. You are treating us with great hospitality, and we feel bound to repay you to the best of our means and ability. So tell me now the reason for your low spirits.'

'You have been kind and gracious guests,' replied Eirik, 'and it does not so much as enter my mind that you have treated me other than perfectly. [H. What troubles me rather is whether once you find yourselves in other parts it will be noised abroad how you never spent a poorer Yule than this now coming in, when Eirik the Red was your host at Brattahlid in Greenland.]'

'That will not be so', Karlsefni assured him. 'On board our ships we have malt and meal and corn, and you are welcome to help yourself to anything you please, and prepare a feast as splendid as your ideas of hospitality would have it.'

Eirik accepted this offer, and a Yule feast was now prepared, and one so choice and costly that men thought they had rarely seen such high living [H. *adds* in a poor country].

Then after Yule Karlsefni put to Eirik a proposal for Gudrid's hand, for as he saw it this lay in Eirik's competence, and he thought her a beautiful and accomplished lady. Eirik answered yes, he would welcome his suit—she deserved a good match, he said. 'And it is likely that she will be fulfilling her destiny', were she given to him. He had heard nothing but good of Karlsefni, he said. His proposal was now put to her, she declared herself content with whatever Eirik decided for her, so without more ado the match was made, the feast augmented, and the wedding held. There was great and merry entertainment at Brattahlid the winter through, with much playing of board-games and storytelling, and many things to comfort and cheer the household.

This same winter long discussions took place at Brattahlid. Karlsefni and Snorri resolved to go and find Vinland, and men debated this a good deal. The upshot was that Karlsefni and Snorri fitted out their ship, meaning to go and find Vinland in the summer. Bjarni and Thorhall resolved to make the journey with their ship and the crew which had served with them. There was a man by the name of Thorvald, a son-in-law [*sic*] of Eirik the Red. Thorhall was nicknamed the Hunter; for a long while now he had been out on hunting expeditions with Eirik in the summers, and had much business in his charge. He was tall of

stature, dark and ogreish, was getting on in years, of difficult
disposition, taciturn and of few words as a rule, underhand and
offensive of speech, and always busied to a bad end. He had
had little truck with the Faith since it came to Greenland. Thorhall had hardly a friend to his name, yet Eirik had long been
accustomed to consult with him. He was aboard ship with Thorvald and his crew, for he had an extensive knowledge of the
unsettled regions. They had that same ship which Thorbjorn
had fetched to Greenland. They resolved to go along with Karlsefni and his men, and for the most part they were Greenlanders who went. They had a hundred and sixty men on board
their ships. They then sailed away for the Western Settlement
and for Bjarneyjar, Bear Isles. From Bjarneyjar they sailed
with a north wind, were at sea two days, and then found land.
They rowed ashore in boats and explored the country, finding
many flat stones there, so big that a pair of men could easily
clap sole to sole on them. There were many arctic foxes there.
They gave the land a name, calling it Helluland, Flatstone
Land. Then they sailed with a north wind for two days, when
land lay ahead of them, with a great forest and many wild animals. Off the land to the south-east lay an island, where they
found a bear, so called it Bjarney, Bear Island. But the land
where the forest was they called Markland, Wood Land.

Then when two days were past they sighted land, and sailed
to the land. Where they arrived there was a cape. They beat
along the coast and left the land to starboard; it was an open
harbourless coast there, with long beaches and sands. They put
ashore in boats, came across the keel from a ship, so called the
place Kjalarnes, Keelness. Likewise they gave a name to the
beaches, calling them Furdustrandir, Marvelstrands, it was such
a long business sailing past them. Then the land became bay-
indented, and towards these bays they headed their ships.

It happened when Leif was with King Olaf Tryggvason, and
he commissioned him to preach Christianity in Greenland, that
the king gave him two Scots, a man named Haki, and a woman
Hekja. The king told Leif to make use of these people if he had
need of fleetness, for they were fleeter than deer. These people
Leif and Eirik provided to accompany Karlsefni. So when they
had sailed past Furdustrandir they put the Scots ashore, ordering them to run into the region lying south, spy out the quality

of the land, and come back before three days were past. They were so attired that they were wearing the garment which they called 'bjafal': this was so put together that there was a hood on top, it was open at the sides and sleeveless, and buttoned between the legs, where a button and loop held it together; while for the rest they were naked. They cast anchor and lay there this while, and when three days were past they came running down from the land, and one of them had grapes in his hand and the other self-sown wheat. Karlsefni said they appeared to have found a choice, productive land. They took them on board ship and went their way until the land was indented by a fjord. They laid the ships' course up into this fjord, off whose mouth there lay an island, and surrounding the island strong currents. This island they called Straumsey [H. Straumey]. There were so many birds there that a man could hardly set foot down between the eggs. They held on into the fjord, and called it Straumsfjord [H. Straumfjord], and here they carried their goods off the ships and made their preparations. They had brought all sorts of livestock with them, and looked around at what the land had to offer. There were mountains there, and the prospect around was beautiful. They paid no heed to anything save exploring the country. There was tall [*or* abundant] grass there. They spent the winter there, and a hard winter it proved, with no provision made for it; they were in a bad way for food, and the hunting and fishing failed. Then they went out to the island, hoping it would yield something by way of hunting or fishing or something drifted ashore. But small store of food was there, though their stock did well there. So now they prayed to God, that he should send them something to eat, but their prayers were not answered as quickly as they craved. Thorhall disappeared, and men set off to look for him; this continued for three whole days. On the fourth day Karlsefni and Bjarni found him on the peak of a crag, staring up at the sky, with both his eyes and mouth and nostrils agape, scratching and pinching himself, and reciting something. They asked him why he had come to such a place. It was none of their business, he retorted, and told them not to look so dumbstruck; he had lived long enough, he said, not to need them troubling their heads over him. They urged him to return home with them, which he did. A little later a whale came in; they hurried to it and cut it up, yet had no notion what kind of whale it was. Karlsefni had a wide knowledge and experience of whales, but for all that did not recognize this one. The cooks boiled this whale and they ate of it and were all taken ill of it, at which Thorhall came forward and said, 'Was it not the case, that Red Beard proved a better friend than your Christ? This is what I get for the poem I made about Thor my patron. Seldom has he failed me.' But the moment men heard this, no one would make use of the food; they threw it over the cliff, and committed their cause to the mercy of God. And then they were enabled to row out fishing, and there was no shortage of provisions. In the spring they went up into Straumsfjord and got supplies from both sources, hunting on the mainland, eggs in the breeding grounds and fishing from the sea.

Now they talked over their expedition and made plans. Thorhall the Hunter wished to proceed north by way of Furdustrandir and Kjalarnes and so look for Vinland, but Karlsefni wished to travel south along the coast, and east of it, believing that the land which lay further south was more extensive, and it seemed to him wiser to explore in both directions. So now Thorhall began making ready out by the islands, and there were not more than nine men going with him, for the rest of their company went with Karlsefni. And one day, when Thorhall was carrying water to his ship, he took a drink, and chanted this poem:

> 'They told me, war-trees bold,
> This land held, once we found it,
> Such drink as men ne'er drank of;
> My curse then—all men hear it!
> This sucking at the bucket,
> This wallowing to spring's welling,
> Fine work for helm-god's war-oak!
> No wine's passed lips of mine.'

Later they put to sea, and Karlsefni saw them out past the islands. Before they hoisted sail Thorhall chanted a verse:

> 'Back sail we now where beckon
> Hands of our own Greenlanders;
> Have steed of seabed's heaven
> Search out the streams of ocean:

> While here these brisk sword-stirrers,
> This precious country's praisers,
> On Furdustrand far-stranded,
> Boil whale for wambling bellies.'

Afterwards they parted company and sailed north by way of Furdustrandir and Kjalarnes, and wished to beat to westward there. They met with a storm and were shipwrecked off Ireland, where they were badly beaten and enslaved. It was then Thorhall lost his life.

VI

Karlsefni sailed south along the land with Snorri and Bjarni and the rest of their company. They journeyed a long time till they reached a river which flowed down from the land into a lake and so to the sea. There were such extensive bars [557 islands] off the mouth of the estuary that they were unable to get into the river except at full flood. Karlsefni and his men sailed into the estuary, and called the place Hop, Landlock Bay. There they found self-sown fields of wheat where the ground was low-lying, and vines wherever it was hilly. Every brook there was full of fish. They dug trenches at the meeting point of land and high water, and when the tide went out there were halibut in the trenches. There were vast numbers of animals of every kind in the forest. They were there for a fortnight enjoying themselves, and saw nothing and nobody. They had their cattle with them.

Then early one morning when they looked about them they saw nine [H. a great multitude of] skin-boats, on board which staves were being swung which sounded just like flails threshing—and their motion was sunwise.

'What can this mean?' asked Karlsefni.

'Perhaps it is a token of peace,' replied Snorri. 'So let us take a white shield and hold it out towards them.'

They did so, and those others rowed towards them, showing their astonishment, then came ashore. They were small [H. dark], ill-favoured men, and had ugly hair on their heads. They had big eyes and were broad in the cheeks. For a while they remained there, astonished, and afterwards rowed off south past the headland.

Karlsefni and his men built themselves dwellings up above the lake; some of their houses stood near the mainland, and some near the lake. They now spent the winter there. No snow fell, and their entire stock found its food grazing in the open. But once spring came in they chanced early one morning to see how a multitude of skin-boats came rowing from the south around the headland, so many that the bay appeared sown with coals, and even so staves were being swung on every boat. Karlsefni and his men raised their shields, and they began trading together. Above all these people wanted to buy red cloth [H. *adds* in return for which they had furs to offer and grey pelts]. They also wanted to buy swords and spears, but this Karlsefni and Snorri would not allow. They had dark unblemished skins to exchange for the cloth, and were taking a span's length of cloth for a skin, and this they tied round their heads. So it continued for a while, then when the cloth began to run short they cut it up so that it was no broader than a fingerbreadth, but the Skrælings gave just as much for it, or more.

The next thing was that the bull belonging to Karlsefni and his mates ran out of the forest bellowing loudly. The Skrælings were terrified by this, raced out to their boats and rowed south past the headland, and for three weeks running there was neither sight nor sound of them. But at the end of that period they saw a great multitude of Skræling boats coming up from the south like a streaming torrent. This time all the staves were being swung anti-sunwise, and the Skrælings were all yelling aloud, so they took red shields and held them out against them. [H. *adds* The Skrælings ran from their boats and with that] they clashed together and fought. There was a heavy shower of missiles, for the Skrælings had war-slings too. Karlsefni and Snorri could see the Skrælings hoisting up on poles [H. a pole] a big ball-shaped object [H. *adds* more or less the size of a sheep's paunch], and blue-black in colour, which they sent flying [H. *adds* from the pole] inland over Karlsefni's troop, and it made a hideous noise where it came down. Great fear now struck into Karlsefni and all his following, so that there was no other thought in their heads than to run away up along the river [H. *adds* for they had the impression that the Skræling host was pouring in upon them from all sides. They made no stop till they came] to some steep rocks, and there put up a strong resistance.

Freydis came out of doors and saw how they had taken to their heels. 'Why are you running from wretches like these?' she cried. 'Such gallant lads as you, I thought for sure you would have knocked them on the head like cattle. Why, if I had a weapon, I think I could put up a better fight than any of you!'

They might as well not have heard her. Freydis was anxious to keep up with them, but was rather slow because of her pregnancy. She was moving after them into the forest when the Skrælings attacked her. She found a dead man in her path, Thorband Snorrason—he had a flat stone sticking out of his head. His sword lay beside him; she picked it up and prepared to defend herself with it. The Skrælings were now making for her. She pulled her breasts out from under her shift and slapped the [H. *adds* naked] sword on them, at which the Skrælings took fright, and ran off to their boats and rowed away.[3] Karlsefni's men came up to her, praising her courage. Two of Karlsefni's men had fallen, and four [H. a great many] Skrælings, but even so they had been overrun by sheer numbers. They now returned to their booths [H. *adds* and bandaged their wounds], puzzling over what force it was which had attacked them from the land side. For now it looked to them as though there had been only the one host, which came from the boats, and that the rest of the host must have been a delusion.

Further, the Skrælings had found a dead man whose axe lay beside him. One of them [H. *adds* picked up the axe and cut at a tree with it, and so they did one after the other, and thought it a great treasure, and one which cut well. Afterwards one of them set to and] cut at a stone, the axe broke, and then he thought it useless because it could not stand up to the stone, so threw it down.

It now seemed plain to Karlsefni and his men that though the

[3] This bizarre incident may owe something to a Norseman's experience or hearsay of the Beothuk Indian taboo against fighting with or harming a woman with weapons. To expose the bosom would be an immediate and simple way for an endangered Beothuk woman to announce her sex and immunity from attack (see Farley Mowat, *Westviking* (1965), pp. 257–8 and 461). On the other hand, the violent-hearted Freydis of both *Grænlendinga Saga* and *Eiríks Saga Rauða* would be very much at home with the female berserks assembled, according to Saxo, for the apocalyptic struggle at Bravellir between the semi-mythological Harald War-tooth and the highly fictionalized Sigurd Hring. She is, in short, a less than well-attested lady.

quality of the land was admirable, there would always be fear and strife dogging them there on account of those who already inhabited it. So they made ready to leave, setting their hearts on their own country, and sailed north along the coast and found five Skrælings in fur doublets asleep near the sea, who had with them wooden containers in which was animal marrow mixed with blood. They felt sure that these men would have been sent out from that country, so they killed them. Later they discovered a cape and great numbers of animals. To look at, this cape was like a cake of dung, because the animals lay there the nights [557 winters] through.

And now Karlsefni and his followers returned to Straumsfjord [H. *adds* where there was abundance of everything they had need of]. It is some men's report that Bjarni and Freydis [H. Gudrid] had remained behind there, and a hundred men with them, and proceeded no farther, while Karlsefni and Snorri had travelled south with forty men, yet spent no longer at Hop than a bare two months, and got back again that same summer. Then Karlsefni set off with one ship to look for Thorhall the Hunter, while the rest of their party stayed behind. They went north past Kjalarnes, and then bore away west, with the land on their port side. There was nothing but a wilderness of forest-land [H. *adds* to be seen ahead, with hardly a clearing anywhere]. And when they had been on their travels for a long time, there was a river flowing down off the land from east to west. They put into this river-mouth and lay at anchor off the southern bank. It happened one morning that Karlsefni and his men noticed up above the clearing a kind of speck as it were glittering back at them, and they shouted at it. It moved—it was a uniped—and hopped down to the river-bank off which they were lying. Thorvald Eirik the Red's son was sitting by the rudder, and the uniped shot an arrow into his guts. He drew out the arrow. 'There is fat round my belly!' he said. 'We have won a fine and fruitful country, but will hardly be allowed to enjoy it.' Thorvald died of this wound a little later. The uniped skipped away and back north, and Karlsefni and his men gave chase, catching sight of him every now and again. The last glimpse they had of him, he was leaping for some creek or other. Karlsefni and his men then turned back. [557 It happened one morning Karlsefni and his men noticed up above a clearing a kind of speck as it were glittering back at them. It moved—it was a uniped—and hopped down to where they were lying [*sc*. Karlsefni and] Thorvald Eirik the Red's son. Then said Thorvald: 'We have won a fine country.' The uniped then skipped away and back north, and shot an arrow into Thorvald's guts. He drew out the arrow and 'There is fat round my belly!' he said. They gave chase to the uniped, catching sight of him every now and again, and it looked as if he was getting away. He leaped out to a creek.] Then one of the men sang this ditty:

> 'Men went chasing,
> I tell you no lie,
> A one-legger racing
> The seashore by:
> But this man-wonder,
> Curst son of a trollop,
> Karlsefni, pray ponder,
> Escaped at a gallop.'

Then they moved away and back north, believing they had sighted Einfætingaland, Uniped Land. They were unwilling to imperil their company any longer. They proposed to explore all the mountains, those which were at Hop and those they [*sc*. now] discovered. [H. They concluded that those mountains which were at Hop and those they had now discovered were one and the same (range), that they therefore stood directly opposite (in line with?) each other, and lay (*or* extended) the same distance on both sides of Straumfjord.]

They went back and spent that third winter in Straumsfjord. There was bitter quarrelling [H. *adds* on account of the women], for the unmarried men fell foul of the married [H. *adds* which led to serious disturbances]. Karlsefni's son Snorri was born there the first autumn and was three years old when they left.

[H. When they sailed from Vinland] they got a south wind and reached Markland, where they found five Skrælings, one of them a grown man with a beard, two women, and two children. Karlsefni captured the boys but the others escaped and sank down into the ground. These boys they kept with them, taught them their language, and they were baptized. They gave their mother's name as Vætilldi, that of their father as Uvægi. They said that kings ruled over Skrælingaland, one of whom was called Avalldamon and the other Valldidida. There were no houses there, they said: the people lodged in caves or holes. A country lay on the other side, they said, opposite their own land, where men walked about in [H. lived who wore] white clothes and whooped loudly, and carried poles and went about with [H. carried] flags. They concluded that this must be Hvitramannaland [H. *adds* or Ireland the Great].[4] And now they came to Greenland and spent the winter with Eirik the Red.

But Bjarni Grimolfsson was carried into the Greenland [H. Ireland] Sea and came into wormy waters, and before they knew it the ship grew worm-eaten under them. They talked over what plan they should adopt. They had a tow-boat which was coated with seal-tar, and it is common knowledge that the shell-worm does not bore into timber which is coated with seal-tar. The voice of the majority was to man this boat with as many of the men as she would take. But when it came to the point, the boat would not take more than half the ship's company. Then Bjarni proposed that they should go into the boat, but go by lot, and not by rank. But every living soul wanted to go into the boat, and she just could not take them all, which was why they adopted this plan of transferring men from ship to boat by lot. And the way the lot fell out, it fell to Bjarni to go into the boat, and roughly half the crew with him.

So those who had drawn lucky transferred from ship to boat. When they got into the boat a young Icelander who had been Bjarni's shipmate, called out: 'D'you mean to leave me here, Bjarni?'

'That is the way of it,' replied Bjarni.

[4] Further to Hvitramannaland: 'He [Ari Masson] was driven off course to Hvitramannaland, which some call Ireland the Great. It lies west in the ocean, near Vinland the Good. It is reckoned six days' sail west from Ireland. Ari failed to get away again and was baptized there. The first to tell of this was Hrafn the Limerick-farer, who had spent a long time at Limerick in Ireland. According to Thorkel Gellisson, Icelanders who had their information from Thorfinn earl of Orkney report that Ari had been recognized in Hvitramannaland but failed to get away. He was held in high regard there' (*Landn*, S. 122). Another who failed to escape from this entirely mythical country was Bjorn, champion of the Breidavik men and lover of Thurid, he 'who was a closer friend to the housewife at Froda than to her brother the priest at Helgafell'. See *Eyrbyggja Saga*, cap. 64.

'This', said he, 'is not what you promised me when I followed you from my father's house in Iceland.'

'I see nothing else for it,' said Bjarni. 'But answer me, what do you suggest?'

'I suggest we change places. That you come here, and I go there.'

'So be it,' replied Bjarni. 'For I see you are greedy for life, and think it a hard thing to die.'

Then they changed places. This man went into the boat, and Bjarni aboard ship, and men reckon that Bjarni perished there in the wormy sea, and those men who remained on board with him. But the boat and those who were in her went their way till they reached land [H. *adds* at Dublin in Ireland], where they afterwards told this story.

Two summers later Karlsefni returned to Iceland, and Snorri [H. Gudrid] with him, and went home to his place at Reynisnes. His mother considered he had made a poor marriage and did not stay in the same house with them that first winter. But once she found Gudrid to be so remarkable a woman, she returned home, and they lived happily together.

The daughter of Karlsefni's son Snorri was Hallfrid, the mother of bishop Thorlak Runolfsson. Karlsefni and Gudrid had a son whose name was Thorbjorn, whose daughter's name was Thorunn, mother of bishop Bjorn. There was a son of Snorri Karlsefni's son by the name of Thorgeir, the father of Yngvild, mother of bishop Brand the first.

And that is the end of this saga.[5]

[5] In place of this last sentence Hauk Erlendsson supplies a genealogy leading to himself: Steinunn too was a daughter of Snorri Karlsefni's son, she who was married to Einar the son of Grundar-Ketil, son of Thorvald Krok, son of Thorir from Espihol. Their son was Thorstein Ranglat, who was father of that Gudrun whom Jorund from Keldur married. Their daughter was Halla, mother of Flosi, father of Valgerda, mother of Herra Erlend Sterki, father of Herra Hauk the Lawman. Another daughter of Flosi was Thordis, mother of the lady Ingigerd the Mighty, whose daughter was the lady Hallbera, abbess of Reynisnes at Stad. Many other distinguished people in Iceland are descended from Karlsefni and Gudrid, who are not catalogued here. God be with us. Amen.

8

Karlsefni's Voyage to Vinland

The Hauksbók Version of part of Thorfinn Karlsefni's Expedition to Vinland

THEN after Yule Karlsefni put before Eirik a proposal of marriage for Gudrid, for as he saw it this lay in Eirik's competence. Eirik gave him a favourable answer, reckoning she must follow her fate, and that he had heard nothing but good of Karlsefni. So that was how it ended: Thorfinn married Gudrid, the feast was augmented, their wedding held and drunk to, and they spent the winter at Brattahlid.

There were long discussions at Brattahlid, that men ought to go and find Vinland the Good, and it was the general opinion it would be found a good and fruitful country out there. And so it came about that Karlsefni and Snorri fitted out their ship to go and find that country in the spring. The man Bjarni and his fellow Thorhall, who have already been mentioned, went with them in their own ship. There was a man by the name of Thorvard, who was married to Eirik the Red's natural daughter Freydis, who went along with them, together with Eirik's son Thorvald, and [that other] Thorhall who was nicknamed the Hunter. He had been with Eirik a long time now, acting as hunter for him in the summers, and during the winters as his bailiff. He was a big, strong, dark, and ogreish man, taciturn, but when he did speak abusive, and he was always advising Eirik for the worse. He was a bad Christian, but he had a wide knowledge of the unsettled regions. He was on board ship with Thorvard and Thorvald (they had that same ship which Thorbjorn Vifilsson had fetched to Greenland). In all they had a hundred and sixty men when they set sail for the Western Settlement and from there to Bjarney, Bear Island. From there they sailed south for two days and then sighted land. They launched their boats and explored the countryside, finding huge flat stones there, many of them twelve ells across. There were large numbers of arctic foxes there. They gave the land a name, calling it Helluland. Then they sailed onwards for two days and changed course from south to south-east, and found a land heavily forested, with many wild animals. Offshore to the south-east lay an island. They killed a bear on it, so called the island Bjarney, Bear Island, and the land Markland.

From here they sailed south along the land for a long while till they came to a cape. The land lay to starboard; there were long beaches and sands there. They rowed ashore and found there on the cape the keel from a ship, so called the place Kjal-arnes. The beaches they called Furdustrandir, Marvelstrands, because it was such a long business sailing past them. Then the land became bay-indented, and into one of these bays they headed their ships.

King Olaf Tryggvason had given Leif two Scots, a man named Haki, and a woman Hekja, who were fleeter than deer. They were on board Karlsefni's ship, and once they had sailed past Furdustrandir they put the Scots ashore, ordering them to run across country southwards to spy out the quality of the land, and come back before three days were past. They were wearing the garment which they called 'kjafal': this was so put together that there was a hood on top, it was open at the sides and sleeveless, and buttoned between the legs with a button and loop; while for the rest they were naked. They waited there a while, and when the Scots came back the one had a bunch of grapes in his hand and the other an ear of new-sown [*sic*] wheat; so with that they went back on board ship and afterwards sailed on their way.

They sailed into a fjord off whose mouth there lay an island surrounded by strong currents. So they called this island Straumey. There were so many eider-duck on the island that a man could hardly take a step for the eggs. The place itself they called Straumfjord, and here they carried their goods off the ships and made their preparations. They had brought all sorts of livestock with them, and the country round was very fine. They paid no heed to anything save exploring the country; they spent the winter there, but made no provision for this all the summer; the hunting and fishing failed, and they were in a bad way for food. Then Thorhall the Hunter disappeared. Before this they had prayed to God for food, but their prayers were not answered as quickly as their needs craved. They were looking for Thorhall three whole days, and found him where he was lying on the peak of a crag, staring up at the sky with his mouth and nostrils both agape, and reciting something. They asked him why he had gone to such a place, but he told them that was none of their business. They urged him to return home with them, which he did. A little later a whale came in. They went to it and cut it up, yet never a man of them knew what kind of a whale it was. Once the cooks had boiled it, they ate and were all taken ill of it. Then said Thorhall, 'Red Beard proved a better friend now than your Christ. This is what I get for the poem I made about Thor my patron. Seldom has he failed me.' But the moment they heard this, they disposed of the entire whale into the sea and committed their cause to God. With that the weather improved, enabling them to row out to sea fishing, and from then on there was no shortage of provisions, for there was hunting of animals on the mainland, eggs in the island breeding-grounds, and fish from the sea.

The story now goes that Thorhall wished to proceed north by way of Furdustrandir to look for Vinland, whereas Karlsefni wished to travel south along the coast. Thorhall began making ready out by the island, and they were not more than nine men all told, for all the rest of the company went with Karlsefni. And when Thorhall was carrying water to his ship and had taken a drink of it, he chanted this poem [See p. 225: They told me, etc.].

When they were ready they hoisted sail. This time Thorhall chanted [See pp. 225–6: Back sail we now, etc].

After this they sailed north by way of Furdustrandir and Kjalarnes, and wished to beat to westwards, but met with a west wind and were shipwrecked in Ireland, where they were beaten and enslaved, and Thorhall lost his life, according to what traders have reported.

9

The Story of Einar Sokkason

Einars Þáttr Sokkasonar
also called
Grænlendinga Þáttr

I

THERE was a man named Sokki, the son of Thorir, living at Brattahlid in Greenland. He was highly esteemed and popular with all. His son's name was Einar, a man of high promise. Father and son had great authority in Greenland, and stood head and shoulders above other men.

On a given occasion Sokki had a Thing summoned, at which he announced that he did not wish their land to remain bishopless any longer, but wanted all his compatriots to make a contribution from their means so that a bishop's see could be established—a proposal to which all the franklins assented. Sokki asked his son Einar to undertake the necessary journey to Norway. He was the fittest person, he told him, to carry out this mission. So Einar said he would go, just as his father wished, and took with him a big supply of ivory goods and walrus hides to push his case with the chieftains.

They arrived in Norway, and it was Sigurd Jerusalem-farer who was king there at the time. Einar came to have audience with the king; he eased his case forward by means of gifts, and afterwards set out his aims and intention, petitioning the king to help him, so that he might get what he was asking for to meet his country's need. The king agreed that this would indeed be a fine thing for Greenland.

Then the king summoned before him a certain man named Arnald, who was a good clerk and well fitted to be a teacher of God's word. The king bade him address himself to this task for God's sake and his, the king's, prayers. 'And I will send you to

Denmark with my letters and seal, to have audience with Ozur archbishop of Lund.' Arnald replied that he was not much tempted to undertake this; first on his own account, in that he was ill fitted for it; second, because of parting with his friends and family; and third, because he would have to deal with such cantankerous people. The king's counter to this was that the greater the trials he suffered at men's hands, the greater would be his merit and reward. Arnald confessed he could not find it in his heart to refuse the king's prayer—'But if it is ordained that I accept the sacred office of bishop, then I want Einar to swear me this oath, that he will help and uphold the rights of the bishop's see and those properties which are given to God, and chastise those that trespass against them, and be the defender of all things that pertain to the see.' The king said he should do this, and Einar agreed to undertake it.

So now the bishop-elect went to see archbishop Ozur, and put his business before him, and the king's letters too. The archbishop welcomed him warmly; they came to know each other's mind, and once the archbishop could see that this was a man in every respect fit for high office he consecrated Arnald as bishop [1124], and parted with him handsomely. Arnald then returned to the king who received him warmly. Einar had brought with him from Greenland a bear which he presented to King Sigurd, and in return gained honour and the king's esteem.

Later they set off in one ship, the bishop and Einar, while Arnbjorn the Norwegian together with such other Norse men as desired to go out to Greenland made ready in a second. Next they sailed to sea, but the wind was not over-helpful to them, and the bishop and Einar came in at Holtavatnsos under Eyjafjall in Iceland. At the time Sæmund the Learned was living at Oddi; he went to meet the bishop and invited him to his home for the winter, and the bishop was grateful, and said he would accept. Einar spent the winter under Eyjafjall.

The story goes that when the bishop rode from the ship with his men, they stopped for a rest at some farm or other in the Landeyjar. They were sitting in the open air when out came an old woman with a wool-comb in her hand. She walked up to one of the men, and 'Eh, buckie,' she said, 'wilt fasten the tooth in my comb?' He took it, saying yes he would, took a riveting-hammer out of a bag, and did a job which pleased the old lady very much. Now this man was none other than the bishop, for he could turn his hand to anything, and this story has been related of him for the proof it gives of his humility.

He spent the winter at Oddi, where he and Sæmund hit it off well together. There was no news of Arnbjorn and the others, so the bishop and Einar concluded he must have reached Greenland. Next summer they left Iceland and came to Greenland, to Eiriksfjord, where they were given a cordial welcome, but to their great surprise could still get no news of Arnbjorn. Several summers passed, then it was generally agreed that they must have perished. The bishop established his see at Gardar and transferred himself there. Einar and his father were his mainstay, whilst they of all their fellow-countrymen stood highest in favour with the bishop.

II

There was a Greenlander by the name of Sigurd Njalsson who of an autumn often went off fishing and hunting in the Wilderness: he was a master of the seaman's art. There were fifteen of them all told, they reached the glacier Hvitserk in the summer, and had come across some human cooking-places and signs of catches too.

'Which would you rather do,' Sigurd asked them, 'turn back or go on? There is not much of the summer left. On the other hand our catch has been a poor one.'

His shipmates said they would rather turn back. It was a dangerous business, they contended, sailing these big fjords under the glaciers.

He admitted that was true. 'Yet someting tells me the bigger part of our catch lies ahead, if we can only lay hands on it.'

They said the decision must be his. They had trusted to his guidance for a long time now, they said, and everything had gone well. He admitted that his own inclination was to press ahead, so that was what they did. There was a man by the name of Steinthor on board their ship. He now struck in, saying: 'Last night I had a dream, Sigurd, a dream I will describe to you. For as we were threading this big fjord here, it seemed to me I got in amongst some precipices and yelled out for help.' Sigurd said the dream was none too good. 'So don't go spurning at what can help you, and landing yourself in such a hole that you can't keep your mouth shut.' For Steinthor was a very headstrong, heedless sort of man.

As they headed up the fjord Sigurd asked: 'Am I right in thinking there is a ship in the fjord?' Yes, they said, there was. Great news would come of this, said Sigurd. They held on towards it up the fjord, and could see that the ship had been beached in a river-mouth and covered over. She was a big sea-going vessel. Next they went ashore, and saw a hall there, and a tent close by. For a start, said Sigurd, they had best pitch their own tent. 'The day is coming to a close, and I want everyone to stay quiet and watchful.' In the morning they walked across and looked the place over. Near them they could see a block of wood: stuck in it was a pole-axe, and there was a man's corpse close by. Sigurd reckoned this man had been chopping wood and had collapsed for hunger. With that they walked to the hall, where they saw another corpse. This one, reckoned Sigurd, had stayed on his feet as long as he could. 'They must have been the servants of those who are inside the hall.' For an axe lay beside this one too. 'I think it a wise precaution,' said Sigurd, 'to break open the hall and let the stench of the bodies which are inside clear off, and the foul air which has been gathering there this long while. And mind, everybody, to keep out of its way, for there is nothing more certain than that it will bring on such sickness as is utterly destructive of man's being. Though it is unlikely the men themselves will do us any harm.'

Steinthor said it was silly to give themselves more trouble than there was call for, and as they were breaking open the hall he walked in at the door. As he came out Sigurd got a look at him. 'The man is all changed!' he said. And at once he began to yell and run off, with his comrades in pursuit of him, and leapt into a fissure in a crag where no one could get at him, and perished there. His dream had come only too true for him, said Sigurd.

Afterwards they broke open the hall, following Sigurd's instructions closely, and got no hurt by it. Inside the hall they saw dead men and a lot of money. Said Sigurd: 'As I see it, it will be best for you to clean the flesh off their bones in these boilers they had. It will be easier then to move them to church. Most likely this will be Arnbjorn, for this second fine ship standing here on the shore, I have heard tell she was his'. She was a vessel with a figure-head, coloured, and a great treasure. But the merchant-ship was badly broken underneath, and in Sigurd's opinion was by now good for nothing. So they took out her bolts and nails, then burned her, and took a loaded transport out from the Wilderness, the tow-boat too, and the vessel with a figure-head. They got back to the Settlement and found the bishop at Gardar. Sigurd told him of their adventures and the finding of the money. 'So far as I can see,' he said 'the best thing that can happen to this money is for it to accompany their bones, and so far as I have any say in the matter, that is how I want it to be.' The bishop assured him that he had acted well and wisely, as everyone agreed. There was a lot of money and valuables along with the bodies, and the bishop described the ship with her figure-head as a great treasure. Sigurd said of that too that it would be best if it went to the see for the good of their souls. The rest of the goods those who had found them divided among themselves in accordance with the law of Greenland.

But when news of these events reached Norway it came to the ears of a nephew of Arnbjorn's named Ozur. There were other men as well who had lost kinsmen of theirs aboard that ship and felt entitled to inherit their money. They made a voyage to Eiriksfjord, where men came down to the shore to meet them; they started buying and selling, and later were found lodgings in men's homes. Skipper Ozur went to Gardar where the bishop lived, and spent the winter there. There was a second merchant-ship up in the Western Settlement at this same time, belonging to a Norwegian, Kolbein Thorljotsson; while yet a third ship was under the command of Hermund Kodransson and his brother Thorgils. They had a substantial body of men with them.

During the winter Ozur had a talk with the bishop, how he had come out to Greenland expecting to inherit after his kinsman Arnbjorn. He asked the bishop to arrange for the inheritance to be paid over both in respect of himself and the rest of them; but the bishop contended he had received the money in accordance with the law of Greenland relative to this kind of mishap; he had not done this, he said, of his own initiative, and he maintained that it was only right and proper that the money should go for the good of the souls of those who had been its owners, and to the church where their bones were buried. It was shabby, he said, to claim the money now. After this Ozur would not stay another day at Gardar with the bishop; he went off to join his crew, and they stuck close together, all of them, over the winter.

In the spring Ozur prepared a lawsuit for the Greenlanders' Thing. This Thing was held at Gardar, the bishop was in attendance along with Einar Sokkason, and they had a strong body of men. Ozur attended too, together with his shipmates. Once the court was set up Einar marched into court with a strong force, and said he thought they would have endless trouble dealing with foreigners in Norway if this was to be the course of events out in Greenland. 'We want to have the law that obtains here!' And when the court went into procession, the Norwegians failed to get anywhere with their case and had to withdraw. Ozur did not like this at all. He felt he had won humiliation for his pains, not money; so what he resorted to was this: he went to where the coloured ship was standing, and cut two strakes out of her, one on each side, upward from the keel. After which he went off to the Western Settlement, where he met Kolbein and Ketil Kalfsson, and told them how things stood. Kolbein agreed that he had been treated shamefully, but what he had resorted to, that was not so good either, he said.

Said Ketil: 'I strongly advise you to move up here to us, for I have heard that the bishop and Einar act hand in glove together. You will never be able to cope with the bishop's plots and Einar's power of action, and we had best all stand together.'

He agreed that was probably the most useful thing they could do. One of the merchants' party there was Ice-Steingrim. Ozur now returned to Kidjaberg, where he had been before.

The bishop grew very angry when he learned that the ship was ruined. He summoned Einar Sokkason before him, and this is what he told him: 'The time has now come for you to make good those oaths you swore when we left Norway, to punish any affront to the see and its possessions on those that wrought it. I hereby declare Ozur's life forfeit, for he has ruined what rightly belonged to us and in every respect treated us with contempt.

There is no concealing that I do not like things the way they are, and I shall brand you a perjurer if you do nothing about it.'

'It is not a good thing to have done, lord bishop,' Einar agreed, 'yet some will say there is excuse of a kind for Ozur—he has suffered so heavy a mulcting—even though these men might not easily contain themselves when they laid eyes on those splendid treasures which had belonged to their kinsmen, yet could not secure possession of them. Indeed, I hardly know what line to take here.'

They parted coolly, and the bishop's face was eloquent of his displeasure. But when folk went to the church anniversary and feast at Langanes, the bishop put in an appearance with Einar at the feast. A lot of people had come along for the service, and the bishop sang mass. Ozur was one of those who attended, and was standing by the south side of the church against the church wall, and talking to him was a man named Brand Thordarson, one of the bishop's servants. He was urging him to give way to the bishop. 'For then', he said, 'I believe all will end well, but as it is the outlook is bleak.' Ozur said he just could not find it in his heart to do that, he had been treated so badly, and they went on arguing the ins and outs of it. Then the bishop and the rest of them left the church for the house, and Einar joined in the procession. But just as they arrived at the hall doors Einar broke away from the party and went off to the churchyard all on his own, seized an axe from the hand of one of the worshippers and walked south round the church, to where Ozur stood leaning on his axe. He instantly struck him his death-blow, then walked back indoors, where by now the tables had been set up. Einar took his place at table opposite the bishop, without saying a word.

Then Brand Thordarson walked into the room and up to the bishop, and, 'Have you heard the news, lord bishop?' he asked.

Not a thing, said the bishop. 'And what have you to report?'

'A man has just dropped down dead outside.'

'Who did it?' asked the bishop. 'And who was the victim?'

Brand said there was a man near him who could tell him all about it.

'Einar,' asked the bishop, 'have you caused Ozur's death?'

'Quite right,' he replied. 'I have.'

'Such deeds are not right,' said the bishop. 'Yet this one is not without its justification.'

Brand asked that the body should be washed and a service sung over it. There was plenty of time for that, replied the bishop, and men sat to table, taking their time over everything, and indeed the bishop appointed men to sing over the body only when Einar pressed for it, urging that this should be done in a way which was seemly and proper. The bishop said that in his opinion it would be the more proper course not to give him church burial at all. 'However, at your request he shall be buried here at a church which has no resident priest.' Nor would he appoint clergy to sing over him before his body was laid out.

'Things have taken a sharp turn now,' said Einar, 'and in no small measure through your contriving. There are a lot of violent men concerned in this, and in my opinion a lot of trouble is heading our way.'

The bishop said he hoped they would be able to stave off all such violence, and offer arbitration and a just solution of the case, so long as it was not pursued in a violent way.

III

The news spread and the merchants came to hear of it. 'My guess was not far out,' said Ketil Kalfsson. 'that this would cost him his head.'

There was a kinsman of Ozur's whose name was Simon, a big, strong man; and Ketil said it was probable, if Simon acted in character, that he would not be overlooking the slaughter of Ozur his kinsman. Simon's comment was that this was not the occasion for big talk.

Ketil had their ship made ready. He sent men to see skipper Kolbein and had him briefed with the news. 'And tell him this, that I am going to prosecute Einar in court, for I know the law of Greenland and am quite prepared to handle these people. Besides, we have a strong force of men, if it comes to trouble.' Simon said he was prepared to take his lead from Ketil, and afterwards set off to find Kolbein, and informed him of the killing and of Ketil's message, that they should join forces with those from the Western Settlement and attend the Greenlanders' Thing. He would certainly come if he could, said

Kolbein; he would like the Greenlanders to discover that it did not pay to go killing their men. Ketil immediately took over the lawsuit from Simon and set off with a fair body of men, ordering the merchants to follow quickly after. 'And bring your goods with you.' The moment he received this message Kolbein took action, ordered his mates to come to the Thing, and explained that they had now so strong a following that it was doubtful that the Greenlanders could encroach on their rights. And now Kolbein and Ketil met and laid their heads together—and each of them a man to be reckoned with. They set off, had a foul wind, but kept moving ahead: they had a big body of men, though as it happened fewer than they had expected. And now men came to the Thing.

Sokki Thorisson had come there too. He was a shrewd sort of man, old by now, and was often appointed to arbitrate in men's lawsuits. He went to see Kolbein and Ketil to tell them he wished to seek for an atonement. 'I want to offer myself as an arbitrator between you,' he said, 'and though I have stronger ties with Einar my son, still I shall act in the case in such a way as will seem pretty fair to myself and to other reliable and sensible men.' Ketil said he thought they would be all for pressing their case to its conclusion. Still he did not entirely rule out the idea of a settlement. 'But we have been treated monstrously, and it has never been our way to let our rights go by default.' Sokki said he thought they would not stand an even chance if it came to a fight, besides which it remained to be seen, he said, whether they would get any more satisfaction even though he, Sokki, was not their judge and arbitrator.

The merchants went into court and Ketil put his case against Einar. Said Einar: 'It will make news everywhere if they overbear us in this case.' And he marched to the court and broke it up, so that they could not proceed with their business. 'It still stands,' said Sokki, 'that offer I made for a reconciliation and to arbitrate in the case.' But Ketil said he thought that any further compensation he awarded would serve no purpose now. 'Einar's lawlessness in this case remains unaffected.' And with that they parted.

The reason why the merchants from the Western Settlement had not put in an appearance at the Thing was that they got a head wind there when they were ready with their two ships. But at midsummer there was to be an arbitration made at Eid, and now these merchants made their way down from the west and lay off a certain headland, where they all met together and held a conference. Kolbein swore it should not have come so near a settlement had they all been there together. 'But now I think it best for us all to attend this meeting, and with all the resources we can muster.' And that was the way of it: they went off and into hiding in a certain hidden bay a short distance from the bishop's see.

It happened at the see that they were ringing for high mass just as Einar Sokkason arrived. When the merchants heard this, they said it was paying Einar great honour that the bells should be rung to greet him. It was a scandal, they said, and were furious at it. But, 'Don't be upset by it,' said Kolbein, 'for it might well turn out that before evening falls this could change to a funeral knell.'

Now Einar and his men came and sat down on a bank there. Sokki laid out the articles to be valued and those items which were intended as compensation. Said Ketil: 'I want Hermund Kodransson and myself to price these articles.' It should be so, said Sokki. Ozur's kinsman Simon was prowling around with a scowl on his face while the price of the articles was being settled. And now an ancient coat of plate-mail was brought forward. 'What an insult,' cried Simon, 'offering such rubbish in payment for a man like Ozur!' He dashed the mail-coat to the ground and marched up to the men who were sitting on the bank, and the minute the Greenlanders saw this they sprang to their feet and stood facing downhill against Simon. And now Kolbein moved up outside them as they all turned forward, then slipped in at their rear, and it was at one and the same moment he got behind Einar's back and cut at him with his axe between the shoulders and Einar's axe lighted on Simon's head, so that they both suffered a mortal wound.

'It is only what I expected,' said Einar, as he fell.

Then Einar's foster-brother Thord rushed at Kolbein, intending to cut him down, but Kolbein swerved out of his way, jabbing with his axe-horn, and catching him in the throat, and Thord was killed instantly. With that battle was joined between them; but the bishop sat down alongside Einar, and he breathed his last on the bishop's knees. There was a man by the name of Steingrim who said they must stop fighting, please; he walked in between them with certain others, but both sides were so mad that he had a sword whipt through him in a twinkling. Einar died up on the bank by the booth of the Greenlanders. By this time there were many men badly wounded, and Kolbein and his party got down to their ship with three of their men killed, and afterwards got themselves across Einarsfjord to Skjalgsbudir, where the merchant-ships were lying and being busily made ready for sea.

There had been a bit of a brawl, commented Kolbein. 'And I can't help thinking the Greenlanders will be no better pleased now than before.'

'It was a true word you spoke, Kolbein,' said Ketil, 'that we should hear a funeral knell before we got away, and I believe that Einar's dead body is being carried to church.'

Kolbein agreed that he was not without some responsibility for this.

'We can expect the Greenlanders to launch an attack on us,' said Ketil. 'I think it best for our people to carry on loading as hard as they can, and for everyone to stay aboard ship by night.'

Which is what they did.

IV

Sokki was deeply distressed by what had happened, and canvassed for help if it came to a fight. Living at Solarfjall was a man named Hall, very level-headed and a good farmer. He was on Sokki's side, and was the last to come in with his following. He said to Sokki: 'This plan of yours, using small boats to attack big, looks most unpromising to me, when you consider the welcome I feel sure they will have prepared for us. Another thing, I don't know how far this muster of yours can be relied on. Those worth their salt will all give a good account of themselves, true, but the rest will be more for hanging back, so your leaders will all get knocked on the head, and our case end up worse than it started. So it seems to me only wise, if there is to be a fight, that everybody now swears an oath that he will either die or conquer.'

At these words of Hall's a good deal of their courage seeped out of them. 'Yet we cannot let it drop', said Sokki, 'while the case remains unsettled.'

Hall replied that he would try for a peaceful settlement

between them. He called out to the merchants, asking: 'Shall I have peace to come over and see you?' Kolbein and Ketil called back that he should, so he went across to them and argued the need to get the case settled after such great and dire events. They declared themselves ready for either alternative, war or peace, just as the others pleased; all these evils, they argued, had come about through the Greenlanders. 'But now that you are showing such goodwill, we pledge our word that you shall compose the issue between us.' He said he would arbitrate and judge in the light of what seemed to him most right, like it as they might, either party. Next, this was put to Sokki, who likewise agreed to Hall's jurisdiction. The merchants must carry on day and night with their preparations to leave, and they stressed that nothing would satisfy Sokki except that they should be out and away at the earliest possible moment. 'But if they dawdle over their preparations and mortify me so, then it is certain they shall have no redress if they are caught.'

On that note they parted, and a place was fixed on for the announcement of the award. 'Our sailing arrangements are not getting on at all quickly,' said Ketil, 'while supplies are running out fast. I suggest we look round for provisions. I know where there is a man living who has any amount of food, and I think it only sense to go and find him.' They said they were all ready, and later hurried ashore one night, thirty of them in a group, all armed. They reached his farm, but it was completely deserted. Thorarin was the name of the farmer living there. 'My suggestion has not turned out so well,' said Ketil, whereupon they turned away from the farm and down the path towards the ships. There was a bushy place they passed. 'I feel drowsy,' said Ketil. 'I am going to sleep.' This was not exactly prudent, they held, but all the same down he lay and went to sleep, while they sat watching over him. A little later he woke up. 'Matters of some moment have been revealed to me,' he told them. 'How would it be if we were to pull up this clump which is under my head here?' They pulled up the clump, and down below it was a big cave. 'To start with, let us take a look what sort of provisions are here,' said Ketil. They found sixty carcasses there, twelve eighty-pound weights of butter, and any amount of dried fish. 'It is a good thing', commented Ketil, 'that I have not led you on a fool's errand.' And they went down to the ship with their plunder.

Now time wore on to the peace-meeting, and both sides turned up to it, both merchants and Greenlanders. Hall made this announcement: 'This is my award between you, that I want Ozur's killing to cancel that of Einar; but because of the disparity between the two men outlawry shall follow for the Norwegians, so that they get neither food nor shelter here. In addition, the following killings shall be held equal: franklin Steingrim and Simon, Krak the Norwegian and Thorfinn the Greenlander, Vighvat the Norwegian and Bjorn the Greenlander, Thorir and Thord. Which still leaves one of our men unpaid for, Thorarin by name, a man with helpless folk dependent on him. He must be paid for with money.'

Sokki said the award was a bitter disappointment to him and his fellow Greenlanders, when men were paired off in such fashion; but Hall was firm that his verdict should stand even so, and it was on those terms they parted.

The next thing, in swept the ice and all the fjords were frozen. It was a pleasing thought to the Greenlanders that they might lay hands on them if they could not get away by the appointed time, but at the very end of the month all the ice swept out, the merchants got away from Greenland, and that was their parting.

They reached Norway. Kolbein had brought a white bear from Greenland and went with this creature into the presence of King Harald Gilli, and presented it to him, and held forth before the king about what cruel treatment the Greenlanders had meted out, slandering them greatly. But later the king heard a different story and thought that Kolbein had been pitching him a lot of lies, so no bounty followed in respect of the bear. After that Kolbein took sides with Sigurd Shamdeacon, attacked the king in his chamber, and gave him a wound [1136]. But later, as they were on their way to Denmark and crowding sail, with Kolbein in the tow-boat and the wind blowing hard, the boat was torn adrift and Kolbein was drowned. But Hermund and the others came to Iceland to the land of their fathers.

And that is the end of this saga.

APPENDIXES

Appendixes

I(*a*). OHTHERE'S NORTHERN VOYAGE

[This concise report of Ohthere's voyage north, during which he rounded the North Cape and reached the White Sea, was inserted by King Alfred in his paraphrase of the early fifth-century *Historiæ adversum paganos* of Paulus Orosius. Ohthere's voyage was undertaken *c*.880 or not long thereafter.]

OHTHERE said to his lord King Alfred that he lived farthest north of all Norwegians.[1] He said that he lived up north in the land alongside the western sea. He said even so that the land extends a very long way north from there, but it is all waste save that in a few places here and there Lapps make their camp, hunting in winter and in summer fishing by the sea.

He said that on one occasion he wished to find out how far the land extended due north, or whether anybody dwelt north of the waste. He proceeded then due north along the land; he kept the waste land to starboard and the open sea to port the whole way for three days. He was then as far north as the whale-hunters travel farthest. He then travelled still due north as far as he could sail in the next three days. Then the land veered due east, or the sea in on the land, he knew not which,[2] save that he did know that he waited there for a wind from the west and a little from the north, and then sailed east along the Land as far as he could sail in four days. He then had to wait there for a wind from due north, for just there the land veered due south, or the sea in on the land, he knew not which. Then from there he sailed due south along the land as far as he could sail in five days. Then at that point a great river opened up into

[1] There is general agreement that he lived somewhere in the Malangen-fjord–Senja–Kvaløy area, about 69° N.

[2] Ohthere (ON Ottar) had reached the North Cape. He would thereafter proceed as far as the White Sea and Kandalaksha Bay.

23. THE WALRUS HUNT (OLAUS MAGNUS)

the land. They then turned up into the river, because they durst not sail on past the river for fear of hostility, because the land on the other side of the river was all inhabited. Before this he had not met with any inhabited land since leaving his own home, but there was waste land the whole way to starboard, except for fishers and fowlers and hunters, and they were all Lapps, and at all times there was the open sea to port. The Permians had cultivated their land very well, but they durst not put in there. But the land of the Terfinns was all waste, except where there were hunters encamped, or fishers or fowlers—and they were all Lapps.

The Permians told him many things both about their own lands and those lands which were round about them, but he did not know how much of it was true, for he did not see it for himself. The Lapps, it seemed to him, and the Permians spoke very much the same language. Mainly he travelled that way, in addition to viewing the land, for the walruses, because they have very fine bone in their teeth (they brought some of these teeth to the king), and their hides are very good for ship's ropes. This whale is much smaller than other whales: it is not longer than seven ells long. But the best whale-hunting is in his own land: these are forty-eight ells long, and the biggest fifty ells long. Of these he said that with five others he killed sixty in two days.

He was a very wealthy man in the goods in which their wealth consists, that is, in wild animals. He still had, when he visited the king, six hundred tame deer for sale. They call these animals 'reindeer'. Six of them were decoy-reindeer. These are very dear among the Lapps, because with them they capture the wild reindeer. He was among the first men in the land. Even so he had no more than twenty cattle, twenty sheep, and twenty pigs; and the little that he ploughed he ploughed with horses. But their revenue is mainly in the tribute which the Lapps pay them. That tribute consists of animals' skins, of birds' feathers and whalebone, and in the ship's ropes which are made from whale- [i.e. walrus-] and seal-hide. Each pays according to his rank. Those of highest rank must pay fifteen marten-skins, five of reindeer, one bearskin, and ten measures of feathers [i.e. down], and a coat of bearskin or otter-skin, and two ship's ropes, each to be sixty ells long, the one made of whale-hide, the other of seal's.

He said that the land of the Norwegians was very long and very narrow. All of it that one can either graze or plough, that lies alongside the sea, and even that is very rocky in places; and to the east, and alongside and parallel to the cultivated land, lie wild mountains. In those mountains live Lapps. And the cultivated land is broadest in the south, and increasingly narrower as it extends further north. In the south it may be sixty miles broad or somewhat broader, and in the middle thirty or broader, and northwards, he said, where it was narrowest, it might be three miles broad to the high ground, and the high ground thereafter in some places as broad as one might cross in two weeks, and in some places as broad as one might cross in six days.

Then parallel to that land in the south, on the other side of the mountains, is the land of the Swedes up to the line dividing it from the north, and then parallel to that land [Norway] in the north, the land of the Cwenas.[3] Sometimes the Cwenas make war on the Norwegians across the mountains, sometimes the

---

[3] Kainulaiset, Kvennir, etc., presumably a Lapp tribe or people. By a confusion with an Old Norse word for 'woman', it later acquired notes of a *terra feminarum*, Kvenland, Cwenaland, etc.

Norwegians on them. And there are very big fresh-water lakes throughout the mountains, and the Cwenas carry their boats overland to the lakes, and make war on the Norwegians from there. They have very small ships, and very light ones.

Ohthere said that the district he lived in was called Halogaland. He said that no one lived north of him. Then there is a mart south in the land which they call Sciringesheal [Skiringssalir, Kaupang]. He said that a man could sail thither in a month, if he camped by night and had a favourable wind every day, and all the time he must sail along the land. And to starboard is first Ireland,[4] and then the islands which are between Ireland and this land. Then there is this land until one comes to Sciringesheal, and all the way to port is Norway. To the south of Sciringesheal a very large sea flows up into the land. It is broader than anyone can see across. And Jutland is opposite on the one side, and thereafter South Jutland. The sea lies many hundreds of miles up into the land.

I(*b*). SAXO GRAMMATICUS'S DESCRIPTION OF ICELAND AND NORWAY

[From the Preface to Saxo's History of the Danes, *Gesta Danorum*, of *c*.1185–1216. The Preface is generally held to have been written after he had completed the work. The passages are reproduced from Peter Fisher's translation in *Saxo Grammaticus. The History of the Danes*, vol. I: *English Text*, (1979).]

I shall record, besides the parts and climate of Denmark, those of Sweden and Norway, since the same geographic area embraces them, and because of their kindred languages. This region, lying beneath the northern heavens, faces Boötes and the Great and Lesser Bear; beyond its highest latitude, where it touches the Arctic zone, the extraordinary brutality of the temperature allows no human beings to settle. Of these countries Nature decided to give Norway an unpleasant, craggy terrain; it reveals nothing but a grim, barren, rock-strewn desert. In its

[4] Some commentators prefer Iceland (*Iraland*, *Isaland*) but the change, though tempting, is not essential. See Bjørnbø's reconstruction, p. 4.

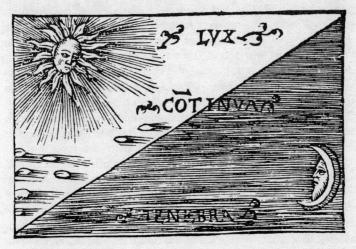

24. DIES CONTINUUS, NOX UNA CONTINUA (OLAUS MAGNUS)

furthest part the sun never withdraws its presence; scorning alternate periods of day and night it apportions equal light to each.

To the west is Iceland, an island surrounded by the vast Ocean, a land of meanish dwellings yet deserving proclamation for mysterious happenings beyond credibility. There is a spring here which by the virulence of its gaseous waters destroys the original nature of any object. Certainly anything tinged by the vapour it emits is petrified. This phenomenon might well be more dangerous than wonderful, for such hardening properties are inherent in the gentle fluidity of the water that anything brought to steep in its fumes instantly assumes the qualities of stone, merely retaining its shape. There are reports of a great many other springs in the same locality, whose water at times swells to enormous volume, overflows the basins and frequently spouts jets high into the air; at other times their flow subsides till it is sucked into pits deep down in the earth, scarcely penetrable to the eye. Thus in full activity they splash everything near with bright spray, but when they drain away the sharpest sight cannot perceive them. Again there is a mountain in this island which gives off a meteoric light from the surging flames which it belches forth without cease. This is no whit inferior to the previous marvels I have described, in that a land enduring bitter cold can produce abundant fuel for such heat, to feed its undying fires with secret supplies, from which it stokes its blaze to eternity. At certain definite times, too, an immense mass of ice drifts upon the island; immediately on its arrival, when it dashes into the rocky coast, the cliffs can be heard re-echoing, as though a din of voices were roaring in weird cacophony from the deep. Hence a belief that wicked souls condemned to a torture of intense cold are paying their penalty there. If a piece is severed from this mass and fastened with the most bulging knots, it slips its ties as soon as the main body of ice breaks away from the land. It is dumbfounding to think that, whether they load it with the tightest shackles or bind it round intricately, it still pursues the floe of which it formed a part, inevitably escaping the closest supervision. Another kind of ice is well-known there, interspersed among rocky mountain ridges. This periodically turns upside-down, with its surface sinking below and the under parts moving to the top. There is a story, to prove this statement, of certain men who happened to be running across an ice-field when they pitched into the depths of gaping crevasses which appeared before them; shortly afterwards they were discovered lifeless and not the merest chink remained in the ice. For this reason many believe that they were swallowed into a sling-shaped ice pocket and when this reversed later it delivered up their bodies. Rumour has it that whoever sips at a certain unwholesome fountain which gushes there falls dead as if he had drunk poison. Other springs are said to have the quality of ale. There are kinds of fire too which, though unable to harm wood, may consume a fluid such as water. There is also a rock which flies over the mountain steeps by its own natural movement rather than any external propulsion.

Now to describe Norway rather more thoroughly I must tell you that it shares its eastern frontier with Sweden and Götaland and is bounded on each side by the neighbouring Ocean. To the north it faces an undefined and nameless territory, lacking civilisation and swarming with strange unhuman races; a vast stretch of sea however separates this from the opposite shores of Norway and, since navigation there is hazardous, very few have set foot upon it and enjoyed a safe return.

The inner bend of the Ocean pierces Denmark and passes on

25. LAND OF FIRE AND ICE (OLAUS MAGNUS)

to border the southern quarter of Götaland in a broad curve;[5] the outer sweep increases in breadth as it streams eastwards along the coastline of northern Norway till it is walled by an unbroken arc of land and terminates in a sea which our ancestors called Gandvik [the White Sea].[6] Between Gandvik and the waters to the south there is a thin strip of mainland situated between the lapping seas; if this natural barrier had not been created against the almost meeting waves, the tides, washing together in a channel, would have made an island of Sweden and Norway. Within the eastern area of these countries live the Skrit-Finns. In their passion for hunting, these people habitually transport themselves in an unusual manner, having to trace slippery roundabout routes to reach the desired haunts in

[5] 'The Latin is *Oceani superior flexus*, literally 'upper bend of ocean.' Saxo appears to see a movement towards the outer rim of earth and the encircling Ocean as a downward one, and that towards the earth's centre as an upward one. Thus in the next line he writes: *inferior meatus*, literally 'the lower course', which is here translated 'the outer sweep'. *Saxo Grammaticus. The History of the Danes*, Vol. II: *Commentary*, by Hilda Ellis Davidson and Peter Fisher, (1980).

[6] *Gandr*, a word of ill savour: Gandvik, Magic or Spooky Bay, probably because of the Laplanders' reputation for sorcery and witchcraft.

remote parts of the mountains. No cliff stands too high for them
to surmount by some skilfully twisting run. For first they glide
out of the deep valleys by the feet of precipices, circling this way
and that, frequently swerving in their course from a direct line
until by these tortuous paths they achieve the destined summit.
They normally use animal skins instead of money to trade with
their neighbours.

Western Sweden faces Denmark and Norway, but to the
south and along much of its eastern side the Ocean adjoins it.
Beyond, to the east, can be found a motley conglomeration of
savage tribes.

II. THE ONLY KING WHO RESTS IN ICELAND

[These two chapters from *Ólafs Saga Helga* recount the last
stages of King Olaf's dealings with his enemy and kinsman
Hrœrek, one of the five kings of Uppland. Olaf captured all
five, took the tongue from one, the eyes from Hrœrek, and the
others he banished. After that he never let Hrœrek out of his
sight, though he treated him well enough. However, Hrœrek in
all his moods was constant for revenge, and before our portion
of his story opens had attempted both assassination and escape.

The Icelander Thorarin Nefjolfsson is known not only for his
unsuccessful attempt to reach Greenland with King Hrœrek,
but for a famous crossing from (Stad in) Mœr in Norway to
Eyrar (i.e. Eyrarbakki) in the south-west of Iceland (see p. 11
above).]

84

It happened on Ascension day [15 May 1018] that King Olaf
went to high mass. The bishop walked in procession round the
church, leading the king, and when they came back to the
church the bishop led the king to his seat in the north of the
choir. As usual King Hrœrek was seated next to him. He had
his face under his over-cloak. When King Olaf had sat down
King Hrœrek put his hand on his shoulder and felt it. 'Fine
clothes you wear now, kinsman,' said he. 'This is a high festi-
val,' replied King Olaf, 'held in remembrance of Jesus Christ's
ascension to heaven from earth.' 'I am not quite clear,' said

King Hrœrek, 'what you tell me about Christ, so that I can keep it safe in mind. Much of what you tell me seems none too credible, though to be sure many wonders happened in the old days.'

When mass had begun King Olaf stood up, raised his hands above his head and bowed towards the altar, and his cloak fell back from off his shoulders. King Hrœrek sprang up quick and hard and struck King Olaf with a knife of the kind called 'rytning'. The blow came on the cape by the shoulders as the king was bending forwards; the clothes were badly cut, but the king was unwounded. When King Olaf knew of this assault he sprang forward on to the floor. King Hrœrek struck at him a second time with the knife, but missed him. 'Are you fleeing then, Olaf Digri,' he cried, 'from me, a blind man?' The king ordered his men to seize him and lead him out of the church, which was done.

Following this incident King Olaf was urged to have King Hrœrek killed. 'It is pressing your luck hard, king, to keep him about you and spare him, whatever mischief he gets up to. Day and night his one thought is to take your life, while once you let him out of your sight we see no one who will keep so close an eye on him that there will be no chance of his escaping. And if he gets loose he will promptly raise an army and do great harm.'

'What you say is true enough,' replied King Olaf. 'Many a man has got his death for less provocation than Hrœrek's. But I am loath to tarnish the victory I won over the Upplanders' kings, when in a morning I caught them all, and seized their kingdoms in such fashion that I need not be the death of a single one of them, for they were all my kinsmen. At the moment I find it hard to tell whether Hrœrek will put me in a position where I must have him killed or not.'

Hrœrek had put his hand on King Olaf's shoulder to find out whether he was wearing a mail shirt.

85

There was a man called Thorarin Nefjolfsson, an Icelander whose family lived up north, not of high birth, but full of sense and wise conversation, and ready to speak his mind in the highest company. He was a great traveller and had spent much time in foreign parts. Thorarin was very ugly, and the main cause of this was the deformity of his limbs. His hands were big and ugly, and his feet were far worse.

Thorarin was staying in Tunsberg when the events just narrated took place. He and King Olaf were not unacquainted. At the time Thorarin was fitting out the merchant-ship he owned, for he proposed sailing to Iceland in the summer. King Olaf had Thorarin as his guest for a few days and had plenty to talk to him about. Thorarin slept in the royal quarters. Early one morning it happened that the king was awake while the others in the room were asleep. The sun had just risen, and it was quite light indoors. The king could see how Thorarin had stuck one of his feet out from under the bedclothes. He studied the foot for a while, then those in the room woke up.

'I have been awake some time,' the king told Thorarin, 'and have seen a sight well worth seeing, a man's foot so ugly that I cannot think there is an uglier in this town.' And he told the others to take a look, whether it appeared that way to them; and all who looked vowed that it was so.

Thorarin understood very well what they were talking about. 'There are few things', he replied, 'whose match you cannot hope to find, and it is very probable that is the case here too.'

'For my part,' said the king, 'I am convinced that so ugly a foot just cannot be found, no, even if I have to bet on it.'

'I am willing to bet you I shall find an uglier foot here in the town,' said Thorarin.

'Then let the one proved right claim anything he likes of the other,' said the king.

'So be it,' replied Thorarin, and stuck his other foot out from under the bedclothes. It was no whit handsomer than its fellow, and its big toe was missing. 'See for yourself, king, another foot which is uglier to the extent that one of its toes is missing. I have won the bet.'

'No, no,' said the king, 'the other foot is uglier to the extent that it has five nasty toes, and this only four. So I have a claim to make of you.'

'Dear are the king's words,' said Thorarin. 'And what claim are you making?'

'This,' said he, 'that you carry King Hrœrek to Greenland and hand him over to Leif Eiriksson.'

'I have never been to Greenland,' replied Thorarin.

'If you have not,' said the king, 'then it is high time a traveller like you did.'

At first Thorarin made little answer in the matter, but when the king kept pressing his request he did not entirely evade the issue, but said this: 'I will let you hear, king, the demand I had it in mind to make, had our bet been won by me. It was this: I wanted to ask for a place among your men. And if you grant me that, it will be all the more my duty not to dawdle over what you ask of me.'

The king agreed to this and Thorarin became his retainer. He saw to his ship, and when he was ready to sail took charge of King Hrœrek. As he took leave of King Olaf he asked the king: 'Now should it turn out, sire, as is not improbable and happens often enough, that we cannot complete the Greenland passage but must run for Iceland or some other land, how shall I part with this king to your satisfaction?'

'If you come to Iceland,' said the king, 'you must deliver him into the hands of Gudmund Eyjolfsson or Skapti the Law-speaker or some other chieftain who wishes to accept my friend-ship and the tokens that go with it. But if you are driven to other lands lying nearer home, then so arrange matters that you know for sure Hrœrek will never return alive to Norway. But do this only if you see there is nothing else for it.'

When Thorarin was ready and had a good wind he sailed the whole outer course away beyond the islands, and north of Lidandisnes stood out to sea. For a while he did not get a good wind, but made it very much his business not to come to land. He sailed south of Iceland, then knew where he was, and so west of the land into the Greenland sea. There he got great storms and heavy seas, and late in the summer came to Iceland, to Breidafjord. Thorgils Arason was the first man of any importance to come to them, and Thorarin told him of King Olaf's message, his offer of friendship, and the tokens relating to the taking over of King Hrœrek. Thorgils showed himself friendly in return, inviting King Hrœrek to his house, where he stayed with Thorgils for the winter. But he did not like it there, and asked Thorgils to have him conveyed to Gudmund. He seemed to have heard, he said, that at Gudmund's was the most splendid style of living in Iceland, and it was to him he had been sent. So Thorgils did as he asked and provided men to convey him to Gudmund at Modruvellir. Gudmund gave him a good welcome because of the king's message, and it was there he spent his second winter. Then he liked it there no longer, so Gudmund found him a place to live at a little farm called Kalf-skinn, where there were very few people, and there he spent his third winter. And ever since he lost his kingdom, he said, that was where he liked being best, for there he was held the first man by all. The following summer Hrœrek took the sickness which brought him to his death, so it is said he is the only king who rests in Iceland.

III. UNGORTOK THE CHIEF OF KAKORTOK

[This bloodthirsty tale, together with its illustrations by the Greenlander Aron of Kangeq, is reproduced from Henry Rink, *Tales and Traditions of the Eskimos*, translated from the Danish by the author (London, 1875), pp. 308–17. There is an equally bloodthirsty version, of obscure provenance, and told from the Icelandic or Norse point of view, preserved in Reykjavík. See the footnote on p. 100 above.]

It once happened that a kayaker from Arpatsivik came rowing up the firth, trying his new bird-javelin as he went along. On approaching Kakortok, where the first *Kavdlunait* [plural of *kavdlunak*, foreigner, Norseman] had taken up their abode, he saw one of them gathering shells on the beach, and presently he called out to him, 'Let us see whether thou canst hit me with thy lance.' The kayaker would not comply, although the other continued asking him. At last, however, the master of the place, named Ungortok [Ungor = Yngvar?], made his appearance, and said, 'Since he seems so very anxious about it, take good aim at him;' and soon the kayaker sent out his spear in good earnest, and killed him on the spot. Ungortok, however, did not reproach him, but only said, 'It certainly is no fault of thine, since thou hast only done as thou wast bidden.' When winter came, it was a general belief that the Kavdlunait would come and avenge the death of their countryman; but summer came round again; and even two summers passed quickly by. At the beginning of the third winter, the same kayaker again rowed up to Kakortok, provided with the usual hunting tools, bladder and all. This time he again happened to see a Kavdlunak gathering shells, and somehow he took a fancy to kill him too. He rowed up towards him on that side where the sun was shining full upon the water, and launching his spear at him, killed him at once, upon which he returned home unobserved, and told how he had done away with one of the Kavdlunait. They reproached him with not having let their chief know of this; and the murderer answered them, 'The first time I only killed him because I was asked over and over again to do so.' Some time after this occurrence, a girl was sent out to draw water in the evening; but while she was filling the pail, she noticed the reflection of something red down in the water. At first she thought it to be the reflection of her own face; but turning round, she was horrified at seeing a great crowd of Kavdlunait. She was so confounded that she left the pail behind, and hurried into the house to tell what had happened. At the same time the enemies posted themselves in front of the door and the windows. One of the inmates instantly ran out, but was soon killed with an axe, and cast aside. They were all dispatched in this way: only two brothers remained unhurt. They happily escaped out on the ice. The Kavdlunait, however, soon caught sight of them saying, 'Those are the last of the lot; let us be after them;' and at once began the pursuit. The leader now said, 'I am the quickest of you; let me start after them;' and he followed them out on the ice, where the speed of the brothers had been greatly reduced owing to the younger one having got new soles to his boots, which made them slippery, and caused him often to lose his footing. At length they reached the opposite shore, and Kaisape, the elder, succeeded in climbing the icy beach; but the younger fell, and was quickly overtaken. Ungortok cut off his left arm, and held it up before his brother, saying, 'Kaisape! as long as thou livest thou won't surely forget thy poor brother.' Kaisape, who was not armed, could render him no assistance, but quickly took to his heels. He crossed the country for Kangermiutsiak, where his father-in-law was living. Here he remained all winter, and was presented with a kayak. In summer he kayaked southward to learn some magic lay that had power to charm his enemies. He again wintered at Kangermiutsiak; but when the summer came round he went away to the north, in order to find himself a companion. At every place he came to, he first inquired if there happened to be a couple of brothers, and then he went on to examine the inside fur of their boots to see whether they had any lice in them; and he travelled far and wide before he found two brothers, of whom the younger one was altogether without lice. This one he persuaded to assist him, and made him return with him to Kangermiutsiak. He was now very intent on catching seals; and all he caught he had the hairs removed from the skins, which were then used for white skins. This done, he went out in search of a large piece of driftwood, and at last found one to suit his purpose. He now proceeded to excavate it with his knife until it was all hollow like a tube, and made a cover to fit tightly at one end; and both sides he furnished with little holes, for which he also made stoppers of wood. Being thus far ready, he first put all the white skins inside the hollow space, shut it up at the end with the cover, and likewise closed the little side holes. He then put it down into the water, upon which all the kayakers joined in towing it down the inlet to Pingiviarnik, where they landed it; and having got out the skins, attached strings to them, then hoisted and spread them like sails, so that the boat came to have the appearance of a somewhat dirty iceberg, the skins being not at all alike white. The people now got in: it was pushed off from land, and Kaisape gave the order, 'Let the skins be spread!' This was accordingly done; and the people on shore were astonished to see how very like it was to an iceberg floating slowly along. Kaisape, who wanted to take a survey of the whole from shore, said to the crew, 'Now ye can take the boat out yourselves, while I step ashore to have a look at it.' When he beheld the work of his hands, he was well pleased with it, and ordered the boat to land again. The skins were all spread out to dry in the sun; and when this had been done, he remarked that he had not yet forgotten his brother. They were now ready to go to Kakortok and have their revenge, but for some time they were obliged to station themselves at Arpatsivik, awaiting a favourable wind to carry them up the inlet. When the fair wind had set in, the firth gradually filled with broken bits of ice of different form and size. Now was the time for Kaisape to spread all sail and get in. Several boats followed in his wake, but the crews landed a little north of Kakortok to gather fagots of juniper;

while Kaisape and his helpmates, well hidden in the hollow wood, and keeping a constant look-out through the peep-holes, drifted straight on towards the house. They saw the Kavdlunait go to and fro, now and then taking a look down the inlet. Once they distinctly heard it announced, 'The *Kaladlit* [plural of *kalâ-lek*, a Greenland Eskimo] are coming': upon which they all came running out of the house; but when the master had reassured them saying, 'It is nothing but ice', they again retired; and Kaisape said, 'Now, quick! they won't be coming out for a while, I think.' They got out on shore; and, well loaded with

26.

juniper fagots, they all surrounded the house. Kaisape filled up the doorway with fuel, and then struck fire to it, so that all the people inside were burned; and those who tried to make their escape through the passage were also consumed. But Kaisape cared little for the people in general; his thoughts all centred in Ungortok; and he now heard one of his helpmates exclaiming, 'Kaisape! the man whom thou seekest is up there.' The chief had by this time left the burning house through a window, and was flying with his little son in his arms. Kaisape went off in pursuit of him, and approached him rapidly. On reaching the lake, the father threw his child into the water that it might rather die unwounded. Kaisape, however, not being able to overtake his antagonist, was forced to return to his crew. Ungortok ran on till he reached Igaliko, and there established himself with another chief named Olave. On finding that Kaisape would not leave him at peace there, he removed to the head of the firth Agdluitsok, where he settled at Sioralik, while Kaisape established himself at the outlet of the same firth. The following summer he again left in pursuit of Ungortok, who, however, succeeded in getting to the coast opposite the island of Aluk. Kaisape traced him right along to the north side of the same island, where he took up his abode; and he now consulted the Eastlanders with regard to some means of killing Ungortok. At last one stood forth, saying, 'I will get thee a bit of wood from a barren woman's boot-shelf, out of which thou must shape thine arrow.' Having pronounced some spell upon it, he handed it over to Kaisape, who acknowledged the gift saying, 'If it comes true that this shall help me, I will be bound to give thee my aid in hunting and fishing.' He now went on making as many arrows as could be contained in a quiver fashioned out of a sealskin; and last of all, he added the precious charmed one, and then with his helpmates left for the great lake in front of Ungortok's house, where Kaisape stuck all the arrows in the ground at a certain distance from each other; and finally also the charmed one. He let his companion remain below by the lake, and cautiously mounted some high hills by himself, from whence he could see Ungortok striding to and fro outside his house. He heard him talk to himself, and mention the name of Kaisape. However, he resolved to await the coming of night to carry out his purpose. In the dusk he stole away to the house, and looked in at the window, holding his bow ready bent. Ungortok was passing up and down as swiftly as a shadow, on account of which it was impossible for him to take a sure aim. He therefore levelled his bow at Ungortok's wife, who lay sleeping with a baby at her breast. Ungortok hearing a noise, gave a look at his wife, and perceived the arrow sticking fast in her throat. Meantime Kaisape had quickly run back to the margin of the lake to fetch another arrow, while Ungortok sped after him with uplifted arm holding the axe that had formerly killed his brother in readiness for himself. Kaisape launched his second arrow at him, but Ungortok escaped it by falling down and making himself so thin that nothing but his chin remained visible; and before long Kaisape had spent all his arrows, without having hit his mark. Ungortok broke them in twain, and threw them into the lake. But at last Kaisape caught hold of the charmed arrow, and this went straight through the protruding chin down into the throat. As Ungortok did not however, expire immediately, Kaisape took flight, but was shortly followed by the wounded Ungortok. Kaisape had been running on for a good long while, when all of a

27.

sudden he felt his throat getting dry, and fell down totally exhausted. Remembering Ungortok, however, he soon rose again, and running back to see what had become of him, found his dead body lying close by. He now cut off his right arm, and holding it up before the dead man, repeated his own words, 'Behold this arm, which thou wilt surely never forget!' He also killed the orphan child; and taking the old Eastlander with him, he travelled back to Kangermiutsiak, where he sustained the old man, whose bones, according to report were laid to rest, in that same place.

IV. A WINTER TOO MANY: NIPAITSOQ V54

[The farm ruin known as Nipaitsoq V54 lies on the south-west side of Ameragdlafjord in the old Norse Western Settlement in Greenland. Radiocarbon dates of AD 1410±50 (Clark's calibration AD 1405±50) and AD 1500±65 (1440±65) from structural turves in the farmhouse suggest that the site was occupied until the end of the Norse settlement in the area, normally dated to c.AD 1350. It has been known and documented since Bruun, 1918; was a key site for research into a multi-causal explanation for the demise of the Norse settlements (1948–62); was further investigated during the 1976–7 Inuit–Norse Project; and over the last seven years has been the object of intense and sophisticated palæo-ecological study by teams drawn from many countries. The paragraphs that follow have been excerpted, by kind permission of the authors and the Board of Regents of the University of Wisconsin System, from 'A Study of the Faunal and Floral Remains from Two Norse Farms in the Western Settlement, Greenland', by Thomas H. McGovern, Hunter College, New York; P. C. Buckland, Diana Savory, Guðrún Sveinbjarnardóttir, Birmingham University, UK; Claus Andreasen, Grønlands Landsmuseum, Nuuk/Godthaab; and P. Skidmore, Museum and Art Gallery, Doncaster, UK (*Arctic Anthropology*, 20.2 (1983), pp. 93–120). The article's scrupulous documentation and its entire treatment of Niaqussat V48 have been omitted for reasons of space.]

In plan, the house complex belongs to what Roussell (1941) has termed the centralized house, where dwelling and livestock premises are constructed in a single block. It consists of a number of houses built in a cluster around what seems to be a central passage. This building technique developed in Greenland, apparently to provide protection against the cold weather. At Nipaitsoq, the main entrance to the farm faced south, looking away from the fjord. The rooms to the west of the passage lie side by side, oriented approximately east–west. Most of the rooms to the east of the passage lie roughly parallel to it and to each other.

The rooms are small, the largest one (VI) being only about 6.6 m in length. Room III has a central hearth and a bench along the end wall opposite the door. A row of loom weights was found along one wall. Included in the bones were some hand-polished pieces, some chewed by dogs, and many burned fragments. The presence of the bench, the loom weights, and the central hearth point to this as the living and working room, the *stofa*. In the room next to III, room VI, very few bone fragments were found, but large numbers of feathers were noted during excavation. Room IV, which lies across the end of the central passage, contained the largest number of bones of all the rooms, including several which were articulated, a number of bird bones, and several mouse skeletons. The room also contained a quantity of mussel shells and the remains of a tub with traces of white material in the bottom . . . On the basis of white material in a tub in one of the rooms at Stöng in Iceland, this similar deposit in Greenland is interpreted as the remains of a dairy product, *skyr*. On the basis of the bones, shellfish, and the tub with white substance, room IV has been identified as the larder. Room V seems to be a byre, since cattle dung was identified in it. This may be the case, provided that access to room V did not depend entirely upon going through room IV, since it would seem curious to have the cattle pass through the larder. Norse cattle, however, were kept inside throughout the winter, and there are examples at other sites of turf and stone walls simply being broken down to get the cattle and their collected dung out. The wall was then rebuilt.

Archaeological Interpretation

Having examined the general picture provided by the midden at Niaqussat, we may offer a tentative interpretation of the contents of the samples from rooms III, IV and VI in the farm at Nipaitsoq. The biotic elements in the samples consist of material used in flooring and that which was trampled into, and living within, the floors. The floral remains provide no detailed information as to the uses of individual rooms. However, if the crowberry seeds, present in all the house samples, are accepted as the result of feces deposition, the other seeds could have been introduced in hay or flooring materials along with casual introduction by footwear, clothing, or herbivore dung. Willow charcoal, charred seeds of grasses, and charred leaves of crowberry appear in the sample taken close to the hearth in room

III. It is possible that, as in post-medieval Iceland, dung was used as fuel. The high frequency of small fragments of burned bone around the hearth suggests that bone was used as fuel also. Similar deposits have recently been noted in an early Norse structure on Papey, a small island off the east coast of Iceland, where provision of fuel must always have been difficult.

The six astragali, polished by usage, may represent a child's game. In much of Europe, these might have been used as gaming pieces for the common children's game of knucklebones or fives. There is little evidence for such a game being played in Scandinavia, but children in Iceland, for example, used the bones when playing 'farms' and casting fortunes. The relatively large number of bones chewed by dogs in this room would suggest that this was their normal abode.

The paleoecological evidence from room VI is of more value, particularly in view of the less definite nature of the archaeological data. Few bone fragments but large numbers of feathers were noted in the room during excavation (Andreasen 1982: 179). Many were recovered from the sample, and by using the key of Day (1966) and comparing with modern reference material, many of them could be identified to the level of the Order Galliformes. Within this order, it is unfortunate that it is not possible to distinguish chicken feathers from those of ptarmigan. Although there is a reference to a cushion filled with chicken feathers in Eirik the Red's Saga [see p. 213 above], the circumstances to which this refers are special in that it is a fortuneteller who is supposed to be seated upon such a pillow. The zooarchaeological record has yet to prove the existence of chickens in Norse Greenland. It is more probable that the feathers in room IV come from ptarmigan, whose bones are common on the site. Other feathers from the deposit can be closely matched with those of Alcidae, a family which includes the guillemots, whose bones occur in some numbers. The dominance of down and downy feathers in the sample suggest that the room was not used for the preparation of birds for eating, but that the down was presumably used in cushions and bedding. In northern regions during the medieval period, those were most commonly filled with straw, hay, moss, and animal hair. Feathers and down were, however, also used from early

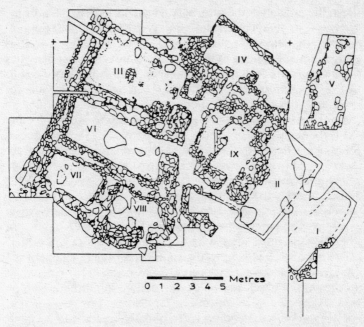

28. NIPAITSOQ V54

Plan of the excavated part of the house. The farm is of a centralized type common in Greenland, and especially frequent in the Western Settlement

times. It is known from Icelandic medieval church documents that it was regarded as a sign of wealth to own eiderdown bedding, and the use of down may have been largely reserved to the principal landowners and Church personnel in Greenland, as it was in Iceland . . . Mosses were present in several samples but were too poorly preserved for identification. It is the occurrence of the pill beetles (Byrrhids) and, to a lesser extent, the weevil *Otiorhynchus articus* which implies the existence of considerable quantities of moss in the room, the insects having been accidentally incorporated during its collection. The possible uses to which mosses (Bryophytes) might be put have been discussed by Seaward and Williams (1976; see also Buckland 1980). But it is most probable that, like feathers, the mosses were used for filling bedding. Therefore, the room might best be interpreted as the sleeping quarters of the farm. A sample from the midden of the farm V45, located 25 km to the north at the head of Itivdleq, produced several fragments of seaweed. Seaweed is known to have been used for bedding as well as food, animal fodder, and fuel . . . Indications of other activities in the room are few, and the single apostome of a larval caddis fly, *Limnephilus* sp., may have been casually introduced, although there are other indications of aquatic vegetation in room IV. However, one element common to rooms III, IV and VI is the suggestion of human feces provided by the fly puparia. Flies associated with the decay of vegetation, which was probably spread over the twig floors to provide a more comfortable surface, are dominant in the living quarters, rooms III and VI.

In room IV there are apparent contradictions between the purely archaeological evidence and the paleoecological remains. The latter, however, largely relate to the last phase of the room, perhaps after it had ceased to be the farm's larder. The crux of the evidence is the abundance of the puparia of the fly *Heleomyza serrata*, a species not recorded from Greenland at the present day. It is widely distributed in northern Europe and also occurs in Iceland and eastern North America. The species is markedly synanthropic, frequently breeding in accumulations of human feces, and was presumably spread across the North Atlantic in the ships of immigrants. This species, often characteristic of localities where hygiene is lacking, is dominant in two of the samples from Room IV and evident in lesser numbers in all samples. Faunal evidence supports the archaeological implications that the overall environment within the farm was decidedly squalid. In a place where it was essential to conserve as much heat as possible, it is probable that visits to the outside world during winter were kept to an absolute minimum and the use of one room for defecation, even if it was not strictly a latrine, is not surprising. One matrix sample from room IV, from around two house mouse skeletons, contains an assemblage of fly puparia, including taxa associated with carrion and more noticeably with decaying vegetation as well as feces. While the carrion may well have been merely dead mice, it should be noted that articulated feet of cattle and reindeer and a seal flipper also occur in the deposit, material which could as easily represent waste from food preparation as storage. Such rubbish might normally be cleared out onto the midden, where the farm dogs would see to its final fragmentation . . . The final use of the larder may, therefore, have been as a barn to store fodder for the cattle in the adjoining room V. Among the foetid hay, the accumulation of rotting meat and human feces would probably have been less offensive. The spreading of feces and rotting vegetation into other rooms, however, should be noted.

The Distribution of Animal Bones Within V54

Recent ethnoarchaeological studies indicate that the final distribution of bone fragments on a site is likely to reflect several processes (Binford 1978). These include the initial dismemberment of carcasses, division into cuts of meat, long- and short-term storage, preparation and consumption of meals, refuse disposal, and bone redeposition by dogs. Caution should, therefore, be exercised in reconstructing past human activity from bone distribution patterns recovered by archaelogical excavation. Excellent conditions of preservation, careful recovery methods, and clear boundaries to rooms, however, make the Nipaitsoq collections particularly suitable for an assessment of the use of individual rooms.

The distribution of bones within the farm indicates that activities in rooms III and IV resulted in far more deposition of bone fragments there than elsewhere. The marks of carnivore, presumably dog, teeth on bone fragments were recorded and the frequency of such chewed bones was found to vary from room to room. The dogs seem to have had greater access to room III than IV. Room IV also contained a number of articulated parts of bodies, mainly the feet of cattle, reindeer, and ptarmigan as well as seal flippers. If the dogs had had access to this room in the final stages of the farm, they would have swiftly destroyed or scattered these articulated elements. The distribution of different skeletal elements of major species in rooms III and IV may also reflect variations in function, not totally obscured by canine redeposition. The feet and tibiotarsi of at least 37 ptarmigan and the hooves of a minimum of five cattle were found in the final floor of room IV, as were parts of at least one newborn calf. The concentration of cut-off cattle hooves, without corresponding numbers of marrow-bearing metatarsi and metacarpi, and the bird legs suggest butchery waste. The articulated reindeer feet and seal flipper may likewise represent such waste. It is possible that these represent the remains of cuts of meat brought in from the external meat store (*skemma*) some 350 m to the northeast of the main house block. Such *skemmur* seem to have held the major portion of the Norse Greenlanders' air-dried meat, and haunches hung in the *skemma* might well retain some lower limbs.

While room III also contained a number of disarticulated foot bones of reindeer, sheep/goat, and seals, it lacks the concentration of cattle phalanges and ptarmigan bones that characterize the room IV collection.

Room III produced a considerable number of small chips of reindeer antler (not included in the bone count), most of which showed cut marks. These fragments are not found in the other rooms' bone collections, and they would seem to be the residue of the sort of antler-working that produced the distinctive two-sided combs of later Norse Greenland (cf. Roussell 1941: Fig. 163, nos. 214, 328). Room III also contained the greatest concentration of walrus bone and tooth fragments. These are mainly the peg-like post-canines and fragments of the dense maxillary bone surrounding the main tusk roots. This debris seems to be the remains of final finishing of walrus ivory from animals probably caught in *Nordrsetur*, the northern hunting grounds in the Disko Bay area over 500 km to the north. Maxillae seem to have been chopped from the skulls (which can weigh up to 18 kg whole) and taken back to the settlements so that the valuable tusks could be carefully chiseled out at leisure. While the tusk ivory itself is very rare in Greenland, the less valued other teeth seem to have been extensively used as raw material for buttons and tiny walrus and polar bear amulets.

Discussion

It is tempting to equate the paleoecological evidence for a low level of household hygiene with conditions of poverty and deprivation, but such need not be the case. The rank nature of the floors may, indeed, have been encouraged, since the decaying vegetation would not only have been absorptive, but would also have acted as an insulator from the cold ground below. The processes of decay would also release a certain amount of heat, a point which Coope has recently made in discussing similar floors in medieval Dublin. There is also the risk of attributing to the Norse farmer an anachronistic twentieth century attitude, which might appear to him strangely unfamiliar if not distasteful. The connection between poor hygiene and health was rarely noted in the medieval period. The body louse, *Pediculus humanus* L., for example was not unfamiliar to the Norse Greenlanders, and its bites would have been accepted as a fact of life. The Greenland farms appear to have been no more squalid than contemporary York or Dublin, although the troglodytic existence imposed by the harsh dark winters must have (by our standards) made life nasty, brutish, and short.

Final Phase Deposition at V54, a Speculative Reconstruction

The unusual nature of the bone deposit in the final floor of room IV, with its concentration of cattle feet and ptarmigan and hare bones so different from the usual midden deposit, may suggest that some unusual butchery and food preparation took place during the last occupational phase at the farm. If the butchery of at least five cattle did take place inside the building, then it probably took place all in the same winter. Norse butchery parties would be unlikely to choose to work in the cramped and dark interior of the farm building if outdoor temperatures were not significantly below freezing. The rapid freezing of a large animal carcass during dismemberment would present serious problems to the metal-poor Norse Greenlanders, who seem to have lacked meat saws and whose iron knives were often whetted to tiny stumps.

The partially articulated newborn or late fetal calf in room IV would seem to suggest that its birth and butchery occurred just before abandonment of the farm, which then might be placed in late winter or early spring. The concentration of ptarmigan and hare bones may also suggest late winter conditions, as these fat-poor and small-bodied species are often used as second choice famine food in late winter throughout the Arctic. The byres of Nipaitsoq could have held no more than six to eight cattle, so the minimum of five animals represented by the feet in room IV may well have comprised most, if not all, of the farm's cattle herd. The decision to butcher and consume perhaps the majority of the farm's cattle could only have been made under conditions of unusual stress, as the age-structure of most of the excavated Norse cattle bone collections reflects a herding economy normally centered on the production of secondary products rather than beef.

The fragments of dog bone scattered in rooms III, VII, and IX were disarticulated, but all could have come from a single individual (one of the long-limbed deerhounds identifed by Degerbøl 1936; cf. McGovern 1979). An isolated skull, found in room IV, was tentatively identified as that of a wolf, but it may have belonged to one of these large dogs. One of the dog tibiae shows cut marks, and it is at least possible that the farm's dogs, as well as its cattle, were eventually butchered for human consumption.

Thus, it seems possible that V54 was finally abandoned after a particularly hard winter in which the stock gradually died or were deliberately slaughtered. The floral and microfaunal evidence for an unsavory mixture of room functions may be, in part, a reflection of the gradual breakdown of the farm's normal operation in a period of severe stress, although it should be emphasized that the evidence from middens elsewhere in the Western Settlement reflects an equally squalid existence.

Dedication. The authors would like to dedicate this paper to the memory of Dr. Kristján Eldjárn and Dr. Sigurður Thórarinsson, pioneers in the archaeology and paleoecology of the Scandinavian North Atlantic.

V. THE NORSE GREENLANDERS AND ARCTIC CANADA

[It has seemed best to bring together here under one head the modest evidence, reasonable assumption, and unlikely speculation relating to a Norse knowledge of, and contact with, the lands and peoples of Eastern, Central, and High Arctic Canada. The discussion starts from the general assertion (repeated from my main text, p. 116 above) that once the Norsemen had plotted their homes and shared out pasture in the grassy areas of south-west Greenland, and were in process of exploring and exploiting their new surroundings, they would quickly feel assured that out west lay *something*. From their own mountain tops, from ventures out to sea, from all their lore of sea and sky and birds and fish and sea-mammals, from their experience of refraction and mirage, even from their inaccurate yet indicative mythological world-picture, they would guess at the presence of yet more land to the west, and nothing would stop them going to investigate it.]

It may reasonably be assumed that the Norse settlers in Greenland soon acquired a degree of acquaintance with the islands and peninsulas of Arctic Canada. They had ships, resolution, land-hunger, and an urgent need to make a living by exploiting each and every natural resource within their reach. Some have argued that the Norsemen were almost immediately *au fait* with the Hudson Bay area, with Baffin, Devon and Ellesmere islands, and their intricate network of waterways. But unless the documents are interpreted with determined ingenuity they yield no trace of it. That the Greenlanders moved up their own coast as far as Disco and Upernavik, and once to Melville Bay, we know—but the full process took time. That they crossed the water and proceeded south by way of Labrador is part of our present theme—and it happened quickly. What happened in addition is unclear. As hunters, fishers, and garnerers of all good things, the Norsemen must have made many unrecorded but vaguely traceable, or at least deducible, voyages over a period of three or four hundred years, not only to regions in the general latitude of the two Greenland colonies, *c*.58–64° N., but farther north (of which two cairns discovered in Jones Sound 76° 35′ N., and two more on Washington Irving Island 79° N., may be the visible proof—though the 'Norse eider-duck shelters' reported by Otto Sverdrup have more recently been interpreted as slab box-hearths of the Palaeo-Eskimo inhabitants of a much earlier period). One judges it certain that the Norsemen at times wintered away from home, doubtless at regularly frequented bases, and surely in moderate numbers, but that their journeyings were inconclusive in terms of settlement seems all too clear.

It was Jón Dúason's thesis, as prescribed in his huge *Landkönnun og Landnám Íslendinga i Vesturheim* (Reykjavík, 1941–8)—cold-shouldered by his compatriots, but espoused by the Canadian Tryggve Oleson in his official history, *Early Voyages and Northern Approaches* (1963)—that quite a number

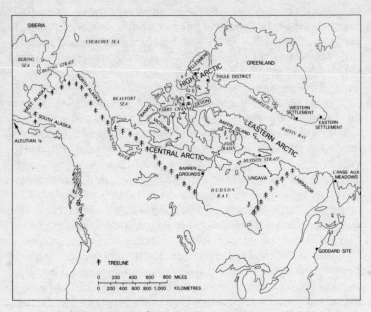

29. NORTHERN NORTH AMERICA, SHOWING LOCATIONS
MENTIONED IN THE TEXT

of Norsemen from Greenland went over to an Eskimo way of
life in both Canada and Greenland, and that by intermixture
with the Dorset people whom they found there became the
ancestors of a new race, the Thule Eskimos, who eventually
took over the whole of Greenland from the white man. Thus
they see three Norse or part-Norse entries into Arctic Canada.
The first was by way of Norse voyages of exploration and
exploitation—something we have just discussed. The second
was by way of a racial blending of Norse (Viking) hunters and
trappers with the Dorset Eskimo, which produced the Thule
people. The third was when the Thule people made life so difficult for the remaining white men in Greenland that they threw
in their lot with the Thule Eskimos and departed across the
Davis Strait into Baffin Island and became part, a fast-diminish-
ing part, of the bloodstream of the inhabitants there before the
next wave of European voyages and acquisition.

This invites a number of comments. First, there is a wealth of probability and a few pieces of evidence for Norse voyages there. Second, archaeologists, anthropologists, and Arctic prehistorians will have nothing to do with the Dúason–Oleson theories of the origin of the Thule Eskimo and the subsequent movements of that people. The only piece of documentary evidence that might seem to lend its weight to the emigration of the Norse Greenlanders to North America is the highly suspect so-called annal of 1342 included by an unverifiable process in the *Annalium Farrago* written in Latin *c.*1637. A shakier foundation-stone for the theory could hardly be found (see pp. 95–6 above). Otherwise there is nothing in Scandinavian written sources that lends unambiguous support to the Dúason–Oleson theory, and there is much that contradicts it.

Again, from everything we know of the Scandinavians in Iceland and Greenland, they were uncompromisingly tenacious of their family genealogies and their status as Europeans. (We are not, of course, here talking about white hunters and sailors attaching themselves to native women, wherever found.) Also it would require the most compelling and incontrovertible evidence to make one believe that within a period of two centuries a fair proportion of Norse Greenlanders could depart the Settlements, produce a hybrid race, and that this race could subsequently inherit the colonies of the fellow-countrymen of these same Norse Greenlanders, with apparently no one on either side aware of their blood-tie and family relationship. But as a reference to the literature of the subject shows, the evidence, whether archaeological, anthropological, or linguistic, far from being incontrovertible, has been and still is the subject of keen debate and sharp division.

Finally, a number of Thule Eskimo folk-tales contain references to a mysterious people called the Tunit, or Tornit. Dúason–Oleson think these were the Norsemen, but just about everybody else thinks they were the Dorset Eskimos. Neither a Norse–Dorset nor a Norse–Thule miscegenation has established itself as an explanation of all such highly debatable phenomena as long or rectangular houses, bear-traps, cairns, nails and knives, fragments of cloth, wood, or iron, eider-duck shelters, suspected correspondences of vocabulary, tall or blond or bearded Eskimos, whenever and wherever encountered in the Canadian Arctic. A vestige may be found, but a presence cannot be proved. Thus the claims first made in the 1960s and thereafter pressed with vigour by Thomas Lee for a Norse or part-Norse settlement or settlements in the Ungava Bay region of North Quebec have suffered an accelerating erosion, most fatally of all in respect of the so-called Norse or Norse-Eskimo long-houses found there (see Thomas E. Lee, Dekin, Plumet *et al.*, in Patrick Plumet's bibliography in 'Les Vikings en Amérique. La Fin d'un mythe', in Boyer (ed.), *Les Vikings et leur civilisation. Problèmes actuels* (1978), pp. 60–87). So-called Norse-Eskimo skulls have fared no better. There are recent reports of small finds made since 1978 of Norse material (including cloth and chain-mail sections) on Ellesmere Island 79° N., reinforcing the discovery of earlier fragments in the same general area. They are of the approximate dates 1190, 1280, 1310, 1520, but at present even though their Norse nature is accepted it is not possible to say whether their presence on Ellesmere Island is attributable to trade between Inuit (Eskimo) groups in Greenland and Canada or between the Inuit and Norsemen. In the present state of knowledge the mildest verdict possible upon the Dúason–Oleson thesis is 'not proven'.

What, then, does this leave us with? With very little, and that little open to more than one explanation. The visible evidence of Norse–Eskimo contact consists for the most part of small pieces of smelted metal, both iron and copper, a few fragments of Norse cloth and chain-mail, and a severely limited number of made objects, found over a wide area from Hudson Bay and Hudson Strait, by way of southern Baffin Island, northwards to Devon and Ellesmere Islands. It was from this last, on Skræling Island and Eskimobyen just north of the forty-kilometre narrows of Smith Sound separating Ellesmere Island from the Thule region of Greenland, that Peter Schlederman reported in 1980 finding fragments of chain-mail armour, pieces of woollen cloth, knife-blades of smelted iron and iron boat-rivets, the base of a wooden barrel, pieces of oak-wood, and some miscellaneous bits of smelted iron and copper. Radio-carbon dating suggests that the site was occupied between the thirteenth and fifteenth centuries, and possibly in the twelfth century too. The twelfth century is likewise the most probable site-occupation date of Robert McGhee's find of copper fragments, a small pendant of high-antimony low-tin bronze, and some iron. Two of the finds are especially notable, that by Patricia Sutherland on the west coast of Ellesmere Island, some 2,000 kilometres distant from the Norse colonies in south-western Greenland, of a portion of a Norse bronze balance of a kind commonly used by Norse traders to weigh coins and small objects generally; the other, by Deborah and George Sabo, from near Lake Harbour on the south coast of Baffin Island, of a small wooden figurine, 5.4 centimetres tall, which appears to represent a man dressed in European clothes: a long robe slit up the front and with a cross incised on the breast. It would appear to be the work of a Thule Eskimo artist.

Remarks on the Arctic Finds
by Robert McGhee

[From an article, 'Contact between Native North Americans and the Mediaeval Norse: A Review of the Evidence', *American Antiquity*, 49. 1. (1984). A full bibliography accompanies the article.]

We know of no North American archaeological site where direct contact with the Norse can be demonstrated: all of the objects of European origin recovered from native occupation sites had probably reached these sites after travelling greater or lesser distances through aboriginal trading networks. Yet the number and distribution of such finds suggests that contacts must have occurred more frequently than recorded in the Norse historical accounts. For example, the few pieces of smelted metal from Dorset sites, and perhaps the Maine coin as well, strongly suggest unrecorded contacts with the Dorset Palaeo-Eskimos of Labrador during the thirteenth or fourteenth centuries. The wooden figurine apparently representing a person in European clothing, recovered from a thirteenth century Thule site in southern Baffin Island, suggests an unrecorded contact with the Thule Eskimos of the region; this specimen was almost certainly carved locally, since the Greenlandic Eskimos depicted Norsemen in a very conventionalized carving style of which the author of this carving appears to have been ignorant. The scatter of metal objects in Canadian Arctic Thule sites which appear to date to the thirteenth or even the twelfth century appear to indicate contact at a time earlier than the first mention of Eskimos in the Norse historical accounts.

It should be remembered, as pointed out by McGovern, that all of the European objects so far recovered from North American aboriginal archaeological sites could have originated from a single Eskimo attack on a small Norse hunting party in the *Nordrsetur*. On the other hand, the small sample of Dorset and Thule sites which have been excavated in Arctic Canada, and the relative frequency with which objects of probable Norse origin occur in excavated sites, suggests that a much larger number of such objects remains buried in High Arctic and Eastern Arctic sites. It has been argued that the current archaeological evidence, although very limited, is more compatible with a model of wide-ranging but sporadic contact between the Norse and natives of northern North America, than with a model of long-distance trading of Norse goods obtained by one or a few raids in Greenland.

Such contacts may have been encouraged by the Norse requirements for ivory, the primary trading commodity which Greenland exchanged with Europe in return for metal, grain and luxury goods, as well as the commodity with which they paid annual tribute to Norway, and tithes and crusade taxes to Rome. For example, in 1327 the Greenland See paid tithes in the amount of approximately 400 walrus tusks, representing a larger number of animals than the annual take from the entire west coast of Greenland (rarely more than 150 animals) during the early part of the present century. Since walrus do not occur in the vicinity of the Norse Greenlandic colonies today, and almost certainly did not during the relatively warm period in which the colonies existed, most of the ivory was obtained during summer hunts in the *Nordrsetur* over 400 km to the north of the colonies. McGovern has emphasized the strain which such hunts must have placed on the Greenlandic Norse economy. Dorset and Thule culture archaeological sites of the period indicate that these groups possessed quantities of ivory, and later historical accounts indicate that the descendants of the Thule people were eager to trade ivory and skins for small metal objects. Although chronically short of metal themselves, the Norse could probably have afforded to trade scraps and exhausted metal tools in return for ivory. Schledermann suggests that the amount and nature of Norse material recovered from northwestern Greenland and eastern Ellesmere Island hints at a Norse presence in the area, either as hunters or traders. The recent discovery that a Norse iron arrowhead recovered from a Western Settlement farm is made of meteoric iron, almost certainly from the Cape York meteorites in northwestern Greenland, either supports the view that the Norse reached this area or indicates that trade in metal was mutual between the Eskimo and Norse occupants of Greenland. The bronze balance arm from western Ellesmere Island, a characteristic trader's artifact and the only one known archaeologically from west of Iceland, again hints at possible contact between Eskimos and Norse traders. The figurine from Baffin Island suggests that the Norse came ashore in that area, and trade would seem a possible motive for such a landing.

In short, contacts between North American natives and the Norse probably occurred more frequently and over a greater area than recorded in historical accounts. Our present archaeological knowledge is too inadequate to indicate whether such contacts occurred for purposes of peaceful trade or mutual plunder. It seems likely that the two motives were generally combined, each side being willing to trade and equally willing to plunder if it could be accomplished with relative safety. It is unlikely that anything like a regular trading relationship was ever established between the two groups; if it had been, we would expect to find much greater amounts of European material in aboriginal sites of the period. Contacts were probably sporadic and opportunistic, and likely occurred most frequently during Norse voyages to Labrador in order to obtain timber. Such voyages probably occurred sporadically from the eleventh to fourteenth centuries, and could have led to encounters with Eskimos on the eastern Arctic islands, Dorset Palaeo-Eskimos in northern Labrador and Point Revenge Indians in central Labrador.

VI. OF SPIES AND UNIPEDS

1. *Haki and Hekja*

Much learning has been expended on the two Scottish slaves who in both versions of *Eiríks Saga Rauða* (pp. 223–4 and 234 above) were dispatched southwards through Markland by Thorfinn Karlsefni to spy out the land, and returned with a burden of grapes and wild wheat. They are oddly named, of doubtful attire and unacceptable origin, and their entrance into the narrative could hardly be more arbitrary. But their role, or office, becomes clearer if one re-reads (I owe the suggestion of old to my friend Björn Thorsteinsson) the Book of Numbers, 13: 1–3 and 17–27, whose substance is this:

And the Lord spake unto Moses, saying, Send thou men, that they may search the land of Canaan, which I give unto the children of Israel: of every tribe of their fathers shall ye send a man, every one a ruler among them . . . And Moses sent them to spy out the land of Canaan, and said unto them, Get you up this way southward, and go up into the mountain: And see the land, what it is; and the people that dwelleth therein, whether they be strong or weak, few or many; And what the land is that they dwell in, whether it be good or bad; and what cities they be that they dwell in, whether in tents, or in strong holds; And what the land is, whether it be fat or lean, whether there be wood therein, or not. And be ye of good courage, and bring of the fruit of the land. Now the time was the time of the firstripe grapes. So they went up and searched the land from the wilderness of Zin unto Rehob, as men come to Hamath. And they ascended by the south, and came unto Hebron . . . they came unto the brook of Eshcol, and cut down from thence a branch with one cluster of grapes, and they bare it between two upon a staff; and they brought of the pomegranates, and of the figs. The place was called the brook Eshcol because of the cluster of grapes[7] which the children of Israel cut down from thence. And they returned from searching of the land after forty days. And they went and came to Moses, and to Aaron, and to all the congregation of the children of Israel, unto the wilderness of Paran, to Kadesh; and brought back word unto them, and unto all the congregation, and shewed them the fruit of the land. And they told him, and said, We

---

[7] Esh'kol, Esh'kōl, cluster or bunch (of grapes). The Vulgate, Liber Numeri, cap. xiii, 24–5 and 27–8, has 'Pergentesque usque ad torrentem Botri, absciderunt palmitem cum uva sua, quem portaverunt in vecte duo viri. De malis quoque granatis et de ficis loci tulerunt; qui appellatus est Nehelescol, id est torrens Botri . . . venerunt ad Moysen et Aaron et ad omnem coetum filiorum Israel . . . ostenderunt fructus terrae; et narraverunt, dicentes: Venimus in terram, ad quam misisti nos, quae revera fluit lacte et melle, ut ex his fructibus cognosci potest.' It would be these words, or something very close to them, with which a northern *frǽðimaðr*, learned man, scholar, historian, historiographer, saga-man, scribe, or whatever, would be familiar during the time when the Vinland sagas were composed.

came unto the land whither thou sentest us, and surely it floweth with milk and honey; and this is the fruit of it.

(And see Judges 18: 2 and 8–10.)

2. *The einfœtingr*

There have been many explanations offered of the uniped, the one-legged creature who shot an arrow into Thorvald Eiriksson's entrails and killed him north of Kjalarnes in Markland (see pp. 229–30 above). A. H. Mallery in *Lost America* (1951), p. 95, thought he was an Eskimo dancing on one foot; and Munn, *Wineland Voyages*, p. 28, quotes Professor Howley of the Newfoundland Archaeological Survey: 'this uniped was undoubtedly an Eskimo woman of short stature, and dressed in the conventional Eskimo woman's attire with a long tail coat, she would undoubtedly look to the men who chased her as if she had only one leg.' Hermansson, *The Problem of Wineland*, pp. 53–4, thinks the *einfœtingr* was either one-legged or made to appear so by reason of his dress or outfit. Mowat, *Westviking* (1966), p. 277, sees him as a limping Beothuk Indian. But to the *frœðimenn*, the book-wise scholars and antiquaries of twelfth- and thirteenth-century Iceland, he was pretty certainly what *Eiríks Saga* called him: a one-legged, one-footed creature or monster. Learned in the seventh-century encyclopaedic and educative writings of Isidore of Seville, they would be well aware that the home of such creatures was in Africa. They knew too that the Vinland region was a northward extension of Africa, so what more natural than to find one of them there, or what more proper than to suppply one in his absence? The well-aired legendary lore of ancient scholars dies slowly, or not at all; and when the explorer Jacques Cartier came to Canada in the 1530s he was soon informed of a region where each and every one of whose inhabitants had only one leg (A. M. Reeves, *The Finding of Wineland the Good*, p. 177. I owe the reference to Matthías Thórðarson, *Ísl. Forn.* vol. iv, p. 231 n. 4).

VII THE L'ANSE AUX MEADOWS SITE

by Birgitta Linderoth Wallace

[Birgitta Wallace has a twenty-year acquaintance with the L'Anse aux Meadows site, and is presently Director of the

Parks Canada Project there. She is a leading authority on Norse finds (and 'finds') in North America. Appendix VII was written for publication in *The Norse Atlantic Saga*, and in view of the unique interest of the L'Anse aux Meadows site as the first Norse, Viking, and therefore European, settlement in the New World, it has seemed appropriate to print the author's supporting bibliography in full.]

The L'Anse aux Meadows site was discovered in 1960 by Helge Ingstad and excavated under the direction of Anne Stine Ingstad from 1961 to 1968. The Ingstads investigated eight Norse buildings and a charcoal pit kiln as well as a number of native features. Their results were first published in a preliminary report in 1970 (A. S. Ingstad 1970); the final report came in 1977 (A. S. Ingstad 1977). A second volume of the latter, dealing with the historical evidence and written by Helge Ingstad, is yet to come.

In 1968 the National Historic Sites and Monuments Board of Canada recommended that the site be recognized as historically significant, and the site came to be administered by Parks Canada. An International Advisory Committee was established to plan further archaeological research and protection of the site. Members included Helge and Anne Stine Ingstad and scholars from the Scandinavian countries and Canada.

In 1977 the site became a National Historic Park; an area of 8,000 hectares of land and sea around it was included in the park to protect its setting. In 1975 a temporary display centre opened in the park; a permanent visitor reception centre followed in the summer of 1985. The centre will have most of the significant artefacts on display. Full-scale replicas of three of the Norse buildings have also been built. Over the past decade the site has attracted world-wide attention, and in 1978 it became the first site to be placed on the United Nations World Heritage List.

The International Advisory Committee for L'Anse aux Meadows recommended further excavations on the site, and a Parks Canada team excavated here from 1973 to 1976. Anne Stine Ingstad declined directorship of these investigations; the work was instead led first by Bengt Schonback, then by the author of this appendix. Among the goals of the continued excavations was an attempt to establish the presence or absence of a cemetery or other features that would bear upon the question of site function and length of occupation. More information was also sought on iron-working and the relationship of the Norse to the native cultures on the site. The major areas excavated by Parks Canada were the bog immediately adjacent to the Norse buildings and a large area about 300 m to the south-west. In the process many new analyses were undertaken to complement those already made by the Ingstad expedition: additional pollen analysis, extensive wood identifications, seed analysis, further faunal analysis, petrological analyses, a study of tool marks on wood and geological investigations are but a few of the studies performed. In addition, many more radio-carbon dates were obtained. Inventories of the modern flora and fauna were also established. This appendix draws on information from these studies as well as the work already done by the Ingstads.

Located on the northernmost tip of Newfoundland's Great Northern Peninsula, the site of L'Anse aux Meadows commands a magnificent view of the northern entrance to the Strait of Belle Isle. To the east Labrador looms in the distance; to the far north Belle Isle forms a misty blue outline. Closer by, Beak Point extends a low, flat arm towards two small, equally flat islands, and behind them the craggy profile of Great Sacred Island forms a distinctive landmark for anyone approaching from the sea.

We know now that the L'Anse aux Meadows site was a short-lived base camp for explorations leading the Norse at least as far south as the southern shores of the Gulf of St Lawrence. Its location was probably considered to be the entrance to Vinland. A major activity on the site was ship repair, and the site probably served as a winter station where the returning crew could rest and spend the winter before continuing to Greenland or extending the explorations in the summer.

About 1 km north of the site the small village of L'Anse aux Meadows has been home to English-speaking fishermen since about 1850. Between the sixteenth century and 1904 French fishermen landed intermittently; the remains of their shore station on Beak Point are now all but gone. Before them, Indians and Eskimos had used the site for more than 5,000 years.

So when the Norse arrived on a summer day sometime around AD 1000, they were neither the first, nor the last, to make L'Anse aux Meadows their home. The native groups included both Eskimos and Indians, ranging from Maritime Archaic Indians and the Groswater culture (the latter may or may not be Eskimo) in the millennia preceding Christ, to middle Dorsets in the fifth to eighth centuries AD, followed by at least two, possibly three, Indian groups, one of which is more or less contemporary with the Norse. We thus now know that if the Norse ever faced Skrælings at L'Anse aux Meadows, these Skrælings would have been Indian, not Eskimo.

Modern L'Anse aux Meadows is situated on deep Medée Bay on the northern side of Beak Point, but the archaeological remains of the Norse and most of the native inhabitants lie on the shores of the shallow Épaves Bay on the southern side of the point. While the majority of the native occupants preferred the very shore, the Norse, as in Greenland and Iceland, stayed away from the storm-ridden waterline and settled about 200 m inland. Their buildings are strung out in a line on a narrow, raised, beach terrace, bordered on the sea side by a basin-shaped sedge peat bog through which a small brook winds its way to the sea, and on the east by a raised sphagnum bog. To the north is a grassy plain; to the south tight stands of tuckamore seek shelter against a rocky ridge rising 30 m above the site. The buildings hug the western edge of the terrace. Only one, a small forge, stands alone away from the others, on the opposite side of the brook, closer to the shore.

All buildings were made of sod over a wooden frame, the sod covering the roofs as well as the walls. Both sod strips, blocks, and diagonally cut half-blocks were used in the construction. Most of the walls were built in a skin technique with a core consisting of sand and gravel, stabilized with cross-strips of sods and held in place with a facing of sod strips and blocks. This building method is the traditional Icelandic–Greenland form of construction, the core also serving as drainage for the steeply peaked sod roofs which intersected with the walls, not at the outer edges as in most buildings, but at their very centres.

For the sake of convenience, the buildings were given letter designations by the Ingstads, in order of excavation, and these designations will be used here. Buildings A, D, and F are dwellings, buildings E and G workshops, building J a forge, and building B a combined dwelling and workshop. Building C may have been used for storage. The buildings are grouped into three complexes, each consisting of a large dwelling and a workshop. The complex closest to the brook, the A–B–C complex, has one additional structure, building C. As stated previously, the small forge lies by itself, away from the other buildings.

The A–B–C Complex

The southernmost complex consists of the large dwelling A, a small combined dwelling and workshop B, and an unidentified building C. House A had slightly out-bowed side walls and perfectly straight end walls. Its western side wall was irregular, narrowing towards the northern end to follow the contours of the terrace. The main entrance was in the centre of the side wall, facing the terrace. With a total interior length of 26.6 m, the building was substantial. It contained four rooms, all in a row, with a total floor area of about 100 m². Three of the rooms, numbered I, II, and IV, were sleeping/living rooms as indicated by the presence of the elongate central fireplaces flanked by wooden sleeping/seating platforms along the walls. The fourth room was used as a workshop. This room contained more than 70 per cent of all the finds, and of these, almost half were slag. Clearly smithing took place here. This is wholly in line with West Norse practices where forges were frequently incorporated into dwellings (cf. Myhre *et al.* 1982: 328–31, 353; Laing 1975: 193). Forging pits were often located by the door (Olsen and Schmidt 1977: 138), and one finds such a pit directly to the left of the door as one enters the room.

House B was a small, one-roomed structure of rectangular shape. As in many small Norse buildings, the main hearth was not in the centre but by an end wall, in this case the southern one. The hearth was a shallow pit in the floor behind which the wall was protected by a large stone slab. In line with the hearth, but 40 cm north of it, was a stone-lined firepit, presumably used for cooking, although a large piece of smithy hearth slag was found in it. Towards the other end of the house was a bog-ore roasting pit, with a small ember pit by its edge, and, close by, what might have been a large barrel, as indicated by markings in the soil.

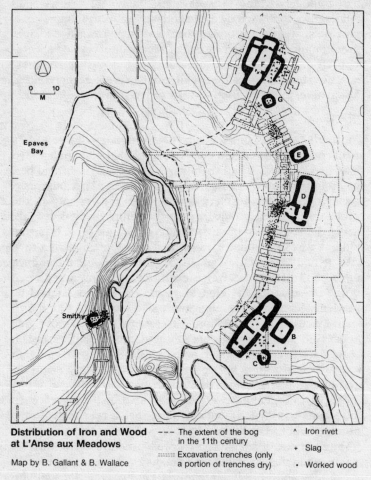

Distribution of Iron and Wood at L'Anse aux Meadows

Map by B. Gallant & B. Wallace

– – – The extent of the bog in the 11th century

::::: Excavation trenches (only a portion of trenches dry)

^ Iron rivet

+ Slag

· Worked wood

30. THE L'ANSE AUX MEADOWS SITE, NORTHERN NEWFOUNDLAND

Building C was of rounded shape, rather like a pear, opening towards house A. It contained no features except a charcoal concentration in its inner part. Its use is unclear. It may have been for storage as no storage room has been otherwise identified in the complex.

The D–E Complex

The D–E complex is the smallest one. Its dwelling, house D, measured only 15.5 m in interior length and consisted of three rooms, rooms I and III in a row, with room II added to its seaward side. This building, too, had bowed side walls and straight end walls. One entrance was in the eastern side wall, close to the southern corner and facing the terrace; a second entrance from the bog side led into the room added to the side of the building. The largest room, III, was a sleeping/living room. Room I was used for storage. The room projecting towards the sea, room II, was a workshop situated at the very edge of the sedge peat bog. Here the evidence for activity lies primarily in a midden outside rather than inside the room. (This distinction is the result of differential preservation, because artefacts are of wood which survived in the wet bog but perished inside the drier house.) Many hundreds of pieces of worked wood were found here. Most of the wood was debitage from wood-working, chiefly the debris from the trimming and cutting of planks and logs. Only a few were finished artefacts. Among them is a piece tentatively identified as the floor-board for a small boat (A. E. Christensen, personal communication to C. Lindsay). The board has two holes for treenails, with one treenail still in place, held secure with a small wedge driven into its head. The board itself is spruce, the treenail Scots or Red pine. Neither of these latter species grows in northern Newfoundland, and Scots pine was only later introduced into the New World from Europe. Unfortunately, the cell structures of the two pine species are so similar that it is virtually impossible to distinguish them one from the other. If, however, the treenail is Scots pine, it must be of European origin. Other objects include a decorative finial, also of Scots or Red pine, a pedal-shaped piece of unknown use, and a boat rib. Common to all the pieces is that they had been damaged and discarded, presumably to be replaced by new ones made in or around house D. Scattered treenails in this area and long spruce roots wound up into a coil awaiting use also indicate that new pieces were manufactured here. In character the wood objects and debitage remind one of the recently discovered ship-repair place at Maglebrænde on northern Falster in Denmark where wood-working debris and broken and discarded artefacts were a major feature (Skamby Madsen 1984).

Building E was a pit building, dug into the terrace. The walls rose only slightly above the ground and consisted of gravel and sand removed from the pit, lined with sod, and held in place by interior posts. In one corner was a fireplace, consisting of a cist-like oven. No artefacts were found inside the building, but in the bog outside it were what appear to be wooden netting sticks, pieces of twined spruce-root ropes, a sewn container of birch-bark, and several birch-bark rolls. Such birch-bark rolls occur commonly on Viking-Period and later sites as wrappings for stones used as net sinkers. A group of small stones found in the north-west corner of the building may in fact be the sinkers for these rolls. It seems likely that the activities in this building included the repair of fishing gear.

The F–G Complex

The F–G complex consisted of the large dwelling F and the small workshop G. With three rooms in a row, two rooms added on the western side, and a workshop on the eastern side, house F is the largest building on the site. Once again the side walls are bowed, the end walls straight. Entrances are in the eastern side wall, close to the corners. The central rooms I, II, and III were all for sleeping and sitting. The largest of the western side rooms, V, contained a cooking-pit but no other features, and must have been used primarily for storage. The smaller room joining it, room IV, was a kitchen of the kind used in the West Norse sphere for the preparation of large quantities of meat at butchering times, preserves of all kinds, brewing, and laundering. Its dominant feature was a stone oven, consisting of a cist topped by a heavy packing of small stones.

House F had one room, room VI, added to its eastern side which was not a room in the same sense as the others but a lean-to structure, the natural ground serving as the floor. The addition was open-ended on the side facing the bog. Of all the finds in the building, 60 per cent were found inside this shed or directly outside it. Of these artefacts, 59 per cent were rivet fragments, 41 per cent slag. Many of the rivets had been deliberately cut. The shanks had been clipped, and the rivet roves cut diagonally with a chisel blow so that they could be pried loose and removed. Of a total of over 52 smithy rivet fragments found on the site, no fewer than 47 came from the F–G complex, of which 29 were from the room VI area. A similar situation was encountered in the ship-repair area of the seasonal commercial centre of Paviken, Gotland, Sweden (Lundröm 1981: 75–9). The numbers do not seem impressive until compared with the finds on West Norse sites in general. Hardly any iron nails were employed in West Norse buildings, where doors, furnishings, planking, and rafters were joined by treenails or mortised together (cf. Roussell 1936: 24,78; Rolfsen 1974: 92). During the excavation of as many as 63 house sites in Rogaland, Norway, only 15 nails or parts thereof were recovered (Rolfsen 1974: 92), and iron nails or rivets are relatively rare in Icelandic and Greenland finds. Wherever nails and rivets do occur in concentrations such as those at L'Anse aux Meadows, they are associated with the repair or construction of ships and boats (ibid.), or boat planks used as firewood (Hamilton 1956: 116). Room VI in house F contained less charcoal than any of the other rooms of the building, so the presence of rivets here cannot stem from the use of boat planks for fuel, and the clipped condition of the rivets is a sure indication that the room was used as a boat-repair shed. The many iron rivets that held the strakes together in Norse ships rusted quickly in the salt water, and had to be replaced frequently, so it is understandable that such work was needed at a site where ships formed the only link with the homeland.

Building G, slightly smaller than building E, had a fireplace by one wall, like the one in house B. The finds here were chiefly iron rivets, slag, and roasted bog ore. It may therefore have served some aspect of the boat-repair function in room VI on house F to which it abuts.

Pit buildings like buildings E and G, with their characteristic fireplaces, are extremely common in Iron Age Scandinavia, particularly in the Viking Age. They were primarily workshops, frequently for women, where they worked at upright looms and sat with their spinning, sewing, and needlework. Being small, such a room was easy to keep warm, and because little cooking took place here, they were perhaps relatively smoke-free, so for still-sitting work they may have been more comfortable than the large houses.

The Forge

Among the most intriguing finds at L'Anse aux Meadows was iron slag. The area is rich in limonites or bog iron, and early analyses performed for the Ingstad expedition (A. S. Ingstad 1977: 373, 424) seemed to indicate that the slag was the by-product of the reduction of these into iron. Over the years of work on the site, about 10 kg of slag were collected (another couple of kilos may have remained uncollected). More than 90 per cent of this slag came from the small building at some distance from the other buildings and separated from them by the brook. When iron slag is encountered on Scandinavian sites in concentrations like this, the furnace that produced it is without exception found directly below or beside it. This is also the case at L'Anse aux Meadows, and the building is actually a furnace building.

The furnace building is a pit structure like E and G. Unlike them, it is open-ended, the open side facing the bog in a close parallel to furnace buildings in Norway (cf. Martens 1972: 98). The open construction would have helped to alleviate the discomfort of the heat from the furnace for people working around it. The furnace itself consisted of little more than a shallow, clay-lined pit, topped by a frame of stone slabs joined with clay. The furnace was situated approximately in the centre of the building. After the firing, it was destroyed and the iron removed; while parts of the broken frame were tossed down the slope towards the brook, together with a great deal of slag. The pit itself was later reused as a forge pit.

A short distance to the south-east of the furnace building the Ingstad expedition found a charcoal pit kiln of the type found by the hundred in Norway (cf. Martens 1972: 98; Johansen 1973: 88), and which has survived in Iceland into modern times (Friðgeirsson 1968). The charcoal produced here was used to fire the furnace.

A comprehensive metallurgical analysis made by Parks Canada's Conservation Division in Ottawa of all the iron metal from L'Anse aux Meadows has produced the following results:

Of all the slag found, about 33 per cent was smelting slag, 14 per cent smithy slag, 22 per cent cinder or slagged furnace lining, 17 per cent refractory, the rest indeterminable (Unglik and Stewart 1979).

The temperature in the furnace had been between 1,150 and 1,200 °C, the process direct reduction.

The iron smelted was local bog iron.

The ratio of iron obtained was low in relation to the slag, about 1 kg of iron for every 5 kg of slag.

The fuel used was wood charcoal.

The Artefacts

The artefacts found in association with the Norse buildings are singularly unvaried. As touched on previously, the majority are work debris and fall within three categories: iron slag, carpentry debitage, and iron rivets. Domestic and personal items are few and consist mostly of small objects which would have been easily lost by their owners. This indicates that the site was abandoned in an orderly fashion and the belongings removed with the owners.

Among the small personal objects is a ring-headed bronze pin for the fastening of a garment such as a cloak. The type was a Scottish-Celtic invention but had become popular in much of Scandinavia by the Viking Age; this particular type seems to occur in the West Norse area, most belonging to the tenth century (Fanning 1979). The pin could have been used by either a man or a woman. A small glass bead found outside house D by the Parks Canada team could likewise have been worn by either a male or female. A spindle whorl of soapstone and a small needle-hone of quartzite, both found close together in the work-shed of house F, are, however, part of a woman's tool-kit. The spindle whorl is of a flattened, semi-spherical shape, a form particularly common in the Viking Age (Petersen 1951: 304). The needle-hone with its elongate-form, four-sided cross-section, tapering ends, and no suspension hole, is likewise a characteristic Viking Age form (Roesdahl 1977: 60). A bone needle with a flat trianguloid head with a drilled hole through the centre, found in the fireplace of the sleeping/living room in house D, is likewise a woman's tool, such as would probably be used in a single-needle knitting technique to produce such basic items as mittens and socks.

The majority of the artefacts are, however, from distinctly male activities. Iron smelting and forging, carpentry, ship repair, all these were male pursuits. Fishing and hunting were also carried out by men. The evidence for fishing has been described in conjunction with building E. There was also evidence of hunting in the preform of a small arrow of wood, of the same shape as antler arrowheads found in the late tenth-early eleventh century farm of Narssaq in Greenland (Vebæk 1964). The fact that it is of wood could indicate that it is simply a toy. This latter possibility is tempting because a small bow also found at L'Anse aux Meadows could have been a toy, if not a fiddle bow. Sixteen wooden skewers the size of large pencils could have been used for many purposes. Such skewers are common on Scandinavian sites from the late Viking Period and the ensuing Middle Ages.

Date of the Site

The shape of the large dwellings suggests that they were built in the last years of the tenth or in the first half of the eleventh century, probably in the first quarter or so, before the standardized Icelandic building style known as the Thjórsardalur type became fully evolved. The presence of pit buildings may be yet another date-indicator. In Iceland and mainland Scandinavia pit buildings become increasingly uncommon as the eleventh century wears on (cf. Roesdahl 1980: 66). Although few of the artefacts found at L'Anse aux Meadows can be closely dated, all fit well into an early eleventh-century context.

No fewer than 133 radio-carbon dates have been obtained for the L'Anse aux Meadows site. Of these, 55 pertain to the Norse occupation. The latter radio-carbon dates vary between about AD 700 and 1000 (tree-ring recalibrated values). This does not mean that the settlement dates from 700 to 1000. All too often a radio-carbon date of the *sample* is confused with the date of the archaeological event. Much of the time, the two are not the same. All depends on what material is being dated. If it is peat, for instance, the peat material contains many compressed vegetation zones, which have died and ceased to absorb radiocarbon successively. The actual date of a peat level may in fact be as much as three hundred years younger than the material dated, depending upon the size of the sample and the number and type of inclusions. A date on wood or wood-charcoal may likewise be misleading since the heartwood of the tree ceases to absorb carbon 14 long before its sapwood. Spruce can produce sapwood for up to 600 years (Jacoby and Ulan 1981: App. 1–11). This means that if the piece dated is heartwood, it can be as much as 500–600 years older than the event that finally killed the tree; hence the radio-carbon date is correspondingly centuries older than the event it was supposed to date. Hardwoods such as birch and poplar, on the other hand, rarely become older than 300 and 100 years respectively, and hence a radio-carbon date on a piece of poplar, for example, is more likely to be contemporary with its felling.

The most useful dates are those on short-lived material such as berry bushes and young twigs. At L'Anse aux Meadows we find that those radio-carbon dates which lie in the eighth- to ninth-century range include a good quantity of softwoods such as spruce, larch, and pine, especially spruce, while those of a tenth- to eleventh-century determination are on birch and poplar. Four other dates, on the other hand, on heather and young twigs, yielded an average date of AD 980±90 (S—1111, 1113, 1340, and 1355).

Length of Occupation

How long was the site occupied? Not long. One way to gauge length of occupation in archaeological contexts is to assess the amount of accumulated garbage. On the Greenland Norse sites, garbage middens are huge, often up to 150 m long and 1 to 2 m deep in their deepest parts, as exemplified by the middens excavated by Thomas McGovern at Niaqûssat (W48) in the West Settlement (McGovern, personal communication). Niaqûssat was a small and relatively poor farm not too far from Sandnes; it lasted approximately 300 to 350 years. Had the occupation at L'Anse aux Meadows been equally long-lived, we should expect middens of similar proportions, while a century of use should have produced middens of at least a third the size.

At L'Anse aux Meadows, however, there are hardly any middens of a size worth mentioning. The largest midden is the wood debitage in the bog, but it is no larger than could have been produced in a few days. Food remains and kitchen debris such as bone and ashes from the fireplaces would, or course, have been dissolved by the tannic acid in the bog, so it is only natural that none were found. A chemical analysis of the peat, undertaken to determine whether they were ever present, indicated that they were not. The largest pile of kitchen debris is outside room III of house F, where there were both ashes and burnt bone, but this midden is only about 2 × 3 m in size and 25 cm deep. While it is impossible to determine exactly how many years of occupation it represents, it is safe to say that it is a question of a few years or, at the most, a couple of decades rather than centuries.

Nor do sod buildings such as those built by the Norse last very long in an area such as northern Newfoundland. In southern Iceland sod buildings have to be rebuilt completely after about twenty years (Nilsson 1943: 293). At L'Anse aux Meadows even modern painted wooden houses do not last much longer, and the Parks Canada full-scale replicas of Norse sod buildings are requiring repair already after two years of use. Had the Norse settlement lasted more than a quarter of a century, there should at least be traces of more than one generation of buildings. As none have been found, the settlement must have endured less than twenty-five years.

Size and Nature of Occupation

Various formulae have been applied to archaeological sites to determine size of population, using measurements such as floor space or overall site area (Naroll 1962; Wiessner 1974), none satisfactorily. In the case of L'Anse aux Meadows, the most accurate measurement would be available sleeping space, since we have a good idea of the appearance of West Norse sleeping arrangements. Applying this criterion we can estimate that there was room for thirty people at most in each of buildings A and F, twenty in house D, with an additional four or six in house B.. The total maximum number of inhabitants would therefore have been around eighty-five.

Was the settlement permanent or seasonal? A permanent settlement would have necessitated burials. At this time the Norse were Roman Catholics so burials in consecrated communal cemeteries were a must. A wide area around the L'Anse aux Meadows site has been surveyed for their presence, but no evidence for them has been found. This is also an indication that the site cannot have been occupied for long, much less on a permanent basis. More than likely, the body of any deceased person would have been returned to Greenland or Iceland for a permanent resting-place, the same way bodies were collected from outlying farms in Greenland and brought to centrally located cemeteries.

In a seasonal settlement we would expect the buildings to be booths or shielings, but the L'Anse aux Meadows structures are more substantial than any of these, and so solidly built that they were clearly meant to withstand winter conditions. They are in fact exactly like those of a normal Norse homestead, but with the most important ingredient missing. There are no byres at L'Anse aux Meadows, only dwellings and workshops. Nor is the grouping of the buildings, with three dwellings close together, that of a farm but rather that of a commercial centre.

The question remains whether or not the three complexes were occupied simultaneously. Their even spacing on the terrace indicates that all three were physically present at the same time and that property lines were respected. While the three large dwellings vary in layout, they are all from the same period, a period that was marked by some flexibility in the placement of additions to the sides of the main buildings. Presumably the dissimilarities stem from a difference in function, so that the rooms were placed where they were needed. Another indication of the contemporaneity of the complexes is the high degree of specialization among them, with activities which complemented each other, each producing components useful for boat repair. This, in turn, may suggest that the co-ordination, initiative, and investment lay in the hands of one single leader, most likely one of the key figures in the early Greenland settlement. What we are dealing with at L'Anse aux Meadows is thus a sort of port of trade, geared to the repair of boats and ships. The large buildings provided facilities for housing, feeding, and protecting the Vinland explorers and space for the storage and trans-shipping of their goods.

Is L'Anse aux Meadows Vinland?

In order to assess the evidence for an answer to this question we must backtrack to Helluland. Helluland is a singularly apt description of the Canadian Arctic above the 58th parallel, but cannot easily be applied to any area south of it; therefore Helluland cannot have extended south of this line.

It is not clear if Markland began where Helluland ended, or if the two were actually thought of as separated by an open sea. At any event, Markland must have lain within the confines of what is now Labrador. It can hardly have encompassed the whole area, which, with its 110,000 square miles, is enormous in Norse terms—the entire East Settlement covered less than 5,000 square miles.

It would have been logical if Newfoundland as a third land mass was Vinland. Coasting along the shores of Labrador from the north, the sailor for the first time finds himself with land on *two* sides as he enters the Strait of Belle Isle. The strait is narrow here, and the two coasts can be clearly distinguished. L'Anse aux Meadows lies on one of the northernmost points of this new land mass suddenly appearing on the port side. The landmarks of Cape Bauld, Great Sacred Island, and Beak Point make it easy to find. On a bright, sunny, summer day it is an inviting site, reminiscent of many areas of Iceland, and with a splendid view of the strait.

But even without a slavish acceptance of every word of the sagas, there are certain broad suggestions which make it impossible to equate northern Newfoundland with Vinland. All scattered references to Vinland make it plain that, compared with Markland, Vinland was more bountiful, the weather was warmer, the tides were higher, the resources more exotic, and, above all, more varied. As one source put it: the further south one travelled, the better the land became.

The Norse did continue south, beyond L'Anse aux Meadows. In the Norse wood-debris concentrations were two butter-nuts, *Juglans cinerea*, a form of walnut. The northernmost limit of butter-nuts is the mouth of the St Lawrence and north-east New Brunswick: the nuts have never grown in Newfoundland. They are too large to have arrived on the site with birds, and they are too heavy to float, so they cannot have come with the currents (which are primarily north–south in this area anyway). Thus they must have arrived on the site with humans, and their presence in the Norse activity areas indicates that those humans were Norse. The Norse at L'Anse aux Meadows must therefore have visited areas at least as far south as the southern portion of the Gulf of St Lawrence. Interestingly enough the northern limit of butter-nuts coincides in part with that of wild grapes. It is therefore entirely within the realm of the possible that the Norse in this area may have had first-hand experience of the land of wild grapes.

Why then L'Anse aux Meadows? Why were Norse remains found here and not in New Brunswick, Quebec, or Nova Scotia? Perhaps one day some evidence of the Norse will be found in these places as well. Looking at a map, one can easily see that L'Anse aux Meadows would have filled the important function of a base for exploration and exploitation of resources farther south. The sailing season is short in northerly waters, and ships cannot have entered Davis Strait much before the beginning of July, even if ice conditions were less severe in the eleventh century than now. By the same token, the return could not be contemplated after early October.

The distance from Greenland's west coast around Godthaab to the southern Gulf of St Lawrence by way of Helluland and Markland—the only route Norse navigators could choose, given the fact that longitude could not be determined—is about 1,400 nautical miles, an impressive distance which would have required up to two weeks of sailing (faster on the way there because of the currents, but correspondingly slower on the return). The loss of a month of the navigable season meant that the Vinland-farers would have only two months at their disposal for exploration and collecting. By establishing a base camp at L'Anse aux Meadows they could extend that season significantly. By leaving a contingent behind to lay up supplies of food and firewood needed for the winter, they could extend it further and stay south until well into November, returning to L'Anse aux Meadows in good time for Christmas.

Such a use is consistent with the fact that much of the room in the buildings is devoted to sleeping/living spaces, yet these appear to have been used only sparingly, judging from the scarcity of artefacts. The location of L'Anse aux Meadows is well chosen for such a base camp. From here, at the entrance to the Strait of Belle Isle, one can circumnavigate practically the entire Gulf of St Lawrence without ever losing sight of land. From here it is also easy to follow the coastline eastward to the rest of Newfoundland. Whatever the case, it seems that L'Anse aux Meadows must have marked the entrance to Vinland, the land of all good things, becoming better and better as they left Markland behind.

But the settlement did not last, perhaps not even beyond one winter. The reason is clear. The distance there was fully as long as that to Europe, and everything that could be obtained in Vinland could also be had in Europe. Europe had so much more to offer: luxury articles, ready-made tools, grain, salt, spices, family and friends, and ecclesiastical ties. L'Anse aux Meadows was soon abandoned as an impractical venture and Vinland became a distant dream, shrouded in legend.

Bibliography

DALTON, G., 1978. 'Comments on Ports of Trade in Early Medieval Europe', *Norwegian Archaeological Review*, vol. II, no. 2, pp. 102–8.

FANNING, T., 1979. 'Some Aspects of the Bronze Ringed Pin in Scotland', in D. Clarke and A. Grieve (eds.), *From the Stone Age to the Forty-Five*. Edinburgh.

FRIÐGEIRSSON, Sr., EINAR, 1968. 'Að gjöra til kola', *Árbók hins íslenzka fornleifafélags*, pp. 108–10. Reykjavík: Thjóðminjasafn Íslands.

HAMILTON, J. R. C., 1956. *Excavations at Jarlshof, Scotland*. HMSO, Edinburgh.

INGSTAD, ANNE STINE, 1970. 'The Norse Settlement at L'Anse aux Meadows, Newfoundland. A Preliminary Report from the Excavations 1961–1968', *Acta Archaeologica*, vol. 49, pp. 110–54; 36 figs., bibl. Copenhagen: E. Munksgaard.

—— 1977. *The Discovery of a Norse Settlement in America: Excavations at L'Anse aux Meadows, Newfoundland, 1961–1968*, vol. 1; 430 pp., figs., tables, plates. Oslo: Universitetsforlaget.

JACOBY, GORDON C., and ULAN, LINDA D., 1981. 'A Review of Dendroclimatology in the Forest-Tundra Ecotone of Alaska and Canada', unpublished typescript; 39 pp., 6 figs., refs. New York: Columbia University.

JOHANSEN, ARNE, 1973. 'Iron Production as a Factor in the Settlement History of Mountain Valleys Surrounding Hardangervidda', *Norwegian Archaeological Review*, vol. 6, no. 2, pp. 84–101; 8 figs., bibl.

LAING, LLOYD, 1975. *The Archaeology of Late Celtic Britain and Ireland* c.*400–1200 AD*, 451 pp., illus. London: Methuen & Co. Ltd.

LUNDSTRÖM, PER, 1981. *De kommo vida . . . Vikingars hamn vid Paviken, Gotland*, 114 pp., 22 figs., 12 colour plates. Stockholm: Statens sjöhistoriska museum.

MARTENS, IRMELIN, 1972. 'Møsstrond i Telemark — En Jernproduserende Fjellbygd før Svartedauden', *Viking*, vol. 36, pp. 83–114.

MYHRE, BJØRN, STOKLUND, BJARNE, and GJÆRDER, PER (eds.), 1982. 'Vestnordisk byggeskik gjennem to tusen år. Tradisjon og forandring fra romertid til det 19. århundrede', Arkeologisk museum i Stavanger,. *Skrifter*, 7; 287 pp., illus. Stavanger: Arkeologisk museum.

NAROLL, RAOUL, 1962. 'Floor Area and Settlement Population', *American Antiquity*, vol. 36, pp. 210–11.

NILSSON, ALBERT, 1943. 'Den sentida bebyggelsen på Islands landsbygd', in M. Stenberger (ed.), *Forntida gårdar i Island*, pp. 271–306, figs. 160–80. Copenhagen: E. Munksgaard.

OLSEN, OLAF, and SCHMIDT, HOLGER, 1977. 'Fyrkat. En jysk vikingeborg, Vol. I: Borgen og Bebyggelsen', *Nordiske Fortidsminder*, Serie B—in quarto, vol. 3, publ. by Det Kgl. nord. Oldskriftselskab; 241 pp., 135 figs., 1 fold-out map. With 'The Fyrkat Grain, A Geographical and Chronological Study of Rye', by Hans Helbæk; 41 pp., 15 figs. Copenhagen.

PETERSEN, JAN, 1951. 'Vikingetidens Redskaper, *Det norske Videnskaps-Akademi i Oslo*, II, Hist.-filos. klasse no. 4. Oslo.

ROESDAHL, ELSE, 1977. Fyrkat. En jysk vikingeborg, Vol. II: Oldsagerne og gravpladsen', *Nordiske Fortidsminder*, Series B—in quarto, vol. 4, publ. by Det Kgl. nord. Oldskriftselskab; 233 pp., illus. Copenhagen.

—— 1980. *Danmarks Vikingetid*, 324 pp., 104 figs. Copenhagen: Gyldendal.

ROLFSEN, PERRY, 1974. 'Båtnaust på Jaerkysten', *Stavanger museums skrifter*, 8. Stavanger: Arkeologisk museum.

ROUSSELL, AAGE, 1936. *Sandnes and the Neighbouring Farms*. MGr., Copenhagen, vol. 88(3).

Skamby Madsen, Jan, 1984. 'Snekkeværft', *Skalk*, No. 2, pp. 3–9; illus.

Unglik, Henry, and Stewart, John, 1979. 'Metallurgical Investigation of Archaeological Material of Norse Origin from L'Anse aux Meadows, Newfoundland', 481 pp., illus. Ottawa: Parks Canada typescript report.

Vebaek, C. L., 1964. 'En Landnamsgaard i Nordbobygderne i Grønland'. *Naturens Verden*, 200–24, Copenhagen.

Wiessner, Polly, 1974. 'A Functional Estimator of Population from Floor Area', *American Antiquity*, vol. 39, no. 2, I; pp. 343–50.

VIII. TEXTS AND EDITIONS

[The matter of this appendix relates to the translations prepared for *The Norse Atlantic Saga*, pp. 101–203 (1964), and reproduced with a number of improvements on pp. 143–248 in the present volume. The Supplementary Note deals with the more significant editions and discussions which have appeared during 1964–85.]

1. *Íslendingabók*

Íslendingabók, or *Libellus Islandorum*, 'The Book of the Icelanders', was written by Ari Thorgilsson the Learned (1067/8–1148), probably between 1122 and 1125, and certainly before 1133. It appears to be the revision of an earlier work of his, written for the bishops then holding office in Iceland, and is a concise, indeed severely condensed, history of Iceland from the Settlement to his own day, critical, accurate, based on reliable sources of information, and much concerned with chronology. Its faults are a certain arbitrariness of subject-matter and lack of proportion between its parts, but these were inherent in Ari's design and purpose. It richly deserves the praises heaped upon it from the earliest times to our own day as an indispensable sourcebook of Icelandic (and in one of its chapters Greenlandic) history and the oldest sustained narrative prose in any Scandinavian language. It is preserved in two transcripts of the seventeenth century, and despite the lateness of this date preserved with care and accuracy. The best edition is by Halldór Hermansson, *The Book of the Icelanders* (*Íslendingabók*), *Edited and Translated with an Introductory Essay and Notes*, Islandica, xx (New York, 1930).

2. *Landnámabók*

Landnámabók, 'The Book of the Landtakings *or* Settlements', as its name implies, is a schematized record of the colonization of Iceland. It preserves a wealth of information regarding some 400 of the principal settlers, usually telling where they came from, where they took land, what happened to them, and through what descendants and what vicissitudes their families persisted. The settlements are dealt with in an orderly progress clockwise round the island. Its matter is for the most part as entertaining as it is useful, for along with genealogical and historical fact it offers us anecdote, folk-tale, contemporary belief, and superstition. It is possible, but not proven, that Ari Thorgilsson, the author of *Íslendingabók*, was also the author of an original, no longer extant, *Landnámabók*. If he was, he was helped in his undertaking by Kolskegg the Learned (who died before 1130), who wrote about the settlements in east and south-east Iceland, and no doubt by many informants whom he met either on his travels or at public assemblies. Even if he was not its author, it is generally agreed that his writings or *schedulæ* (for he wrote more than *Íslendingabók*) were important for its compilation. The five versions of *Landnámabók* now extant date from the thirteenth to the seventeenth century, and derive from the lost version prepared by Styrmir the Learned (*c.* 1170–1245), the so-called *Styrmisbók* of *c.* 1225. The relationship of *Styrmisbók* to the assumed *Landnámabók* of Ari cannot be determined. The two complete but far from identical versions of *Landnámabók* preserved from medieval times are those of Sturla Thórðarson (*Sturlubók*), most likely written between 1260 and 1280, and Hauk Erlendsson (*Hauksbók*), written some time before Hauk's death in 1334. The third medieval version, *Melabók*, survives in a few fragments only, though rather more of it can be recovered from the seventeenth-century *Þórðarbók*, which was compiled by Síra Thórður Jónsson of Hitardal (d. 1670) from *Melabók* when it was less defective than it is now and Björn Jónsson's *Skarðsárbók*, in its turn compiled from *Sturlubók* and *Hauksbók*.

The relationship between the different versions of *Landnámabók* is still less than clear, despite the studies of. Björn M. Ólsen and Jón Jóhannesson's *Gerðir Landnámabókar* (Reykjavík, 1941). But the purposes of the present volume are unquestionably best served by a reliance on the version prepared by the famous thirteenth-century historian Sturla Thórðarson, and on Hauk's enlarged version, based as he tells us that it was on *Sturlubók* and *Styrmisbók*. The standard edition of *Landnámabók* is that of Finnur Jónsson (Copenhagen, 1900, 1921, and 1925); the most recent that of Einar Arnórsson (Reykjavík, 1948). The best edition of *Skarðsárbók* is by Jakob Benediktsson (Reykjavík, 1958). My own selection owes much to Jón Helgason's *Fortællinger fra Landnámabók* (Copenhagen, 1951). *Landnámabók*'s account of Eirik the Red has been excluded because its entire substance will be known from the opening sections of *Grænlendinga Saga* and *Eiríks Saga Rauða*.

3. *Grænlendinga Saga* and *Eiríks Saga Rauða*

Grænlendinga Saga is preserved in the form of three interpolations relating to Eirik the Red, his son Leif, and the Greenlanders, inserted in the 'Large' Saga of King Olaf Tryggvason, itself preserved in *Flateyjarbók*, an extensive codex written down in the last decades of the fourteenth century. Of the source of these chapters (that is, from what manuscript their scribe Jón Thórðarson copied them) we know nothing. The age of *Grænlendinga Saga*, as opposed to the age of the codex in which it is preserved, has been the subject of much inquiry. It has been ascribed to the fourteenth century, to various decades of the thirteenth, and even to the end of the twelfth. The strongest argument for an early date has been offered by Jón Jóhannesson (not later than *c.*1200; see *Aldur Grænlendinga Sögu*, in *Nordæla*, Reykjavík, 1956, English translation Saga Book XVI, 1962, and *Íslendinga Saga*, I, Reykjavík, 1956, English translation 1974).

Eiríks Saga Rauða, which is sometimes called *Þorfinns Saga Karlsefnis* (*Þórðarsonar*), is preserved in two vellum manuscripts and five seventeenth-century manuscripts which derive

from these. The vellums are AM 544 4to, which is part of the
big codex *Hauksbók* [*H*] made before 1334 for Hauk Erlendsson and already referred to as containing Hauk's version of
Landnámabók; and AM 557 4to [557], sometimes called *Skál-
holtsbók*, of the fifteenth century. They tell the same story, in
the same order of events, but with frequent and sometimes considerable differences of wording. This is because *H*, in part written out by Hauk himself, is a deliberate 'improvement' of its
original, whereas 557 comes from a pen which far from seeking
to improve it is not even concerned to do it justice, and as a consequence abounds in gaucheries and inadvertencies. Considered as literature then, the *H* version outshines 557, but as
Sven B. F. Jansson has demonstrated in his comprehensive
study (*Sagorna om Vinland*, i, (Lund, 1944)), 557 despite the
late date of the manuscript in which it is preserved is beyond all
doubt an earlier and more authentic version of *Eiríks Saga
Rauða* than its polished rival.

Eiríks Saga Rauða must have been composed after 1263, if
we trust to the reference in the concluding genealogy of both *H*
and 557 to 'bishop Brand the first', which is intelligible only in a
context of bishop Brand the second (of Holar 1263–4), and if we
further believe that its opening chapters were taken from Sturla
Thórðarson's recension of *Landnámabók*. It is, however, possible that the reference to bishop Brand is a late addition, and
that there was an older version of *Eiríks Saga Rauða* known to
and used by Sturla, so the dating cannot be certain. On grounds
of style and composition the saga has been held by different
judges to be of both the first and the last quarter of the thirteenth century. Of recent authorities Matthías Thórðarson,
Eiríks Saga Rauða (Íslenzk Fornrit, iv) (Reykjavík, 1935; re-
issue of 1957), pp. lxxxiv–lxxxv, places it in the first third of the
century, and Stefan Einarsson, *A History of Icelandic Literature*
(New York, 1957), p. 138, hesitantly in the first quarter;
Sigurður Nordal, *Sagalitteraturen* (Nordisk Kultur, viiiB)
(Copenhagen, 1952), pp. 244 and 248–9, lists it among sagas
written 1230–80; Halldór Hermannsson, *The Vinland Sagas*
(New York, 1944), p. viii, subscribes to the general view that
'our Saga was written in the latter half of the thirteenth century', as does Jón Jóhannesson in those works of his already
cited.

Probably we should conclude that the version of the saga from which *H* and 557 derive was written not long after 1263, but that this was not necessarily the original *Eiríks Saga Rauða*. *Grænlendinga Saga* appears to be not of later date than *Eiríks Saga Rauða*, and might indeed be earlier, for it either knows nothing of or completely disregards the tradition stemming from Gunnlaug Leifsson's Life of Olaf Tryggvason that Leif Eiriksson discovered Vinland. Instead it grants the honour of the discovery to Bjarni Herjolfsson, while giving Leif a more convincing role as Vinland's first explorer. Nothing is gained by exalting either saga at the expense of the other, but *Grænlendinga Saga* is assuredly a very important document indeed. Both sagas seem to be put together from older and partly oral tradition, *Eiríks Saga Rauða* somewhere on Snæfellsnes, and *Grænlendinga Saga* possibly in Skagafjord. They do not derive from a common original; and while the possibility that the author of *Eiríks Saga Rauða* used a detail or two from *Grænlendinga Saga* cannot be ruled out, it seems safer to conclude that the two sagas were written independently and in ignorance of each other. That the author of *Grænlendinga Saga* described the Leifsbudir area largely in terms of Karlsefni's Hop was not because he had read *Eiríks Saga Rauða*, but because he filled a deficiency in his own sources from tradition associated with Karlsefni. Had he known *Eiríks Saga Rauða* he would have used it more fully and more skilfully, and differently.

For *Grænlendinga Saga* I have used the text, and in the matter of the narrative relating to Leif's conversion and evangelism the arrangement, of Halldór Hermannsson, *The Vinland Sagas* (1944). In the case of *Eiríks Saga Rauða* I have translated 557, at the same time presenting the significant variants of *H*. On occasion in contexts not affecting the narrative or argument of this book where 557 makes less than full sense or is the victim of its scribe I have felt free to resort to *H* without indication, and inevitably any save a literal translation must obscure scores of minor differences of expression. I have used the parallel texts of 557 and *H* in Sven B. F. Jansson's *Sagorna om Vinland*, and consulted at all times Halldór Hermansson, *The Vinland Sagas*.

4. *Einars Þáttr Sokkasonar*

In this soberly told short saga we get a good look at life in Greenland in the second and third decades of the twelfth century. It is preserved in *Flateyjarbók*, and has been translated from Matthías Thórðarson's text in *Íslenzk Fornrit*, iv, pp. 273–94 (where it is entitled *Grænlendinga Þáttr*).

BIBLIOGRAPHICAL NOTE

A thoroughgoing bibliography of the Atlantic voyages and settlements would be an enormous compilation, beyond the scope and intention of this book. In general, sources and authorities have been named in their context, and the books now listed are by way of supplement.

The sagas relating to Iceland, Greenland, Vinland, will be found in the three series, *Íslenzk Fornrit*, (Reykjavík, 1933–); *Altnordische Saga-Bibliothek* (Halle, 1891–1929); and *Íslendingasagnaútgáfan* (Reykjavík, 1946–50). The standard edition of the Annals is still Gustav Storm's *Islandske Annaler indtil 1578* (Christiania, 1888). All known material relating to Greenland was collected in the three volumes of *Grønlands Historiske Mindesmærker* (*GHM*) (Copenhagen, 1838–45, reprinted 1976). These and the relevant volumes of *Meddelelser om Grønland* (*MGr*) (Copenhagen, 1878–) are indispensable to the study of Norse Greenland. Of periodicals and series the following are particularly rewarding: the *Saga-Book* and other publications of the Viking Society for Northern Research, London; *Medieval Scandinavia*, Odense; *Skirnir* and *Gripla*, Reykjavík; while the two encyclopedias *Nordisk Kultur* (Copenhagen, 1931–56) and *Kulturhistorisk Leksikon for nordisk Middelalder* (Copenhagen, 1956–) are repositories of authoritative information.

Supplementary Note, *1986*

The Old Icelandic texts have all been edited anew during the past twenty years. *Íslendingabók* and *Landnámabók* appeared in Jakob Benediktsson's edition for *Íslenzk Fornrit*, i, 2 vols. (Reykjavík, 1968). The same scholar has presented a summary in English of his views on *Landnáma*'s textual history in *Saga-*

Book, xvii. 4 (1969) pp 275–92, and in a review in *Saga-Book*, xix. 2–3 (1975–6), pp. 311–18, of Sveinbjorn Sveinsson, *Studier i Landnámabók. Kritiska Bidrag till den Isländska Fristatens Historia* (Lund, 1974). The problems of historicity and credibility remain acute. 'We do not know what Sturla and Haukr thought they were doing, when they substituted extracts from sagas and other sources for older and presumably more trustworthy sources. Did they think they were writing history or fiction? Or were they not able to resist telling a good story when they knew one? . . . *Landnámabók* was thus a book that was in the making for centuries; it is like a medieval church that one generation after another goes on building and altering, until it becomes very different from what the first builders had intended . . . This is of course true of many other books than *Landnámabók*. And it is a point that should be kept in mind when people speak of the authors of sagas, for instance. Many of them were also altered, but the main story persisted, it lived on, and the older version influenced the person who altered it, established certain limits, set up a distinct pattern. So it is also with *Landnámabók*. The main scheme of the book is unimpaired by all the additions and alterations' (Benediktsson, *Saga-Book*, xvii. 4 (1969), p. 292).

The Greenland and Vinland material was edited anew by Ólafur Halldórsson in *Grænland í Miðaldaritum* (*GríM*) (Reykjavík, 1978). The editor argues cogently that *Grænlendinga Saga* and *Eiríks Saga Rauða* are independent of each other, and assigns both sagas to the beginning of the thirteenth century. The volume contains the first complete edition of *Grænlands annál* (1623), and sets out a case for ascribing that important but irregular, belated, and in matters of authorship and provenance often puzzling compilation to Jón lærði Guðmundsson (i.e. not to Björn Jónsson á Skarðsá). Ólafur offers us too a new translation into Icelandic (*Grænlandslýsing*) of Ivar Bardarson's equally puzzling and equally important description of mid-fourteenth century Greenland, *Det gamle Grønlands beskrivelse*. The volume closes with a summary in English by Peter Cahill.

The following short list of books is designed for the English-language reader:

Finn Gad, *The History of Greenland*, Vol. I, (*Grønlands Historie*, I, trans. Ernst Dupont) (1970).

E. Guralnick (ed.), *Vikings in the West*, (Chicago, 1982): 'Historical Evidence for Viking Voyages to the New World' (Gwyn Jones); 'The Lost Norse Colony of Greenland' (Thomas H. McGovern); 'The Discovery of a Norse Settlement in America' (Helge Ingstad); 'The Norse Settlement at L'Anse aux Meadows' (Anne Stine Ingstad); 'Norsemen and Eskimos in Arctic Canada' (Robert McGhee); 'Viking Hoaxes' (Birgitta Wallace).

Helge Ingstad, *Land under the Pole Star* (1966).
The Discovery of a Norse Settlement in America. Vol. I, *Excavations at L'Anse aux Meadows, Newfoundland*, A. S. Ingstad (Oslo 1977); Vol. II, H. Ingstad (forthcoming).

H. M. Jansen, *A Critical Account of the Written and Archaeological Sources' Evidence Concerning the Norse Settlements in Greenland, MGr*, (Copenhagen, 1972).

Jón Jóhannesson, *A History of the Old Icelandic Republic: Íslendinga Saga*, trans. Haraldur Bessason (University of Manitoba, 1974). (This work appeared as *Íslendinga Saga, I, Þjóðveldisöld*, (Reykjavík, 1956), and was followed by a posthumous collection of Jón's writings, *Íslendinga Saga, II, Fyrirlestrar og Ritgerðir um Tímarbilið 1262–1550* (Reykjavík, 1958). (My references are to the English translation of vol. i, save on the rare occasions when the reference includes vol. ii, when I refer to the Icelandic editions.)

M. Magnusson and H. Pálsson, *The Vinland Sagas: The Norse Discovery of America* (1965).

General Works

P. Foote and D. M. Wilson, *The Viking Achievement* (1970).
Gwyn Jones, *A History of the Vikings*, revised edn. (1984).

The Maps

Note 1. The routes shown on Maps 2, 4, and 8, whether they indicate the sea voyages of the Norsemen or the coastal progress of the Eskimos, are approximate only. In the case of the former, even where the old sailing directions have been preserved, detail is usually lacking.

Note 2. The maps used in the 1964 edition have where possible been updated, but cartographical, archaeological, and ethnological work currently in progress will certainly expand and refine our present knowledge of racial distribution and contacts in Greenland and North America. Meantime I repeat my thanks to Lauge Koch, C. L. Vebæk, Jørgen Meldgaard, and my three transatlantic contributors for their counsel and practical help.

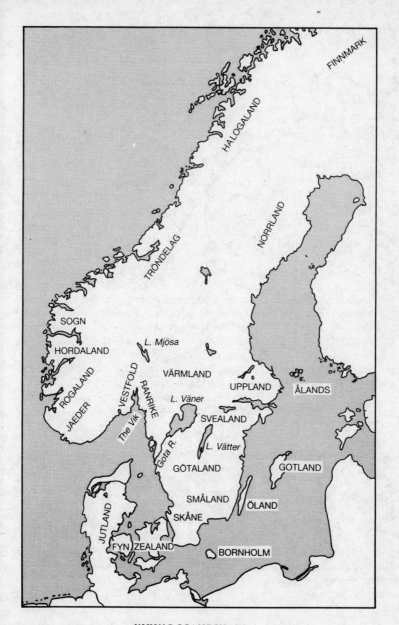

VIKING SCANDINAVIA

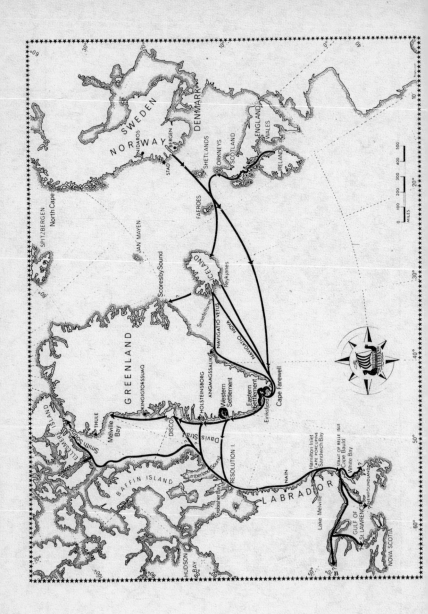

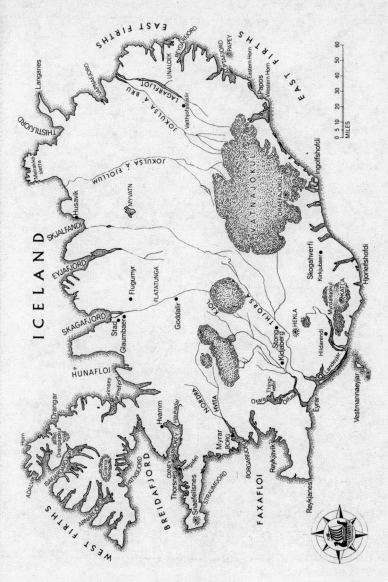

ICELAND

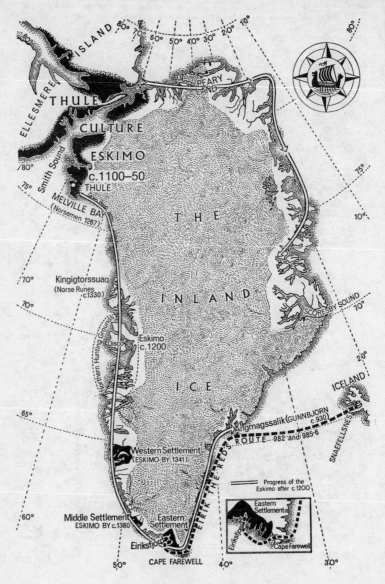

NORSE GREENLAND, AD 985–1500

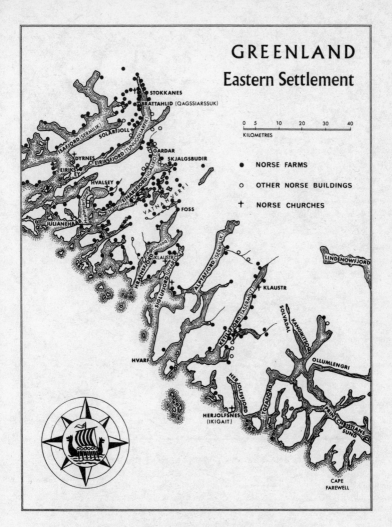

GREENLAND, THE EASTERN SETTLEMENT

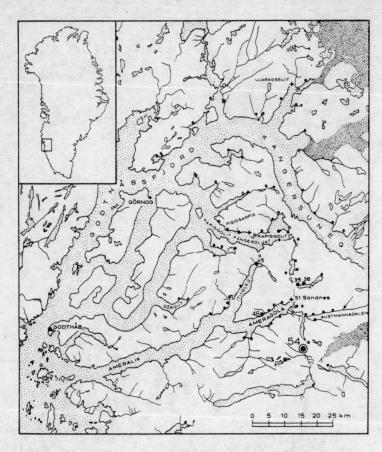

GREENLAND, THE WESTERN SETTLEMENT

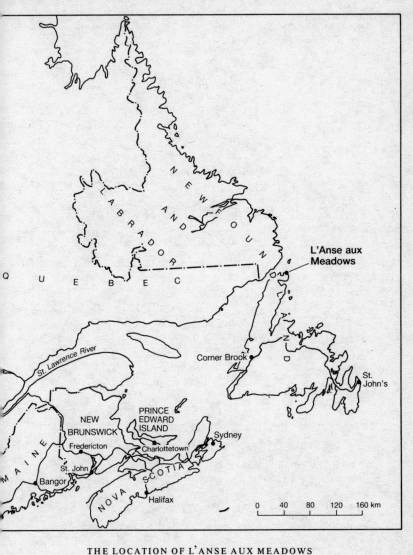

L'Anse aux
Meadows

Corner Brook

St.
John's

St. Lawrence River

NEW
BRUNSWICK

PRINCE
EDWARD
ISLAND

Sydney

Fredericton

Charlottetown

St. John

NOVA   SCOTIA

Bangor

Halifax

MAINE

QUEBEC

LABRADOR

NEWFOUNDLAND

0   40   80   120   160 km

THE LOCATION OF L'ANSE AUX MEADOWS

Main route to VINLAND (Leif, Thorvald, Karlsefni).

Probable route of Thorvald and Karlsefni north-west from Leifsbudir-Straumfjord

E Indicate the approximate position of the native ESKIMO and INDIAN population c. 1000 A.D.

LM L'Anse aux Meadows

0 10 20 30 40 50 60 70 80 90 100
MILES

Cape Harrison

Hamilton Inlet

THE STRAND

Cape Porcupine

North West River

LAKE MELVILLE

English River

SANDWICH BAY

Goose Bay

L A B R A D O R

ALEXIS RIVER

ST. LEWIS RIVER

Battle Harbour

BELLE ISLE

ST. AUGUSTINE RIVER

Pistolet Bay
Sacred Bay
Great Sacred Island
Cape Bauld
LM

Q U E B E C

STRAIT OF BELLE ISLE

THORVALD'S MEN

HARE BAY

LITTLE MECATINA RIVER

N E W F O U N D L A N D

KARLSEFNI AND SNORRI

WHITE BAY

MARKLAND AND VINLAND

Index